CHRISTIAN EPIGRAPHY

AN ELEMENTARY TREATISE

WITH A COLLECTION
OF ANCIENT CHRISTIAN INSCRIPTIONS
MAINLY OF ROMAN ORIGIN

BY

ORAZIO MARUCCHI

PROFESSOR OF CHRISTIAN ARCHAEOLOGY IN THE
ROYAL UNIVERSITY OF ROME

TRANSLATED BY

J. ARMINE WILLIS

ARES   PUBLISHERS   INC.
CHICAGO   MCMLXXIV

Unchanged Reprint of the Edition:

ARES   PUBLISHERS   INC.
150 E. Huron Street
Chicago, Illinois 60611
Printed in the United States of America
International Standard Book Number:
0-89005-070-8
Library of Congress Catalog Card Number:
74-82057

PREFATORY NOTE

FEW words are needed to introduce Dr. Marucchi's *Manual of Christian Epigraphy* to the English reader. Issued originally as one of the well-known series of Hoepli's *Manuali*, it is the work of one of the great De Rossi's most distinguished disciples. It is primarily concerned with the inscriptions of Rome, though important monuments from elsewhere find a place in it. The author's plan has been to select from the bewildering mass of extant material sufficient specimens of all the main classes of Christian inscriptions to familiarise the reader with the current formulae, and, by the help of special chapters—*e.g.* on the Consular Fasti and the Calendar—to interpret methods of dating and to appreciate the bearing of the monuments upon history. Under such guidance it becomes possible to realise the importance, the interest, and the beauty of these early documents, and to cope with their frequent obscurities and their sometimes baffling barbarisms. Dr. Marucchi writes from the Roman Catholic standpoint, and makes his Biblical quotations normally from the Latin Vulgate.

M. R. JAMES.

CAMBRIDGE, *October* 1911.

PRELIMINARY NOTICE

MY purpose in compiling this *Manual of Christian Epigraphy* has been to supply students with some general information concerning this important branch of Christian archaeology, and at the same time to provide them with a classified collection of inscriptions which may be useful to them for the illustration of lectures.   In forming this collection I have made use principally of Roman inscriptions, as the oldest, the most numerous, and the·most important; but I have not omitted to quote here and there inscriptions from other parts of the ancient world.

The book being intended specially for educational purposes, and not as a "Corpus Inscriptionum" proper, I have thought it needless to give the bibliography of each inscription, contenting myself with noting whether the inscription quoted still exists or not: in the former case I indicate the place where it is now preserved; in the latter, the source from which the text of it has come down to us.

So, also, when quoting any inscription of which

the original is in fragments, for the sake of some name or some phrase which it contains, I have contented myself with referring to a portion of the inscription only.

I hope that this work may prove especially useful to young students who are taking up archaeology; and I trust also that I may have thus satisfied the desire expressed at the second Congress of Christian Archaeology held in Rome in 1900, for the issue of an elementary Manual of Christian Epigraphy.

I owe my special thanks to two young and able students of archaeology, scholars of my own, MM. George Schneider and Henry Josi, for their kind assistance in the compilation of this Manual.

O. MARUCCHI.

ROME, *January* 1910.

CONTENTS

PART I

GENERAL STATEMENT

PART II

A COLLECTION OF CHRISTIAN INSCRIPTIONS, MAINLY
FROM ROME, IN THEIR VARIOUS CLASSES

APPENDIX

NOTE

For brevity's sake the name only is quoted in the case of some mutilated inscriptions.

INTRODUCTION

GENERAL INFORMATION

General Characteristics of Ancient Roman Inscriptions

ANCIENT Christian inscriptions must be looked upon as a special class in the vast mass of inscriptions of the old Roman world; and any manual of ancient Christian Epigraphy must therefore necessarily be preceded by some elementary information on Roman Epigraphy in general. But the demands of strict necessity will be sufficiently met by some information as to ancient nomenclature and social conditions, with a few general observations on sepulchral inscriptions; without this, Christian inscriptions could not be understood, much less distinguished from those of paganism.

The Roman citizen had three names, the *praenomen*, the *nomen*, and the *cognomen*. The *nomen*, properly called *gentile*, was that of the founder of the family, and passed on to all his issue; these were hence said to belong to the same *gens* (gentiles). But as in the course of time the *gentes* split up into various *familiae*, the *cognomen* was adopted to distinguish one *familia* from another; and hence there were differing cognomens within the same gens.

B

But, further, each member of any one family had to be distinguished from the others; and for this purpose the praenomen was used. Thus, for example, from the root-ancestor *Fabius* issued the gens called *Fabia*, and this came to be divided into various familiae, as the *Vibulana*, the *Ambusta*, the *Labeona*. Then the individuals of the same family, *e.g.* the *Vibulana*, were distinguished one from the other by a praenomen, say, Marcus, Caius, Lucius, etc.; thus *Caius Fabius Vibulanus* indicates a member of the gens Fabia belonging to the familia Vibulana and distinguished from others of that *familia* by the praenomen Caius. Of the three names the first is the praenomen, the second is the gentile name, the third is the cognomen.

The habitual use of these three names continued to the fall of the Republic. But from the beginning of the imperial era the cognomen was often substituted for the praenomen, to distinguish the individual; thus, even in the first century of the Empire, Titus Flavius Vespasianus, Titus Flavius Domitianus, Tito Flavius Clemens, had for their distinguishing names the cognomens Vespasianus, Domitianus, Clemens, respectively. The habit spreading in the course of time, the praenomen became at last entirely neglected and was no longer noticed in inscriptions, as the use of it seemed an act of superfluous pedantry. This custom begins to make its appearance about the time of the Antonines.

It follows, therefore, that inscriptions on which these three names are to be found set out in order most probably belong to the pre-Antonine epoch; and consequently, if these inscriptions should be proved to be Christian, they would date back to the earliest age of Christianity.

The praenomens which were intended to distinguish one member of a family from another generally had their origin in some special circumstance in the family circle ; *e.g.* the first-born of the sons was called Primus, the third Tertius, the tenth Decimus, etc. ; he who was *prima luce natus* was called Lucius, he who was *mane natus* Manius ; *Gnaeus* from *naevus,* a wart or body mark ; Cajus from γαίω, I rejoice, to indicate the joy caused by his birth ; and so forth.

The commonest praenomens in inscriptions are not put out at length, but are always abbreviated into one or more of their initial letters. But to avoid confusion some are only indicated by the first letter, others by the two first, others by the first syllable, others by some conventional mark, as may be seen in the subjoined table.

These praenomens, however, were not in use in all the *gentes* alike without distinction. Some are more frequently found in one *gens,* some in another, owing to the desire in each *gens* to perpetuate within itself the praenomen of some illustrious ancestor.

COMMONEST PRAENOMENS

A = *Aulus*	N = *Numerius*
C = *Cajus*	P = *Publius*
D = *Decimus*	Q = *Quintus*
L = *Lucius*	S = *Sextus*
M = *Marcus*	T = *Titus*
M*l* = *Manius* [1]	TI = *Tiberius*

[1] To distinguish *Manius* from *Marcus* the former was represented by M followed by a special mark.

Less Common Praenomens

Ap	= *Appius*	Min	= *Minatius*
O	= *Olus*	Nov	= *Novius*
C or K	= *Kaeso*	Op	= *Opiter*
Ep	= *Epidius*	Ov	= *Ovius*
Her	= *Herius*	Pac	= *Pacujus*
Mam	= *Mamercus*	Pes	= *Pescennius*

Pupus was supposed to mean a *child*, but it is a real praenomen, inasmuch as an inscription has been found of a youth over fourteen years of age, with the praenomen of Pupus, and the indication of his tribe. Moreover, its appearance even in the epitaphs of children proves nothing, for, as we know, the praenomen was given by the Romans eight days after birth, *i.e.* on the day of lustration.

Sal	= *Salvius*
Sept	= *Septimus*
Ser	= *Servius* or *Sergius*

Ser. generally stands for *Servius*, as appears from many instances, but two inscriptions from Tusculum show that it may also stand for *Sergius*. Both these praenomens, however, may, in the opinion of many, be referred to an older form *Senguius*, corrupted by some into *Servius*, by others into *Sergius*; much as the old form *ninguis* has become *nivis*. Sp = *Spurius*, which, however, is sometimes represented by a single S.

St and Sta	= *Statius*
Tert	= *Tertius*
V	= *Vibius*

THE COGNOMEN OF FEMALES

In very early times women had praenomens like men; later they went out of use; but about the third and fourth centuries of the Empire some ladies of the highest rank resumed them. In the times before the decadence, when women had no praenomen, the inscriptions give their gentile name and cognomen only; the agnomen or surname was reserved for family use; or else a name of endearment was formed from the father's nomen, such as Fabiola, Priscilla, Domintilla, Plautilla, etc.

OF GENTILE NAMES

The gentile name was that of the original ancestor of the family, which was passed on to all his descendants. These names were formed by adding *-ius* to the name of the individual, *e.g. Pompo*, Pomponius, etc. This termination in *ius* is the old mark to distinguish the gentile name from the cognomen, and exceptions to the rule were believed either not to exist or to be negligible.

Panvinius recognised only four exceptions, in the gentile names *Perpenna, Norbanus, Peduceus, Poppeus*. But since the days of Panvinius many others have come to light, not ending in *-ius*. The principal exceptional terminations are the following: *erna, -inna, -ina, -as, -io, -ax, -acus, -eus, -enus, -aeus* (Magiaeus, Decimaeus), *-is* (Aurelis, Caecilis). But some of these are only apparently exceptional, *e.g.* names ending in *-eus* are only the ordinary form, archaistically pronounced; and those in *-aeus* (with the diphthong) come from an *-ejus* form, as from *Poppeius* is formed *Poppaeus*.

The other irregular terminations indicate that the bearers of the names were foreigners in Rome. Thus names in *-erna* or *-ina* are Etruscan, those in *-as* or *-anas* are Umbrian, those in *-enus* Picenian, those in *-acus* Gallic.

With respect to names in *-anus*, which have hitherto been little understood, Hübner has suggested an ingenious explanation. Taking his stand on ancient geography, he thinks that these names generally represent a local connexion, especially with places in Latium or near Rome; he suggests that they were borne by strangers who had migrated to Rome, and were there of course addressed by the names of their respective birth-places, *e.g. Albanus, Bovillanus*, etc., and that these names then became the permanent gentile names of their families.

The cognomen is an addition to the gentile name not in itself absolutely required. In fact, in primitive ages it did not exist, but as the familiae of a gens increased in number, the habit of the cognomen came in. It was generally derived either from some mark peculiar to the founder of the familia or from some event in its history; nearly all the cognomens of the most illustrious familiae, as the Scipiones, the Nasicae, the Cicerones, etc., have been already explained by ancient writers. As for its form, it may be best described negatively, as generally eschewing the gentile termination *-ius*; beyond that its terminations are as various as its origins. Among these the termination in *-anus* calls for some remark. Some are derived from local names, as *Norbanus*

[if this be a cognomen, not a gentile name—TR.];
Aelianus is formed from the gentile *Elius*, *Caecilianus* from the gentile *Caecilius*.

In these cases the ending in *-anus* signifies a
transfer from one gens to another. This transfer
was effected in two ways. The first method was
by adoption : the member of the gens Cornelia who
was adopted into—say—the gens Fabia, changed
his gentile name, and was no longer Cornelius,
but Fabius ; but he kept his former nomen with
the addition of *-anus*. This, however, was not
compulsory, as sometimes they retained their
original *nomen*. But in process of time the prolongation by *-anus* was used out of mere vanity,
as a way of bringing in the gentile name and
cognomen of maternal relations in addition to
the bearer's own ; in this way one person might
have several dozen names and cognomens, without
any indication which were his own and which
were additions ; and this confusion is more and
more noticeable in the course of the third and
fourth centuries. Foreigners, too, who had obtained
Roman citizenship, and soldiers who had gained
an honourable discharge, adopted the gens of the
person through whom the favour was obtained,
but often retained their own cognomen with the
prolongation of *-anus*. Praenomens ceased to be
used to distinguish individuals after the beginning
of the Empire, when cognomens took their place ;
hence every one came to have a different cognomen.
This nomenclature, however, was only used in
family transactions and in inscriptions of a private
nature ; and hence Christian inscriptions, being
almost exclusively records of family events, generally give the cognomen to distinguish the individual.

Where the cognomens were many in number, the last, according to Sirmondo, was the distinctive one; but Borghesi has proved by irrefragable arguments that the same person was in the habit of putting his cognomens in any order he pleased; and his final opinion is that every one was at liberty to select the cognomen he preferred as the distinctive one, and even to place it where he liked among his other names.

Some persons had a right to more than one cognomen; in that case one was the cognomen, the other was called agnomen, a word meaning the same as cognomen, *i.e.* additional name. Last come the surnames, familiar sobriquets, but in no sense legal or recognised; none the less, in the third and fourth centuries they had become so common that some people of mark were known to the vulgar by their surname only. This is why we read on the cornice of the pedestal of the statue erected in honour of the celebrated orator Lucius Avienius Aurelius Symmachus the word *Eusebii*, this being, according to Borghesi, the surname of that champion of dying polytheism. This surname was called *signum*, and was sometimes set out at full length in inscriptions, *e.g. Projectus Signo Musculus* [Projectus, surnamed Musculus]; or else it is introduced by *qui et*, *sive*, *vel*, or *qui vocitatur*, e.g. *Manlius Januarius qui vocitatur Asellus*, etc. These surnames were sometimes of foreign origin, as in the case of foreigners admitted into a Roman *gens*, who might retain their name of origin as a surname; *e.g.* the full name of the celebrated Herodes Atticus was Claudius Herodes Atticus, Herodes (his original Athenian name) being retained as a surname.

It follows that the presence of praenomen and gentile name alone is a mark of the highest antiquity; later on we find praenomen, gentile, and cognomen; then from the beginning of the Empire gentile and cognomen alone came into use, though not in inscriptions. In the third and fourth centuries the cognomen, alone or in conjunction with another cognomen, became very common, but only on quasi-private and domestic inscriptions, *e.g.* those of Christians, and not even on these when of official or solemn character. In the fourth century a gentile name was at times adopted as a cognomen; thus the gentile Petronius became the cognomen Petronius, and similarly Honorius was used as a cognomen. Finally we may note that the gentile name Flavius was used as a sort of praenomen in the later days of Roman nomenclature.

OF THE STATUS OF INDIVIDUALS

Kindred is created either by natural relationship or by affinity or by community of *gens*. By natural relationship I mean the bond that unites husband and wife, father and son; by affinity, that which connects, say, the relations of the husband with those of the wife. Community of *gens* was the link between all of the same gens, *i.e.* descended from the same stock.

A father had absolute authority over his sons, extending even to their lives; but this, which was called *patria potestas*, differed from the *dominium* of the master over his slave. A man of free birth might be subject to *patria potestas*, but never to *dominium*. Indeed, a pure-bred Roman citizen was bound to state the name of his father as evidence of his purity of birth : this was termed *ciere patrem*, and was expressed by the letter F (initial of *filius*) preceded by the *praenomen* of the father in the genitive case, *e.g. Marci filius, Titi filius*, etc. Often if the individual was under the *potestas* of his grandfather, the grandfather's name was also quoted in the genitive case with the letter N (initial of *nepos*) prefixed.

Women also recorded the names of their fathers to prove their purity of birth; and sometimes in lieu of the father's name, or even in addition thereto, the mother's name is given. This was specially the custom among the Etruscans; indeed, one of the few inscriptions that exhibit this variation was found at the Etruscan city of Chiusi. It runs as follows :

C · VENTIUS · C · F · CAESIA · NATUS

Sometimes in cases of two persons of the same names the words *pater* and *filius* are attached; this has nothing to do with the habit of *ciere patrem* to prove purity of birth, but was simply done to avoid confusion. Similar distinctions were also expressed by the addition of *major* and *minor*, *senior* and *junior*, which were used even in the case of brothers.

In many inscriptions the epithet *naturalis* is applied to *filius*; not however to be understood in the sense of illegitimate, but solely as the opposite of adoptive.

The father of the family in referring to his issue would use the expression *ii qui in potestate mea sunt*.

A woman entered the family of her husband on marriage, and came under his *potestas*; hence she was bound to give his name (in the genitive case) to show his possessory right over her. Thus we read in the famous inscription of Caecilia Metella on the Via Appia:

CAECILIAE
Q · CRETICI · F
METELLAE
CRASSI

i.e. Caecilia Metella, daughter of Quintus Creticus, wife of Crassus, and the use of Crassus in the genitive indicates that he was the person to whom she "belonged."

Matrimony creates affinity, and this implies a sort of kinship between the relations of husband and those of wife ; this is expressed in inscriptions by the words *patraster, matrastra, filiaster, filiastra ;* sometimes even *tata* and *mamma,* though these more probably mean *nutritor* and *nutrix* (tutor and nurse).

In a legal Roman marriage the woman became Caja, and is entitled *uxor, compar, marita, comes, sodalis, adjutrix, convivia, collaboronia,* the last being rare forms. The wives of those who had not contracted marriage *jure Romano—e.g.* those of strangers, of Latins, and also of Romans who were not entitled to the privilege—could not use the name *uxor,* but had various styles—*e.g. hospita, focaria,* and even *concubina ;* but the last, of course, without any connotation of immorality.

Among slaves marriage simply did not exist ; they were looked upon as on a level with brutes, among whom there could only be cohabitation, importing no rights either to the man or to the woman or to the offspring.

Christians, on the contrary, made no distinction between freeman and slave ; they recognised only the one term, *conjugium*, for all forms of marriage, without distinction, and repudiated every other name.

Women often had descriptive names in inscriptions. Thus *Univiria* is one who had but one spouse, *Virginia* one who never had a second husband ; and a man also might be called *Virginius*.

As for marriages between free women and slaves the following observations may be made. A free woman marrying a slave without his master's consent became the slave of the latter ; if with his consent, she became a freed-woman ; but in senatorial families these marriages were strictly forbidden.

The Romans allowed divorce, which might be *cum dissidio, i.e.* where the parties separated on unfriendly terms, or *sine dissidio*, where the divorce took place amicably. Just as the most solemn form of contracting marriage was *confarreatio*, so a solemn divorce was called *diffarreatio*.

In some inscriptions children and also freedmen are called *incrementa*, i.e. *incrementa familiae*. In others a man is described as *jus trium—quatuor—liberorum habens*, or more generally *jus liberorum habens*, expressed by the initials I.H.L. To understand this it must be explained that the father of legitimate and surviving children, to the number of three in Rome, four in Italy, and five in the provinces, was exempted from several taxes ; and some who had no children were granted the same rights as a favour.

Besides natural paternity, there was also paternity

by adoption. Every citizen had the right to adopt the son of another citizen (of course, with consent of the latter). The adopted son became by law the very son of his new father, and took his praenomen and gentile name, keeping, however, his own name with the addition of *-anus*. Thus P·CORNELIUS·P·F·SCIPIO·AEMILIANUS was the name of the second conqueror of Africa, who was the actual son of Paulus Aemilius and was adopted by P. Cornelius Scipio.

In the second century began the fashion of *polyonomia, i.e.* of taking, by the method of adoption, several names, both gentile and cognominal; these were placed between the true gentile and cognomen. Thus we have the well-known Vatican inscription of a certain Quintus Roscius, in which there are a good dozen names. But this fashion did not prevail among the Christians; and hence an inscription containing several names may be at once set down as pagan.

As for foreigners who obtained citizenship, they took the gentile name of the person through whom they had obtained this privilege.

A Roman citizen would also state the tribe in which he was enrolled: this was done by placing the tribal name (abbreviated) between the name of the father and the cognomen, *e.g.* P·AELIO·P·F·PAL·TIRONI, which reads, "to Publius Aelius Tiro, son of Publius Aelius Tiro, and member of the *Palatine* tribe."

However, as the tribal name is never indicated in Christian inscriptions, it is needless to say more about it.

OF SLAVES AND FREEDMEN

The slave (*servus*) among the Romans was not a human being, but a chattel belonging to his master, and thus he had no rights either civil or domestic; he could not contract matrimony, but mere *contubernium* (cohabitation), and had no rights over wife or children. He had no family name, but a mere personal name, which either indicated his nationality, as *Syrus, Scotha,* etc., or some distinguishing trait, as *Agilis, Dexter,* etc.

In Christian inscriptions the humiliating description *servus* is never found, except occasionally in the phrase Servus Dei, δοῦλος τοῦ Θεοῦ.

Among the Christians, indeed, there was no distinction between slaves and master, as Laetantius finely says, " With us there is no difference between master and slave ; for we consider that we are all equal " (*Divin. Inst.* v. 14, 15).

Slaves when emancipated became " freedmen " and took the gentile name of their patron ; after which, and before their own cognomen, they placed his praenomen : thus, M · TULLIUS · M · L · TYRO means that the slave Tiro had belonged to Marcus Tullius Cicero, and on becoming his freedman had taken his gentile name and praenomen, keeping the name he had borne as a slave for his own cognomen. Sometimes, but exceptionally, the patron's name was placed after the servile cognomen, and this was specially the case with the freedmen of the Emperors. When in inscriptions concerning a freedman two L's are found, the first must be read with the name of the patron, while the second may indicate generally that the bearer belonged to the class of Freedmen. When a slave belonged to two or more masters, on emancipation he had just the same number of patrons, and entered the praenomens of all of them in inscriptions ; then if several had the same name, its initial would be repeated—once if they were two, twice if they were three.

Sometimes the patron is mentioned, not by his praenomen alone, but by all his names, or again by his cognomen only, according to the taste of the writer ; sometimes from mere caprice, sometimes in the case of persons of importance, lest they should not be recognised under a mere praenomen which they shared with many others.

Slaves of municipalities or colonies when emancipated described themselves as freedmen of that municipality or colony, *e.g.* MUNIC·VERONENS· LIB ; or as freedmen of its inhabitants, *e.g.* VERONENSIUM · LIB. As for their gentile name and praenomen, they sometimes formed it from the name of the city, or of the magistrate who had acted on behalf of the municipality or college ; sometimes they took the gentile name *Publicius*.

Slaves belonging to institutions or to temples when emancipated were described as freedmen of the institution ; thus we find *Stationis aquarum Lib.*, *Fani Herculis Lib.*, etc.

In some inscriptions we find FAM · ET · LIBERTORUM · CAI, etc., where *familia* means slaves and manumitted freedmen. In others the freedmen of freedmen are mentioned, which need cause no surprise, as freedmen could purchase slaves, who, on manumission, would become their freedmen. A special record of the patron of a man's own patron would be made when the former was a person of note, and particularly when he was Emperor.

In some inscriptions "future" freedmen are mentioned, evidently meaning those who were to be manumitted by deed or by will.

The sons of freedmen were called *libertini*; but they were full citizens, as free as any, and they depended in no way on their fathers' patrons.

In an election list discovered on a wall in Pompeii we read of a *princeps libertinorum*; which would seem to mean the ruler of the Jewish Synagogue in that city. Indeed, the Italic Jews who had been imported as slaves from Asia, specially by Pompey, and then emancipated were called *libertini*, and formed "the Synagogue of the Libertines," mentioned in the Acts of the Apostles. Manumission, or the ceremony by which slaves were set free, is often named in inscriptions, including those of Christian origin, as Christians often manumitted their slaves, and considered manumission an act of piety and mercy.

The Social Classes and the Occupations of Ancient Rome

Above all classes of citizens stood naturally pre-eminent the imperial house, *domus Augusta*.

The Emperor, his family, and the members of the imperial household formed a class by themselves. The Emperor was the protector of the State, the commander-in-chief of the army, the senior consul of the republic (for in Rome the republic continued to exist, in theory at least, up to the conquest by the barbarians). All the Emperors bore the title of *Augustus*, a name of good omen and bearing a religious significance. The name of *Caesar* was also common to them all, in honour of the first of the Emperors : and on inscriptions of the Empire we constantly find the name of the Emperor accompanied by the two letters P. F. *Pius Felix* (not to be confused with *Publii Filius*).

On the strength of the Emperor's bearing the name of Augustus, all his household were called *domus Augusta,* and all those who had any connexion with the *domus Augusta* were bound in describing themselves to mention the name of the Caesar or the Augustus. A slave must describe himself as *Caesaris nostri,* or *Augusti nostri servus* ; freedman, as *Augusti libertus, Caesaris libertus.* The *domus Augusta* or *domus Caesaris* is mentioned also in the Epistle of St. Paul to the Philippians, where he says, "All the saints salute you, principally they who are of Caesar's household."

Next after the imperial household came the two great classes of patricians (*nobiles*) and plebeians. The distinction between the two was founded on birth, not on property ; hence there might be some patricians poorer than some plebeians. When a plebeian was ennobled by imperial grant, he was described as "adlectus inter patricios," and in respect of his recent promotion he was a "homo novus."

Those in whose "familia" there was no taint of slave-blood were called "ingenui": hence there might be *nobiles* who were not *ingenui.*

Furthermore there were the orders or classes of civil life: the "ordo senatorius," the "ordo equestris"; and the "plebs."

To the senatorial order belonged all members

of senatorial families, with the title "viri claris-simi." This rank of "clarissimus" was the mark of the senatorial order, and was indicated by the letters C. V. or V. C. (vir clarissimus) of a man; C. F. (clarissima femina) of a woman; C. P. (c. puer) of a child.

This title is found even in Christian records. Thus in the Acts of the Martyrdom of S. Caecilia we read that in reply to the judge's question as to her social position, she said, "*Ego sum Caecilia, ingenua nobilis clarissima*"; a very precise answer, and probably taken down verbatim by a short-hand writer at the trial.

It also appears on Christian inscriptions.

Members of the "ordo equestris" or knights had the title "viri egregii" (V. E.): "egregius puer" is rarely found, "egregia foemina" scarcely ever. In later times we find occasionally the title "vir perfectissimus" (V. P.).

Lastly, after the "ordo equestris" we have the *plebs*, which must not be confused with the *populus*. The *plebs* was in fact only a fraction of the whole, while the name *populus*, though originally confined to the patricians, came after-wards to designate the entirety of patricians and plebeians.

Each of these orders, the senatorius, equestris, and plebs, had its own duties, which had to be performed by all who wished to pass through what was known as the "cursus honorum." There was a "cursus honorum" for the senatorial order, another for the equestrian, and another for the plebs. We will say a few words only of the most important of these, the senatorial.

A youth of senatorial rank who wished to

launch himself on the "cursus honorum" must
begin with the "viginti viratus." The "viginti
viri" were a board of twenty with special duties.
They furnished the "decemviri litibus judicandis,"
who were ten judges for the decision of civil cases
of minor importance ; from them also came the
"triumviri capitales," three judges in criminal and
capital cases. There were also "quatuorviri
viarum curandarum," with very important duties,
inasmuch as the charge of the roads included
everything accessory to them, the opening of new
roads, the improvement of old ones, etc. Last
came "triumviri monetales," who had the special
supervision of the mint, "moneta"; a name given
to it by the Romans because it originally stood on
the Capitol close to the temple of Juno Moneta,
the goddess of advice (*monere*).

The "triumviri monetales" had the right of
coinage ; and on the coins, commonly called
consular or family coins (from the name of the
"familia" stamped on them), were placed the
names of the triumviri followed by the letters
A. A. A. F. F.; *i.e.* "Auro, Argento, Aeri, Flando,
Feriundo." In order to complete the first step in
the "cursus honorum" of the senatorial order, the
viginti viratus, the youthful initiate need not have
performed all the above-named functions in
succession : it was enough that he had performed
one of them for a reasonable time. Next came
the Quaestorship ; the young man would become
quaestor, or administrator of the public revenue ;
and the quaestorship gave admission to the Senate.
Once in the Senate, he had open to him an
immense field of activity, which might lead to the
highest offices of the Empire. Thus he could

become praetor, or chief of the judiciary, *praetor urbanus* if dealing with the citizens of Rome, *peregrinus* if with foreigners or provincials. The praetor entrusted with a province had a "quaestor" to deal with its finances. From the praetorship a man rose to the consulship; the consuls could not be less than forty years of age. The consulship, like all other magistracies, lasted for a year, and began on 1st January. The consulship was one of the most important charges in the State, and solemn festival was held on the election of new consuls. They had the privilege of giving their names to their year of office, whence they were called *eponymi*. These were the regularly elected consuls; besides these there were those selected (*subrogati*) in cases of resignation or death, who were called *suffecti*. In Christian inscriptions, as we shall see, the names of the consuls are often given to indicate the date.

Those who had served as consuls were called "viri consulares." Some of the more important offices could only be held by *viri consulares, e.g.* the governorship of the greater provinces.

Besides the consulship there were many other offices, civil, military, and ecclesiastical, to which a senator might aspire. Among the ancients these three careers were not distinct as in our days, but interchangeable, so that a man might be at one and the same time a priest and a general. But there were some priestly offices reserved exclusively for senators, *e.g.* that of Flamen Dialis; so also no one who was not "vir clarissimus" and of consular rank could belong to the College of Augurs.

To the information given above, without which it would be impossible to understand the nomen-

clature in use in ancient inscriptions, may be added
some observations on the sepulchral inscriptions of
pagans, which will help to explain the more ancient
Christian inscriptions, inasmuch as these last are
without exception sepulchral. This is also necessary
because it is by means of the expressions used
in pagan sepulchral inscriptions that we learn to
distinguish the pagan from the Christian.

Sepulchral Inscriptions

The special characteristic of these is the dedication to the "manes," sometimes expressed at
length, DIIS · MANIBUS, but oftener by the initials
D · M only; in Greek, θεοῖς καταχθονίοις, or
initials Θ·K. After the dedication, which indicates
the nature of the monument, comes the body of
the inscription, in which are found the names of
the person or persons buried there, and their
relationship; and hence this class of inscriptions is
invaluable as illustrating the nomenclature of the
ancient Romans and their domestic and family
relationships. There we find praenomens, gentile
names, cognomens; and illustrations of the practices
as to adoption and manumission, as to slaves and
freemen, all in short which went to build up the
ancient Roman family, and of which we have given a
short exposition above. Sometimes special symbols
are to be met with : *e.g.* V or Θ ; V preceding a name
indicates that the person is still living, *vivus* : Θ on
the other hand that he or she is dead, θανών or
θανοῦσα. Often at the end of sepulchral inscriptions
may be read the technical language of donation or
testamentary gift, or a statement of the ownership

of the site, or of the inviolability of the monument, etc.: *ex testamento, ex arbitratu,* or *sibi suisque, sibi posterisque suis, libertis libertabusque posterisque eorum.* Fairly frequently too is found the following abbreviation : H. M. D. M. A., signifying *huic monumento dolus malus abesto,* a formula of deprecation, which was intended to protect the sepulchral monument from the spells of witchcraft. Another formula often found at the end of a sepulchral inscription is one which declares the monument to be free from the claims or liabilities of heirs, *hoc monumentum heredem non sequitur* (H. M. H. N. S.).

To every sepulchral monument was attached an adjacent plot of land, which, together with the monument itself, belonged to the owner of the tomb (*area quae cedit monumento*); this plot was marked off by boundary stones, and was sometimes enclosed by rough masonry or by regular walls ; its size was indicated by the words, *e.g. in fronte pedes XLV, in agro pedes XXV*; which means that the sepulchral area in question had a frontage of 45 feet to the public road on which the monument was placed, and a depth of 25 feet into the field which lay behind it. And the formula is so usual as to be nearly always abbreviated into its initial letters IN FR. PED... IN AGR. PED... or IN F. P... IN A. P...

The custom of burial or inhumation seems to have been very ancient in Latium ; though it must be admitted that the custom of cremation or incineration was also of considerable age. Cinerary urns were in use from the earliest times, and this custom of cremation or incineration became very common under the Republic and the early Empire ;

so much so that only a few exceptional families
omitted to conform to it; in Rome the Gens
Cornelia always maintained the fashion of inhumation.   This is why the well-known tomb
of the Scipios, discovered on the Via Appia,
contained no cinerary urns, nor columbaria, but
only sarcophagi, in which lay the bodies of members
of the family, entire.   There was the sarcophagus
of Scipio Barbatus, with an inscription showing
the date 456 after the foundation of the city; there
were also those of Scipio Asiaticus, and of many
other notabilities of that illustrious family.   But
with the exception of that family, all others followed
the custom of cremation or incineration, even up
to the days of the Empire.   The tombs, however,
varied in shape.   Some were constructed for one
person alone ; others were vast mausoleums, others
were chambers for the sepulchral urns, others
columbaria with little niches, small compartments
for an immense number of urns ; the last was the
commonest and the most ordinary form of tomb,
being used for folk of little account, generally
slaves or freedmen, or members of some club for
mutual help ; while the tombs of the nobility and
aristocracy, though used in connexion with cremation, had not generally the look of columbaria (dove-
cots), but of halls with urns and niches, ornamented
with marbles and even with statues.   A very frequent
form of burial tombstone was the short column or
cippus, which generally carried a cinerary urn, or
stood on the spot in which that urn was placed :
hence it is that we often see in museums these
columns in the form of posts with sepulchral inscriptions on the front, and sometimes also on the sides
or back ; the posts being solid acted as pedestals and

supports for the cinerary urn. This practice was
in vogue about up to the time of the Antonines,
that is to the middle, as nearly as possible, of
the second century of our era, when inhumation
began gradually to take the place of cremation :
then of course the larger sepulchral urns, or rather
marble coffins which we call sarcophagi, came into
use ; and thus a return was made to the early
method which had been so long abandoned. For
this reason sarcophagi, though such numbers of them
are to be seen in museums, are never very ancient.
With the exception of the sarcophagi of the Scipios
and those of the prehistoric cemeteries, we have not
a single sarcophagus of the age of the Roman
Republic, or even of the first period of the Empire ;
they all belong to the second, third, or fourth
century.

It was in the second century, about the time of
the Antonines, that this method of burial began to
spread ; and it soon became so general that cremation was gradually abandoned. This is why the
carving which we find on these marble coffins
never exhibits the refinement and elegance which
would have characterised them in the last years
of the Republic, or in the first of the Empire.
Even on the older sarcophagi the reliefs and the
sculptures, beautiful as they are, already show the
germ of that decadence in art which is distinctly
visible in the second century. And with these
chronological inferences the inscriptions themselves
are in complete harmony, being all evidently of the
second, third, or fourth century.

Having drawn attention to these general points
in connexion with the various forms of tomb among
the ancient Romans, we may make some remarks

on the more notable sepulchral inscriptions. These are those which we call "sepulchral testaments," lengthy statements of the intentions of the owner of the tomb, of his wishes with respect to it, his intentions as to its decoration, its protection and defence against profanation, and as to the rites and ceremonies to be performed in the monument on given days and especially on anniversaries. The monuments of most importance from this point of view are the *Donation of Flavius Syntropus*, which was discovered on the Via Latina, and a fragment of which is preserved in the Vatican Museum; the *Testament of Dasumius*, found in two pieces on the Via Appia and now standing near the German Institute; and the famous *Testament of Basle*, of which the original is lost, but an ancient copy of it was found in a codex of the Basle Library in 1863. In these sepulchral testaments the dimensions of the tomb are given, its ornamentation is described, and directions are given as to the ceremonies, the funeral sacrifices, and the banquets which are to be celebrated there on given days, and especially on anniversaries; thus these testaments are of great value for the study of the usages and customs of the ancient Romans, and for the description they give us of these monuments of which we now see only the remains in the majestic ruins which line the great Roman roads and especially the Via Appia. So by the aid of these inscriptions we can reconstruct those shapeless masses which line the great suburban roads; from the indications which still remain to us in these ruins, our fancy may rebuild them, with their boundary walls, their halls, their marble ornaments, and their statues. Thus in the fine sepulchral inscription of Claudia Semnis now in the Vatican Museum, after the names of the lady and her husband we read as follows: HUIC · MONU-MENTO · CEDET · HORTUS · IN · QUO · TRICLIÆ · VINIOLA · PUTEUM · ÆDICÜLÆ · IN · QUIBUS · SIMULACRUM · CLAUDIÆ · SEMNES · IN · FORMAM · OMNIUM · DE-ORUM · ITA · UTI · CUM · MACERIA · A · ME · CIRCUM · STRUCTA · EST · H · M · H · N · S. From these words it may be gathered that the monument was surrounded by a cultivated en-closure, that part of it was a sort of garden, where there were trellised walks, a small vineyard, a well, and some shrines, all intended for the service of the tomb, and especially for the funeral banquets which were to be held close by. The decoration of these shrines was very peculiar. It appears from the inscription that they contained statues of the owner of the tomb in various characters, and re-presenting various divinities. Finally, the whole block—monuments, sepulchral building, vineyard, garden, and all—was enclosed in a boundary wall.

Another inscription, also Roman, gives some further information: ITER · PRIVATUM · A · VIA · PUBLICA · PER · HORTUM · PER-TINENS · AD · MONUMENTUM · SIVE · SE-PULCRUM · QUOD · AGATHOPUS · AUG · LIB · INVITATOR · VIVUS · ET · JUNIA · EPICTETUS · FECERUNT · AB · IIS · OMNI-BUS · DOLUS · MALUS · ABESTO · ET · JUS · CIVILE. This inscription tells us that there was a private road branching out from the high road, which ran in front of the tomb of Agathopus, an imperial freedman who held the office of *invitator*, a functionary who issued the invitations for the imperial dinners. We are told that the monument is surrounded by a garden ; then comes the formula, *ab iis omnibus dolus malus abesto*, that is, "be far from it all deceit and evil "—to which is added, "and litigation "—"jus civile." Another inscription is of special importance as showing that all the testator's directions respecting the monument, his instructions as to its elevation, and his testamentary dispositions concerning the actual tomb, had been reduced to writing in a sort of official statement, and recorded in a public document with attested exhibits : HUIUS · MONUMENTI · EXCEPTIO · CHIROGRAPHO · CONTINETUR : *i.e.* any limitations which may have been declared of this testamentary disposition were contained in a chirograph, or deed in writing ; such deeds were usually deposited with the Vestal Virgins, whose duty it was, *inter alia*, to take custody of wills, and other confidential papers, such as are now kept by notaries public. We sometimes find on funerary inscriptions threats of penalties against those who profane the tomb. Tombs were by Roman law sacred and inviolable; it was enough that a corpse had been laid in a place to make it "consecrated," *locus religiosus*. These words have not the same meaning as *locus sacer*. A temple was a *locus sacer*; a tomb also might be so called, in respect of the religious and sacred rites performed there ; but *per se* the resting-place of a corpse, were it temporary or even momentary, was always *locus religiosus*, and as such came under the jurisdiction of the *collegium pontificum*, of which the pontifex maximus was president. For that reason no alteration could be made in the tomb, nor could it be moved to another spot without the consent of the college of pontiffs. Hence it is that on some inscriptions we find it stated that the tombs had been constructed *permissu pontificum*. From consecrated and holy places the doers of evil and the defilers of holy things were banished by special adjurations and special formulae; we read *locus sacer sacrilege cave malum*, even on an inscription placed close to a Christian cemetery. Thus threats were addressed to all who might profane the monument; not to speak of heavy fines payable to the treasury of the pontifical college (*arcae collegii pontificum*), or to that of some particular club, or even to that of the city, or of the local municipality (if in a city other than Rome). For example, in an inscription at Pola: AVIDIA · MAXIMA · DOMUM · AETERNAM · VIVA · SIBI · POSUIT · SI · QUIS · ALIUM · CORPUS · SUPERPOSUERIT· DET· FISCO· CCC· MILIA. Here it was forbidden to place one body on the top of another in this tomb; the penalty for so doing being 300,000 sesterces payable to the privy purse. In another inscription we read: LOCUM (*sic*) · HUIC · SI · QUIS · MANUS · INTULERIT · VIRGINIBUS · VESTALIBUS · SOLVET · POENA, etc. "Any one doing any damage, or laying a hand (*manum sacrilegam*), on this monument, shall pay so much to the Vestal Virgins," these being, as we have already seen, the official custodians of these wills and sepulchral instruments. HOC · SEPULCRUM · SI · QUIS · VENDIDERIT · VEL · ABALIENAVERIT · DARE · DEBET · REIPUBLICAE · PUTEOLANORUM · POENAE · NOMINE · XX · MIL · N.: "Any one selling or alienating in any way this tomb shall pay the municipality of Pozzuoli 20,000 sesterces";

inasmuch as the tomb could not be sold, it could not be alienated at all, and remained for all time the property of the family, not being even attached to the family estate. *Hoc monumentum haereditatem non sequitur*: "This monument does not go with the inheritance." Their object was to establish the principle that the monument was to remain inviolable and sacred, not to be sold, or in any other way alienated.

Besides the private sepulchral inscriptions, there is a special class, that relating to clubs or guilds, and more particularly to the so-called burial guilds, *collegia funeraticia*, associations of people combining for the simple object of having a tomb in common and of securing that all should have proper funeral rites. Some of these associations only aimed at owning a tomb; for the most part they were named either after some divinity, or after their founder and organiser, or after the place in which they met. Thus we have a note of a guild called that of Sergia Paulina ; *Collegium quod est in domo Sergiae Paulinae*, as may be read in an inscription in the *Galleria lapidaria* of the Vatican, meaning the guild that met in that lady's house. In another we find the description, *collegium cultorum clypeorum Sesti Abulli* ; the members of which were those who had the charge of the shields, military ornaments, and targets of this gentleman ; the name was taken without any special reason as a means whereby to distinguish them from any other similar association. Now these guilds had their own burial-places, and very often we find in columbaria tombs belonging to just such associations as these. A remarkable monument of a guild of this sort is that of the guild of Aesculapius and Hygeia discovered at Civita

Lavinia, and now in the National Museum of the Terme in Rome.

These burial guilds were perfectly free not only to own a burial-place, but to meet in the tomb itself on certain days, to hold funeral feasts, and celebrate religious rites in special memory of their founders and benefactors. They also possessed a calendar of their own, a guild calendar. The origin, organisation, and history of these burial guilds is of material import to the study of the rise of Christianity. In fact, in the opinion of De Rossi, there was a time in the early centuries in which the Christian Church, in some places at least, copied the system of the guilds. This is inferred from certain passages in Tertullian, from which we may gather that in Africa, for instance, the Christians used to make a monthly payment, exactly like the members of the guilds; that the tombs were called *areae*; and that, like the guilds, the Church had a recognised title of *Ecclesia fratrum*, as may be read in a well-known inscription. All this would explain, according to De Rossi, how it was that the Christians, even in the days of the severest persecutions, were able to own cemeteries, though not of course on the same magnificent scale then as in later times, and to hold them, at first perhaps in the private right of the families that nominally owned them, but afterwards under the actual aegis of the laws which protected the burial guilds. The Christians were able to own not only underground vaults and tombs, but also meeting-houses near these same tombs, wherein to assemble and celebrate their love-feasts and other religious ceremonies; indeed, in the neighbourhood of the very ancient cemetery of Domitilla one of these places has been discovered, in which they used to celebrate these feasts, not the funeral banquets of the pagans, but the love-feasts of the Christians held in memory of the dead, to keep alive their feelings of mutual affection. And so these feasts, which the pagans celebrated as the anniversaries of the benefactors who had bequeathed money for the benefit of the guild, were for the Christians most undoubtedly the anniversaries of martyrs; and the guild calendar became in Christian hands the embryo and nucleus of a Christian martyrology.

The burial guilds were not the only bodies in Rome which owned sepulchral monuments, often of remarkable grandeur; there were other associations of entirely different character, *i.e.* combinations of persons affected by no religious tie or by the bond of a special ritual which united the members of the guilds, and existing solely for the purpose of getting a site in a sepulchre of some sort. They were, so to speak, commercial associations, the members of which subscribed for shares, and the payment on the shares secured a site in the common sepulchre. And for the most part the tombs of these curious old burial-clubs were in the shape of columbaria, as, for instance, those which may be seen on the first section of the Via Appia, near the Porta San Sebastiano. These consist of three magnificent columbaria, one of which certainly belonged to one of these burial-clubs, inasmuch as the members whose names are recorded are of different families; it is not a family columbarium, nor that of any association either sacred or religious or funerary; the names belong to all professions and pursuits—merchants, freedmen, servants, slaves, artisans, in short, every class of society is represented. The clubs had a regular organisation, a master (magister), a secretary (ab epistolis), and a treasurer (arcarius); the members made their payments every month, and drew lots eventually for the position of the niche in the columbarium which they were to occupy. Hence in the inscriptions of columbaria of this sort we find notices of these positions. *Sors prima, sors secunda, sors tertia . . . ordo primus, secundus.* The places were all numbered, and the lots bore corresponding numbers; the man who drew a certain number eventually occupied the place which it indicated. There are several inscriptions in which these details are mentioned; the most important is that of a certain Licinius Alexa, the *curator* or managing director of this association which had erected a common burial-place: L · LICINIUS · L · F · L · L · ALEXA · CURATOR · SOCIORU · SECUNDUS · IS · MONUMENTUM · EX · PECUNIA · COLLATA · SOCIORUM · AEDIFICAVIT · ARBITRATU · SUO · IDEMQUE · TECTORIA · PERFECIT · ET · IS · TRICLINIUM · SOCIORUM · EX · SUA · PECUNIA·OPERE·TECTORIO·PERPOLIT · ET · AMICIS · DONUM · DEDIT · ET · EX · AMICORUM · AERA · COLLATO · IMAGO · EI·FACTA·EST·ET·SINE·SORTE·PRIMO· AB · SOCIS · QUAS · VELLET · OLLAE · SEX · DATAE · SUNT · EIQUE · OB · OFFICIUM·ET·MAIESTATEM·EIUS·IN · PERPETUUM · IMMUNITAS · DATA · EST. The inscription states that this Lucius Licinius Alexa, a freedman by condition, was the managing director of this society, and that by means of the funds collected either by subscriptions or as calls

on the shares he had erected the sepulchral
monument, and beautified it with a coat of cement,
and perhaps also of colour ; he had added a dining-
table for the convenience of the funeral banquets
which always formed an essential part of all ancient
funeral rites, and, finally, he had made a volun-
tary gift of the whole to his friends. He had
added the decorations at his own expense, and
on that account, as a mark of gratitude for his
generosity, the society had dedicated a statue in
his honour (meaning probably that a marble bust
of him had been placed in one of the niches of
the columbarium, as we see in some existing
examples); and not only had they erected a statue or
bust to him, in grateful recognition of what he had
done, but they had further granted him the privilege
of selecting his own position for his tomb, without
drawing lots as ordinary members did. In consequence of this he might dispose of six places for himself and his dependants ; furthermore, he was for
ever freed from all liability, that is, from the payment
of ordinary calls on members, out of regard for the
expenses which he had incurred on the monument.

From what has been here said the importance
of this class of sepulchral inscriptions is obvious,
both on the score of their number and of their
offering the widest field for the special study of the
nomenclature in use among the ancients and of
their domestic relations. And the study of these
inscriptions is also of the greatest value for that of
primitive Christian epigraphy.

Indeed, as has been already observed (p. 21), the
oldest Christian inscriptions are all of a sepulchral
character, and they contain certain forms of expression which are common to pagan inscriptions also.

D

On the other hand, the Christian inscriptions with a historical bearing, of which we shall next treat, are of a relatively late date, and have little to do with pagan inscriptions of a historical or panegyrical character; on these latter, therefore, we need not offer any special remarks.

ADDENDA TO THE INTRODUCTION [1]

P. 2. Under the Empire, plebeians, who in earlier times used praenomen and nomen only, adopted a distinguishing cognomen.

P. 7. Praenomens were no longer used to distinguish individuals after the second century of the Empire.

P. 8. At the beginning of the Empire every one bore praenomen, gentile name, and cognomen ; later the practice began of using gentile name and cognomen only. With respect to the name described as "distinctive," Diehl has argued in a recent work that it is of the nature of a "collegial" name (*i.e.* denoting membership of a fraternity, etc.).

P. 9. The gentile name *Flavius* was used in late times by barbarians who had obtained citizenship from the Flavian Emperors of the fourth and fifth centuries.

P. 13. The indication of the tribe is not found in Christian inscriptions, because it soon fell out of use.

[1] On revising the whole work some months after the preceding Introduction had been in print, I noticed that some of my remarks on Roman inscriptions were wanting in fullness and clearness, and might hence create some confusion in the minds of their readers. I have therefore thought it well for the sake of greater lucidity to append to the Introduction these few observations, with references to the pages on which they arise.

P. 14. Imperial freedmen bore the title AUG ·
LIB (Augusti libertus) and adopted the praenomen
and gentile name of the Emperor, hence the
general date of the inscriptions of these freedmen
can be ascertained from their contents.

P. 17. The Emperor was the head of the State.
The letters P · F (*Pius Felix*) on inscriptions referring to the Emperor came into use in the time of
Commodus. The republican order continued to
exist in theory till the reign of Diocletian, when
a complete change was made.

P. 17. Next after the imperial household came
the two great orders of patricians and the plebeians.
In imperial days there were three classes in
Society : *ordo senatorius, ordo equestris*, and *plebs*.
The order of the *plebs*, in its widest sense as the
third order of Society, included all citizens who did
not belong to the senatorial or equestrian orders.

P. 18. As to *cursus honorum*, it should be
observed that the titles of the plebs did not confer
rank, but imposed duties.

P. 19. Of the various duties of the *viginti viratus*,
it was not usual to perform more than one. From
the praetorship a man rose to the consulship after
fulfilling certain special duties. Under the Empire
the consulship was held for a few months only,
after which *suffecti* were at once nominated.

P. 21. Some consider that the Θ prefixed to
names in some sepulchral inscriptions is equivalent
to the word *obitus*.

P. 23. The Gens Cornelia kept up the practice
of inhumation up to the time of Sulla.

CHRISTIAN EPIGRAPHY

PART I
GENERAL STATEMENT

CHAPTER I

PRELIMINARY NOTES ON THE ORIGINAL SOURCES
OF THE STUDY OF ANCIENT CHRISTIAN EPI-
GRAPHY AND ON THE BIBLIOGRAPHY CON-
CERNING IT.

A VAST number of ancient Christian inscriptions have
unfortunately been lost through the destruction of
monuments, and the dispersion of the inscribed
marbles which were once so abundant in cemeteries
and basilicas; the text, however, of many of these
lost inscriptions, so indispensable for the purpose
of our studies, has been preserved to us in ancient
manuscripts or in archaeological works; before
attempting, then, the study of the various classes of
Christian inscriptions, it is incumbent on us to
indicate with clearness the sources from which we
derive our knowledge of the text of ancient in-

37

scriptions ; some of these sources are also common to a certain extent to the study of classical epigraphy, as they consist of records in which both Christian and pagan inscriptions are preserved.

The first trace of a scientific study of Christian as of pagan epigraphy is to be found in the collections of the principal inscriptions of historical or literary importance which were made by sundry anonymous writers in the early middle ages with a view to the formation of an anthology, and as models for reproduction or imitation.

Archaeological collections of this sort began to be formed, according to De Rossi, in the fifth century A.D. ; and to this period belongs the so-called parchment of Scaliger, which contains the first specimen of an anthology of inscriptions.

Next comes the collection of Reichenau, hitherto known as the *Einsiedeln*, which was made towards the close of the eighth century. It was edited by Mabillon in the *Analecta vetera*, A.D. 1685, and again more accurately by Haenel.[1]

De Rossi re-edited this invaluable work, and added an important appendix, which had escaped the notice of previous editors, and which gave a description of the ceremonies practised by the Roman pontiff during Holy Week, about the date of Charlemagne.

Then comes the codex known as the Palatine, in the Vatican Library (No. 833), compiled about the

---

[1] *Archiv für Philolog.* v. pp. 116-38 : cf. also Urlich's *Codex urbis Romae topographicus*, p. 59 *et seq.* Of the itinerary which accompanies this sylloge a critical edition was published, with learned notes, by Lanciani in the *Transactions of the Academy dei Lincei* (vol. ix.) ; and again very recently it was the subject of a very learned paper by Hulsen in the *Transactions of the Pontifical Academy of Rome*, vol. ix.

ninth century, of which the greater part has been edited; De Rossi restored to it its proper name of *Corpus laureshamense veterum syllogarum*, and demonstrated that it was a combination of various "syllogae," which he was able to resolve into its elements by rare analytical acumen.

Another very valuable collection is the *Sylloge Centulensis*, containing Christian hymns from Rome, Spoleto, and Ravenna anterior to the eighth century, which is preserved to us in a codex of the Monastery of Corbie, now in the Imperial Library of St. Petersburg. This sylloge, which was discovered in the Petersburg codex by De Rossi, has a special interest in connexion with the Christian epigraphy of Rome, inasmuch as it contains hymns of great historical importance, as we shall see in its proper place.

Other epigraphic collections are: the sylloge of St. Gall and those of Verdun, Würzburg, Klosterneuburg, and Gottweih; the sources and the history of all these, together with a commentary, may be found in the work of De Rossi.[1]

Besides general syllogae, there are special collections confined to a single town, or to some well-known Christian building. Thus the city of Tours, celebrated for the shrine of S. Martin, has its own sylloge, copied as an appendix to the collection of Klosterneuburg, and first published by De Rossi; the inscriptions of Milan, Pavia, Piacenza, Vercelli, and Ivrea have been incorporated into the codex Laureshamensis; the city of Nola, which became famous in the Christian world for the cult of Paulinus, gives us the whole series of its inscriptions in the

[1] *Inscriptiones christianae urbis Romae septimo saeculo antiquiores*, vol. i. part ii. (Rome, 1888).

codex of Cluny. The Vatican Basilica, which is so rich in monuments and records of the nature of inscriptions, was above all others bound to encourage their transcription by collectors; and we do in fact possess several Vatican syllogae, all of which contain inscriptions of Popes and great Roman personalities, of the greatest value for the history of the Middle Ages. The latest of these by Pietro Mallio (twelfth century) includes a topographical description of the older basilica, with its numerous oratories, altars, tombs, statues, and pictures, which is of the highest interest.

From all this it may be gathered that the study of ancient inscriptions which was begun in the fifth century underwent a marked revival in the Carlovingian age, when, in the midst of the general decadence, culture experienced a short revival through the influence of the learned Alcuin and his scholars. At that time many travellers and pilgrims visiting Rome and the other sanctuaries of Christendom were diligent not only in collecting information about the most striking monuments, but also in copying the actual texts of the most remarkable inscriptions, whether pagan or Christian; and with these they enriched those diaries of their journeys which we now find in the old parchments of European libraries. Moreover, such collections became the object of much study and imitation from a literary point of view; insomuch that we find the actual wording of some inscriptions reproduced in Christian basilicas of the remotest countries of the East and West.

But this first impulse of the early Middle Ages, and especially of the Carlovingian period, towards the study of inscriptions died out after the ninth century; the general ignorance was such that in the thirteenth and fourteenth centuries Latin inscriptions had become indecipherable puzzles— a fact which may be partly attributed to the growing use in those days of the so-called Gothic character. The following illustrations will suffice: in 1300 a pilgrim passing through Perugia succeeded in persuading everybody that an ordinary Latin sepulchral inscription of the third century was in the Etruscan tongue; again, Odofred, a doctor of Bologna, confused the *lex regia* of the time of Vespasian with that of the Twelve Tables! This incredible ignorance of ancient records is reflected in the *Liber mirabilium urbis Romae*, a ridiculous farrago of the wildest legends concerning the monuments of the eternal city, the names of which are arbitrarily changed, even when they were plainly to be read on their dedicatory inscriptions.

The first in the midst of this welter of barbarism to devote himself to the study of classical antiquity in general, and of inscriptions in particular, was the famous tribune Cola Rienzi, who, in the words of his contemporary biographer, "all day meditated amid the carved marbles which surround one in Rome; and there was none like unto him for reading ancient epitaphs." Inflamed by the memories of the ancient grandeur of Rome, he looked to these majestic inscriptions of consuls and of emperors for arguments whereby to excite the people to mighty deeds, in the hope that Rome might return to its pristine power. The last of the Roman tribunes was the real founder of epigraphic science in Italy, and, as De Rossi shows, it is to him that we owe the sylloge of inscriptions which in some codexes bears the name of Nicola Signorili. Next after this came the collection of Giacomo Dondi, known as Giacomo dell' Orologio (A.D. 1375); and after an interval of fifty years comes a third compilation by Poggio Bracciolini, the famous scholar of the time of Martin V. As the dawn of the revival of letters grew brighter, the love of the past and the cultivation of the study of epigraphy increased. In the pontificate of the great Pope Nicholas V., the illustrious patron of liberal studies, Maffeo Vegio, canon of the Vatican Basilica, was indefatigable in copying numerous ancient inscriptions, both Christian and pagan; and besides these he left among his papers very valuable notes on the great basilica to which he belonged.

Ciriaco d' Ancona, Marcanova, Pontano, Pomponio Leto, Frà Giocondo of Verona continued the noble rivalry for the preservation of the precious texts of ancient inscriptions from oblivion; and their handwriting is lovingly looked for by modern epigraphists, who continue to draw upon them more and more copiously for archaeological information.

But all these writers devoted themselves almost exclusively to the collection and transcription of pagan inscriptions; it is only very occasionally that they contain any allusions to those of Christianity.

The first to compile a real sylloge of the Christian inscriptions of Rome was Pietro Sabino at the close of the fifteenth century; he dedicated it to King Charles VIII. in that ill-omened year 1494, in which that Prince swooped down upon Italy and inaugurated the miserable period of our subjection to the foreigner.

The only complete copy of the sylloge of Pietro Sabino is preserved in a codex of St. Mark's Library in Venice (Cod. Lat. x. 195); a codex in the Vatican Library containing his collection of the Christian inscriptions of Rome only, with a noble dedication to the Saviour (Cod. Ottob., Vat. 2015).

This sylloge, which is of great importance in the history of Christian epigraphy, was published for the first time in its entirety by De Rossi in his work on Christian inscriptions.

After the syllogae come the printed works on epigraphy, beginning with Mazzocchi in the sixteenth century and continued by others. But these earlier works contain pagan inscriptions only, as Christian antiquities were still neglected by the archaeologists of the Renaissance.

However, about the close of that century and the beginning of the seventeenth the study of Christian archaeology really shook off its long slumbers, first by the efforts of Panvinio, and next by those of Ugonio and Bosio.

In that period we begin to find Christian inscriptions printed by the side of pagan in works on epigraphy ; and even important groups of exclusively Christian inscriptions may now be met with in works treating of the Catacombs and other sacred monuments.

The following is a list of them in chronological order :—

GRUTER : *Inscriptiones antiquae totius orbis romani in corpus absolutissimum redactae* (1603). Pagan and Christian inscriptions.

BOSIO : *Roma sotterranea.* Cemetery inscriptions.

ARINGHIUS : *Roma subterranea.* Cemetery inscriptions.

SARAZANI : *S. Damasi papae opera*, etc. (1638).

RIVINUS : *S. Damasi carmina sacra* (1652).

CIAMPINI : *Vetera monimenta* (1690).

FABRETTI : *Inscriptionum antiquarum*, etc. (1699). Pagan and Christian inscriptions.

BUONARROTI : *Osservazioni sopra alcuni frammenti di vetri antichi* (1716). Principally Christian inscriptions.

BOLDETTI : *Osservazioni sopra i sacri cimiteri* (1720). Christian inscriptions from catacombs.

LUPI : *Epitaphium Severae martyris* (1734). Christian inscriptions.

MURATORI : *Novus thesaurus veterum inscriptionum* (1739-42). Pagan and Christian inscriptions.

MARANGONI : *Acta S. Victorini illustrata*, etc. (1740). Christian inscriptions.

MERENDA : *S. Damasi papae opuscula*, etc. (1754). Christian inscriptions.

GORI : *Thesaurus veterum dipticorum* (1759). Pagan and Christian inscriptions.

GAETANO MARINI (†1815). Thirty-one volumes MSS. in the Vatican Library. Christian inscriptions.

A. MAI : *Scriptorum veterum nova collectio*, vol. v. (1831). Christian inscriptions.

MARCHI : *I monumenti primitivi dell' arte cristiana*, etc. (1845). Christian inscriptions principally from catacombs.

LE BLANT : *Inscriptions chrétiennes de la Gaule* (1856).

BOECK : *C. I. Graecarum*, vol. iv. (1859). Greek Christian inscriptions, ed. Kirchhoff.

In 1847 Mommsen laid down the scheme for his colossal work, *Corpus Inscriptionum Latinarum*, in which Christian inscriptions were also included, with the exception of those of Rome, which were entrusted to G. B. De Rossi. Consequently the volumes already published contain Christian as well as pagan inscriptions of the various districts dealt with. Those, however, of Spain and of Britain have been edited separately by Hübner, as will appear below.

DE ROSSI : *Inscriptiones christianae urbis Romae septimo saeculo antiquiores,* vol. i. (1861).

DE ROSSI : *Roma sotterranea cristiana,* vol. i. (1864) ; vol. ii. (1867) ; vol. iii. (1877).

LE BLANT : *Manuel d'épigraphie chrétienne d'après les marbres de la Gaule.* Paris, 1869.

HÜBNER : *Inscriptiones Hispaniae christianae* (1871).

HÜBNER : *Inscriptiones Britanniae christianae* (1876).

L. BRUZZA : *Le Inscrizioni antiche di Vercelli* (1876). Pagan and Christian inscriptions.

DE ROSSI : *Il Museo epigrafico lateranense* (1877).

BAYET : *De titulis Atticae christianis antiquissimis commentatio historica et epigrafica* (1878).

DE ROSSI : *Inscriptiones christianae,* vol. ii. part i. (1888).

F. S. KRAUS : *Die christliche Inschriften der Rheinlande* (1890-94).

BUECHELER : *Anthologia epigraphica* (Anthol. Latinae pars post., fasc. i. Lipsiae, 1895).

IHM : *Damasi epigrammata* (1895).

FORCELLA-SELETTI : *Iscrizioni cristiane di Milano* (1897).

HÜBNER : *Inscriptiones Hispaniae christianae, supplementum* (1900).

G. B. DE ROSSI : *Bullettino di archeologia cristiana.* Christian inscriptions from various quarters, and particularly Rome. (1863-1894.)

Nuovo Bullettino di archeologia cristiana (Editor, O. Marucchi. Contributors : Bonavenia, Franchi de' Cavalieri, Gatti, Kanzler, Wilpert), 1895 and onwards. Also contains inscriptions from various quarters, and particularly Rome.

Römische Quartalschrift (A. de Waal), 1887 and onwards.

Bullettino di archeologia e Storia dalmata. Christian inscriptions principally from Dalmatia.

N.B.—The general collection of Greek-Christian inscriptions is in hand.

Among these various works that of De Rossi is the one really fundamental, and we will therefore give a brief summary of it.

Summary of the work of De Rossi on the Christian Inscriptions in Rome.—In 1861 De Rossi published the first volume of his great work, in which, after a luminous and masterly review of the whole story of epigraphic science in the Middle Ages, in the Renaissance, and in modern days, he went on to give illustrative comments, confining himself, however, to the Christian inscriptions in Rome of which the date is fixed by names of consuls or otherwise. He prefaced it with a copious treatise on the methods of indicating the dates, on the rules and formulae for " consular " dating by the consul-ship, on the consular fasti, and on sundry solar and lunar cycles in use among the ancients and occasionally mentioned in the inscriptions ; next he took in chronological order all the many Christian inscriptions in Rome, mostly sepulchral, which gave their own dates with certainty. These are very rare in the first three centuries of the Church, during the period known as that of the persecutions, but become very common in the fourth century of our era ; they continue to be numerous in the fifth century, and begin to diminish in numbers again in the sixth. Finally, in the second half of the sixth century, when the consular dignity ceased to be bestowed on private individuals, all notifications of consuls disappear, and the series of inscriptions treated by the author closes with the last inscriptions of that period.

In this splendid volume may be found the most accurate information as to the formulae and the symbols in use among ancient Christians, not only in each century, but in the various parts of each century. A wonderful light is thrown upon the civil and religious history of Rome and of the Roman world by these inscriptions, where in the very names of the emperors and consuls may be read the story of the varying fortunes of the two Empires, the usurpations of tyrants, the invasions of barbarians, and the gradual passage from classical civilisation into the rudeness of the middle age.

This first volume may be considered as practically the foundation of the whole work, inasmuch as it contains the chronological canons by which the age of undated inscriptions may be fixed by comparison with others whose date is known ; this chronological critique of inscriptions is indispensable to the scholar, and without it any further investigation of our subject would be of little use.

In the sequel of the work De Rossi proposed to publish inscriptions bearing on doctrine and on history, the epitaphs of martyrs, popes, and celebrated men, together with memorial notices of the erection of great basilicas and baptisteries, as well as of less important buildings. His plan was obviously on a vast scale, bearing on the history of the Church, of the Empire, of public bodies and of families, and also on the topography of the great metropolis.

But the precious material for such a work is, alas ! to a great extent lost, for the slabs which bore a large number of the texts in question are no longer in existence, while of others we have only copies preserved to us on the old codexes. For this reason De Rossi determined to write a prefatory treatise on these ancient MSS. collections of which we spoke at the beginning of the present chapter; and the publication of these syllogae is the main purpose of his second volume (part i.), issued in 1888.

The further continuation of the work has now been entrusted to the learned epigraphist Comm. Giuseppe Gatti, who proposes to publish the valuable lists of inscriptions already drawn up by the great archaeologist, together with numerous and important additions of his own, and such corrections as further discoveries require.

PRINCIPAL COLLECTIONS OF CHRISTIAN INSCRIPTIONS EXISTING IN ROME

To the student who proposes to investigate the originals of the more numerous and important Christian inscriptions of Rome, it will be useful to know where the principal groups are to be found. They are as follows :—

The Lateran Museum of Christian Inscriptions.

The Galleria Lapidaria of the Vatican Museum (on the walls opposite the pagan inscriptions).

The Museum of Inscriptions in the Monastery of S. Paolo fuori le Mura.

The " Christian " room in the Museo Kircheriano.

The new " Christian " room in the Museum of the Capitol.

The Monastery of S. Lorenzo fuori le Mura.

The porch of Santa Maria in Trastevere.

The grand staircase of the basilica of Santa Agnese fuori le Mura.

The Roman catacombs, where all inscriptions found in the excavations made by the Commission of Sacred Archaeology are kept and systematically registered.

The following cemeteries are of the greatest importance for the number of inscriptions which are still preserved there :—

The cemetery of Priscilla on the Via Salaria (especially for the older inscriptions).

The cemetery of Callisto on the Via Appia.

The cemetery of Domitilla on the Via Ardeatina.

The cemetery of Commodilla on the Via Ostiensis.

The cemetery of S. Peter and S. Marcellinus on the Via Labicana.

After these general observations as to the original materials for the study of ancient Christian epigraphy, we will now go on to consider the actual inscriptions of primitive Christianity. And in order to carry this out in logical order we will first give some general information as to the form of the ancient Christian tombs on which the inscriptions were placed, and next as to the conventional " formulae " and symbols which they exhibit in the various periods. These general statements will be followed by an examination of the various classes of inscriptions.

CHAPTER II

GENERAL FACTS CONCERNING CHRISTIAN INSCRIPTIONS

THE first Christian inscriptions are almost exclusively sepulchral; we must therefore begin by a few words on the form of the tombs used by the ancient Christians.

From the very origin of the Church the Christians, while insisting, on the one hand, in keeping their burial-place separate from that of idolaters, desired, on the other, out of brotherly love, to share it with their brethren; and to their common burial-place they gave the name of Cemetery (κοιμητήριον, from κοιμᾶσθαι, to sleep); the word is connected with the idea of the sleep of death and with the resurrection, and was never used by pagans. The name, however, was used not only of a group of tombs (which is its commonest meaning), but also at times of a single tomb.

Christian cemeteries came into existence with Christianity, owing to the repugnance always felt by the faithful to the use of a burial-place in common with the pagans, over whose tombs superstitious rites were practised.

Furthermore, Christians objected to the practice of cremation, owing to their belief in the resurrection of the body, and their obedience to the Jewish custom of burial which was followed in the case of the Saviour. Hence, when possible, Christians excavated their tombs underground, in imitation of the tomb of Christ, which was *excisum ex petra.* But in low-lying land and on the seashore, as at Carthage and elsewhere, or where the land did not lend itself to it, they were obliged to construct cemeteries in the open air, which were then known as "sepulchral areas." But subterranean excavation was preferred where it was possible, as, for instance, in Rome, where the subsoil of tufa lent itself easily to the work. Thus the cutting of the cemeteries which we call catacombs had been begun actually in the days of the Apostles. They were originally private property and bore the names of their owners, *e.g. coemeterium Lucinae, Domitillae, Priscillae, Praetextati*, etc. But in process of time some of the cemeteries came into the possession of the Church, *i.e.* the community of the faithful, and after Constantine this must have been almost universally the case.

Here we may give some general information, applicable particularly to the older Roman cemeteries.

The underground cemeteries are formed of a vast network of subterranean galleries (*cryptae*), from which open at intervals the passages to chambers (*cubicula*); the tombs are cut in the walls of both galleries and chambers. The simplest are the *loculi*; the more ornate, with an arch above them, are the *arcosoli*.

For the shape of the galleries and cubicles with tombs in their walls see Plate I. The shape of the arched tomb or arcosolium is given on Fig. 1 (next page).

In the walls, and especially in the back walls of

the cubicles, is generally found the tomb of the shape called *arcosolium*, because it is formed of a tomb cut out of the tufa (*solium*) with an arch above forming a niche (*arcus*). Along the passages these arcosolia also occur, and these, being more imposing and more spacious than the simple *locus*,

FIG. 1.

were constructed as burial-places for the wealthier brethren. The idea that this style of tomb was used only for martyrs, or that they served as altars, is a mere vulgar error, and it could only have been true in exceptional cases.

The front of the *locus* was closed by tiles, by bricks, or by marble slabs; and the whole was then fixed in with mortar.

On this front was placed the inscription—cut, if the substance was marble; painted, or sometimes written with charcoal, if it was tile. It was usual also to place thereon various objects as distinguishing marks, *e.g.* a terra-cotta lantern, a glass vessel, or other small memorial. This is the commonest form of tomb, and the one generally used from the time of the Apostles, certainly to the fifth century. Hence the dates of Christian inscriptions from the underground cemeteries are generally within these limits, *i.e.* between the first and the fifth centuries.

But there are also other types of tomb, such as the *formae*, which are graves cut in the floor of the vault containing more than one body, one above the other, and covered with thick slabs like the arcosolia ; the stones, on the other hand, that closed the *loculi* might be of very moderate thickness, as they were not intended to bear any weight. It follows that, generally speaking, delicately cut inscriptions on slabs of oblong shape may be held to belong to loculi, and as a rule cannot be later than the fifth century.

The inscribed stones in open-air cemeteries, like those in the cemetery chapels, are of great thickness, as they form part of the pavement ; so that you may to a certain extent tell from the very appearance of the stone whence it came. Inscriptions painted in red or black all belong to cemeteries, as do also "graffiti," or marks scratched on the mortar. Graffiti are divided into two classes, sepulchral and memorial. Sepulchral graffiti are those made in the mortar with a pointed instrument at the time of inhumation ; memorial or historical graffiti are those made on the cement of the walls often long after the permanent closing of the tomb. They were the work of pilgrims and visitors from the fourth to the eighth centuries ;

sepulchral graffiti, on the other hand, can only be primitive, *i.e.* from the first to the fifth centuries.

The first Christian inscribed stones come almost exclusively from cemeteries or tombs, and vary in shape and thickness according to the character of the tombs to which they belong; thus they are long and thin when they belong to *loculi*, rather thicker when they formed the covers of arcosolia, larger and very thick when they covered *formae*.

Inscriptions taken from subterranean loculi are, as we have already said, not often later than the fifth century. Many of these may be dated back to the second century, and a very few to the first; those of the third century are more numerous, and by far the largest number are of the fourth.

Inscriptions on *formae* are generally of the fourth, but may be of the fifth and sixth centuries. Those from suburban cemeteries are not later than the sixth century, after which time the custom of burial outside the walls was almost entirely given up, and people began to bury in the great basilicas, inside the city, a fashion which lasted up to about the middle of the nineteenth century. In the more important suburban basilicas, however, burials continued even beyond the sixth century.

The age of an inscription may be told (1) by its contents, and (2) palaeographically by the style of the lettering.

The oldest inscriptions are also the shortest and simplest. Very often there is nothing cut or painted on the tomb, except the gentile name, with perhaps some simple ejaculation; sometimes, too, with the sobriquet, or "distinctive" name of the deceased.

Besides ordinary names the ancient Christians often used these sobriquets, which generally bore some religious meaning—*e.g.* Pistis, *faith*; Elpis, *hope*; Agape, *love*; Irene, *peace*; Agne, *chaste*. From these are derived corresponding masculine names, Irenaeus, Agapitus, etc.

The oldest group of inscriptions in the Roman catacombs is that in the cemetery of Priscilla, which is the most ancient in Rome, and goes back to almost Apostolic times.

This very early group contains two classes:

(*a*) Inscriptions on tiles painted in vermilion or written with charcoal.

(*b*) Inscriptions carved on marble.

Those of the first class are the oldest, some of them possibly of the first century. They bear some sort of similarity to the well-known election notices, the so-called " Programmi," which were found painted in vermilion on the outside walls of houses in ancient Pompeii.

In this class of inscriptions some, not to say most, bear nothing but the name.

Additions to these inscriptions are often found, always very short, and mostly greetings or prayers.

The commonest phrases are: *Pax tecum* or *Vivas in Deo* or *in Domino.*

The customary Latin formula *in pace* has a very common equivalent in Greek, ἐν εἰρήνῃ.

The form *in pace*, whether in Latin or in Greek, is not an absolutely certain indication of a Christian origin, as the Jews often used it, and usually in the Greek language; but as a rule they did not use it alone and without additions, but added some words peculiar to their own nation:

ἐν εἰρήνῃ
κοίμησις αὐτοῦ,

" his sleep be in peace."

But it is not hard to tell the Jewish from the Christian inscriptions — first, because the former are much the rarer, and, secondly, because on the former certain Jewish symbols are nearly always found carved or painted, *e.g.* the seven-branched candlestick, etc.

The pagans also occasionally used the word *pax*, but never alone; they always added some other phrase which immediately points to a pagan origin. Thus they would write *pax ossibus tuis*, meaning the same as *sit tibi terra levis*. Another useful means of recognising an inscription as Christian is the syllable DEP, for *depositio* or *depositus*; this mark is very frequent, and is placed before the date, *e.g.* III KAL IAN, December 30th, or as the case might be.

These words *depositus* and *depositio* are of exclusively Christian use, because they imply the hope of resurrection. Indeed *depositus* means something quite different to *situs*, the word used by the pagans, which expresses the gloomy notion of an abandonment in that place for all eternity; whereas *depositus* suggests something being given into temporary keeping, and means that the body is committed to the care of the earth till the resurrection day.

The pagans, however, more frequently used the word *defunctus*; the Christian use of it is rarer.

After *depositus* it was customary to put the date, owing to the practice of celebrating the anniversaries of the dead, a practice which gave rise to the services for the commemoration of martyrs.

To the antiquity of these commemorations the letter of the church of Smyrna on the martyrdom of S. Polycarp bears witness. This states in so many words that letters notifying the martyrdom of that holy bishop (A.D. 155) had been written to other churches, in which the day and hour on which the martyrdom took place had been carefully noted, with a view to this annual commemoration. (Eusebius, *H.E.* iv. 45.)

In the oldest inscriptions, however, the word *depositus* is not found; it begins to be general in the third century. In the fifth century we begin to find the word *situs* on Christian inscriptions, but not in the pagan sense.

We may now say a few words on the emblems used by Christians in their inscriptions.

CHAPTER III

SYMBOLS were largely used by Christians from the earliest times. This is not the place for a lengthy disquisition on symbolism, which would more properly belong to a treatise on ancient Christian art; but we may say a few words on symbolism in its more restricted sense, meaning what are called ideographic signs to express conceptions and thoughts—in short, ideas—such as the hieroglyphic characters of the ancient Egyptians. The symbolism by figure which is met with in ancient Christian inscriptions is exactly of that sort.

It was indeed from Egyptian symbolism that some of the Christian ideographic signs were derived, e.g. that of the dove, which signifies the soul freed from the trammels of the body, the soul in bliss; it may be compared to the bird denoting *Ba* in hieroglyphic character, which signifies the soul of the deceased. Another connexion might be found with the same ancient system of symbolism in the praying figure, which signifies the soul of the deceased praying in heaven.

The Christians made use of these symbols in their inscriptions to avoid the open exhibition of their religious beliefs before the eyes of the pagans.

Thus we have a series of ideographs, of which the most frequent are the following.

The oldest and one of the commonest of all is *the anchor*, which is represented in various ways. In this symbol, however much the lower part may vary, it never changes in essential shape; much less does it ever omit either of the two upper transverse arms representing the cross. Thus in the anchor we have a twofold meaning, that of the cross and that proper to the anchor, which, taken alone, signifies the hope of the shipwrecked for safety. In Christian symbolism, therefore, the double signification is the hope of the faithful centred in the Cross of Christ, or the hope of eternal salvation through the merits of the Redeemer (Plate II. 2, 4, 8).

The first Christians had another reason, besides their desire to keep their tenets secret, for using the anchor instead of the cross: they retained for a long time their natural repugnance to display the instrument which was then still used for the capital punishment of criminals in what was very naturally thought the most disgraceful and infamous fashion. Another reason which influenced them in maintaining this attitude of reserve was the fear of exposing the venerated sign of redemption to the gibes and brutal jeers of pagans.

Next to the anchor and its varieties came into use what is called the "gamma cross," a name given it because it was formed by four gammas meeting in a cross (Plate II. 7). After that the famous "monogram" appears; this in its turn underwent various changes, starting from its simplest and oldest form as a combination of the two Greek initials of the names *Jesus Christos*. Very shortly afterwards began the use of the other form, known as the " decussated monogram," as containing the mark X, the symbol for *decussis* (10 asses) in the Roman coinage (Plate II. 3, 6). This monogram must be read ΧΡΙΣΤΟΣ, and is obviously a combination of the two initials of the Sacred Name. We may reject with decision the mistaken idea, which has been repeated even by some modern critics, of reading it as *Pax Christi*, or, worse still, as *pro Christo* or *passus pro Christo*. This monogram was also called "Constantinianum"; not that Constantine invented it, but because he adopted it as a military device, placing it on the Labarum. This monogram also dates back to the earliest times, and was used by pagans as well as by Christians, though, of course, with a different meaning. For them this intersection of the two Greek letters X and P stood for ΧΡΥΣΟΣ, gold. In this precise sense the monogram was used in Ptolemaic times, and it is also met with as a stamp on coins.

The Christus monogram was in some but not frequent use in the earlier centuries also, and only in the place of the word Christ or instead of a cross ; in other words, as a sort of shorthand. But after the victory of Constantine over Maxentius (A.D. 313) it began to be used as a symbol of victory and triumph. Hence De Rossi laid down this canon, that an inscription bearing the decussated monogram with no context must as a rule be attributed to the age of Constantine or later.

This monogram underwent a notable change towards the end of the fourth century, and was drawn in a shape much nearer to that of a cross ; hence it is called the "monogrammatic cross" (Plate II. 1).

Although the use of the cross for capital punishment had been abolished by Constantine through
reverence for the instrument of Christ's passion,
the old objection to the use of the symbol lasted
well through the fourth century, so that it was not
till after the definite triumph of Christianity under
Theodosius (A.D. 384) that the true shape of the
cross begins to come into ordinary use, although
instances of it are very occasionally found in primitive inscriptions.

Two inscriptions from the cemetery of S. Peter
and S. Marcellinus on the Via Labicana, which are
not later than the third century, infringe the above
rule by inserting among the letters of the name a
Greek T, which is, in fact, a slightly disguised
cross of the Greek type, in which the upper
member is wanting. Thus the symbol would be
equivalent to an anchor and to the formula *Spes in
cruce Christi*.

Another symbol very usual in the first three
centuries, and indeed chiefly found in them, is the
fish, painted or carved on the stone, or scratched
on the mortar of the loculi (Plate III. 2, 4).

The fish (ΙΧΘΥΣ) is the most ancient symbol of
Christ, the food of the faithful as imaged in the
multiplication of the loaves and fishes, a miracle
which was interpreted as a type and a forecast of
the Eucharistic feast ; as such we find this symbol
referred to in some of the oldest inscriptions, and
figured in the frescoes of cemeteries from the
second century onwards.

Another reason for the mystical interpretation of
the fish may be found in the story of Tobias : as
by means of a fish the father of Tobias recovered
his sight, so from Christ we receive our light.

This is the meaning of the words of Prosper of Aquitania, *Praebens se universo mundo ictyn e cujus interioribus remediis quotidie illuminamur et pascimur.* To these fancies may be also added the well-known explanation given in the sibylline books of the word ΙΧΘΥΣ, a fish, as an acrostic of the words Ἰησοῦς — Χριστός — Θεοῦ — Υἱός — Σωτήρ, "Jesus Christ, Son of God, Saviour."

In some inscriptions we find the symbolical meaning of the fish clearly indicated, for instead of the figure of the fish we see the word ἰχθυς with a stop between each letter, as if to remind the reader of the acrostic. In other inscriptions the fish is dotted disconnectedly all over the stone; in others, again, it stands alone with the name of the deceased: in that case it evidently stands for the name of Christ, and, in fact, in other exactly similar inscriptions we find the monogram XP in the place of the fish. Hence the two symbols are equivalent; and in both inscriptions after the name we should read the words *in Christo.* But Christian symbolism is not always so simple as this: it sometimes assumes much more complex forms, of the most usual of which we will now give some account, with illustrations.

In some inscriptions we find the fish and the anchor combined, which undoubtedly means *spes in cruce Christi filii Dei salvatoris mundi*, or *spes in Christo*. When this combined symbol is found alone it may signify the crucifixion. But very often Jesus Christ was denoted by a dolphin, that being the fish which was vulgarly held to be the friend and preserver of man. Similarly we have seen an "encolpium" or neck-pendant in the shape of a dolphin with the words σωτήρ μου, "my Saviour."

In the cemetery of Callistus a fresco exists representing a dolphin twined round a trident.[1] This symbolical figure most certainly stands for the crucifixion of Christ.

Sometimes, but not very often, the idea of the crucifixion is represented in another way, *i.e.* by a lamb below an anchor. Of this we have an example in an inscription of very early date in the cemetery of Callisto, in which we find the name *Faustinianus*; below this there is a dove with a twig, denoting the soul enjoying eternal bliss, and close to it an anchor lying on its side, and above it a lamb looking at the dove (Plate III. 1).

But the fish does not always represent Christ; sometimes it stands for the believer. It is this last symbolism which inspires the fancy of Tertullian, when he says that as the fish lives and can only live in the water, so the believer lives and can only live in and by virtue of the water of baptism; and as the fish is born therein, so the believer is born again therein to eternal life, which is the true life. *Nos pisciculi secundum* ἰχθυν *nostrum Jesum Christum in aqua nascimur et nonnisi quam in aqua permanendo salvi facti sumus.*

Generally when several fish are found together each stands for an individual believer.

And we often find the same idea better developed in other inscriptions on which we see two little fishes moving towards an anchor; these represent the believers going to Christ, their one salvation. The same idea is sometimes still more clearly set forth by fishes suspended by small chains

---

[1] The trident was another veiled way of representing the cross; for if you remove the two side teeth of the trident a true cross remains.

to the stem of the anchor, a combination which certainly signifies the intimate union of the faithful with Christ.

Another ideographic symbol connected with the sea and the harbour which we find in use is that of the ship, which represents the life of this world as a ceaseless journey, full of disaster.

Sometimes the ship is the mystical ship of the Church. In some inscriptions a dolphin is near the ship, clearly intended to recall the thought that through the tempests of this life Christ the Saviour ever follows us with His love.

To this group of symbols also belongs the lighthouse, in the shape of a rude tower, at the top of which a flame is sometimes represented; this certainly points to the final reception of the ship into the waters of the true haven of safety, heaven (Plate III. 5).

The ship is a very important symbol when there are figures or inscriptions in it or near it. There is an instance of this in a bas-relief on a sarcophagus found at Spoleto, in which we see a boat propelled by four rowers, Mark, Matthew, Luke, and John. This we may easily understand as representing the Church, the mystical ship, borne to harbour by the evangelists under their chief pilot Jesus Christ.

Again, on a sarcophagus in the cemetery of S. Valentine in Rome is shown the sea, with a man standing on the shore intent on fishing; on the sea is a boat steered by a figure under which we read the name "Paulus," while on the bows the name Thecla is carved. In this important bas-relief we meet with a symbolic representation of the idea that the deceased lady whose body lay in that sarcophagus was led to the harbour of Salvation through the lessons of Paul, even as Thecla reached it by the same means. This valuable record has been described by me in the *Nuovo Bullett. di arch. crist.*, 1897, p. 103.

The Church is once more represented by a boat on the sea in a fresco belonging to the cemetery of Callisto. In this picture the boat is represented with a sail made in the shape of a cross, evidently signifying the Church sailing through the stormy sea of the world under the banner of the cross of Christ.

Another symbol is the vase, alone, or combined

FIG. 2.

with doves. The vase when alone symbolises the good works of the Christian ; but if there are doves with it, and if they are drinking from it, and especially if the vase is a large one, then the idea represented is quite different, that of the soul rejoicing in celestial bliss. The same idea is figured by a dove pecking a bunch of grapes.

All these symbols, and many others less commonly found, were used to expand the ancient inscriptions, which in themselves were so concise as to tell the reader little or nothing. They go back to very early times, and are generally not later than the fourth century.

Sometimes by the side of the praying figure we

F

have another of great significance, that, namely, of the Good Shepherd bearing the lamb on his shoulders. This symbol is very frequent in paintings, and also, to a rather less extent, in "graffiti." When the Good Shepherd is represented with the figure in prayer, it denotes the soul praying to the Good Shepherd in heaven (Plate V. 4). Sometimes the figure in prayer is in the midst of doves, which signifies the soul received into the company of the mystical flock of the Shepherd (Plate IV. 3).

Besides these symbols there are others which relate to the games and shows of the ancients: ideographically considered they signify these games and shows; but as Christian inscriptions they have another meaning.

Thus a palm branch on a monument means victories won, and when used by pagans means neither more nor less than the winning of chariot-races. No doubt Christians too have made use of this sign for the same purpose, but this very rarely occurs. This use of it is justified by the fact that there were jockeys (*i.e.* racing charioteers) among Christians as well as among the pagans, as is known from more than one instance. Thus an inscription in the cemetery of S. Sebastian, on which a palm branch is carved, says that the charioteer in question had won a hundred races *in glauca, i.e.* in the blue faction. But, as we said above, these instances are rare.

Christianity then soon took possession of this class of symbols; indeed, from apostolic times onwards Christians in their conversation used expressions which, though taken from the games, had a specially Christian significance.

The first who speaks thus is S. Paul himself, when he says *non coronabitur nisi qui legitime certaverit*—meaning, in a Christian sense, "none shall receive the reward of life eternal but he who has fought out his life under the banner of Christ."

The mistaken notion was once held that the palm branch always signified martyrdom. I say mistaken, because there exist clear proofs that it is not true; indeed, we often find drawings of palm branches on inscriptions which go back to the great Peace of the Church, while, on the other hand, there are very many inscriptions which undoubtedly record martyrs and yet do not show a palm branch. The idea is therefore baseless, though still held by some.

The other symbolic sign is the crown. This had two forms, either a plain circle or the "athletic" crown, the *brabium* or *corona justitiae*, of which S. Paul speaks.

The first was of ordinary shape, *i.e.* a ring covered with bay-leaves; the second had the form of a piece of twisted stuff or of a cap, such as was actually given to winners on a race-course.

There is connected with the ideas of the palm branch and victory a well-known monogram, of which we have many instances, and which may be described as formed by a combination of the letters P and E (℞). We find it used by Christians and pagans alike, and it is seen on monuments connected with the circus. Thus, for example, we find the monogram in question over the pictures of charioteers or of a horse. So also it is found over the busts of gladiators.

The true meaning of this monogram is not yet

known, and opinions upon it vary. All allow that
the P is the initial of *palma*, the more so as the
two are often found near one another, and indeed
in some cases the monogram is surrounded with
palm branches. There are various and more or
less plausible interpretations of this monogram;
some treat it as formed of two letters, and thus
taken it might stand for either *palma Elea* or
palma emerita. But the most probable view is
that the monogram consists, not of the two

FIG. 3.

letters PE only, but of three letters, PFE, inasmuch as in several instances an F is clearly
visible, and hence the more generally received
reading of it is *palma feliciter*.

Sometimes, but rarely, we find in these inscriptions the figure of a horse (Plate IV. 1), which
clearly refers to the race of life and the words of
S. Paul, *cursum consummavi*, etc.

Another very rare symbol is that of the gladiator
with one or other of his weapons. The clearest
and most certain example of this is on a leaden
vessel discovered at Tunis, which was probably
used as a baptismal font. On this, along with
many other symbols, such as the Good Shepherd,
and the monograms, we find the figure of a

gladiator, a symbol which we must interpret from a Christian point of view.

In this case it would stand for the Christian who has fought the battle of life with courage, and has come out a conqueror. In the cemetery of S. Sebastian too, at the back of a burial-chamber, we see surrounded by other symbols the figure of an athlete, to which we must assign the same meaning as to that on the vessel from Tunis. Another symbol found on a "graffito" over an inscription is the bushel measure, a large hollow vessel in the shape of a truncated cone, at the top of which some ears of corn show, denoting that good and complete measure has been given. This symbol was to remind the faithful of the full and overflowing measure with which God rewards good deeds done and sacrifices made for His name's sake.

Among these ideographic symbols we sometimes find a combination of the sheep, the emblem of the believer; with the peacock, the emblem of immortality (Plate V. 1); with a suppliant in the midst of saints (Plate IV. 7) (a symbol of which we shall speak in its place); or with the figure of an animal representing ideographically the name of the deceased, *e.g.* a lion in the inscription on one Leo (Plate V. 2), a ship in the inscription of a certain *Nabira*, etc. Lastly, these symbols sometimes represent episodes from the Old or New Testament, like those in pictures or sculptures. A good instance of this may be seen in a marble of the Lateran Museum, representing various symbolical groups, such as Adam and Eve, Daniel among the lions, etc. (Plate IV. 9). Notice also the scene of the Epiphany (Plate V. 3). We may also remark as a peculiarity, that sometimes, instead of the names of the deceased, monograms were used, or rather complexes of the letters that formed the name, as in the two examples of Rufilla and Rusticus given in Plate IV. 6, 8.

Interpunctuation

By this we mean the marks used to separate words in old inscriptions, both Christian and pagan. They have an extraordinary variety of shapes. Most frequently they are in the shape of small triangles, more rarely in that of round dots. But often the points are made in the shape of leaves, which, as we know, were called by the ancients *hederae distinguentes*, though they have been mistaken by some for representations of the heart. But the ancients, if I may say so, were absurdly whimsical in the matter of these points, for which they used various shapes and geometrical figures, placing them not only between words, but even between syllables, or even between the letters of the same word. In some inscriptions the points are shaped like palm branches, in others like arrows; and the latter have sometimes been erroneously supposed to represent the instrument of martyrdom (Plate VI. 2).

CHAPTER IV

METRICAL INSCRIPTIONS

CHRISTIAN metrical inscriptions, in contrast with those of pagan origin, are generally not only lacking in elegance, but often rough and even incorrect in scansion, and they might therefore be called rhythmical rather than really metrical. From the first to the fourth century inscriptions of this sort are nearly all sepulchral, and very short and simple. They often present us with a patchwork of ancient poetry, and whole or halves of verses borrowed from classical authors; so that they differ little, if at all, from pagan inscriptions of the same sort; but when they are the composition of Christian poets solely, as sometimes occurs, they are of greater value, as expressing the thoughts, the beliefs, and the dogmas of the then Christian world. After the peace of Constantine we begin to find inscriptions placed in the basilicas used for public worship, poems by Pope Damasus in honour of martyrs, and eulogies of men of note. Some of these poems, when better known, were imitated by later writers, who borrowed whole sentences from them. All this constitutes, so far as it goes, a magnificent chapter in ancient Christian literature; indeed we may call it a patristic history built up of inscriptions, seeing that these noble lines deal with doctrine and ecclesiastical tradition, exactly like the writings of the Fathers, and that it was precisely for the purpose of instructing the faithful in these matters that they were so often placed on the walls of the most-frequented tombs and sacred edifices.

Inscriptional poetry of the age preceding Constantine often reproduces verses from Vergil, as, for instance, that well-known line from the *Aeneid : abstulit atra dies et funere mersit acerbo.* A valuable inscription of the third century, which was to be seen in the Villa Borghese, contains the words, *miserere animae non digna ferenti*; and not only is this a Christian inscription, but it commemorates a martyr of whom it says, *sanguineo lavit Deus ipse lavacro.*

Among the poetical inscriptions of the first centuries two hold incontestably the place of honour— (1) that of Abercius of Hierapolis in Phrygia and (2) that of Pectorius of Augustodunum (Autun) in France ; of these we shall speak at the proper time.

Of inscriptions referring to doctrine we have some instances in Rome, *e.g.* those of Maritima and Agape in the cemetery of Priscilla, and that of Julia Euarista from a vault in the Via Latina. Christian metrical inscriptions previous to Constantine are often in the metre called *quasi-versus,* introduced by the poet Commodianus in the third century of our era. He wrote shortly after the persecution of Decius (A.D. 250), and the purpose of his poems was to instruct pagans and edify Christians.[1] In the same style is the well-known

---

[1] On the poet Commodianus see the recent treatise of Ludwig, *Commodiani carmina*, Leips., 1877 and 1878. Cf. Boissier in the *Revue archéologique*, November and December 1883.

inscription of the deacon Severus in the cemetery
of Callisto, and also the acrostic of Theodulus,
an employé in the office of the Praetor Urbanus,
discovered in the same cemetery. After the Peace,
metrical inscriptions increase in number. Constantine adorns the walls of his basilicas with
poetry, Pope Damasus in Rome and Ambrose in
Milan celebrate the glories of the martyrs in elegant
epigrams, Paulinus of Nola magnifies the deeds of
his hero Felix in poetry, and, in the midst of his
meditation on Holy Scripture, Jerome writes a
metrical epitaph on the noble lady Paula; Bassus
the consul composed a panegyric on Monica, the
mother of Augustine, and the mighty bishop of
Hippo himself writes affectionate verses to the
memory of the deacon Nabor, who was killed by
the Donatists. The mausoleums of the Christian
nobility are adorned with metrical inscriptions; we
need only refer, as a representative example, to the
magnificent inscriptions on the tomb of the Anicii
near the Vatican Basilica.

The same fashion is continued in the fifth
century; thus we find metrical inscriptions of Spes
and Achilles, bishops of Spoleto; of Sidonius
Apollinaris, prefect of Rome in 467 and later bishop
of Clermont; of Ennodius of Pavia. Sixtus III.
adorned the Liberian Basilica and the baptistery
of the Vatican with poetical inscriptions. Lastly,
Symmachus followed the example of Damasus, the
poet of the martyrs. In the following century
Pope Vigilius rebuilt the Christian monuments in
Rome which had suffered during the Gothic
War, and restored the effaced verses of Damasus
on the original slabs; he records in verse his own
pious labours as well as the liberation of the

land from the dominion of the barbarian in the following line : *Hostibus expulsis omne novavit opus.* Other laudatory poems are found in that age of decadence ; but the inscription on the tomb of Gregory the Great in the basilica of S. Peter may be considered as reflecting the last ray of the "grandeur which was Rome."

In the seventh century culture continues to wane, manners become barbaric throughout the whole West, the beautiful language of Latium gradually changes, ignorance and misery increase. It is not surprising if in this condition of affairs the literature of inscriptions also degenerates, and metrical inscriptions become every day rarer. The most important products of that rude age are those few monumental inscriptions which occur on the mosaics of the basilicas. Finally, with the seventh century begins the age of mediaeval inscriptions, at which we stop.

PART II

A COLLECTION OF CHRISTIAN INSCRIP-TIONS, MAINLY ROMAN, IN THEIR VARIOUS CLASSES.

CHAPTER I

PRIMITIVE INSCRIPTIONS, WITH PRIMITIVE CONVENTIONAL ABBREVIATIONS

THE most ancient Christian inscriptions are those in the cemetery of Priscilla in the Via Salaria ; and with these we propose to begin our list ; but we shall add others taken from other quarters.[1]

I

MODESTINA	A Ω

Cemetery of Priscilla.   Painted on tiles in red.

The name alone appears, followed by the two letters A and Ω, which, according to the symbolism

[1] If this book were a *corpus inscriptionum*, it would be necessary to add in all cases the bibliography of the inscription. But, as the inscriptions are only given as illustrations, it is

75

taken from the Apocalypse, denote the beginning and the end ; as much as to say that the deceased believed in Him who was the beginning and end of all things, *i.e.* in God and in His Christ.

2

ZOSIME	PAX TE CVM (anchor)

Cemetery of Priscilla.   In red on tile.

The formula *pax tecum* was used in the remotest times, being derived from the greeting of Christ to the Apostles, "pax vobis."   The anchor painted beside it is the emblem of Christian hope, while at the same time it suggests the shape of the cross. It therefore represents the hope of the deceased in the redemption of Christ.

3

PAX TECVM VALERIA
(anchor)   (palm)

Cemetery of Priscilla.   In red on tiles.

Observe the same words and the same symbol as above.

unnecessary to do this, and it will suffice if we state in each case the place in which it was discovered and that in which it is at present to be seen.

4

> CAELESTINA
> PAX

Cemetery of Priscilla.   In red on tile.

The complete formula *pax tecum* is to be understood.

5

> AVRELI · VARRO
> DVLCISSIME · ET
> DESIDERANTIS
> SIME COIVX · PAX
> TIBI BENEDICTE

Cemetery of Priscilla.   Marble.

A remarkable expression of affectionate greeting and of kindly wishes.   The epithet *benedicte* alludes to the Saviour's words, "venite benedicti patris mei."

6

> ΑΓΑΠΗΤΟC
> ΕΝ ΕΙΡΗΝΗ

" Agapito in peace."

Cemetery of Priscilla.   In red on tile.   (Plate VI. 1.)

The name Agapito is one of those used by Christians, and is derived from " Agape," meaning "the beloved, the dear one."

7

LVMENA	PAX · TE	CVM · FI
(anchor) (palm)	(arrow)	(anchor) (arrow)

Discovered in the cemetery of Priscilla in 1802; now preserved in the church of Mugnano near Naples.

There are three tiles, each of which contains a portion of the inscription. It is of great age, as may be inferred from the style and the lettering, and must have originally been arranged thus:

PAX · TE	CVM · FI	LVMENA

(Plate VI. 2.)

The most natural explanation of the misplacement of the three tiles is that they belonged to an early tomb, and were taken thence to close another of later date.[1] The arrows are only punctuation marks.

8

EI	PHNH · COI · OYPCA

" Ursa, peace be with thee."
Galleria Lapidaria of the Vatican.

In all these inscriptions where the formula *pax tecum* or *tibi* occurs it may be noted that the verb

[1] Cp. Marucchi, *Nuovo Bull. di arch. crist.*, 1906, p. 190.

understood is *sit*, not *est*, expressing a wish or a prayer, not a mere statement of fact.

9

MARCIANVS · HIC · DORMIT · IN · PACE

Cemetery of Priscilla.   Painted in black on tile.

The expression *hic dormit* is a profession of belief in the doctrine of the final resurrection of the body, and recalls the words of the gospel "Lazarus amicus noster dormit" (John xi. 11). It is related to the name given by Christians to their burial-places, *coemeterium*, or *dormitorium*, as opposed to the *domus aeterna* of the pagans.

10

HIPERCHIVS
HIC · DORMIT

Cemetery of Priscilla.   Marble.

A fine laconic inscription.

Sometimes the inscription indicates that the tomb is intended as a resting-place for the deceased, as in the following instances.

11

DORMITIONI ISIDORAE

Cemetery of Priscilla.   Marble.

12

(Hermes.)	DORMITIONI T · FLA · EVTY CHIO · QVI VI XIT · ANN · XVIIII MES · XI · D · III HVNC · LOCVM DONABIT · M · ORBIVS · HELI VS · AMICVS KARISSIMVS KARE • • BALE (two fishes)	(Hermes.)

Cemetery of Commodilla (De Rossi, *Roma sott.* i. p. 186).

In this inscription notice should be taken of the affectionate greeting KARE · BALE, and the use of the three names, praenomen, gentile name, and cognomen, a mark of great antiquity.

13

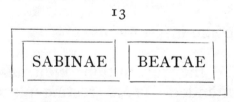

| SABINAE | BEATAE |

Cemetery of Priscilla.   In red on tiles.   (Plate V. 5.)

The epithet *beata* must not be read in the sense now given it, of one held in veneration by the faithful after her death.   It alludes only to the celestial bliss which the deceased is supposed to enjoy.

14

ΠΕΤΡΟ Ϲ	PETRVS · AVSANONTIS FILIVS

Cemetery of Priscilla.   In red on tiles.

This, like other inscriptions containing the name of Peter, is of great significance, as the name was of exclusively Christian use, having been adopted in memory of the Apostle Peter.

It is worthy of note that the repetition of this name in Greek and in Latin is peculiar to the cemetery of Priscilla, where there are other reasons, historical and topographical, for believing that there was a special cult commemorating the first preaching of S. Peter in Rome.

15

LIVIA NICARVS

LIVIAE PRIMITIVAE

SORORI FECIT

Q · V · AN · XXIIII · M · VIIII

(fish)   (shepherd)   (anchor)

Inscription on a Sarcophagus
now in Paris in the Museum of the Louvre.

This comes from the primitive cemetery which grew up round the tomb of S. Peter in the Vatican; and its great age is a further proof of the great antiquity of that cemetery.

16

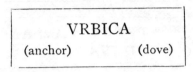

In the Cemetery of Callisto.   Marble.   (Plate II. 5.)

The graffiti over this inscription are of great significance.   They represent the soul of the deceased Urbica in the shape of a dove admitted to the mystical garden of Paradise as a reward of her belief and hope in the Cross of Christ.

17

Cemetery of Callisto.   Marble.   (Plate II. 2.)

Here we find the name alone, and the oldest form of the anchor symbol.

18

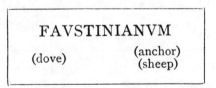

Cemetery of Callisto.   Marble.   (Plate III. 1.)

Here also the ideographic signs have their import.   The lamb below the anchor represents Christ under the Cross, and the dove represents the soul of Faustinianus winging its way to heaven as a reward for his belief in the resurrection.

19

EPAFRODITO · DVLCISSIMO

Cemetery of S. Agnese.   Marble.

20

LEONTI P
AX   A   FRA
TRIBVS
VALE

Cemetery of Priscilla.   Marble.

This expresses the greeting of the Christian brethren to the deceased Leontius, and thus is connected with the prayers offered by the congregation of the faithful over the tomb at the moment of burial.

This same greeting, though found in many pagan inscriptions, does not here bear the heathen meaning of an eternal farewell, but rather suggests the hope of the Christian by the use of the beautiful words " Pax a fratribus."

Another very ancient ejaculation is that which prays that the deceased may live in God, as in the following :

21

AGAPE VIVAS IN DEO

Cemetery of Priscilla.

22

> EVCARPE
> IN DEO
> VIVES
> (anchor)

Cemetery of Priscilla.   Cut on a brick.

Here we find, combined with the ejaculation, an anchor as emblem of the Cross, the idea being that expressed by the Apostle Paul that the Cross is the *life* and the *salvation* of the Christian.

23

> ☧
>
> STAFILI
> PAX TECVM
> IN DEO
> HAVE VALE

The two words HAVE and VALE [1] are noticeable; their combination is full of meaning, and uncommon in Christian inscriptions.

24

> AEMILIANE ROMANE
> VIBATIS IN DEO

Cemetery of Priscilla.   Marble.

---

[1] Le Blant, *L'Épig. chrét.* p. 10.

Specimens of these primitive inscriptions, painted in red or black on brick or tiles, which come almost exclusively from the cemetery of Priscilla, may be seen in Plate VI.

To summarise the above short notes on the inscriptions of the earliest group, the distinctive characteristics of primitive Christian epigraphy may be easily recognised: viz. a great sobriety in the emblems and in the style; the almost exclusive use of short, but none the less strong and affectionate, ejaculations, the one most frequently in use being the apostolic greeting, *pax tecum, pax tibi.* The symbolism is confined almost entirely to the use of the anchor and (occasionally) of the palm branch. The increased use of symbolic and doctrinal language, on the other hand, is a mark of the third century, which from this point of view was the Augustan age of Christian epigraphy. And it is with the inscriptions bearing on doctrine that we shall specially deal in the following chapter.

CHAPTER II

General features—The Unity of God—The Divinity of Christ—
The Holy Spirit—The Trinity

General Features of Doctrinal Inscriptions

By doctrinal inscriptions we mean those that refer
in some way, either directly or by inference, to the
dogmas of Christianity.

It is not suggested that a complete statement can
be composed of the doctrinal theories of the first
ages of Christianity out of the inscriptions in the catacombs; to this the spirit of these inscriptions does
not lend itself, seeing they are exclusively sepulchral,
and therefore composed with a special intention
and object; moreover, they are entirely of a private
character, expressing the feeling of the early
Christians towards the beloved dead. If any of
them therefore allude to doctrine, it can only be
because the doctrine thus alluded to is a natural
and essential part of the writer's conception as to a
future life and as to the fate of the departed. For
this reason all the doctrines of Christianity cannot be
illustrated from inscriptions, but only those which
have some connexion with the life beyond the
grave. These are : the belief in the Unity of God;

in the Trinity; in the divinity of Christ; in the Resurrection; the belief in the efficacy of the prayers of the living for the dead, and *vice versa* of the dead for the living, which is tantamount to the doctrine of the Communion of Saints. There are some instances, however, of inscriptions touching the sacraments that are more closely connected with a future life—notably, Baptism, which opens the door to eternal bliss; and its companion, Confirmation.

Sometimes, but less frequently, allusion is also made to the sacrament of the Eucharist, which is the pledge of eternal life.

§ I

Doctrinal Inscriptions referring to the Unity of God

In the midst of the universal polytheism of old times, the Jews and the Christians alone acknowledged and worshipped one God. Some of the pagan philosophers admitted the conception of a single God, but the idea was always vague and confused.

Christians gloried in the fact that they worshipped the One True God, and hence they claimed to be described as of *cultores Dei*. For this reason Christian inscriptions refer sometimes to the Unity of God, as the watchword and pledge of their faith, in such expressions as: IN NOMINE DEI—EN ONOMATI TOY ΘEOY— VIVAS IN DEO—ZHC EN ΘEΩ—PAX TIBI IN DEO.

The following inscriptions begin with a solemn Christian invocation, *In nomine Dei* :

25

```
IN · NOMINE · DEI · GORGON
IN · PACE · CVM · PARENT
ET · MENSIS · N · VI · ETDE
QVI · VIXIT · ANNOS · DVO
```

Lateran Museum.

26

```
... IN · NOMINE · DEI · IN · P
... III · D · XXII · DECESIT
... NO · CON · PARENTES · TO
(to)TI · TRES · HIC · CAPVT · AD · CAPVT
```

Cemetery of Cyriaca.   Lateran Museum.

This inscription is remarkable for the expression used in the last line, which speaks of three deceased, (*to*)TI TRES, who were buried in the same tomb; this must assuredly be the meaning of the words *caput ad caput.*

The inscriptions that follow express the prayers of the survivors, that the dead may enjoy eternal life in God in the abode of the Saints; the formula is therefore, grammatically speaking, not indicative but optative.

27

```
BONO ATQ DVLCISSIMO COIVGI CASTORI
NO QVI VIXIT ANNIS LXI MENSIBVS V · D · X
BENEMERENTI VXOR FECIT · VIVE IN
      (ivy leaf)        DEO        (ivy leaf)
```

From Cemetery of Callisto.   Lateran Museum.

28

```
FAVSTINA · DVLCIS
BIBAS · IN · DEO
(vivas in Deo)
```

From S. Agnese.   Lateran Museum.

29

```
FORTVNATA · VIVES
IN · DEO
```

Lateran Museum.

30

```
ΕΥΤΥΧΙC
CΩΤΗΡΙΗ
CΥΜΒΙΩ
ΚΑΛΩCΗ
ΥΙΩΜΕΝΗ
ΕΠΟΙΗCΑ
ΖΗC · ΕΝ · ΘΕΩ
(thou livest in God)
```

S. Ermete.   Lateran Museum.

31

VRSINA
VIBES · DEO

Lateran Museum.

32

(palm branch)   VI DVA P FELICISSIMA
IN · DEO · VIVES   (ivy leaf)

Cemetery of Cyriaca.   Lateran Museum.

The following inscription asserts more specifically
the doctrine of the Unity of God, which, as has
been pointed out at the outset, is the fundamental
idea of Christianity as opposed to paganism :

33

· · · · · · · · · · ·
ORO · A · BOBIS
FRATRES · BONI
PER · VNVM · DEVM
NE · QVIS · TITVLVM
MEVM · MOLESTET

From the Cemetery of S. Hermes.   Kircherian Museum.

§ 2

Inscriptions referring to Christ and the Trinity

Some inscriptions bear witness to the doctrine of the divinity of Christ by placing His name in the position occupied elsewhere by that of God, *e.g.* :

34

IN NOMINE · ☧ *(Christi)*
QVIESCIT ·

Lateran Museum.

This inscription is probably anterior to Constantine, as the monogram of Christ is used as an abbreviation for His name (*Compendium Scripturae*).

Other inscriptions, however, explicitly assert the divinity of Christ.

35

AEQVITIO · IN · ☧ DEO · INNOFITO
BENEMERENTI · QVI · VIXIT
AN · XXVI · M · V · D · IIII · DEC · III · NON · AVG

Lateran Museum.

In the first line read "In Christo Deo."

In the following Greek inscription Christ is positively called God:

36

ЕРМΛІСКЕ · ΦΩC · Ζ
НС · ΕΝ · ΘΕΩ · ΚΥΡΙΕΙ
Ω · ΧΡΕΙCΤΩ · ΑΝΝ
ΩΡΟΥΜ · Χ · ΜΗCΩ
ΡΟΥΜ · ΣΕΡΤΕ

"Oh Hermaiscus, thou Light, thou shalt live in the Lord God Christ." He lived ten years and seven months.

Lateran Museum.

This fine inscription tells us of a boy by name Hermaiscus, who had been baptized and confirmed shortly before his death, and is therefore addressed as φῶs, light, that being one of the names given at baptism.

37

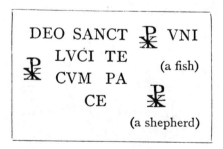

Via Latina.   Seen by Bosio ; now lost.

Here too the name of Christ is shortly expressed by the monogram, and it must be read, *Deo Sancto Christo uni.*

In the following very ancient Greek inscription the first line names the Eternal Father, the first person of the Trinity; and it concludes with a fine form of doxology, or hymn of praise:

38

Ο ΠΑΤΗΡ · ΤΩΝ · ΠΑΝΤΩΝ · ΟΤC · ΕΠΟΙΗCΕC · K̄

ΠΑΡΕΛΑΒΗC · ΕΙΡΗΝΕΝ · ΖΟΗΝ · K̄ · ΜΑΡΚΕΛΛΟΝ

COI · ΔΟΞΑ · ΕΝ · ☧   (anchor)

" Oh Father of all, thou that hast created Irene, Zoe, and Marcellus, receive them to thyself. To Thee be glory in Christ."

Cemetery of Priscilla.
In the floor of the gallery of the vaults of the Acilii.

In the next inscription mention is made of the first and second persons of the Trinity.

39

HIC · POSITVS · EST · FLORENTI
NVS · INFANS · QVI · VIXIT · ANNOS
SEPTEM · ET · REQVIEM · ADCE
PIT · IN · DEO · PATRE · NOSTRO
ET · CHRISTO · EIVS

Sabaria in Pannonia.

The following inscriptions make more special mention of the divinity of Christ:

40

IN · D · CRISTO
. . . OMITIA OPE FILIE CARISSIMED
. . . E NI INNOCENTISSIME PVELLE QVI
. . . II DIES VIIII ORAS V IN PACE CVM

"In Deo Christo."

Cemetery of Cyriaca.   Lateran Museum.

41

BONΩCH
BONΩCΩ
ΤΩ
ΚΟΙΜΩΜΕΝΟΙ
ΕΝΚΩΗΜ

"Who sleeps in our Lord."

Cemetery of Domitilla.

42

ΠΡΙΜΑ · ΜΕΤΑ · ΙΔ ι
ΑΕ · ΘΥΓΑΤΡΟC · ΚΟΙ
ΜΩΜΕΝΙ · Εν · θε
ω · ΚΥΡΙω . . . . . χριστω

"Who sleep in the Lord God Christ."

Cemetery of Domitilla.

43

ΕΡΜΙΟΝΗΝ · ΓΛΥΚυταττην
ΟΙ · ϹΟΙ · ΓΟΝΕΙϹ · ΕΓΡΑѰΑΝ
ΕΝ · ΘΕΙ . . . ΙΗ ☧ · ΒΑϹΙΛΕ
ΗΜΗΡΑϹ · ΚΒ · ΑΠΕΘανεν

Cemetery of Priscilla.

The third line must mean, "In the Divine Kingdom of Christ."

The two next inscriptions contain the name of Jesus, which is very rarely found in ancient Christian inscriptions.

44

	REG	INA VIBAS	
(palm)	IN	DOMINO	(palm)
		ZESV	

From the Via Salaria Nuova.   Lateran Museum.

45

ΕΝ · ΘΕΩ · ΤΕϹΟϹ
ΧΕΡΕΤΕ

" Hail in God Jesus."

Cemetery of Salona in Dalmatia.

46

```
AGAPE · NERAIDI · NVTRICI
ET ☧ PRIBATVS · SVE · IN · PACE
IN · DO · MI · NO · NOS · TRO · D · C · T
```

Venice.　Correr Museum.　(From the Roman catacombs.)

In the last line points are placed to separate the syllables of the words "In Domino nostro," and also to indicate that the single letters at the end are abbreviations. Therefore read "In Domino nostro Deo Christo."

47

```
ΚΛ · ΦΙΛΩΤΑ · ΓΛΥΚΥΤΑΤΩ
ΑΔΕΛΦΩ · ΘΕΟΔΩΡΩ · ΖΩΜΕΝ
ΕΝ · ΘΕΩ   (fish)
```

"Claudius Philotas to his beloved brother Theodorus. May we live in God (Jesus Christ, Son of God the Redeemer)."

Cemetery of Priscilla.

Here the name of Jesus Christ is expressed by the figure of the fish, of which we shall see other instances.

48

```
CALLODROME BENE
DICTA IN ☧
GREMIVM TOTIVS BONI
TATIS AVTRIX CASTISSIMI
PVDORIS ❧ CIRCA MARI
TVM SATIS RELIGIOSA
VIXISTI ANNIS XVIIII
MARITVS
CONIVGI · DIGNE
❧
LEAE INNOCEN
TISSIMAE CESQVEN
TI · IN · PACE · Q · B · AN · XXI
M · VI · MARITVS CONIVGI
```

Cemetery of the Giordani in the Via Salaria.

Remarkable for the expression at the beginning, "Benedicta in Christi gremium."

49

```
      SOZON · BENEDICTVS
      REDIDIT · AN · NOBE
      BERVS ☧ ISPIRVM
IN · PACE · ET · PET · PRO · NOBIS
```

Cemetery of the Giordani.

In this case also the monogram is used instead of the name of Christ; read, therefore, "Verus Christus (accipiat) spiritum (tuum) in pace et pete pro nobis."

50

PVELLE VRBICE · CON
QVIA EIVS OBSEQV
SEMPER NOBISCON
IN MATRIMONIO QVEVI
P · M · XXX RECESSIT DIE XIII · KAL
IN PACE ET IN NOMINE ☧ FILII EIVS

"In nomine Christi filii ejus."

From MSS. belonging to Bruzio.

51

... VIVAS
... ET IN DIE
*judicii a*DEAM
*cum fide ad tribu*NAL CHRISTI

Cemetery of S. Agnese.

This inscription is very valuable for its contents ; the only parallel to it is in the fragment of a "graffito" found in a niche opposite the so-called tomb of S. Felicissimus and Agapitus in the *spelunca magna* of the cemetery of Praetextatus, which is to this effect, *succurrite ut vincam in die judicii.* The idea is similar to that expressed in this inscription, which is a strong testimony to the belief of primitive Christianity in the Resurrection to come, and the final judgment.

The next inscriptions illustrate the well-known emblem of the fish (ἴχθυς) which was in general use in the second and third centuries. The fish is the emblem of Christ the Son of God the Saviour, as in the famous acrostic of the word ΙΧΘΥΣ, Ἰησοῦς Χριστὸς Θεοῦ Υἱὸς Σωτήρ.

52

D (corona) M

ΙΧΘΥC · ΖΩΝΤΩΝ

(fish)　　　(anchor)　　　(fish)

LICINIAE AMIATI BE

NEMERENTI VIXIT

"The fish of the living."

From the Vatican Cemetery.　Kircherian Museum.

53

BETTONI IN PACE DEVS CVM SPIRITVM TVVM ΙΧΘΥC
DECESSIT VII IDVS FEBR (anchor) ANNORVM XXII

"God (Jesus Christ Son of God the Saviour) be with thy Spirit."

Cemetery of Callisto.

54

I · K · Θ · Υ · C
BONO · ET · INNOCENTI · FILIO
PASTORI ❧ Q · V · X · AN · IIII
M · V · D · XXV · I · VITALIO
ET · MARCELLINA · PARENT
(palm)

Lateran Museum.

Sometimes the symbol for Christ is so placed as to enable one to read it as the actual name, as in the following, " Deo Magno Christo Sacrum ":

55

D · M · ☧ · S
VITALIS · DEPOSITA · DIAE · SABATI · KL · AVG
Q · VIXIT · ANNIS · XX · MES · JIII
FECIT · CVM · MARITO · ANN · X · DIES · XX

Cemetery of Cyriaca.   Lateran Museum.

In Christian sepulchral inscriptions the word *Spiritus* is often found, and generally means the soul of the deceased.   But when the expression is *Spiritus Sanctus*, it undoubtedly refers to the third person of the Trinity.

56

CAR · KYPIAKO. . . .
FIL · DVLCISSIMO. . . ,
VIBAS · IN · SPIRITO · SAN(*cto*)

" Live in the Holy Spirit."

Cemetery of Callisto.

57

ΠΡΩΤΩϹ
ΕΝ · ΑΓΙΩ
ΠΝΕΥΜΑ
ΤΙ · ΘΕΟΥ
ΕΝΘΑΔΕ
ΚΕΙΤΑΙ
ΦΙΡΜΙΛΛΑ
ΑΔΕΛΦΗ
ΜΝΗΜΗϹ
ΚΑΡΙΝ

" Here lies Protus in the Holy Spirit of God.
Erected in memory of him by his sister Firmilla."

Cemetery of S. Hermes.   Kircherian Museum.

In another we find the three persons of the Trinity named.

58

. . . . LO. . . .

. . . . PAR. . . .

. . . . CVNDIANVS *qui credidit*

in CRISTVM · IESV*m vivet in*

*patr*E · ET · FILIO · ET · ISP*irito Sancto*

"Secundianus, who believed in Jesus Christ, shall live in the Father, and the Son, and the Holy Spirit."

Cemetery of Domitilla.

CHAPTER III

INSCRIPTIONS BEARING ON SACRAMENTS

§ I

Baptism and Confirmation

THE sacrament of Baptism, the initiation into Christianity, was looked upon as a mystery, the significance of which was not to be revealed to the profane; thus the Law of the Secret applied to it. For this reason certain formulae were used to express it in inscriptions which were intelligible to the initiated only; thus a person was said *accipere* or *recipere* or *percipere*, the words *gratiam baptismi* being understood. The following are instances:

59

PASTOR ET *Tit*IANA (dove) MARCIANA ET (fish)
CHREST(*e*) (*Marci*) ANO FILIO BENEMERENTI (*in*)
✳ D N FEC(*erunt*) QVI VIXIT ANNVS XII M II ET *dies* . . .
QVI GRA*tia*M ACCEPIT D N DIE XII KAL *o*CTOBRES
. . . .VIO PATERNO II COSS ET REDE(*dit*) XI KAL[1]
VIBAS INTER SANCTIS HA*men*

Cemetery of Callisto.

(Boldetti, *Osservazioni*, p. 80.   De Rossi, *Inscr.* i. p. 16.)

---

[1] " Et *reddidit* (spiritum) XI Kalendas (octobris)."

This inscription is important for its age, as it bears the date A.D. 268. De Rossi completed the fourth line, "qui gratiam accepit Domini nostri," *i.e.* who received baptism; and the next line suggests that the deceased, a lad of twelve years of age, died almost on the day of his baptism; thus he seems to have been baptized when in peril of death.

The fact is that baptism was usually administered to adults only; young persons, much more babies, were only baptized in the case of serious illness. And therefore a record of baptism in a sepulchral inscription is almost exclusively confined to the case of the death of the baptized person (whether child or adult), shortly after receiving that Sacrament: otherwise there was no reason for recording it.

Here are some other inscriptions indicating baptism in the same symbolical fashion :

60

```
TYCHE · DVLCIS
VIXIT · ANNO · VNO ·
MENSIBVS · X · DIEB · XXV
ACCEPIT · VIII · KAL.. .
REDDIDIT · DIE · S · S
```

" *Accepit* (gratiam) et *reddidit* (spiritum) die suprascripta."

Cemetery of Priscilla.

This belonged to a girl of under two years of age, *Tyche* (Fortuna) by name, who died on the day of her baptism.

61

```
BENEMERENTI · ANTONIAE · CYRIACETI · QVAE · VIXIT
ANNIS · XVIIII · M · II · D · XXVI |
ACCEPTA · DEI · GRATIA · QVARTA · DIE |
VIRGO · OBIIT · IVLIVS · BENEDICTVS · PATER |
FILIAE · DVLCISSIMAE |
ET · INCOMPARABILI · POSVIT · D · XII · KAL · DEC
```

"Accepta Dei gratia quarta die virgo obiit."

Cemetery of Callisto.

This belonged to a virgin of eighteen years, Antonia Cyriacete by name, who died four days after receiving baptism.

62

```
POSTVMIVS · EVTENION · FIDELIS
QVI · GRATIAM · SANCTAM  CONSE
CVTVS · EST · PRIDIE · NATALI · SVO
```

Buonarroti, *Vetri cimiteriali* (Funerary glass).

Postumius Eutenion is here called *fidelis*, because he had been baptized; this had been done on the day before his death, which is called his *dies natalis*, *i.e.* the date of his birth into the true life.

63

```
FVIT · MIHI · NATIBITAS · ROMANA · NOMEN · SI · QVÆRIS
IVLIA · BOCATA · SO · QVE · VIXI · MVNDA ·
CVM · BYRO · MEO · FLORENTIO ·
CVI · DEMISI · TRES · FILIOS · SVPERSTETES
MOX · GRATIA · DEI · PERCEPI ·
SVSCEPTA · IN · PACE · NEOFITA
```

Cemetery of Callisto.

Valuable for giving the dialect form *bocata so* for *vocata sum*. This *Julia* appears to have died immediately after receiving baptism.

64

```
AuREL · MARCELLINVS · MARITVS · AVR · ERITI coniugi
diGNISSIMAE · BENEMERENTI ·
CVM · QVA · VIXIT · in pace con
soRORIBVS · IN · SE · GRatiam DEI · PERCIPIENTES ann...
dieBVS · XLII · AVR · MARitus fecit
```

Cemetery of S. Hermes.

Note the expression "in se gratiam Dei percipientes," showing that both husband and wife had been baptized.

65

```
ResTITVTA PIENtissima....
(a)CEP (dove) TA Dei gratia?
```

Cemetery of S. Peter and S. Marcellinus.

The dove, the emblem of the soul, is here inserted into the middle of the words indicating baptism.

66

> ## ΚΑΛΩC · ΗΞΙΩΜΕΝΟC
> ## THN · XΛPIN · TOϓ · ΘΕΟϓ

" . . . who has been made worthy to receive
duly the grace of God."

(Marini, Atti degli Arvali, xx.)

67

> ℞ VRSO · ET · POLEMIO · CONSS   (A.D. 338)
> NOMINE · PVELLA · FELITE · IN · ANNIS
> PM · TRIGINTA · PERCIPET · SEPTIMV · KAL · APRIL
> ET · DECESSIT · IN · PACE ·
> POST · TERTIV · KAL · MAI
>
>   DIE · MERCVRI · ORA · DIEI · NONA

Cemetery of Domitilla.

(Marucchi, Nuovo Bull. 1899, p. 279.)

The deceased, Phelite (? Philete) by name, is
here called *puella* on the score of her spiritual
infancy only, as she was thirty years of age at her
death. It records that she *percepit* (gratiam) on
March 26th, 338, and died on May 3rd of the
same year. Now in 338 Easter-day fell exactly on
March 26th; and she must have been baptized
upon that festival, perhaps when she was already
ill, for she died little more than a month later.
Observe that the day of the week (Wednesday) and
the hour of her death (the ninth) are also recorded.

68

```
NATVS · PVER · NOMINE · PASCASIVS
DIES · PASCALES · PRID · NON · APRIL
DIE · IOBIS · CONSTANTINO
ET · RVFO · VV · CC · CONSS · QVI · VIXIT
ANNORVM · VI · PERCEPIT
XI · KAL · MAIAS · ET · ALBAS · SVAS
OCTABAS · PASCAE · AD · SEPVLCRVM
DEPOSVIT · IIII · KAL · MAI · FL · BASILIO
                          V · C · COnsule
```

(Fabretti, *Inscript. domesticae*, chap. viii. No. 70.)

This child, Pascasius by name, was born April 4th, 457, on the Thursday after Easter, and lived six years. He was baptized on April 21st, 463 (Easter Eve), and died in the octave of Easter, on April 29th of the same year. Thus as he died a neophyte, and still wearing the white robe of baptism, he is described as laying down his white garments on his tomb, "albas suas in sepulcro deposuit."

69

```
                  ☧
... IGNA SE BIBO INMERVM LOCVM P
... ORDLA A DP STOLIS SVIS
      (sic)
```

" . . . et Benigna se vivo emerunt locum . . . Concordiana (?) depositis stolis suis."

Cemetery of Callisto.

(De Rossi, *Roma sotterranea*, iii. p. 405.)

This inscription (which contains errors in spelling) records the purchase of a site for a tomb during life. *Se bibo* stands for *se vivo*, and *inmerum* for *emerunt*. Here also may be noted the same expression as in the last, to the effect that the deceased had laid down her baptismal robe upon her tomb, "depositis stolis suis."

70

DEPOSITVS · PVER · MAVRVS · ANNO
RVM · QVINQVAE · MENSORVM · TRES
NONAS · AVGVSTAS · BIMVS · TRIMVS
CONSECVTVS · EST
☧

The Passionei Collection at Fossombrone.

In my opinion this must be read to mean that Maurus was baptized when he was *bimus* (*et*) *trimus*, *i.e.* two years and three years old, or five years : he did in fact survive to the age of five years and three months.[1]

71

FLORENTIVS · FILIO · SVO · APRONIANO
FECIT · TITVLVM · BENEMERENTI · QVI · VIXIT
ANNVM · ET · MENSES · NOVEM · DIES · QVIN(*que*)
QVI · CVM · SOLIDE · AMATVS · ESSET
A · MAIORE · SVA · ET · VIDIT
HVNC · MORTI · CONSTITVTVM · ESSET · PETIVIT
DE · ECCLESIA · VT · FIDELIS
DE · SAECVLO   RECESSISSET

Lateran Museum.

[1] I cannot agree with the explanation given by Father Scaglia, that Maurus was baptized at the age of two, and confirmed at the age of three. (*Notiones arch. Christ.* ii. 1ª, p. 169.)

The babe Apronianus lived for one year and nine months; his grandmother, seeing that he was in peril of death, wished him to be baptized so as to die in the faith, "petivit de ecclesia ut fidelis de saeculo recessisset."

Confirmation is the complement of baptism; it was administered immediately after that sacrament in a special part of the baptistery called *consignatorium*, because *signare* then meant the same as our word confirmation. Hence Tertullian says that on issuing from the laver of baptism we receive the holy unction, "egressi de lavacro perungimur benedicta unctione."[1]

In an inscription at Tolentino there is a specific mention of the laver and the unction, that is of baptism and confirmation, administered to husband and wife together by a bishop.

72

QVOS · PARIBVS · MERITIS · IVNXIT ·
MATRIMONIO · DVLCI
OMNIPOTENS · DOMINVS · TVMVLVS ·
CVSTODIT · IN · AEVVM
CATERVI · SEVERINA · TIBI · CONIVNCTA · LAETATVR
SVRGATIS · PARITER · CHRISTO · PRAESTANTE · BEATI
QVOS · DEI · SACERDOS · PROBIANVS ·
LAVIT · ET · VNXIT

At Tolentino.

Sometimes the idea of the combined rites of baptism and confirmation was expressed by simply saying that a brother had been *signatus*, or more

[1] *De baptismo*, chap. vii.

precisely, *signatus munere Christi*, as in the following inscription from Bolsena:

73

NVPER PRAECLARO SIGNATVS MVNERE CHRISTI
QVI QVONDAM DVRA GENITORVM MORTE DIREPTVS
SVSCEPIT GRATOS MELIORI SORTE PARENTES
SED TRAXIT FORTVNA DIEM NEC DISTVLIT HORAM
NAM GENIALI SOLO PRAECLVSIT TEMPORA VITAE
NOMEN ALEXANDRI PATRIAM GENVS
SI QVAERIS HIC EST
HIC VIXIT ANNIS . . . . III IDVS SEPTEMB

Bolsena.   Cemetery of S. Christina.

Observe here the expression "suscepit gratos
meliori sorte parentes," referring to the *susceptores*,
whom we now call sponsors.

74

D · P
VALE | QVI | LEGERIS | LIBENS | PICENTIAE
LEGITIMAE | NEOPHYTAE | DIE · V · KAL · SEP
CONSIGNATAE | A | LIBERIO | PAPA
MARITVS | VXORI | BENEMERENTI
DVPLICEM | SARCOPHAGVM | CVM · TITVLIS
HOC · LOCO | POSVIT

"Vale qui legeris libens.   Picentiae legitimae
neophitae die. V. cal. sept. consignatae a Liberio
papa.   Maritus uxori benemerenti duplicem sarco-
phagum cum titulis hoc loco posuit."
This once existed at Spoleto, where it was transcribed by Cyriacus of Ancona in the fifteenth century.

(De Rossi, *Bull. di arch. crist.*, 1869, p. 23.)

Pope Liberius, the predecessor of Damasus, was Pope from 355 to 366 A.D., therefore this inscription must come within that period.   Although the Pope administered baptism and confirmation in Rome on Easter Eve in the Lateran Basilica, we need not be surprised to find that this neophyte Picentia was confirmed by Pope Liberius at Spoleto.   We know that Liberius was exiled beyond the Alps in the course of the Arian dispute, and he was bound to pass by Spoleto, which was on his road to the north ; so that he might have administered the sacrament of Confirmation there on his way.   And it is very likely that the name of Liberius was mentioned here as a testimony to his persistent opposition to Arianism.   He has indeed been accused of accepting Arian articles, and of being recalled from exile by the Emperor Constantius on that account ; but this is a calumny, for we know that on his return to Rome he had a triumphant reception, while the anti-pope Felix, who had been appointed by Constantius, was left with scarcely a follower.   This would not have occurred had Liberius put his hand to a heretical Creed. Furthermore, Liberius in his sepulchral inscription (which we shall quote later among the historical inscriptions) is described as the " champion of orthodoxy," which could not have been said of him had he fallen into heresy.

This inscription of Picentia is quoted with immediate reference to the rite of confirmation, but it has also a very important bearing on the history of Pope Liberius.

Now let us pass to the monumental inscriptions

which decorated baptisteries and their adjacent chapels; these are somewhat later in date than those quoted above, inasmuch as in the first centuries no great basilicas existed. Buildings of this sort were erected in times of peace; hence it is in the fourth and fifth centuries that monumental inscriptions make their appearance on the great baptisteries of the Vatican, Lateran, and Ostian basilicas, in those of S. Lorenzo in Damaso, of S. Anastasia at the foot of the Palatine, etc.

These buildings used to contain some inscriptions of the school of Damasus, some earlier than Damasus, others of a later date; but of the originals of these very few now exist, and most of them are known to us through the collections only. It would take too long to set them all out, and we need only quote three of the most remarkable.

One of the most important monumental inscriptions relating to baptism is preserved in the Collection of Verdun which was compiled by an anonymous pilgrim at the end of the eighth century. Many Roman inscriptions are copied therein in topographical order. Thus, after taking a number of inscriptions from the Via Salaria, the pilgrim reaches the cemetery of Priscilla, where, he says, "isti versiculi scripti sunt ad fontes," *i.e.* the inscription stood near a baptistery. Mention is made therein of the visible signs of the grace conferred by baptism, and then comes a marked allusion to the local traditions of S. Peter, who has the power to bind and to loose. The form of the poem is good and the ideas are elevated; it runs as follows:

I

75

Sumite perpetuam sancto de gurgite vitam ;
Cursus hic est fidei mors ubi sola perit.
Roborat hic animos divina fonte lavacrum,
Et dum membra madent, mens solidatur aquis.
Auxit apostolicae geminatum sedis honorem
Christus, et ad coelos hanc dedit esse viam ;
Nam cui siderei commisit limina regni
Hic habet in templis altera claustra poli.

The first verses are an invitation to baptism—
Receive, says the poet, eternal life from the holy
laver ; here is the way of Faith. The next sentence,
" where death alone dies," means that here dies the
sin which begets death—*per peccatum mors* ; baptism
being considered as the burial of the old man, that
the new man may be raised therefrom. The next
verse contains an evident allusion to the ancient
baptism by immersion, when the *baptisterium* was
simply a bathroom. The lines contain an invitation to the catechumens to come to baptism, and
a short description of its results. Then come two
rather obscure couplets. The poet wishes to find
some relation between baptism and the chair of
S. Peter. "Christ has increased the doubled
honour of the Apostolic see." By "doubled
honour" must be meant the twofold power of
Peter to bind and to loose, as appears from the
last verse, where the keys are named. By giving
this twofold power to the Apostolic see, Christ has
made it the way by which to rise to heaven ; for
" he to whom Christ gave the charge of the
Kingdom of Heaven is none but he who here on
earth, in basilicas, in baptisteries, and in this spot,
wields his twofold power to bind and to loose."

These expressions are to be understood to assert the doctrine of "one Church, one baptism." The same idea is expressed in an inscription in the Vatican baptistery in these words:

76

Una Petri sedes, unum verumque lavacrum ;
Vincula nulla tenent quem liquor iste lavat.

Next after the inscription of which we have spoken, the Itinerary of Verdun quotes another, and makes the following comment: *Isti versiculi sunt scripti ubi pontifex consignat infantes, i.e.* those born again by baptism. This evidently refers to the *consignatorium*, the chapel adjacent to the baptistery, where confirmation was administered.

This second inscription runs as follows:

77

Istic insontes coelesti flumine lotos
Pastoris summi dextera signat oves.
Huc undis generate veni quo Sanctus ad unum
Spiritus ut capias te sua dona vocat.
Tu cruce suscepta mundi vitare procellas
Disce, magis monitus hac ratione loci.

The first couplet states the use to which the place is put, saying that it is here that neophytes are confirmed. By the Chief Pastor is meant the Pope, not any ordinary bishop, whence it follows that this was a Papal baptistery.

In the second couplet the neophytes are invited to receive the Holy Spirit. "Oh thou who hast been born again of water, come with thy fellows hither where the Holy Spirit calleth thee, to receive His gifts." This is an invitation to the neophytes clothed in their white robes, who came attended by their *susceptores* to ask for confirmation.

The last couplet contains admonitions to the newly confirmed: "Thou who hast received the sign of the Cross"—that is, the sign made by the bishop on the forehead at confirmation—"learn to conquer the temptations of the world, remembering not only the sacrament thou hast received"—for this might have been received anywhere—"but *hac ratione loci*, *i.e.* keeping ever present to thee the holy influence of the spot in which thou hast been confirmed."

Now this allusion to some famous local tradition can only refer to the great tradition of the baptism administered by S. Peter near the cemetery of Priscilla.[1]

This allusion to S. Peter led De Rossi to believe that the inscription came from the baptistery of the Vatican. But this cannot be admitted, having regard to the topographical accuracy of this collection, which proceeds regularly without skipping; moreover, the compiler states that he transcribed it along with the other inscriptions which stood in the cemetery of Priscilla. Here, then, we may recognise the earliest record of a place set apart specially for the administration of baptism.

We pass to another celebrated inscription in the Lateran baptistery. The Lateran in the earliest times was the ancestral house of the noble family of the Plautii Laterani. Under Nero one of that family was condemned to death, and his property was confiscated, whereby the palace passed into the

---

[1] On this record see various articles of mine in the *Nuovo Bullettino di archeologia cristiana*, 1901, etc.

private demesne of the Emperor, and became one of the imperial palaces. In the days of Constantine it was granted to Pope Miltiades, who established his residence there; and thereupon the basilica, which was dedicated to the Saviour, became the Cathedral of Rome. The palace was once occupied by Fausta, the wife of Constantine, who directed the existing baptistery to be built close by, very likely as her private bath-house. For this reason it was called *Baptisterium*, or *Baptismum Constantini*; whence the legend arose that Constantine was baptized there by Pope Silvester, whereas he was in fact baptized shortly before his death at Nicomedia. Sixtus III. in the fifth century embellished the baptistery, and added an inscription cut on the octagonal marble architrave. The inscription is perfectly preserved, and may be admired even to this day: the lettering somewhat resembles that of the period of Damasus.

78

Gens sacranda polis hic semine nascitur almo
Quam faecundatis spiritus alit aquis.
Virgineo foetu genitrix Ecclesia natos
Quos spirante Deo concipit amne parit.
Coelorum regnum sperate, hoc fonte renati
Non recipit felix vita semel genitos.
Fons hic est vitae et qui totum diluit orbem
Sumens de Christi vulnere principium.
Mergere peccator sacro purgande fluento
Quem veterem accipiet praeferet unda novum.
Insons esse volens isto mundare lavacro
Seu patrio praemeris crimine seu proprio.
Nulla renascentum est distantia quos facit unum
Unus fons, unus spiritus, una fides.

*Nec numerus quemquam scelerum nec forma suorum
Terreat, hoc natus flumine sanctus erit.*

This elegant inscription is most valuable from a doctrinal point of view, as stating the effect of baptism, and the theological conception of that sacrament.

Among other inscriptions in the baptisteries we must not forget those of S. Paul *extra moenia*, where besides a baptistery there was also a confirmation-chapel. Another inscription relating to baptism stood in the church of Anastasia at the foot of the Palatine, which was probably the parish church of the Palatine in the fourth and fifth centuries.

There was a baptistery in the basilica of S. Lorenzo in Damaso also, and the inscription thereon is set forth in the Collection of Verdun, where the church is entitled *S. Laurentius in Prasina*, because it stood near the training-stables of the prasine, or green, faction of the circus.

Many other inscriptions of this class are known, and might be quoted here. But rather than increase the length of this chapter by quotations which are already long enough, we will refer our readers to the *Inscriptiones* of G. B. De Rossi, vol. ii., where they may easily be found under the head "Baptisteria eorumque epigrammata."

§ 2

Inscriptions relating to the Eucharist

The inscriptions as to the Eucharist are few, but the eucharistic emblems found in the paintings and sculptures of the catacombs are many. Of eucharistic texts two only are at present known.

The rarity of these depends on various causes, but principally on the fact that the authors of the inscriptions were more concerned to dwell on the efficacy of prayer for the dead, on the resurrection, etc. ; and only referred to other doctrines when it was desired to bring them into connexion with that line of thought. Besides this, the "discipline of the secret" imposed silence as to the dogma of the Eucharist, which lent itself somewhat to the slanders and jeers of the pagans.

The well-known Apology of S. Justin gives an excellent description of the liturgy of the Eucharist as in use about A.D. 155. The Eucharist is there called the heavenly food of the body of Jesus Christ, and mention is made of the mixing of the wine with water, called κέρασμα. S. Justin speaks of the consecration almost in the same terms as S. Paul, whence it would seem that the rule of the "secret" had been a trifle relaxed in the quiet times. The prayers preceding and following the communion are recorded, and also the kiss of peace; but the actual communion formula is not recorded by S. Justin; we find it, however, preserved by other writers, notably by Tertullian.

According to De Rossi, the oldest painting of the Eucharist is that in the crypt of Lucina; being expressed entirely by symbols, it must represent an older idea than the *Fractio panis* of the cemetery of Priscilla. It presents to us two symmetrical groups, showing a fish on a green ground and bearing on his back the bread and wine; no better emblem could be found of the union of the eucharistic elements with the body of the Redeemer.

There are abundant proofs that the Eucharist is here intended. The body of Jesus Christ in the Eucharist is called by S. Paulinus, *panis verus et aquae vivae piscis.*[1] And we know that in the poorer churches baskets were used to carry the Holy Eucharist: *nihil illo ditius qui corpus Domini in canistro vimineo, et sanguinem portat in vitro.*[2] The fish was undoubtedly a symbol of the Saviour from the second century onwards, and the celebrated acrostic ΙΧΘΥϹ did much to popularise its use.[3] Renan could see in this painting nothing but an allusion to the fish eaten by Christ and His disciples on the lake of Tiberias. De Rossi, on the other hand, has shown that that story has nothing to do with this group of figures, but is to be found in the paintings of banquets in the cemetery of Callisto, which are much later than the frescoes in the crypt of Lucina.

This picture was not intended merely to represent

[1] Epist. xiii.
[2] St. Jerome, Epist. cxxv., *ad Rusticum.*
[3] Cf. De Rossi, "De Christianis monumentis ichtyn exhibentibus," *Spicileg. Solesm.* vol. iii.

the miracle of the multiplication of the loaves and fishes; if that had been the only meaning, the presence of the flask of red wine in the middle of it would have been inexplicable. The symbol of the eucharistic fish is often repeated in funerary art. Next to the above-mentioned comes the painting of the *Fractio panis* in the cemetery of Priscilla; this goes back to the reign of Hadrian or of Antoninus Pius, and the age of S. Justin, and consequently the Greek chapel in which it stands may be considered to be the oldest church in Rome. This fresco represents the ceremony of the division of the bread. On the left the priest and the bishop break the bread into pieces, having the cup in front of them ; five other persons and a female figure are seated round a table on which loaves and fishes are placed. According to Wilpert, this is a correct representation of the eucharistic rite as celebrated on that spot in the second century; and certainly the actors in it are realistically drawn. But it cannot be said to be a simple study of real life, for the baskets standing on each side have evidently a symbolical meaning, as in the picture of the Miracle of the Loaves and Fishes ; and again, the feet of the priest are on the same level as the table, which would be practically impossible. Lastly, the love-feast is here depicted as combined with the Eucharist, a combination which was no longer in use in the second century. For these reasons we conclude that here actuality and symbolism are combined, and that the part truest to fact is the action of the priest.

Another eucharistic picture is that of the tripod with the loaf and the fish. Of this we have two instances in the cemetery of Callisto. In one of them nothing is seen but a tripod alone in the midst of seven baskets, representing the Miracle of the Loaves; in the other a man extends his hand as if in blessing, in the presence of a woman in prayer. In this scene De Rossi saw the very act of consecration. The tripod is the *mensa Domini*, and has the shape of a dining-table, as is usual in the case of primitive altars; and the place it occupies on the wall, between baptism and the eucharistic feast, is an additional proof of its meaning. The woman in prayer suggests the Church praying before the consecrated elements. Wilpert thought that the latter picture might represent the Miracle of the Loaves and Fishes; but in that case the presence of the table could not be explained, nor the absence of the baskets; while the neighbouring picture of the sacrifice of Abraham rather bids us look here for an allusion to sacrifice.

Pictures of tables alone are rare, but pictures of feasts are common enough, especially in the third century. There is always a fish on the table, and the number of persons is invariably seven. In one of the Chambers of the Sacrament,[1] near the table with the loaf and fish, is a painting of the feast on the lake of Tiberias, done in conventional fashion with idealised figures. Here there can be no doubt as to the meaning; in the words of S. Augustine, *Piscis assus Christus est passus*. S. Prosper of Aquitania says that the Redeemer offers of Himself to all as " a fish of salvation that gives daily light and nourishment." The word also suggests some allusion to the fish which healed the blind Tobias and restored his sight.

[1] Five chambers in the cemetery of Callisto decorated with pictures of the sacraments.

The baskets of loaves are one of the oldest representations of the Eucharist, but we find them also in the *Fractio panis* of the cemetery of Priscilla ; the Miracle of the Loaves and Fishes, to which they refer, belongs also to a later period. To that same later series the representation of the Miracle of the Marriage at Cana belongs ; it is somewhat common on sarcophagi, but rare in paintings. Wilpert found an example of it in the cemetery of S. Peter and S. Marcellinus. In that catacomb and in some others may be seen pictures of feasts, which, however, must be carefully distinguished from those of which we are now speaking. The figures therein are not invariably seven, but vary in number. Some have taken them to represent scenes at love-feasts, but this is scarcely likely, as primitive Christian art seldom dealt with scenes of actual life. More probably they are fanciful representations of the heavenly feast promised by the Redeemer, which he calls *Mensa Patris mei.* It must be observed, however, that on some pagan tombs there are also banqueting scenes almost identical, showing the loaf and the fish ; but these are simply pictures of funeral banquets, and the fish indicates that these banquets were fairly costly. It would appear, therefore, that in this case also the Christian artists had probably taken their inspiration from pagan art as far as the artistic composition of the scene was concerned.

A fine picture of the heavenly feast is to be seen in the entrance to the cemetery of Domitilla, and, although it is much damaged, it is still possible to recognise two persons seated at a table bearing a fish and some loaves, and on one side of them the servant, *dapifer*, holding a plate. This picture

dates from the first century. Banqueting scenes
are repeated six or seven times in the cemetery of
S. Peter and S. Marcellinus, and they go back to
the third and fourth centuries. There are always
two women near the table presiding over the
banquet, whom the inscriptions bid us recognise
as personifying Peace and Charity: IRENE DA
CALDA, AGAPE MISCE MI. This word
MISCE reminds us of the custom of mixing of
wine with water in ancient banquets and also in the
Sacrifice of the Eucharist.

The feast of the five wise Virgins is more rarely
represented; an instance of it is found on an
arcosolium of the greater cemetery of S. Agnese.
In the midst is the suppliant figure, on one side
are the five virgins with their lamps alight, on the
other four virgins seated at a table ; the fifth is the
suppliant. In this we may see the marriage feast
of the Celestial Bridegroom. In a fresco of the
cemetery of Cyriaca the five Virgins are represented,
but without the table.

The vessel full of milk is another symbol of the
Eucharist; of this we have a proof in one of the
celebrated visions of the martyr S. Perpetua.
There appeared to the saint in a garden the Good
Shepherd with His flock around Him, and also
other people, to whom the Shepherd, who was milking His sheep, gave a small dish of curds, while all
the bystanders bowed their heads and said *Amen.*

Among the paintings of the cemetery of Callisto
there is the Good Shepherd with the vessel of milk
and two sheep. In the cemetery of Domitilla
there is a picture of a sheep near a vessel of milk
tied to a stick, the symbol of the Shepherd. The
same scene is repeated in front of the *tablinum* of the

house of S. John and S. Paul, whence it may be gathered that this symbol was in use in the fourth century also.

The bunch of grapes, which has the same meaning, is scarcely ever found in paintings, but is often carved on tombstones. Manna, which is a symbol of the Eucharist, is represented on an arcosolium of the cemetery of Cyriaca.

It was necessary to give this preliminary information before offering any remarks on the two celebrated sepulchral inscriptions relative to the Eucharist, known as those of Pectorius and of Abercius.

The inscription of Pectorius was found at Autun in 1839, and was published and annotated by Pitra.

It is a very valuable record, going back perhaps to the beginning of the third century, and containing expressions of great importance from a doctrinal point of view :

Ἰχθύος ο[ὐρανίου θε]ῖον γένος ἤτορι σεμνῷ
  Χρῆσε λαβὼ[ν πηγὴ]ν ἄμβροτον ἐν βροτέοις
Θεσπεσίων ὑδάτ[ω]ν. τὴν σὴν φίλε θάλπεο ψυχ[ὴν]
  Ὕδασιν ἀεινάοις πλουτοδότου σοφίης,
Σωτῆρος δὲ ἁγίων μελιηδέα λάμβαν[ε βρῶσιν]·
  Ἔσθιε πινάων ἰχθὺν ἔχων παλάμαις.

"Thou, the divine offspring of the heavenly IXΘYC, keep a pure heart, while thou receivest the source of God-given waters, immortal gift to mortals. Comfort thy soul, oh friend, with the ever-flowing waters of wealth-giving wisdom ; and receive the honey-sweet food of the Redeemer of the Saints ; eat in thy hunger, holding IXΘYN in thy hands."

Then he goes on:

"Satisfy thyself with IXΘYC. My desire is to thee, my Saviour; to thee I pray, thou light of the dead. Ascandius, father, my heart's beloved, and with thee my darling mother and my brethren, in the peace of IXΘYC remember thy Pectorius."

Here the faithful are bidden to feed on holy food, and to receive into their hands the consecrated elements, according to ancient liturgical usage.

The inscription of Abercius, bishop of Hieropolis in Phrygia, is still more important.

The life and doings of Abercius are known to us from his "Acts" found in the Collection of Metaphrastes, a Byzantine biographer of the saints of the tenth century. These Acts, which have been frequently published, have been again recently reissued by the Bollandists. The story tells us that he was bishop of Hierapolis in Phrygia, under the Emperor Marcus Aurelius; that he undertook very long journeys into the East and the West that he might preach the Gospel everywhere, and visit the more famous churches; and that he was compared to the Apostles for the activity of his ministry. In these journeys he visited Rome among other places, and after his return to the East he determined to bequeath to posterity a record of his wanderings, in the form of an epitaph in verse to be inscribed on his tombstone. The Greek text of this inscription is set forth in the codexes of Metaphrastes, and has therefore been long known. But Tillemont had discredited the Acts of Abercius as purely legendary (and they certainly contain some very queer, if not fabulous, matter); the consequence was that even the text of the inscription quoted therein fell into disrepute among scholars; the more so as the poem differed entirely from every other Christian sepulchral inscription then known, and contained novel and suspicious expressions. The doubts of the learned were further increased by the objection that the name of Abercius was not to be found in the list of the bishops of Hierapolis.

The first to restore the credit of the verses of Abercius, in the face of all these objections, and to pronounce them genuine, was the famous Cardinal Pitra, who wrote long and learned works on the Christian symbolism of the early centuries; and in support of this defence he made use of the above-quoted inscription of Pectorius, discovered at Autun, in which there are some expressions resembling those in the Phrygian inscription. Following Pitra, De Rossi held the epitaph of Abercius to be genuine, and made liberal use of it in the learned comments on the earliest symbolical paintings discovered in the Roman catacombs, which he published in the second volume of his *Roma sotterranea.* But when the genuineness of the record had once been accepted by archaeologists, they began to discuss the restoration of the text of some noteworthy passages, and Garrucci in particular introduced some remarkable emendations, holding that some of the verses were interpolations.

Matters stood thus, when in 1882 Professor Ramsay, of the University of Aberdeen in Scotland, who had undertaken a journey in the East for the purpose of studying the ancient geography of Asia Minor, discovered in Phrygia a sepulchral cippus with an inscription in Greek concerning a

Christian of the name of Alexander. De Rossi was the first to notice that the inscription discovered by Ramsay was an imitation of that of Abercius, through the identity of some of the phraseology, and from the fact that the name of Alexander had been substituted for that of the bishop (Abercius) in defiance of prosody. This was a *prima facie* confirmation of the theory that the verses of Abercius had once really existed; and it further showed that his monument might very well be of the date attributed to it by the "Acta," *i.e.* the second century, for the stone of Alexander, which was copied from it, bears the date 300 of the Phrygian era, which corresponds to A.D. 216.

The discovery of this marble cippus gave birth to a desire to find the actual original of the much-disputed verses of Abercius, and De Rossi publicly called upon Ramsay in his journal, the *Bullettino*, to make another visit to Asia Minor and search diligently for any fragments of this precious text which might be still in existence. The Scottish professor accepted the courteous challenge, and on his return to Phrygia succeeded in discovering a large portion of the desired text. The cippus was found built into a wall of the Thermae, exactly as stated in the "Acta," but not in the well-known city of Hierapolis, as misread in the codexes, but in the less-known Hieropolis. And this correction of detail absolutely does away with, as any one may see, the objection that has been raised to the authenticity of the inscription on the score of the absence of the name of Abercius from the list of bishops of the first-named city.

But the discovery of the original inscription,

though partly destroyed by decay, is yet more important, as proving that the text as given by Metaphrastes is in the main correct, and that the lettering of the inscription, being exactly that of the period of Marcus Aurelius, is therefore the very same which the good bishop ordered to be cut under his own eyes.

The existing fragment is now preserved in the Lateran Museum, and is reproduced in Plate VIII. 1.

We will now give the Greek text as restored by De Rossi, with some short notes on this remarkable record of Christian antiquity.

Abercius is supposed to be speaking; and he gives his autobiography in a few lines:

First face:

1 Ἐκλεκτῆς πόλεως ὁ πολεί-
της τοῦτ᾽ ἐποίησα

2 ζῶν ἵν᾽ ἔχω καιρῷ
σώματος ἔνθα θέσιν

3 οὔνομ᾽ Ἀβέρκιος ὢν ὁ
μαθητὴς ποιμένος ἁγνοῦ

4 ὃς βόσκει προβάτων ἀγέλας
ὄρεσιν πεδίοις τε

5 ὀφθαλμοὺς ὃς ἔχει μεγάλους
πάντη καθορῶντας

6 οὗτος γάρ μ᾽ ἐδίδαξε
[τὰ ζωῆς] γράμματα πιστά.

Second face (Lateran Museum, Plate VIII. 1):

7 ΕΙΣ ΡΩΜΗν ὃς ἔπεμψεν
ΕΜΕΝ ΒΑΣΙΛείαν ἀθρῆσαι

8 ΚΑΙ ΒΑΣΙΛΙΣαν ἰδεῖν χρυσόσ-
ΤΟΛΟΝ ΧΡυσοπέδιλον

K

9 ΛΑΟΝ ΔΕΙΔΟΝ ἐκεῖ λαμπρὰν
  ΣΦΡΑΓΕΙΔΑΝΕχοντα

10 ΚΑΙΣΥΡΙΗΣΠΕδον εἶδα
  ΚΑΙΑΣΤΕΑΠΑντα Νίσιβιν

11 ΕΥΦΡΑΤΗΝΔΙΑβας παν-
  ΤΗΔΕΣΧΟΝΣΝΟμίλους

12 ΠΑΥΛΟΝΕΧΟΝΕΠΟ
  ΠΙΣΤΙΣ πάντη δὲ προῆγε

13 ΚΑΙΠΑΡΗΘΗΚΕ τροφήν
  ΠΑΝΤΗΙΧΘΥΝΑπὸ πηγῆς

14 ΠΑΝΜΕΓΕΘΗΚΑΘαρον ὃν
  ΕΔΡΑΞΑΤΟΠΑΡΘένος ἁγνή

15 ΚΑΙΤΟΥΤΟΝΕΠΕδωκε φί-
  ΛΟΙΣΕΣΘίειν διὰ παντός

16 οἶνον χρηστὸν ἔχουσα
  κέρασμα διδοῦσα μετ᾽ ἄρτου.

Third face:

17 ταῦτα παρεστὼς εἶπον
  Ἀβέρκιος ὧδε γραφῆναι

18 ἑβδομήκοστον ἔτος καὶ
  δεύτερον ἦγον ἀληθῶς

19 ταῦθ᾽ ὁ νοῶν εὔξαιτο ὑπὲρ
  Ἀβερκίου πᾶς ὁ συνῳδός

20 οὐ μέντοι τύμβῳ τις ἐμῷ
  ἕτερόν τινα θήσει

21 εἰ δ᾽ οὖν Ῥωμαίων ταμείῳ
  θήσει δισχίλια χρυσᾶ

22 καὶ χρηστῇ πατρίδι Ἱερο-
  πόλει χίλια χρυσᾶ.

For the convenience of readers we append a translation into English.[1]

[1 This rendering is made, not from the original, but from the author's translation into Italian, in order to reproduce as nearly as possible his view of the meaning.—Tr.]

"I, a citizen of an eminent city, have made a tomb for myself, while yet alive, in which my body shall lie when the time shall have come. My name is Abercius, a disciple of the chaste Shepherd who feedeth the flocks on the mountains and plains, and hath great eyes that look on all things. He instructed me in the sure Word of Life, and sent me to Rome, the royal city, to contemplate that queen girt with golden robe and adorned with golden shoes. There I saw a mighty people famous for their splendid Signet. And I saw the plains and all the cities of Syria and Nisibis, having crossed the Euphrates; and everywhere I found brethren in agreement (with me), having Paul . . . And faith was my guide through all, and everywhere gave me for food the fish (ΙΧΘΥΣ) mighty out of the spring, and pure, which the unsullied virgin took and gave to eat to her friends for ever, having the choicest wine, and ministering it mixed (with water) together with the bread. I, Abercius, being myself present, dictated these things at the age of seventy-two years. Let him who understandeth all this and thinketh in like manner pray for Abercius.

"Let no man place another tomb upon mine; and, if one do so, he shall pay to the treasury of the Romans 2000 gold pieces, and to my beloved native town Hieropolis 1000."

To any one who knows the phraseology of primitive Christian symbolism, the meaning here is obvious. The "chaste Shepherd" is the Good Shepherd of the Gospel, who *animam suam dat pro ovibus suis.* ΙΧΘΥΣ ΠΑΝΜΕΓΕΘΗΣ is the "great fish" of which Tertullian speaks: *nos pisciculi secundum* ἰχθύν *nostrum Jesum Christum in aqua nascimur.* The queen that Abercius saw in Rome is the Christian community in Rome, the Church renowned above all for its founders and its fidelity. In the chaste virgin who has taken the fish from the water we must understand the Virgin Mary, who conceived the Saviour. The discipline of the secret required the use of this mysterious and symbolical language, but to the initiate, "him who understandeth all this and thinketh in like manner," it was perfectly intelligible.

Dr. Gerard Ficker, of Halle, writing some years ago, rejected this interpretation, and went so far as to say that Abercius was a priest of Cybele, and the inscription a pagan one. But his reasoning is of no value. As to his first objection, founded on the shape of the monument, it is well known that monuments in the form of cippi were to be found in Christian cemeteries open to the sky, as elsewhere. Then he insists that a Christian inscription of the second century could not fail to contain some sort of allusion to the doctrine of the Resurrection. But is not a recommendation of oneself to the prayers of the living a sort of allusion to a future life? Moreover, the actual word resurrection is very rarely found on inscriptions in cemeteries.

But Ficker's affirmative arguments are even weaker than his negative; his hypothesis, identifying Cybele with the *virgo casta* and Attis with the Shepherd of the inscription of Abercius, is fantastic. Why, one of the obligations imposed on the worshippers of Cybele was actually abstinence from fish: how then could Abercius have boasted of an act done during his pilgrimage which was a breach of this rule? Nor is it thinkable that the

Christians (who certainly held Abercius in great veneration) should have chosen a priest of Cybele as their bishop. How, exclaims De Rossi, is it possible to treat fancies of this sort as serious, or to discuss them as if they were worth scientific consideration?

We hold, with the majority of scholars, that the inscription of Abercius is a Christian inscription, and indeed the "queen of all Christian inscriptions"; and that it has greater significance than any other from a doctrinal point of view. For it touches on the doctrines of the divinity of Christ, of the Eucharist, of the cult of the Virgin; it asserts a belief in the communion of Saints by its invitation to the faithful to pray for Abercius; and, lastly, it also refers to the Supremacy of the Church of Rome.

This splendid text is throughout redolent of symbolical conceptions, identical with those which we find in the Christian phraseology of the first centuries, when the "discipline of the secret" was so generally practised to conceal the more abstruse doctrines of Christianity from idolaters. The "unsullied pastor" is Christ, who is often represented in ancient Christian art under these allegorical images culled from the parables. The fish is also a symbol of the Saviour, but more recondite, inasmuch as the name of Christ the Saviour is concealed in the Greek word ΙΧΘΥΣ. And the mystical fish, so well known in the Christian symbolism of the first centuries, may be seen repeated in a thousand devices on ancient monuments, and especially in the Roman catacombs. Hence the fish given as food to the faithful with bread and wine is an evident allusion to the sacrament of the Eucharist. The Virgin also, who takes this mystical fish and gives it to her friends, and whose personality is clearly distinguished from that of Faith (ΠΙΣΤΙΣ), is assuredly Mary, who took into herself and conceived the Saviour, as the learned Anglican writer Lightfoot also explains it.

Lastly, the reminiscence of Rome, which Abercius visited, in order to see the royal city and a people illustrious for a "splendid Signet," cannot refer to the material magnificence or to the political grandeur of the Eternal City ; for he would not have said that Christ had commissioned him to observe things of this sort. The words must undoubtedly be understood of the Christian inhabitants of Rome, who were renowned throughout the world ever since the days of Paul for their faith, and must refer to the great authority of the Roman Church, the supremacy of which Irenaeus had just then asserted. And this will appear still more clearly when we remember that Abercius was travelling, as other doctors of Christianity were wont then to do, and as Hegesippus had done, for the purpose of visiting the various churches of Christendom, and of assuring himself of the identity of belief in all parts.

But the views as to the Eucharist expressed in this remarkable inscription find a useful parallel in the inscription of Autun, recorded above, and in the monuments of the catacombs.

Thus the monuments of Hieropolis, of Autun, and of Rome, which may be considered to be practically contemporaneous, are all inspired by the same views of Christian doctrine, and give us the ideas and religious convictions prevailing during

the second and third centuries among the Christian
congregations of three great centres of the ancient
world, Asia Minor, Italy, and Gaul. Indeed, we
may say that the inscription of Abercius, written
in his seventy-third year, about A.D. 170, testifies to
the beliefs prevalent in the first years of the
second century—one might almost say, at the end
of the first. In the long journeys undertaken by
Abercius, he tells us that he found the belief of all
the brethren to be the same as his own, the same
belief which we see set forth on the monuments
of places so far apart. Hence we may see how
complete is the agreement on fundamental points
between the creed of to-day and that of both East
and West in the period nearest to the Apostolic
Age ; a creed which, according to Renan himself,
was identical with catholic doctrine even in the
reign of Marcus Aurelius. It is the confirmation
it affords of truth of this sort that gives their special
importance to these monuments, and above all to
the inscription of Abercius. The fact at any rate
is undeniable, and the more critically we study
historical sources and monuments, the more evident it becomes; while the daily discoveries of
new texts, as well as the recent excavations in the
Roman catacombs, confirm it to an extraordinary
degree. The fact, moreover, is of a nature and
of an importance to call for the most serious consideration from all who would study Christianity,
were it only as a great historical phenomenon, and
who are willing to inquire into its origin and develop-
ment sincerely and loyally with unprejudiced minds.

CHAPTER IV

INSCRIPTIONS RELATING TO THE DOCTRINE OF THE "COMMUNION OF SAINTS"

The Communion of Saints—The Cult of Saints—Inscriptions
of Martyrs

THIS doctrine may be treated under two heads:
the first has to do with the prayers of the faithful
for the departed; the second, with the prayers
addressed to the departed imploring their intercession on behalf of the living.

For greater clearness, therefore, we shall take the
inscriptions relating to them in two corresponding
classes.

§ I

Inscriptions relating to the Prayers of the Faithful for the Departed

The following is one of the most important
inscriptions, as it states its object to be to induce
the faithful on reading it to pray for the salvation
of the deceased:

79

```
          D · P ·
LVCIFERE · COIVGI · DVLCISSIME · OMNEN (sic)
DVLCITVDINEM · CVM · LVCTVM · MAXIME
MARITO · RELIQVISSET · MERVIT · TITVLVM
INSCRIBI · VT · QVISQVE · DE · FRATRIBVS · LE
GERIT · ROGET · DEVM | VT · SANCTO · ET · INNOCENTI
SPIRITO · AD · DEVM · SVSCIPIATVR
     QVE · VIXIT · ANNVS · XXI · MES · VIII · DIES · XV
```

"As a reward for her virtues this tablet has been set up, so that any of the brethren reading it should pray God to receive unto Himself this holy and innocent soul."

Lateran Museum.

Of still greater value is the next inscription, in hexameters:

80

```
EVCHARIS · EST · MATER · PIVS · ET · PATER · EST mihi...
VOS · PRECOR · O · FRATRES · ORARE
HVC · QVANDO · VENitis | ET · PRECIBVS · TOTIS
PATREM · NATVMQVE · ROCATIS | SIT · VESTRAE
MENTIS · AGAPES · CARAE · MEMINISSE | VT · DEVS
OMNIPOTENS · AGAPEN · IN · SAECVLA · SERVET
```

Cemetery of Priscilla.

The inscription used to be on the tomb of a girl named Agape.

The girl is represented as speaking; she begins by recalling the memory of her mother EVCHARIS (excellent grace), and next her pious father, whose name formed a spondee (*e.g.* Marcus or Crassus). Then the writer speaks in his own person, addressing visitors, and the brethren who may come to pray in the cemetery: *Vos precor o fratres orare huc quando venitis et precibus totis patrem natumque rogatis,* i.e. "when you come to offer common prayer (*precibus totis*) to the Father and the Son, remember the beloved Agape, *sit vestrae mentis Agapes carae meminisse,* that God may take her into His glory."

From this it may be certainly inferred that the faithful held liturgical services in the cemeteries, at which prayers were offered for the dead.

This important inscription is not later than the beginning of the third century.

In the following may be recognised an expression taken from a liturgical prayer for the dead:

81

IN PA*ce*
SPIRIT*us*
SILVA*ni*
AMEN

Cemetery of Callisto.

82

EVGENI
SPIRITVVS (*sic*)
IN BONO
(a dove)

"Eugenius, may thy spirit dwell in happiness!"
Cemetery of Callisto.

In a Greek inscription we find the following noble ejaculation :

83

. . . . ℞

H · ΨΤΧΗ · ϹΟΤ · ΕΙϹ · ΤΟΤϹ · ΟΤΡΑΝΟΤϹ

" May thy soul go to heaven ! "

Cemetery of Domitilla.

The following is partly in Greek and partly in Latin, Greek letters being used for the Latin. It contains a prayer to Christ to bear the deceased in mind :

84

(anchor)

ΔΗΜΗΤΡΙϹ · ΕΤ · ΛΕΟΝΤΙΑ

ϹΕΙΡΙΚΕ · ΦΕΙΛΙΕ · ΒΕΝΕΜΕΡΕΝ

ΤΙ · ΜΝΗϹΘΗϹ · ΙΗϹΟΤϹ

Ο · ΚΤΡΙΟϹ · ΤΕΚΝΟΝ . . . . . .

℞

(a dove)

" Lord Jesus, remember our daughter ! "

Cemetery of Domitilla.

In the final words of the following we meet with the beautiful words of the Angelic Salutation:

85

TH · CEMNOTATH · KAI · ΓΛΥΚΥΤΑΤΗ
CΥΜΒΙΩ · ΡΟΔΙΝΗ · ΑΥΡ · ΔΙΟCΙΟδω
ΡΟC · ΤΕΘΕΙΚΑΤ · Ο · ΚΥΡ · ΜΕΤΑ · CΟΥ

"The Lord be with thee!"

Cemetery of Priscilla.

In the two next repose and peace are invoked on behalf of the spirit:

86

ΦΙΛΟΥΜΕΝΗ
ΕΝ · ΕΙΡΗΝΗ · CΟΥ
ΤΟ · ΠΝΕΥΜΑ

"May thy spirit be in peace!"

S. Agnese.   Lateran Museum.

87

ΑΘΗΝΟΔΩΡΕ · ΤΕΚΝΟΝ
Ο · ΠΝΕΥΜΑ · CΟΥ · ΕΙC · ΑΝΑΠΑΥCΙΝ

"May thy spirit be at rest!"

Cemetery of the Giordani.

In the following the close of the epitaph alludes to the doctrine of the Resurrection:

88

. . . .

EIC · ANACTACIN · AIΩNION

"(May thy body be preserved here) till the everlasting Resurrection."

Cemetery of Priscilla.

The most usual formula for offering a prayer for the dead is IN · PACE. But there is another and more solemn expression, REFRIGERIUM, which denotes the relief of a pain which is being endured, a consolation in the midst of affliction.

This word *refrigerium* has always been used in the most ancient and solemn form of petition; and it also maintains its place in the liturgy, for in the Canon of the Mass we still implore on behalf of the dead *locum refrigerii et pacis.*

In the inscriptions this form of prayer is expressed in various ways. Sometimes we find the simple formula IN · REFRIGERIUM; often, too, we find it combined with the more common form IN · PACE. We find also DEVS · TIBI · RE-FRIGERET—DEVS · REFRIGERET · SPIRI-TVM · TVVM—REFRIGERA—BENE · RE-FRIGERA, etc.

The doctrinal value of the word REFRIGERIUM comes out even more clearly in an invaluable relic of legendary history, the "authentic and original

Acts of the Martyrdom of S. Perpetua" (A.D. 203). We mentioned this collection of stories on p. 124; but the present is a suitable occasion for giving a short account of it in connexion with the prayer for *refrigerium*.

The story is in three parts. The first is an account given, perhaps by a deacon, or a clerk of the Church of Carthage, concerning the companions of the Saint in her imprisonment and martyrdom; the second, written by the holy martyr herself, is the journal she kept during her imprisonment; the third gives the story of her martyrdom as related by the writer of the first part. This last part closes with a solemn declaration made by the author that the second part was actually written by the holy martyr with her own hand. The description gives an artless account of all that occurred from the moment the Saint and her fellow-Christians were imprisoned up to the day of her martyrdom. At the end of the same part the Saint relates sundry visions vouchsafed to her during her imprisonment. She prefaces the story of each vision with these words, *et ostensum est mihi hoc*, and closes it with the expression, "and then I awoke." Whether these visions were genuinely such or mere dreams is a matter of indifference to us; for even if we take them to be dreams, they must certainly have borne some relation to the dominating thoughts in the mind of the martyr, and therefore their value as illustrating doctrine remains the same.

In the first of these visions, after the usual formula, *et ostensum est mihi hoc*, she relates how she saw a long staircase reaching to heaven, compassed about by weapons of all sorts, and guarded by a dragon. She had not the courage to mount the stair, but Satyrus, her companion, bade her be of good cheer; then she ascended it, and reached a lovely garden, where she saw an aged and venerable man with white hair, who was milking kine. And when he saw her, straightway he beckoned to her to approach; and when she had drawn near, the old man gave her a morsel of curdled milk (*sicut buccella*), and she received it with hands folded over her lips, while all they who were in the garden said *Amen.* After which Perpetua says that she woke up, and found in her mouth such a sweetness as she had never tasted before.

This is an evident allusion to the Eucharist, as has been pointed out in the preceding chapter.

"After some days had passed since that vision," she goes on to say, "while we all stood together to pray, there escaped from my lips the name of Dinocrates, a younger brother of mine who had died not long before at the age of seven years of a cancer in the face. I wondered," she proceeds, "why I had never theretofore remembered him, and I was sorry therefor; and *all together we set ourselves to pray* for him. A short time after I had another vision, and I saw Dinocrates coming forth from a place of darkness, with countenance all pale and thereon a sore wound which made him foul to look upon. He was much grieved and downstricken, and he went hither and thither wandering as one who suffers much pain. Between me and him there was a great gulf, so that I could not succour him on any wise. In the same place where he was stood also a fountain, and it seemed as though Dinocrates had a burning thirst, for he sought to drink, but could not, because the lip of the basin was very high and he was short of stature. Then I understood that he was in a place of punishment. And so I awoke, and thought straightway of my brother in his suffering, but *I had faith that my prayers would give relief to him*; and straightway we set ourselves to pray for him, till the day came on which they bore us to another prison in the amphitheatre, to await the day of the celebration of the festival of Geta the Emperor's son."

The third vision occurred some days after the second, and was as follows : "I saw before me the same place as at the other times, but wholly transfigured, resplendent with light and in the midst of a fair garden; and Dinocrates joyful and well pleased, dancing here and there, and clothed in white raiment. The lip of the fountain in that garden had been much lowered, and therefrom Dinocrates continually refreshed himself (*et vidi Dinocratem refrigerantem*), while on the edge of the fountain stood a golden flask filled with water. Then," says Perpetua in conclusion, "I awoke, and understood that Dinocrates had been taken from the place of punishment, and was rejoicing in eternal bliss."

In all the ancient literature of Christendom we have certainly no other record speaking so clearly of a belief in Purgatory, of prayers for the dead, and of their power to give relief and refreshment.

We may add a few words as to the conclusion of this precious record. It goes on : " Methought I was in the arena, and the *podium* and the *cavea* were full of people who shouted and desired my death. I turned on one side and saw a huge Egyptian, black of skin, who was to fight with me; affrighted, I turned to the other side and I saw a *lanista* or master of gladiators, who called me to him. Then I slowly drew near to him, and he anointed me with oil, and gave me a staff; then embracing me and kissing me on the forehead, he gave me courage to fight. Renewed in strength I went against the giant and fought against him, and conquered him; and having beaten him down to earth as one dead, I placed my foot upon his head, while all the people wildly applauded my valour. Then I turned again to the *lanista*, and I saw that he beckoned me to him again; and I went to him, and he kissed me, while he gave me the palm of victory and a kiss on the forehead, saying the words *pax tecum*. Thereby I knew full well that in that vision were given me the tidings of my approaching death, and of the nature of the death which I was to die."

Perpetua concludes her priceless journal thus: "Hitherto I myself have said everything; but from henceforth I shall not be able to do so more; therefore that which shall happen to-morrow, another will take care to write down."

Here let us close this parenthesis, and return to our examination of the inscriptions. We can at once give some instances of the formula *refrigerium*. The word is used to express affectionate good wishes for the deceased, and at the same time as a prayer to God for the soul of him who has passed away.

In an inscription dating back to the end of the third century we read this ejaculation:

89

> PRIVATA · DVLCIS
> IN · REFRIGERIO
> ET · IN · PACE

Cemetery of Priscilla.

Here we have the capital distinction between *refrigerium* and *pax* expressed; for the two conceptions were quite distinct. The first is a prayer —and a pious hope—that the departed may enjoy *refrigerium*, or relief from purgatorial pains; the second is a prayer for peace, *i.e.* for everlasting bliss.

Here is another which combines a hope for the eternal happiness of the departed with the prayer for *refrigerium* :

90

> VICTORIA · REFRIGER*et*
> ISSPIRITVS · TVS · IN · BON*o* (*sic*)

" May thy spirit have comfort and happiness."

Cemetery of Domitilla.

The same idea is found in the following prayer from the Office for the Dead in the Greek ritual:

ʿΟ Θεὸς τῶν πνευμάτων . . . .
ἀνάπαυσον καὶ τὴν ψυχὴν τοῦ κεκοι-
μημένου δούλου σου ἐν τόπῳ φωτεινῷ,
ἐν τόπῳ χλοερῷ, ἐν τόπῳ ἀναψύξεως,[1] ἔνθα
ἀπέδρα πᾶσα ὀδύνη, λύπη καὶ στεναγμός.

[1] *In loco refrigerii*, '' in a place of refreshing.

91

PARENTEs · *fi*LIO
BONOSO · FECERVNT
BENEMERENTI · IN
PACE · ET · IN · REFRI
GERIV . . .
QVI · VIXIT · ANN . . .

Cemetery of S. Hermes.

92

AMERIMNVS
RVFINAE · COIV
GI · CARISSIME
BENEMEREN
TI · SPIRITVM
TVVM · DEVS
REFRIGERET

Lateran Museum.   (Plate VII. 1.)

93

BOLOSA · DEVS · TI
BI · REFRIGERET · QVAE · VI
XIT · ANNOS · XXXI · RECESSIT
DIE · XIII · KAL · OCTB · ☧

Lateran Museum.   (Plate VII. 2.)

94

MVRELIVS · IA*nuarius*
CARE · REFRIGERA

Cemetery of Priscilla.

95

EVCARPIA · CARISSI
MA · DEVS · REFRIGERET
SPIRITVM · TVVM

Cemetery of Priscilla.

96

KALEMERE · DEVS · REFRI
GERET · SPIRITVM · TVVM
VNA · CVM · SORORIS · TVAE · HILARAE

(The Good Shepherd)

Cemetery of S. Hermes.   Kircherian Museum.

97

POSVI t · *Hipe* RECHIVS
COIVGI · ALBINVLE
BENEMERENTI · SIC
VT · SPIRITVM · TVVM · DE
VS · REFRIGERET

Cemetery of Priscilla.

This seems to mean that the inscription was put up to secure relief for the departed lady; evidently as suggesting to the faithful that they should pray for her.

98

DVLCISSIMO
ANTISTHENI
CONIVGI · SVO
REFRIGERIVM

Cemetery of Priscilla.

99

S · O . . . .
. . . .
*dulci*SSIMO
. . . . *fil*IO
*p*ATER
SPIRITVM · TVVM
DEVS · REFRIGERET

Cemetery of S. Agnese.

100

*Val*ERIO · VOLVSIANO
. . . VTYCHETIS · FILIO
. . . O · FORTVNATO · QVI · VIM
(?) *igni*S · PASSI · SVNT
. . . GIA · PIENTISSIMIS
. . . REFRIGERET · NOS · *Qui*
*omnia po*TEST　(anchor)

In the Museum of Marseilles.
(Le Blant, *Man. épig.* ii. p. 348.)

This inscription is considered by some to refer to certain martyrs, but the matter is by no means certain. At any rate there is here a prayer for *refrigerium*, in anticipation, on behalf of those who set up the tablet.

Other expressions worthy of note are found in the following :

101

. . . *t*ERRAE RECEPIT CORPVS LIVI
. . . X DECEM ET QVATERQVE BINOS HIC
. . . ESTERREOS TERRE SOLVTVS ANIMA CHRISTO
REDDITA EST

Lateran Museum.

102

```
. . . in PACE · IN · SINO · DEI
    . . . vixit ann XX
    . . . dep IIII · KAL · AVG
```

(De Rossi, *Bull. di arch. crist.*, 1873, p. 75.)

This means the same as "in Christi gremium"; cp. De Rossi.

§ 2

Prayers addressed to the Dead for their Intercession on behalf of the Living

In some inscriptions, with the prayer for the repose of the souls of the departed is combined a prayer for his intercession on behalf of the survivors. The following are some instances:

103

```
(a vase graffito)      (a lamp graffito)
IANVARIA · BENE · REFRIGERA
ET · ROGA · PRO . NOS (sic)
```

"Januaria, be thou refreshed, and pray for us!"

Cemetery of Callisto.

104

. . . .
... VIBAS
IN · PACE · ET · PETE
PRO · NOBIS

" Live in (eternal) peace and pray for us ! "
Cemetery of Domitilla.

We often find the prayer for intercession on behalf of the living standing alone.

105

SABBATI · DVLCIS
ANIMA · PETE · ET · RO
GA · PRO · FRATRES · ET
SODALES · TVOS (*sic*)

Cemetery of the Giordani on the Via Latina.
(Muratori, *Nov. Thes.* p. 1934.)

Note the phrase *fratres et sodales* as meaning Christians.

106

VINCENTIA · IN ☧

PETAS · PRO · PHOE

BE · ET · PRO · VIR

GINIO · E

IVS

Cemetery of Callisto.

By *virginius* is meant the husband who had not been previously married.

107

PETE · PRO · PARENTES · TVOS
MATRONATA · MATRONA
QVE · VIXIT · AN · I · D . LII

Lateran Museum.

108

ATTICE · SPIRITVS · TVVS
IN · BONO · ORA · PRO · PAREN
TIBVS · TVIS

Cemetery of Callisto.

(Muratori, *Nov. Thes.* p. 1833.)

109

SVTI · PETE
PRO · NOS
VT · SALVI · SIMVS

Marangoni, *Acta S. Victorini*, p. 90.

" Pray for us that we may be saved ! "—a fine phrase.

110

```
MARINE · IM · ET . . .
MENTEM        MA . . .
   NOS  (anchor)  CRIA . . .
HABETO        NE · EC . . .
DVOBVS
```

"Oh Marinus, be mindful of us twain!"
Cemetery of Priscilla.

111

```
. . . . ΕΡΩΤΑ
ΥΠΕΡ · ΤΩΝ · ΤΕΚΝΩΝ
ΜΕΤΑ . . . . . ΑΝΔΡΟϹ
```

"Pray for thy children!"
Cemetery of Priscilla.

112

```
ΚΑΤΤΗ ⳨ ΟΙΓΚΑΛ
ΙΟΥΝ · ΑΥΓΕΝΔΕ
ΖΗϹΑΙϹ · ΕΝ · Κ̄Ω̄ · ΚΑΙ
ΕΡΩΤΑ · ΥΠΕΡ · ΗΜΩΝ
```

"Augendus, live in the Lord, and pray for us!"
Cemetery of Domitilla.

113

.......ΙΔΙΩ · ΙΩ · ΦΙΛΗΜΟΝΙ
ζησαντι · καΛΩC · ΕΤΗ · ΔΥΩ · ΜΕΤΑ
των · ΓΟΝΑΙΩΝ · ΕΥΧΟΥ · ΥΠΕΡ · Η
μων · μετα · τΩΝ · ΑΓΙΩΝ

" To . . . son Philemon who lived happily for
two years with his parents.   Pray for us, together
with the Saints ! "

Cemetery of Priscilla.

114

ΚΑΡΑ · ΜΝΗΜΟΝΕΥΕ · ΜΟΥ

" Cara, remember me ! "

Graffito in the cemetery of Priscilla.

115

ΔΙΟΝΥCΙΟC · ΝΗΠΙΟC
ΑΚΑΚΟC · ΕΝΘΑ · ΔΕΚΕΙ
ΤΕ · ΜΕΤΑ · ΤΩΝ · Α
ΓΙΩΝ · ΜΝΗCΚΕCΘΕ
ΔΕ · ΚΑΙ · ΗΜΩΝ · ΕΝ · ΤΑΙ
C · ΑΓΙΑΙC · ΥΜΩΝ · ΠΡΕΥΧΑΙC
ΚΑΙ · ΤΟΥ · ΓΛΥΨΑΤΟC · ΚΑΙ · ΓΡΑΨΑΝ
ΤΟC

(anchor)   (dove)

" The innocent child Dionysius lies here by the
side of the Saints.   Be mindful in thy holy prayers
of him who carved this and of him who composed
it ! "

Cemetery of Callisto.   Kircherian Museum.

116

ATTICE
DORMI · IN · PACE
DE · TVA · INCOLVMITATE
SECVRVS · ET · PRO · NOSTRIS
PECCATIS · PETE · SOLLICITVS[1]

Museum of the Capitol.
(De Rossi, *Bull. di arch. crist.*, 1894, p. 58.)

Found in March 1893 in preparing for the Lazaret at S. Sabina.

The following is very fine; it affirms that our hope of salvation, theologically speaking, rests upon the efficacy of the prayers of the departed for the living:

117

GENTIANVS · FIDELIS · IN · PACE
QVI · VIXIT · ANNIS · XXI • MENS · VIII
DIES · XVI · ET · IN · ORATIONIS · TVIS (*sic*)
ROGES · PRO · NOBIS · QVIA · SCIMVS
TE · IN · ☧

" Pray for us in thy orisons, for we know that thou dwellest in Christ ! "

Lateran Museum.

[1] Compare with this expression S. Cyprian, *De mortalitate*, chap. ix.: "There awaits us a vast number of those dear to us, a large and serried crowd of parents, brothers, sons yearning for us, assured of their own salvation, but still anxious concerning ours."

§ 3

Inscriptions referring to the Cult of Saints

If the intercession of the departed availed anything, much more should the prayers of the martyrs
avail, since of them there was no doubt that they
were in the place of eternal bliss.

The custom of commemorating martyrs is of great
antiquity; we find a record of it as early as the
second century in a letter of the Church of Smyrna
to the Church of Lyons, written in the very year of
the martyrdom of S. Polycarp, A.D. 155.[1]

The martyrs were considered as the intercessors
for the dead and their advocates before the throne
of God; the idea is clearly expressed in the
following inscription, in which martyrs are called
advocates.

[1] Eusebius, *H.E.* iv. 15.

118

CYRIACE

....QVAM NVLLVM AB HIS SORTE ET CON(*diti*)ONE ESSE INMVNEM | *h*OC CONSTET VERVM ID NOBIS DOLORI EST QVOD RARI EXEMPLI | *foemi*NA IN QVA IVSTITIA MIRABILIS INNOCENTIA SINGVLARIS CASTITAS | *inc*ONPARABILIS OBSEQVENTISSIMA IN OMNIBVS | ....NENTISSIMA ORBATIS TRIBVS LIBERIS QVI VNA MECV HVIC SEPVLCRO | CON LAVDIS EIVSDEM INDIDERVNT INMATVRI | ....ITE NOBIS AD QVIETEM PACIS TRANSLATA CVIQVE PRO VITAE SVE | *testi*MONIVM SANCTI MARTYRES APVD DEVM ET CHRISTVM ERVNT ADVOCATI | *que* VIXIT ME-CVM INCVLPABILITER ET CVM OMNI SVAVITATE | *dul*CISSIME ANNIS IIII MENSIBVS QVINQVE DIEBVS DVODECIM | .....

"The holy martyrs shall be advocates for every man before God and before Christ."

Basilica of S. Lorenzo fuori le Mura.

The same conception is often expressed in the catacombs by figures representing the dead standing at the judgment-seat of Christ, defended and protected by the local martyrs. Sometimes the martyrs are represented as actually accompanying the dead to the divine judgment-seat. This idea is remarkably well expressed in the following inscription belonging to the city of Vercelli:

119

DISCITE · QVI · LEGITIS · DIVINO · MVNERE · REDDI
| MERCEDEM · MERITIS · SEDES · CVI · PROXIMA ·
SANCTIS | MARTYRIBVS · CONCESSA · DEO · EST ·
GRATVMQVE · CVBILE | SARMATA QVOD · ME-
RVIT · VENERANDO · PRESBYTER · ACTV | SEPTIES
· HIC · QVINOS · TRANSEGIT · CORPORIS · ANNOS
| IN · CHRISTO · VIVENS · AVXILIANTE · LOCO |
NAZARIVS · NAMQVE · PARITER · VICTORQVE ·
BEATI | LATERIBVS · TVTVM · REDDVNT · MERITIS-
QVE · CORONANT | O · FELIX · GEMINO · MERVIT ·
QVI · MARTYRE · DVCI | AD · DOMINVM · MELIORE
· VIA · REQVIEMQVE · MERERI

It commemorates a priest who was buried close to the Saints, and on whose behalf the intercession of the martyrs Nazarius and Victor is invoked; it describes them as bearing him company till he reached the Lord. "Happy is he who is thought worthy of being accompanied by two martyrs."

The other inscriptions that follow are also inspired by the same idea of commending to the Saints the souls of the departed, that they may introduce them into Heaven.

120

D$\overline{\text{MA}}$ · SACRVM · XL
LEOPARDVM · IN · PACEM
CVM · SPIRITA · SANCTA · ACCEP
TVM · EVM · HABEATIS · INNOCENTEM
POSVER · PAR · Q · V · ANN · VII · MEN · VII

"May the Saints welcome this innocent soul!"
Museum of the Capitol.

121

PAVLO · FILIO · MERENTI · IN · PA
CEM · TE · SVSCIPIAN · OMNIVM · ISPIRI
TA · SANCTORVM · QVI · VIXIT · ANNOS · II · DIES · N · L

" May the spirits of all the Saints welcome thee ! "

From Rome, now at Carseoli in the Museo dei Bagni.

This prayer is still used in our Funeral Service, in the words " Te suscipiant martyres."

And the welcome given by the Saints to the departed is also expressed in paintings found in the cemetery; *e.g.* a very fine one in the cemetery of Domitilla representing S. Petronilla receiving a matron named Veneranda and accompanying her to heaven.

The following also is inspired by the thought that the deceased may be in the company of the Saints :

122

AGATEMERIS · SPI
RITVM · TVVM · INTER
SANCTOS

(dove)   (dove)

" May thy soul be in the midst of the Saints ! "

Cemetery of Callisto.

123

AVRELIAE MARIAE
PVELLAE VIRGINI INNOCENTISSIMAE
SANCTE PERGENS AD IVSTOS ET ELECTOS IN PACE
QVAE VIXIT ANNOS XVI MESIS V
DIES XV.IIII SPONSATA AVRELIO DA
MATI DIEBVS XXV AVRELIANVS . . . . . .
VETERANVS ET SEXTILIA PARENTES
INFELICISSIMAE FILIAE DVLCISSIMAE
AC AMANTISSIMAE CONTRA VOTVM
QVI DVM VIVENT HABENT
MAGNVM DOLOREM
MARTYRES SANCTI IN MENTE HA
VITE MARIA

The conclusion is fine—"Ye holy martyrs, be mindful of Maria!"

In Aquileia.

124

. . . . *ben*EMERENTI · IN · PACE · QVAE · VIXIT
ANNIS · XXX · MESIS · SE
. . . . KAL ·SEPTENBRIS · SANCTE · LAVRENTI
SVSCEPTA · HABETO · ANIM*am ejus*

"May Saint Lawrence receive her soul!"

Cemetery of Cyriaca.   Naples Museum.

Here we have the title of *Sanctus,* which is of later use than *dominus* or *domnus.*

M

125

```
SOMNO · AETERNALI
AVRELIVS · GEMELLVS · QVI
VIXIT · AN . . . . .
ET · MES · VIII · DIES · XVIII · MATER
FILIO · CARISSIMO · BENEMERENTI
FECIT · IN · PACE
CONMANDO · BASILLA · INNO
CENTIA · GEMELLI
```

"I commend to S. Basilla the innocent soul of Gemellus."

Lateran Museum.

126

```
DOMINA . BASILLA · COM
MANDAMVS · TIBI · CRES
CENTINVS · ET · MICINA
FILIA · NOSTRA · CRESCEN . . .
QVE · VIXIT · MEN · X · ET · DIES . . .
```

"Oh martyr Basilla, we commend to thee Crescentinus and our daughter Micina!"

Lateran Museum.

The dead were further commended to the martyrs by the prayer for *refrigerium* on their behalf through the intercession of the Saints, as in the following instances :

127

REFRIGERI · IANVARIVS · AGATOPVS · FELICISSI
MVS · MARTYRES

Graffito from the Cemetery of Praetextatus.

(The prayer is addressed to the martyrs Januarius, Felicissimus, and Agapitus.)

128

REFRIGERET · TIBI·DEVS · ET · CRISTVS
ET·DOMNI·NOSTRI·ADEODATVS [*sic*]
ET·FELIX

Graffito in the Cemetery of Commodilla.

(The prayer is addressed to the local martyrs Felix and Adeodatus.)

129

REFRIGERET · TIBI
DOMINVS · IPPOLITVS

Cemetery of S. Hippolytus.

130

A · DEO · ET · SANCTIS · ACCETA (*sic*)

"She was received by God and by the Saints."

Cemetery of SS. Peter and Marcellinus.

131

RVTA · OMNIBVS · SVBDITA · ET · ATFABI
LIS · BIBET · IN · NOMINE · PETRI
IN · PACE ☧

Cemetery of Priscilla.

(Boldetti, *Osservazioni*, p. 388.)

This is valuable as invoking eternal life for the departed through the intercession of the Apostle Peter, of whose connexion with this cemetery there were many traditions.

Again, in an inscription on glass found in the cemetery of S. Lorenzo, there is an allusion to the local saint :

"Vivet in nomine Laurenti."

(Garrucci, *Vetri ornati di figure in oro*, p. 122.)

132

CORPVS · SANCTIS · COMEN
DAVI · IRENE · TIBI · CVM
SANCTIS · QVINTA · VALE
IN · PACE

"Peace be to thee with the Saints!"

Capua.

133

HIC PASTOR MEDICVS MONVMENT...
FELIX DVM SVPEREST CONDIDIT...
PERFECIT CVMCTA EXCOLVIT QVI...
CERNET QVO IACEAT POENA...
ADDETVR ET TIBI VALENTINI GLODRIA (*sic*) *Sancti*
VIVERE POST OBITVM DAT (*tibi*) DIGNA *Deus*

Cemetery of S. Valentinus.

Notice the words, "addetur et tibi Valentini gloria Sancti," as expressing that the merits of the martyr Valentinus may be applied to the relief of the deceased Felix, priest and physician.

134

PROCVLA · CL · FEMINA
FAMVLA · DEI
A · TERRA · AD · MARTYRES

Lyons.

An ejaculation of triumph, meaning, "Fly from earth to Heaven, the abode of the martyrs!"

135

. . . .
NVTRICATVS · DEO · CRISTO
MARTVRIBVS

Lateran Museum.

The record of a youth who had been brought up in the worship of the true God and of the martyrs.

136

> MANDROSA HIC NOMINE OMNIVM PLENA FIDELIS
> IN X̄P̄O EIVS | MANDATA RESERVANS MARTYRVM
> OBSEQVIS DEVOTA TRANSEGI | FALSI SAECVLI VI-
> TAM VNIVS VIRI CONSORTIO TERQVINOS CONIVN-
> CTA | PER ANNOS REDDIDI NVNC D̄N̄O RERVM
> DEBITVM COMVNEM | OMNIBVS OLIM QVAE VIXIT
> ANN PLM XXXIII DP VIII KAL | FEBRVARIAS CONS
> AGINANTI FAVSTI V C

Monastery of S. Paolo (A.D. 483).

The words " martyrum obsequiis devota " are noticeable, as testifying to the cult of martyrs.

137

(wreath)

> DILECTISSIMO·MARITO·ANIME·DVLCISSIME·ALEXIO
> LECTORI | DE · FVLLONICES · QVI · VIXIT · MECVM
> ANN · XV · IVNCTVS · MIHI · ANN · XVI | VIRGO · AD
> VIRGINE · CVIVS · NVMQVAM · AMARITVDINEM · HABVI
> | CESQVE · IN · PACE · CVM · SANCTIS · CVM · QVOS
> MERERIS | DEP · VIII · X · KAL · IANV

" Sleep in peace beside the Saints, with whom thou hast earned the right to stand ! "

Cemetery of Callisto.

138

```
.... T · ANNIS · XVIIII
.... NOTARIO
.... cuN · MAPTVRIBVS
```

Cemetery of Priscilla.

The last line may mean either that the youth was buried beside the martyrs, or that he was enjoying eternal bliss with them.

139

```
HIC · REQVIESCIT · IN · PA
CE · LVPICINVS
QVI · VIXIT · ANNOS · NV
MERO · XXXV
PLVS · MINVS · QVI · NECSET III
NON · OCTOB
RESVRRECTVRVS · CVM
SANCTIS
☧
```

(Le Blant, *Inscr. de la Gaule*, p. 419.)

140

```
EuseBIVS INFANS PER AETATEM SENE PECCAto
acceDENS AD SANCTORVM LOCVM IN PAce
qui ESCIT
```
(dove)

Cemetery of Commodilla (now in the Casa De Rossi).

141

> HIC · DALMATA · CR
> ISTI · MORTE · REDEM
> TVS · QVIISCET · IN · PA
> CE · ET · DIEM · FVTVRI
> IVDICII · INTERCEDE
> NTEBVS · SANCTIS · L
> LETVS · SPECTIT (*sic*)

(Le Blant, *Inscr. de la Gaule*, p. 478.)

Occasionally the actual day of the martyrdom is recorded.

142

> IIII NON SEPT PASSIONE MARTVR
> ORVM HORTENSIVM MARIANI ET
> IACOBI ΔΑΤΙ MARIN RVSTICI CRISPI
> TAT + MEITVNI BICTORIS SILBANI EGIP
> TIII S̄C̄Ī D̄Ī MEMORAMINI IN CONSPECTVΔNI
> QVORVM NOMINA SCITIS qVI FECIT IN Δ XV
>
>

Near Constantine in Africa.

Sometimes the dates of the festivals of the martyrs are given, to show that the deceased brother was buried on one of those days.

143

> *Locus* FAVSTINIANI ET SORICES *quem*
> *comparav*ERVNT RECESIT NATALE SA*ncti*
> *Laurenti* IN PACE

Cemetery of Cyriaca.

144

ΕΥΣΚΙΑ · Η · ΑΜΕΝΙΠΤΟΣ · ΖΗΣΑ(σα)
ΧΡΗΣΤΩΣ · ΚΑΙ · ΣΕΜΝΑ · ΕΤΗ
ΠΛΙΟ · ΕΛΑΤΤΟΝ · ΚΕ · ΑΝΕ
ΠΑΥΣΕΤΟ · ΤΗ · ΕΟΡΤΗ · ΤΗΣ · ΚΥ
ΡΙΑΣ · ΜΟΥ · ΛΟΥΚΙΑΣ · ΕΙΣ · ΗΝ
ΟΥΚ · ΕΣΤΙΝ · ΕΝΚΩΜΕΙΟΝ
ΕΙΠΕΙΝ · ΧΡΗΣΤΕΙΑΝΗ · ΠΙΣ
ΤΗ · ΤΕΛΙΟΣ · ΟΥΣΑ · ΕΥΧΑ
ΡΙΣΤΟΥΣΑ · ΤΩ · ΕΙΔΙΩ · ΑΝ
ΔΡΙ · ΠΟΛΛΑΣ · ΕΥΧΑΡΙΣ
ΤΙΑΣ ☧

" Euskia, the blameless one, who lived a life of goodness and purity for twenty-five years, died on the feast of our lady Lucia (S. Lucia), for whom no praise is adequate. She was a perfect Christian, well pleasing to her husband, and endued with much grace."

In the catacombs of Syracuse.

145

PECORI · DVLCIS · ANIMA · BENIT
IN · CIMITERV · VII · IDVS · IVL ·
D · POSTERA · DIE · MARTVRORV

Cemetery of SS. Processus and Martinianus on the Via Aurelia.
Lateran Museum.

This records the burial of Pecorius in this

cemetery in the octave of the feast of its patron saints, July 9th.

This inscription has been incorrectly read as referring to the festival of the sons of S. Felicitas (July 10th); a mistake which I corrected later, as above.

146

NATALE

DOMNI · CIRV

(*lae*) *pr*IDIE · KAL

. . . . *oc*TOBRES

"Natale domni Cirulae pridie Kal. Octobris." The festival of a martyr named Cirula on September 30th.

(Africa—Numidia.)

147

Locus FELI	CITATIS
*qui depo*SI (orante)	TA · EST
*natal*E · DOM	NES · THE
clae	

Cemetery of Commodilla.

This records the day of martyrdom of S. Thecla, the well-known disciple of the Apostle Paul.

148

PASCASIVS · VIXIT
PLVS · MINVS · ANNVS · XX
FECIT · FATV · IIII · IDVS
OCTOBRIS · VIII · ANTE
NATALE · DOMNI · AS
TERI · DEPOSITVS · IN
PACE · A ☧ Ω

Cemetery of Commodilla.   Lateran Museum.

This states that Pascasius died eight days before the festival of S. Asterius, a martyr of Ostia.

The inscription also shows that the present habit of distinguishing the days before—or eve of—the feasts of martyrs had then begun.

149

STVDENTIAE · *Depositae*
DIE · *Natali* · MARCELLI
CONS · SALLIES

Basilica of S. Sebastian (A.D. 348).

This Studentia was buried on the feast of S. Marcellus, January 10th.

150

```
HIC · EST · POSITVS · BITALIS · PISTOR · MIA
SHIC · ES · RG · XII · QVI · BICXITAN
NVS · PL · MINVS · N · XLV · DEPO
SITVS · IN · PACE · NATALE · D
OMNES · SITIRETIS · TERT
IVM · IDVS · FEBR · CONSVLA
TVM · FL · VINCENTI · VVC
CONSS
                    (bushel measure)
```

Basilica of S. Paul (A.D. 401).

Vitalis, a baker, is here recorded as having been buried on the feast of the martyr Soter, February 11th, "natale Domnes Sitiretis."

Occasionally reference is made to a commemoration service of the martyrs in the cemeteries, *e.g.* :

151

```
XVI · KAL · OCTOB · MARTVRORV*m in cimi*
TERV · MAIORE · VICTORIS · FEL*Icis (Papiae ?)*
EMERENTI ANETIS · ET · ALEXAN*dri*
```

Museum of the Capitol (new Hall of Christian Inscriptions).

This inscription is valuable because, besides giving the date of the feasts of the martyrs mentioned, it gives the name of the cemetery on the Via Nomentana in which they were buried. This was the larger cemetery of S. Agnese, so called to distinguish it from the smaller, which is situated under the basilica of S. Agnese.

Devotion to the martyrs was specially exhibited by the choice of a burial-place in the neighbourhood of their tombs in the cemeteries or cemetery chapels. And the true mind of the Church in approving this custom is well expressed by S. Augustine, where he says that the dead are benefited, not by the physical juxtaposition to the martyrs, but by the opportunity of getting the special prayers of the faithful who visit their sanctuaries. "Adjuvat defuncti spiritum non mortui corporis locus, sed ex loci memoria vivus precantis affectus" (August. *De cura pro mortuis*, iv. 5).

The inscriptions recording the proximity of the tomb to the sepulchre of the martyr are naturally numerous. The fact was commonly expressed by saying that the tomb was *ad Domnum Caium—ad Domnum Cornelium*, etc.

The following stated that the deceased is buried near the venerated tomb of a martyr:

152

```
BENEMERENTI IOVINE QVE CVM CO
GEM SVVM HABVIT ANNOS V ET De
CESSIT ANNORVM XXI QVE CONPAra
BIT SIBI ARCOSOLIVM IN CALLISTI AD DOMN
DEPOSITA DIE III IDVS FEBRVARIAS
CAIVM FECIT COIVGI MERENTI IN PACI
```

Cemetery of Callisto.

The last line but one is as inserted later.

The inscription says that Jovenis bought herself an arcosolium in the cemetery of Callisto near the tomb of Caius, Pope and martyr.

153

```
SERPENTIV
S · EMIT · LOCV
A · QVINTO · FOSSORE
AD · SANCTVM · CORNELIVM
```

"Serpentius bought himself a tomb from the *fossor* (grave-digger) Quintus near the grave of the martyr S. Cornelius."

Cemetery of Callisto, now near Avellino.

154

```
IanVARIVS ET S(ilana)
loCVM BESOMum
emeruNT AT SANCTA FEL(icitatem)
```

"Januarius and Silana bought themselves a tomb to hold two bodies near the grave of S. Felicitas."

Cemetery of S. Felicitas.

155

```
LVCILIVS PELIO SE VIVV CONPARA(vit)
LOCVM VESCANDENTE IN BASILICA
MAIORE AD DOMNV LAVRENTIVM
IN MESV ET SITV PRESBITERIV
```

The two persons mentioned bought themselves a tomb to hold two bodies near the grave of S. Lorenzo in the middle of the choir of the basilica.

Cemetery of Cyriaca.

156

DRACONTIVS · PELAGIVS · ET · IVLIA · ET · ELIA
ANTONINA · PARAVERVNT · SIBI · LOCV ☧
AT · IPPOLITV · SVPER · ARCOSOLIV · PROPTER ·
VNA · FILIA

"They prepared a sepulchre for their daughter above the arcosolium near the grave of the martyr S. Hippolytus."

Cemetery of S. Hippolytus.   Lateran Museum.

157

. . . .
QVOR SVN NOMI
NAE MASIMI
CATIBATICV
I SECVNDV
MARTYRE
DOMINV
CASTVLV ISCALA

This records a tomb situated in the second story of the cemetery near the steps that led to the grave of the martyr Castulus.

158

GAVDIOSA DE
POSITA IN BAS
ILICA DOMNI
FELICIS

"Gaudiosa, buried in the basilica of the martyr Felix."

Via Aurelia.   (Bosio, *Roma sotterranea*, ii. p. 13.)

159

AD SANCTVM PETRVM APOSTOLVM ANTE REGIA
IN PORTICV COLVMNA SECVNDA QVOMODO
INTRAMVS | SINISTRA PARTE VIRORVM
LVCILLVS ET IANVARIA HONESTA FEMINA

(dove)   A ☧ Ω   (dove)

S. Peter's.   (Bosio, *Roma sotterranea*, ii. p. 8.)

The husband and wife, Lucilius and Januaria, owned the tomb in the porch of the basilica of S. Peter's, near the second column on the left on the men's side.

160

COSTATINOS · EMIS
SE · IANVARIVM · ET · BRI
TIAM · LOCVM · ANTE · DO
MNA · EMERITA · A · FOSSO
RIBVS · BVRDONE · ET · MICI
NVM · ET · MVSCORVTIONE · AVRISOLI
DVM · VN · SEMES · CONS · D · D · N · N · THAE
ODOSIO · ET · VALETINIANO · II

Cemetery of Commodilla, now lost (A.D. 426).

This inscription is full of mistakes. It seems to mean that Januarius and Britia bought a tomb in front of the grave of the martyr S. Merita, from the *fossores*, at the price of $1\frac{1}{2}$ golden solidi, "Constat nos emisse locum ante domna Emerita," etc.

161

```
FL · EVRIALVS · V · H · CONPA
RAVIT · LOCVM · SIVI · SE
VIVO · AD · MESA¹ BEATI
MARTVRIS · LAVRENTI · DES
CENDENTIB · IN · CRIPTA · PAR
TE · DEXTRA · DE · FOSSORE
V . . . . . . . . . CI · IPSIVS
DIE · III · KAL · MAIAS · FL · STILICO
NE · SECVNDO · CONSS ·
```

Basilica of S. Lorenzo on the Via Tiburtina (A.D. 405).

(Marruchi, *Nuovo Bull. di arch. crist.*, 1900, pp. 127-141.)

This states that the tomb of Flavius Euryalus stood near the altar-tomb of the martyr S. Lawrence, on the right hand as one went into the crypt.

With this may be compared the next inscription, from Sirmio, which speaks of a tomb placed on the right of the grave of the martyr Syneros.

162

```
. . . . . . . . . . . . . . . . . . . . . . . . . . .
AD · DOMNVM · SINEROTEM · AD · DEXTERAM²
```

Tombs were also constructed behind the tombs of the martyrs, a position described as "retro sanctos."

¹ *Ad mensam*, close to the altar.
² *Bull. di arch. crist.*, 1884-1885, pp. 144-145.

N

163

> IN CRYPTA NOBA RETRO
> SANCTOS

Cemetery of Cyriaca.   (Boldetti, *Osservazioni*, p. 53.)

This describes a tomb in a newly made gallery behind the tombs of certain martyrs.

164

> FELICISSIMVS · ET · LEOPAR*da emerunt*
> BISOMVM · AT · CRISCENT*ionem martyrem*
> INTROITV

Cemetery of Priscilla.

Felicissimus and Leoparda bought a grave to hold two bodies situated in front of the entrance of the burial-chamber of S. Crescentio.

165

> ERMANOS · POSSID . . .
> VNC · VRBICI · MEMBRA · QVIES . . .
> MIECIVM · LANVGINE · MALAS . . .
> RADIES · ET · FVNERE · MERSIT · ACERBO . . .
> SERINATORVM · CARITATE · PARENTES . . .
> VCTE · POSVERVNT · LIMINA · MARTYR . . .
> IVS · ET · VALERIA · PARENTES · FECERVNT . . .
> . . . RBICVS · PRID · KAL · SEPTEMBRES
>   M
> (dove)   (wreath)   (dove)

Basilica of S. Paul.

This says that the deceased was buried near the martyr, " ad tua limina martyr."

The sites next the tombs of the martyrs, known as "limina sanctorum," were specially sacred spots. Hence, as the following inscription tells us, a pious lady obtained for her great deserts the privilege of burial "intra limina sanctorum"; a place desired by many, though few obtained it; "quod multi cupiunt et rari accipiunt."

166

.... NA IN DOM CVLTRIX
.... P NVTRIVIT
.... VIS
*amatrix pau*PERORVM
quae pro tanta MERITA ACCEPIT
*sepulcrum intra l*IMINA SANCTORVM
.... T ACCEPIT
*quod multi cupiu*N ET RARI ACCIPIVN
Antonio et S VACRIO CS

Velletri.   Borgia Museum (A.D. 381).
(Marini, *Manoscritti*, pp. 904, 907.)

167

Malluit hic propriae corpus committere terrae
Quam precibus quaesisse solum si magna patronis
Martyribus quaerenda quies sanctissimus ecce
Cum trini paribusque suis Vincentius ambit
Nos aditos, servatque domum Dominumque tuetur
A tenebris, lumen praebens de lumine vero

(Le Blant, *Inscriptions de la Gaule*, No. 492.)

168

VRSINIANO · SVBDIACONO · SVBHOC · TVMVLO · OSSA
QVIESCVNT · QVI · MERVIT · SANCTORVM · SOCIARI
SEPVLCRIS | QVEM · NEC · TARTARVS · FVRENS ·
NEC · POENA · SAEVA · NOCEBIT

(Treves.   Cp. *Inscr. de la Gaule*, No. 293.)

The ancient Christians undoubtedly held the
martyrs in great devotion, as is proved to demon-
stration by the monuments.   These show us clearly
how general that devotion was, and how extravagant
sometimes in its outward manifestation, especially
in the fourth and fifth centuries, when magnificent
churches were built over the graves of the martyrs.

Every one wished to be buried near the martyrs ;
hence the more ignorant were led to believe that
this alone was sufficient to secure salvation.

This is why we find an extraordinary number of
tombs near the graves of the martyrs.

These tombs were often made in the walls, thus
ruining or disfiguring the adjacent monuments ;
and the abuses were so scandalous as to call for
the interference of the ecclesiastical authority ;
and it interfered with some effect, as Sabinus, the
archdeacon of the Roman Church, bears witness.
The grave that he selected in S. Lorenzo was not
near that of the martyr, but in the porch of the
church.   This he ordered purposely, to show his
disagreement with those who wanted to be buried in
actual touch with the martyrs.   Damasus expressed
the same objection when he wrote, "Hic fateor

Damasus volui mea condere membra sed cineres timui sanctos vexare piorum."

Such an abuse had to be put down, as I have said already, by the authority of the Church, some of whose dignitaries gave an example of humility by placing their tombs at some distance from the holiest portion of the sanctuary. One of these was the aforesaid Sabinus in the fifth century, whose epitaph in verse expresses this very idea, suggesting that the best way to get into touch with the martyrs is to imitate their virtues. It is a noble epitaph, and runs as follows:

169

SEPVLCRVM · SABINI · ARCHIDIACONI

Altaris primus per tempora multa minister
    Elegi Sancti Janitor esse loci.
Nam terram repetens quae nostra probatur origo,
    Hic tumulor muta membra Sabinus humo.
Nil juvat imo gravat tumulis haerere piorum
    Sanctorum meritis optima vita prope est
Corpore non opus est anima tendamus ad illos
    Quae bene salva potest corporis esse salus.
Ast ego qui voce psalmos modulatus et arte
    Diversis cecini verba sacrata sonis
Corporis hic posui sedes in limine primo
    Surgendi tempus certus adesse cito
Jam tonat angelico resonans tuba caelitus ore
    Et vocat ut scandant castra superna pios.
At tu Laurenti martyr levita, Sabinum
    Levitam angelicis nunc quoque junge choris.

S. Lorenzo fuori le Mura.

§ 4

On the titles " Sanctus " and " Martyr " in Ancient Christian Inscriptions

The title *sanctus* on ancient Christian inscriptions without any context is no mark of "veneration," in our modern sense. Indeed the epithet is not even exclusively Christian, being used by the pagans also: there are numerous passages in ancient writers and many inscriptions in which words like *conjugi sanctae* or even *sanctissimae* occur, which prove this incontestably.

The title denotes veneration when combined with *martyr*. To the latter word, however, the epithet *beatissimus* was often also joined. It must nevertheless be observed that not even *beatus* or *beatissimus*, in the absence of further addition, proves that the deceased was the object of veneration, for it is found in ancient inscriptions applied to ordinary brethren.

Very few of the primitive inscriptions exhibiting the glorious title of martyr date from the actual burial of the martyred saint.[1] There may have been more, but up to the present we have only two that we can quote as discovered in the Roman catacombs: one is the inscription of Pope Cornelius in the cemetery of Callisto (A.D. 253), and that of

---

[1] In a very early inscription painted in red in the cemetery of Priscilla it has been thought that the letter M inserted in the middle of the name was equivalent to the title of *martyr* ; but that is not proved with any certainty.

the martyr Hyacinthus (about A.D. 258) in the cemetery of S. Hermes.

170

```
CORNELIVS · MARTYR
        EP
```

Cemetery of Callisto.   (Plate IX. 3.)

171

```
DP · III · IDVS · SEPTEBR
        YACINTHVS
         MARTYR
```

Cemetery of S. Hermes on the old Via Salaria ; now in the Church of the Propaganda.

It has been hitherto believed that in the early inscription of Pope Fabianus which stands in the Papal crypt of the cemetery of Callisto the word *martyr*, expressed by a combination of Greek letters, was a later addition, though not much later, having been made when his martyrdom was officially recognised.   Recently, however, it has been necessary to modify this view, owing to the discovery of the early inscription of Pope Pontianus, on which may be seen the same monogram for *martyr* as on the inscription of Fabianus; and in the case of Pontianus, as we shall show later, there can be no idea of a later recognition.   We must therefore conclude that in both these cases the title of *martyr* was added during the Time of Peace.   We shall return to these points in a later chapter.

The following early texts also mention the burial of martyrs:

172

> ABVNDIO · PRB
> MARTYRI · SANCT ·
> DEP · VII · IDVS · DEC

Cemetery of Rignano.   Lateran Museum.

This is the inscription of Abundius, priest and martyr, who was buried in the cemetery near Rignano.

173

> SIMPLICIVS · MARTYR
> SERVILIANVS · MARTYR

From the Via Latina ; then in S. Angelo in Borgo ; now lost.
(Bosio, *Roma sotterranea*, iii. p. 27.)

174

> BEATI MART
> VRES
> FELIX ET
> FORTVNA
> TVS

These two martyrs, natives of Vicenza, are supposed to have died in the persecution of Diocletian.

(De Rossi, *Roma sotterranea*, iii. p. 436.)

The inscription of one *Ulvasius martyr* from the cemetery of Domitilla, reported by Bosio, is of doubtful authenticity.

Other inscriptions of martyrs again belong to the Time of Peace.

We will not here cite the inscriptions set up to the martyrs by Pope Damasus, as they will be separately dealt with ; but we may mention the following from Milan ; it has lost its introduction, in which were recorded the names of the martyrs near whom Diogenes and Valeria were buried.

175

. . . . - . . . .

ET · A · DOMINO · CORONATI · SVNT · BAEATI
CONFESSORES · COMITES · MARTYRORVM
AVRELIVS · DIOGENES · CONFESSOR · ET
VALERIA · FELICISSIMA · BIBI · IN · DEO · FECERVNT
SI · QVIS · POST · OBITVM · NOSTRVM · ALIQVEM
CORPVS · INTVLSERINT · NON · ET · FVGIANT
IRA · DEI · ET · DOMINI · NOSTRI

(Seletti, *Inscrizioni cristiane di Milano*, 1897, No. 37, pp. 34-35.)

Similarly the following inscription belongs to the Time of Peace : it contains a record of the most famous African martyrs, the companions of S. Perpetua, and was set up over their relics.

176

+ *Hic* SVNT · MARTY*res*
+ SATVRVS · SATVR*ninus*
+ REBOCATVS · SECV*ndulus*
+ FELICIT PER*pe*T · PAS . . . . .
+ MAIVLVS . . . . .

Found at Carthage by F. Delattre during the excavations of 1907. (See *Nuovo Bull. di arch. crist.*, 1907, p. 250.)

177

TEMPORIBVS · SANCTI
INNOCENTI · EPISCOPI
PROCLINVS · ET · VRSVS · PRAESBB
TITVLI · BYZANTI
SANCTO · MARTYRI
SEBASTIANO · EX · VOTO · FECERVNT

S. Sebastian.   Lateran Museum.

This is a votive inscription cut on a pierced marble screen erected to protect the original tomb of the martyr S. Sebastian. It is of the time of Pope Innocent I. (402-417). It may be noted that this epithet *sanctus* applied to the then living Pontiff does not suggest any formal veneration; on the other hand, in the case of the martyr Sebastian it is so intended.

178

*mar*TYRE AGNETI POTITVS SERBVS
DEI ORNAVIT

Museum of the Capitol.   (New Hall of Christian Monuments.)

This is a fragment of the architrave of the tabernacle of the altar of the ancient basilica of S. Agnese on the Via Nomentana.

179

.... ET · ALEXANDRO · DELICATVS · VOTO *posu*IT
DEDICANTE · AEPISCOP · VRS(*o*)

Cemetery Church of S. Alexander. At the seventh
mile-stone on the Via Nomentana.

A votive inscription still to be seen on the marble
screen standing near the tomb of the martyr S.
Alexander (fifth century).

180

IVNIA · SABINA
C · F · EIVS
FECERVNT

181

SANCTORVM
ORNAVIT

These two last are cut on blocks which formed
the foundation of a small tabernacle on the altar-
tomb of the martyr above mentioned.

The following inscription is cut over a small
foundation-stone like the preceding, and stood on

the altar-tomb of the martyrs Felix and Philippus
in the basilica of the cemetery of Priscilla :

182

> MARTIRVM
> FILICIS · FILIPPI
> · · · · · · · · · · ·

Cemetery of Priscilla ; now in the Louvre.

183

> SANCTIS · MARTVRIBVS
> PAPRO · ET · MAVROLEONI
> DOMNIS · VOTVM · REDD · ☧
> CAMASIVS · QVI · ET · ASCLEPIVS · ET · VICTORIN
> NAT · H̄ · DIE · IIIX · KAL · OCTOBR
> PVERI · QVI · VOT · H̄ · VITALIS · MARANVS
> ABVNDANTIVS · TELESFOR

Lateran Museum.

A votive plaque in bronze, dedicated by an
artist, Camasius, also called Asclepius, and his
pupils, in honour of the martyrs Papias and Maurus.
"Domnis (*Sanctis*) Papro et Mauroleoni (*Papiae
et Mauro*) votum reddit," etc.

184

> PETRVS ET PANCARA BOTVM PO
> SVENT MARTYRE FELICITATI

(Boldetti, *Osservazioni*, p. 431.)

Records a vow made to the martyr Felicitas.

185

SANCTO
MARTYRI
MAXIMO

Catacombs of S. Sebastian.

A dedicatory inscription which must have belonged to some sacred edifice on the Via Appia.

186

⳩

MARTVRES · SIMPLICIVS · ET · FAVSTINVS
QVI · PASSI · SVNT · IN · FLVMEN · TIBERE · ET · POSI
TI · SVNT · IN · CIMITERIVM · GENEROSES · SVPER
FILIPPI

Cemetery of Generosa on the Via Portuensis ; now in the close of S. Maria Maggiore.

This inscription is important as stating that the martyrs Simplicius and Faustinus were thrown into the Tiber, and afterwards buried in the cemetery of Generosa in the plot belonging to Philippus. The inscription, however, is of later date than the others.

Note.—It should be noted that some confusion has at times arisen with respect to some inscriptions in which the title *martyr* seems to appear, when it is in fact only a proper name.

Thus, for instance, there is an inscription in the cemetery of Domitilla in which DEP·MARTYRES occurs; which is only the Greek genitive of the proper name *Martyre*, corresponding to *Martyria*.

Similar to this was the curious mistake made as to the meaning of the following inscription discovered some years ago in the cemetery of S. Agnese on the Via Nomentana, which was supposed to belong to a conjectured martyr Alfenia Narcissa:

187

ALFENIE · NARC*issae*
FILIE · CARISSI*mae*
SIG · MARTYRI

The words *signo Martyri* correspond to such phrases as *signo Musa* or *signo Leucadi*, etc.; and only mean that *Alfenia Narcissa* had the surname *Martyr*.

Finally, it should be observed that the words *martyr* and *sanguis* said to have been found on so-called phials of blood, or on the mortar by which these phials were attached to the tombs of the catacombs, are all modern forgeries; and it should be further noted in this connexion that these phials must not be taken as a general rule to be indications of martyrdom, inasmuch as they did not usually contain blood, but only the liquid perfumes which were so largely used in the rites of Christian burial.

CHAPTER V

HAVING discussed inscriptions illustrating doctrine and commemorating martyrs, we may properly go on to consider those which throw light on the constitution of the early Christian community, in connexion, first with the Church as a whole, next with its officers, and lastly with the various classes and professions of its members.

For those who seek an accurate knowledge of the internal organisation of the primitive congregation of the Faithful the inscriptions which make special reference to these matters are of the highest possible value: hierarchically this community had its own classification, while socially it was fairly representative of all ranks from the highest to the lowest, though this vast and complex system was marvellously fused into one by the spirit of equality and of Gospel charity. The language used in Christian inscriptions, especially of the funerary class, and the descriptions of individuals which they contain, give a lively picture of the community of the Faithful.

The *corpus christianorum*, or collective body of the faithful members of individual churches in the Roman world, was known by the descriptive name of *ecclesia fratrum*, because the Faithful were in the habit of applying to one another the affectionate title of Brother; this may be proved from the following among other inscriptions:

188

AREAM AT SEPVLCRA CVLTOR VERBI CONTVLIT
ET CELLAM STRVXIT SVIS CVNCTIS SVMPTIBVS
ECCLESIAE SANCTAE HANC RELIQVIT MEMORIAM
SALVETE FRATRES PVRO CORDE ET SIMPLICI
EVELPIVS VOS SATOS SANCTO SPIRITV[1]
ECCLESIA FRATRVM HVNC RESTITVIT TITVLVM
M · A · I · SEVERIANI · C · V
EX · ING · ASTERII

Africa—Caesarea in Mauritania.

(De Rossi, *Bull. di arch. crist.*, 1854, pp. 28-29.)

One Euelpius, who describes himself as *cultor verbi*, endowed the *ecclesia sancta* of Caesarea, which in the last line but one he calls *ecclesia fratrum* simply, with a burial plot and a chapel at his own expense. After addressing a warm greeting to the Brethren, whom he describes as *sati sancto spiritu*, he goes on to mention on the marble the *restitutio tituli* effected by *ecclesia fratrum*, probably in consequence of the destruction of an earlier tablet during some persecution.

§ I

Inscriptions of Popes and Bishops

The highest position in the Hierarchy from Apostolic times was that of Bishop of Rome, as it was to the Church of Rome that all other Churches were bound to conform; so says S. Irenaeus in the

[1] *Vos salutat satos sancto spiritu.*

second century, "propter potentiorem principali-
tatem."[1] The Roman Church took precedence of
all others, as Ignatius of Antioch declares in the
same century.[2] The first Popes up to and including S. Victor were interred around the tomb of
the Prince of the Apostles in the Vatican, but we
know nothing of their sepulchral inscriptions. On
the other hand, we have some belonging to the
group of Popes buried on the Via Appia in the
third century, beginning with Pope Zephyrinus,
buried in the cemetery of Callisto. The characteristic of these is their great simplicity, and their use
of the Greek language, which was the official
language of the Church in the first centuries;
after the name they give the formal title, ἐπίσκοπος.
We will give them in chronological order, beginning
with the one assigned by De Rossi to Pope Urbanus,
although it cannot be said that the identification is
made out with absolute certainty.

189

ΟΥΡΒΑΝΟϹ · Επισκοπος?

"Urbanus, bishop."

The inscription is sketched on the lid of a
sarcophagus in the crypt of the Popes. The Pope
Urbanus, to whom it may apply, ruled the Church
from 224 to 231 in the reign of Alexander Severus,
and died in a period of peace.

[1] *Contra haereses*, iii. 3.
[2] "Ecclesia . . . digna quae beata praedicetur digna laude
digna quae voti compos fiat, digne casta *et universo caritatis
coetui praesidens.*" (Epist. ad Romanos, i.)

The following belong without a doubt to Popes of the third century :

190

ΠΟΝΤΙΑΝΟϹ · ΕΠΙϹΚ · M̀Ρ

"Pontianus, bishop, martyr."   (Plate X. 1.)

This inscription was very recently found (January 1909) in an old well in the crypt of S. Caecilia, into which marble tablets and fragments of inscriptions had been thrown in confusion.   Pope Pontianus was exiled to Sardinia in the persecution of Maximinus, and for that reason resigned his high office, "discinctus est."   His body was brought home to Rome later, probably in the reign of the two Philips, 231-236.   The abbreviation for the title of *martyr* was added here in times of peace, and can have nothing to do with the *vindicatio martyris* (the formal claim to the honour) ; for the death of Pontianus had occurred some three years before the removal of his body to Rome, and therefore his martyrdom must by that time have received official recognition.

The next were disinterred in the cemetery of Callisto in the excavations which were carried out there in 1852 and onwards.

191

ΑΝΤΕΡΩϹ · ΕΠ*ισκοπος* . . .

"Anteros, bishop, . . ."   (Plate IX. 1.)

Anteros was elected after the abdication of Pontianus, and was martyred after a very short pontificate in January 236.

192

> ΦΑΒΙΑΝΟϹ · ΕΠΙ · ΜῈΡ

"Fabianus, bishop, martyr."   (Plate IX. 2.)

Fabianus was Pope from 236 to 250, and was martyred in January 250. His death was announced by an encyclical addressed by the Church of Rome to all other congregations of the faithful, " de glorioso ejus exitu." The symbol MP in this inscription, as in that of Pontianus, is evidently by a later hand; in all probability the title of *martyr* was added in times of peace on these two epitaphs, and perhaps on others which have not been recovered. The purpose of so doing was to distinguish the martyr - Popes from those not martyred.

193

> CORNELIVS · MARTYR
> EP ·

"Cornelius, bishop, martyr."   (Plate IX. 3.)

Pope Cornelius was martyred in 253 at Centumcellae (Civita Vecchia), and was laid in a gallery of the crypt of Lucina near the cemetery of Callisto, which gallery was widened later. The inscription is written in Latin, thus differing from those of previous Popes; it is possible that the Latin language was used owing to the connexion between the Pontiff and the world-renowned Roman gens Cornelia. If the title of *martyr* is an addition here also, as has been lately suggested, the addition differs from those in the preceding cases in the fact of having been made contemporaneously with the inscriptions, possibly to correct an omission made in the first cutting.

194

ΛΟΥΚΙϹ ἐπίσκοπος . . .

" Lucius, bishop . . ."

Pope Lucius suffered under Valerian about 255. S. Cyprian calls him *beatum martyrem.*

195

ΕΥΤΥΧΙΑΝΟϹ · ΕΠΙϹ . . .

"Eutychianus, bishop . . ."   (Plate IX. 4.)

Pope Eutychianus (273-283) was not really martyred, although he is venerated as a martyr. He was the last Pontiff buried in the crypt of the Popes.

196

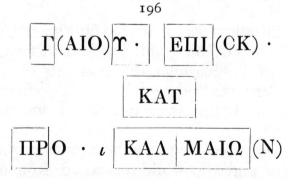

" Burial of Caius, bishop, on April 22nd."

Pope Caius was buried on the other side of the cemetery of Callisto in the region now called that of S. Eusebius. He ruled the Church from 283 to 296, and died on April 22nd. Pope Marcellinus († 304) is recorded in another inscription, which will be given in due course.

The sepulchral inscriptions of ordinary bishops discovered in the Roman catacombs have been even fewer in number.[1] A record of a bishop of Albano has been found in a long inscription in the cemetery of Domitilla.[2]

From the Agro Verano[3] has been recovered the following metrical inscription of a bishop named Leo:[4]

197

```
OMNIA QVAEQVE VIDES PROPRIO QVAESITA LA-
BORE | CVM MIHI GENTILIS IAMDVDVM VITA MA-
NERET | INSTITVI CENSVM CVPIENS COGNOSCERE
MVNDI | IVDICIO POST MVLTA DEI MELIORA SE-
QVVTVS | CONTEMPTIS OPIBVS MALVI COGNO-
SCERE CHRISTVM | HAEC MIHI CVRA FVIT NVDOS
VESTIRE PETENTES | FVNDERE PAVPERIBVS QVID-
QVID CONCESSERAT ANNVS | PSALLERE ET IN PO-
PVLIS VOLVI MODVLANTE PROPHETA | SIC MERVI
PLEBEM CHRISTI RETINERE SACERDOS | HVNC MIHI
COMPOSVIT TVMVLVM LAVRENTIA CONIVX | MORI-
BVS APTA MEIS SEMPER VENERANDA FIDELIS |
INVIDIA INFELIX TANDEM COMPRESSA QVIESCET |
OCTOGINTA LEO TRASCENDIT EPISCOPVS ANNOS |
DEP DIE PRID IDVS MARTIAS
```

[1] Cp. De Rossi, *Bull. di arch. crist.*, 1864, pp. 49 *et seq.*

[2] An *episcopus Albanensis* is mentioned among many other names.

[3] [The Agro Verano, which is frequently mentioned in the course of this manual, was a plot of land behind S. Lorenzo fuori le Mura, and contained a catacomb, in which S. Lawrence is reputed to have been buried; large portions of this were destroyed when S. Lorenzo was built, and a modern cemetery has been laid out there. Many remains of the old catacomb have been brought to light by the grave-diggers of the present day.—TR.]

[4] De Rossi, *l.c.* pp. 54-56.

This inscription has now acquired very great historical importance from the fact that in all probability this bishop Leo was the father of Pope Damasus; if so, he must, of course, have separated from his wife on taking holy orders.[1]

198

+

HIC · REQVIESCIT · IN · PACE · ADEODATVS · EPISC
QVI · VIXIT · ANN | PL · M · LXVII · ET · SED · AN · II · ET
M · VIIII · DEP · SVB · D · PRID · KAL · DECEM·

Cemetery basilica of S. Alexander on the Via Nomentana.

This and the following inscription belong to the bishop of some see in the Campagna of Rome.

199

PETRVS EPISCOPVS IN PACE XIII KL MAIAS

Cemetery of S. Alexander.

(De Rossi, *Bull. di arch. crist.*, 1864, p. 51.)

200

..... EBVS · PARITER · ET · NOMIN*e*
..... M · TERRAMQVE · SIMVL · SOCIOSQVE *reliquit*
*sancte sac*ERDOTII · TENVIT · QVI · SEDE · CORONAM
..... INIS · ET · SEPTEM · REVOLVENTIBVS · *Annis*
.....*plebi* CVNCTA · GEMET · SVISMET · CARV
..... SIS · SEXTI · ITERVM · P · C · SYMMACHI · V · C
INDICTIONE

From Vienne in France.

(Le Blant, *Inscriptions chrét. de la Gaule*, 481 A.)

The title *sacerdos*, as appears from this inscription

[1] Cf. Marucchi, *Nuovo Bull. di arch. crist.*, 1903, Nos. 1-3.

and from that on Bishop Leo, No. 197, indicates episcopal rank.   Indeed, in the inscription on S. Concordius, bishop of Arles, we read :

201

. . . .
LECTVS · CAELESTI · LEGE · SACERDOS

(Le Blant, *Inscr. de la Gaule*, No. 590.)

§ 2

Inscriptions mentioning priests by name are rather more numerous : in some cases the title is simply added to the name of the deceased ; others (and these are of more value to us) give the name of the urban " title " or parish to which the priest was attached.   From the latter we can learn the names of these very early " titles " of the Church of Rome ; and with them, as the most remarkable, we will begin the list.

202

LOC · ADEODATI · PRESB · TIT · PRISCAE

From the Via Ostiensis.

The " title " of Prisca still exists under the same name on the Aventine, as the Church of S. Prisca.

203

> LOCVS PRESBYTERI BASILI TITVLI SABINE

Cemetery of S. Paolo.   (Plate XI. 2.)

The *titulus Sabinae* is the church of the same name on the Aventine.

204

> .... S TITVLI CLEMENTIS VI IDVS APR
> *ra*PVIT RECIA CAELI BLANDA
> .... VE BENIGNA SEMOTA PRVDENS
> .... VIGNAMQVE TVMVLO
> .... A QVIESCIT ....
> *Domino* PRAESTANTE RESVRGET

Cemetery of Cyriaca on the Via Tiburtina.

The *titulus Clementis* is the very early church of S. Clemente on the road to the Lateran.

205

> HIC · REQVIESCIT · IN · PACE · ARGVRIVS · QVI · VIX*it* ...
> DEPS · SVB · D · III · NON · MAIS · CONS · PROVINI ...
> *quem locum* | *compa*RAVIT · FILIA · EIVS · FAVSTA
> · A · PRB · TIT · PRAX*edis*

Cemetery of S. Hyppolytus on the Via Tiburtina (A.D. 395).

The *titulus Praxedis* corresponds to the existing church of S. Prassede on the Esquiline.

206

+ HIC REQVIESCIT M . . . . . . *tituli Sanctorum*
　IOHANNIS ET PAVLI . . . .
　SEMPER CVM OMNES . . . .
　DEPOSITVS IN PACE . . . .
　DOMNO NOSTRO IVSTINO P P　*ang*
　ET IN PACE AETERNAM ET ORET . . . .

　(dove)

SNOƆ · ꓕЯⱯW · ꓶⱯꓘ · IΛ · ꓷ · dǝ *ɐɯıssıɹɐɔ ɹoxu*
IHIW · ꓕIΛꟻ · IꓶX · W · ꓒ · NⱯ · XIΛ · · · · · · · *ɐıuɐ*
OI · WꓱꓶIꞋ ꓒ · INIꓭOꓤꓒ · ꓕꓱ · INIꞋ *ıǝɔɹɐW* *suoɔ*
ꓒ · NI · ꓷ · IX · W · ꓒ · NⱯ · XIΛ · Ò · Ɔ · · · ·

Basilica of S. Stefano on the Via Latina.
(De Rossi, *Inscript. christ.* i. p. 514, No. 1123.)

This stone was used for two tombs successively. The older inscription (which is upside down) bears the names of the consuls of the year 341 ; the later, which bore the name of a priest of the " title " of SS. Giovanni and Paolo (formerly called *titulus Byzantis*), has a consular date which lies somewhere between A.D. 566 and 578.

Other inscriptions of priests with *tituli* or parishes have been recovered in the excavations of the cemetery of Commodilla on the Via Ostiensis ; they show the connexion between that cemetery and the nearest city parish, viz. S. Sabina on the Aventine.   See p. 200.

207

> . . . . . (?) *Nab*IRA QVAE VIXIT
> . . . . . X DEPOSITA IN PA*ce*
> . . . . . *p c* MABORTI VC̄ C̄ŌNS
> . . . . . *a p*ETRO PRIMIC TIT SC̄AE
> *Sabinae* (?) *su*B PR̄B PAVLO

Cemetery of Commodilla.

(Marucchi, *Nuovo Bull. di arch. crist.*, 1904, p. 92, No. 27, and pp. 140-141 ; 1905, p. 39.)

208

> ✝ LOCVS
> TITVLI S(*abinae*)
> CV . . . . .

Ditto.   (Marucchi, *op. cit.*, 1904, No. 27 A.)

209

> CAIANVS EMIT CVM VIVIT
> SIBI ET VXORI SVAE AB ADEO
> DATO FOSSORE SVB PRESEN
> TI SANCTI MAXIMI PRESBITERI
> . . . . P ·

Ditto.   (Marucchi, *op. cit.*, 1905, p. 53, No. 15.)

The priest Maximus had possibly some special jurisdiction over the cemetery of Commodilla.

210

> LOCVS
> ROMVLI
> PRESBYTERI
> TITVLI PVD
> *en*TIANAE

Cemetery of S. Hippolytus on the Via Tiburtina.

This gives the name of a priest of the church of S. Pudentiana, called *ecclesia pudentiana* on the great mosaic of the apse, which dates from Pope Syricius.

To the same parish belongs a large inscription, now in the Lateran Museum, on which the names of the priests Ilicius and Leopardus appear.

211

> SALVO · SIRICIO · EPISC · ECLESIAE · SANCTAE
> ET · ILICIO · LEOPARDO · ET · MAXIMO · PRESBB

(De Rossi, *Bull. di arch. crist.*, 1867, p. 52.)   (Plate XI. 1.)

This also dates from Pope Syricius.

212

> . . . . . *pre*SB · TITVL · LVCI*nae*
> . . . . . CONIVX · MIHI
> *sine ulla c*VLPA · CESQ*uet in pace*

Cemetery of S. Valentinus on the Via Flaminia.

The *titulus Lucinae* of which this cemetery was a dependency is the existing church of S. Lorenzo in Lucina.

213

> *hi*C · RE*Quiescit* . . . . *presbyter* (?)
> *t*ITVLI · EV*sebi*
> *in pa*CE · DEP . . . . . .

Cemetery of SS. Peter and Marcellinus.

The *titulus Eusebii* is the existing church of S. Eusebio.

214

> *hic p*OSITVS · EST · VICTOR · PRAESB · TITVLI
> NICOMEDIS |
> XII · KAL · DECEMB

From the ambo of the basilica of S. Lorenzo in the
Agro Verano.

The *titulus Nicomedis* is entirely unknown.

215

> ✝ HIC · QVIESCIT · ROMANVS
> PRESBITER · QVI · SIDIT
> PRESBITERIO · ANNVS · XXVI
> MENSIS · X · DEP
> X · KAL . . . . .
> (*consulatu*) SEBERINI · VC · CO*ns*

Cemetery of SS. Peter and Marcellinus on the Via Labicana
(A.D. 461 or 482).

There exists a practically identical replica of this
inscription, which must have been returned to the
artist's hands; it is now in the Lateran Museum.

216

> TIMOTEVS
> PRESBYTER

Cemetery of S. Hippolytus on the Via Tiburtina.

This tablet is in the best Damasian lettering, of the shape specially adopted by Pope Damasus in historical inscriptions to the honour of martyrs. It was placed in the crypt of the martyr S. Hippolytus, and remains there still.

217

> PRESBYTER · HIC · SITVS · EST · CELERINVS · NO-
> MINE · DIC*tus* | CORPOREOS · RVMPENS · NEXVS
> QVI · GAVDET · IN · ASTRIS | DEP · VIII · KAL · IVN
> FL · SYAGRIO · ET · EVCERIO

Cemetery of S. Agnese on the Via Nomentana.

At present kept on the grand staircase of the basilica. The epitaph is in verse, and its consular date makes it A.D. 381.

218

> HIC REQVIES
> CIT LEO PRES
> BYTER.....

Cemetery of S. Paolo.

219

> ΔΙΟΝΥϹΙΟΥ
>
> ΙΑΤΡΟΥ
>
> ΠΡΕϹΒΥΤΕΡΟΥ

Cemetery of Callisto. (Plate XII. 2.)

On a priest who also practised the art of healing.

220

> LOCVS VALENTINI PRAESB ·

Basilica of S. Agnese.   (Plate XI. 3.)

§ 3

Inscriptions of Deacons and Sub-Deacons

Diaconus is the title given to the holders of the third grade in the Hierarchy, who assisted the priests and the bishops in their sacred functions.

The deacons of the Roman Church were seven in number; their duties were the custody of the tombs of the martyrs, the chanting of the services, the superintendence of the ecclesiastical districts, and the administration of the property of the Church.   The archdeacon was the chief of them; he acted as personal assistant to the Pope, especially in the administration of the Common *Arca* (Treasury) of the Brethren.   As a general rule the archdeacon succeeded to the honours of the Pontificate.

The best-known evidence in this connexion is the inscription of a deacon named Severus which was found by De Rossi in the cemetery of Callisto. It belonged perhaps to an archdeacon under Pope Marcellinus.

221

CVBICVLVM · DVPLEX · CVM · ARCISOLIS · ET · LVMINARE | IVSSV · PP · SVI · MARCELLINI · DIA- CONVS · ISTE | SEVERVS · FECIT · MANSIONEM · IN · PACE · QVIETAM | SIBI · SVISQVE · MEMOR · QVO · MEMBRA · DVLCIA · SOMNO | PER · LON- GVM · TEMPVS · FACTORI · ET · IVDICI · SERVET | SEVERA · DVLCIS · PARENTIBVS · ET · FAMVLI- SQVE | REDDIDIT · VIII · FEBRARIAS · VIRGO · KA- LENDAS | QVAM · DŌMS · NASCI · MIRA · SAPIEN- TIA · ET · ARTE | IVSSERAT · IN · CARNEM · QVOD · CORPVS · PACE · QVIETVM | HIC · EST · SEPVL- TVM · DONEC · RESVRGAT · AB · IPSO | QVIQVE · ANIMAM · RAPVIT · SPIRITV · SANCTO · SVO | CASTAM · PVDICAM · ET · INVIOLABILE · SEMPER | QVAMQVE · ITERVM · DŌMS · SPIRITALI · GLORIA · REDDET | QVAE · VIXIT · ANNOS · VIIII · ET · XI · MENSES | XV · QVOQVE · DIES · SIC · EST · TRAN- SLATA · DE · SAECLO

This inscription states that Severus the deacon, by the authority of Pope Marcellinus (therefore previous to A.D. 304), made a sepulchral chamber for himself and his sister Severa, to whose virtues he pays a graceful tribute. The inscription has some doctrinal value, as pointing very clearly to a belief in the Resurrection, "hic est sepultum donec resurgat ab ipso," and furthermore as alluding to the gifts of the Spirit, "quique animam rapuit spiritu sancto suo."

The inscription is also noticeable as naming the arcosolia and the sky-lights (*luminare*) which Severus the deacon made in his chamber.

The following gives clear testimony to the dependence of deacons upon the bishops whom they assisted in their sacred ministry:

222

DIACONI · EPI*scopi* . . . .

Cemetery of S. Sebastian.

Now kept in the small local museum.

223

VERECVNDAE · PVDICAE
TOTIVSQVE · INTEGRITATIS · FEMINAE
AVRELIAE · GEMINIAE · CONIVGI
DVLCISSIMAE · FELIX · DIAK

From Porto ; now in Lateran Museum.

On one Aurelia Gemina, wife of a deacon named Felix.

224

Quisque vides tumulum vitam si quaeris operti
Ter morior denos et post bis quattuor annos
Servatum Christo reddens de corpore munus
Cujus ego in sacris famulus vel in ordine lector
Officio levita fui Florentius ore
Qui pater in terris item mihi sancte SACERDos
Contigit et natum tenuit IAM SORTE SECVNDA
HOC SVPERAnte meo discediT SPIRITVS ORAE
ISTE SENi casus gravis est miHI MORTE BEATVS
QVOD PATRIS hospitio bene nunc mea membra quiescunt
DEP · DIE · PR . . . . . .

Agro Verano.   Lateran Museum.[1]

This is a Damasian inscription commemorating one Florentius who was *levita* or deacon.   According to my own investigations as to the family of Pope Damasus, it is highly probable that this Florentius, the son of Bishop Leo (who was also buried in the Agro Verano), was a brother of Damasus.   But I shall have occasion to deal with this matter in the chapter on Damasian inscriptions, in which I shall also go into the history of the family of Damasus, and describe my recent special investigation of this important question.

The mention of sub-deacons or minor deacons is of a later date : it appears that in the Roman Church they also were seven in number, and constituted in early time an actual Minor Order.

[1] The restorations (in italics) are taken from an early transcript.

225

LOCVS · INPORTVNI · SVBDIAC · REG · QVARTAE

Cemetery of S. Agnese.

226

HIC · REQVIESCIT · APPIANVS · SVBDIACONVS
QVI · VIXIT · ANNV | XXXIII · DIES · XXVIIII · D · III
IDVS · APRI · CON · POSTVMIANI · V · C

Cemetery of S. Alexander on the Via Nomentana (A.D. 448).

(De Rossi, *Inscript. christ.* i. p. 324, No. 742.)

227

LOCVS · MARCELLI · SVBD · REG · SEXTE
CQNCESSVM · SIBI · ET · POS |
TERIS · EIVS · A · BEATISSIMO · PAPA
IOANNE | QVI · VIXIT · ANN ·
P · M · LXVIII · DEP · P · C · BASILI
V · C · ANN · XXII | IND · XI ·
VNDECIMV · KAL ·
IANVARIAS

In the crypt of the Vatican.

An inscription of the year 563, in the pontificate of John III.

§ 4

Inscriptions of Inferior Church Officers

The inscriptions that follow all refer to inferior grades among the clergy.

228

GELASIVS EXORCISTA IN PACE
DEP V IDVS M . . . . *ann* XXXXV
ΩΔE EI . . . . . VS DEO GRATIAS

Cemetery of Domitilla on the Via Ardeatina.

The duty of exorcists was to exorcise those possessed by evil spirits, so as to set them free from the power of the devil.

This inscription is of value for the expression *Deo gratias*, which the orthodox of the fourth century used in place of the *Deo laudes* of the Donatists.

229

IN PACE ABVNDANTIVS ACOL
REG QVART ET T̄ VESTINE QVI VIXIT ANN XXV
DEP IN P D NAT S̄C̄I MARCI MENSE OCT ĪN̄D XII

Recovered in the cemetery of S. Agnese.

Acolytes in the Roman Church had the duty of serving at religious functions; and it was their business to carry the Eucharist to those who had been absent from Mass. A celebrated name among the acolytes was that of S. Tarsicius, the youthful martyr in the cause of the Eucharist, who died, according to tradition, in the persecution of Valerian.

The "title" of Vestina corresponds to the modern church of S. Vitale.

The duty of *lectores* or readers was to read the Holy Scriptures publicly in the churches. Even boys were often admitted to this office. Some inscriptions of *lectores* give the name of the parish church in which these officers acted.

230

OLYMPI · LECTORIS · DE · EVSEBI
LOCVS · EST

Cemetery of SS. Peter and Marcellinus.

The word *dominico* or *titulo* must be understood before *Eusebii*.

231

..... LECTOR · DE · SAVI(*na*)
..... IO · QVI · VIXIT
..... NIS · XVI

Cemetery known as that of Balbina on the Via Appia, near the cemetery of Callisto.

A "graffito" inscription on plaster. It records *titulus Sabinae*—the modern church of S. Sabina.

232

```
LOCVS · ADEODATI
LECTORIS · DE · BELA
BRV
DEP · SYRICA · XVII · KAL · AVG
QVAE . VIXIT · ANNOS
P · M · XII . CONS
SEBERINI          (A.D. 460 or 461)
```

Cemetery of Callisto.   Lateran Museum.   (Plate XIII. 1.)

This *lector* belonged to the parochial church of the *Velabrum*, possibly the modern S. Giorgio.

233

☧
(crown)

```
DILECTISSIMO · MARITO · ANIME · DVLCISSIME · ALEXIO
LECTORI | DE · FVLLONICES · QVI · VIXIT · MECVM
ANN · XVI · IVNCTVS · MIHI · ANN · XVI | VIRGO
AD · VIRGINE · CVIVS · NVMQVAM · AMARITVDINEM
HABVI | CESQVE · IN · PACE · CVM · SANCTIS · CVM
QVOS · MERERIS
          DEP · VIII · X · KAL · IANV
```

So-called cemetery of Balbina.

This *titulus Fullonices* is absolutely unknown; it may have taken the name from a neighbouring *fullonica* or laundry.

There is one solitary inscription of one VR-SATVS VSTIARIVS, a gate-porter. (Gruter, 1056, 6.)

234

---

hic POSITVS EST PETRVS VIII IDVS
*mar*TIAS QVI VIXIT ANNIS XVIIII
.... DEP IN PACE PHILIPPO ET SALIA
   COSS DVO FRATRES ....
.... ANTIVS LECTOR DE PALLACINE QVI VIXIT
.... DEP XII KAL SEPT

Cemetery of Priscilla on the Via Salaria (A.D. 348).

(De Rossi, *Inscrip. christ.* i. No. 97.)

The parochial church of *Pallacine* is the modern church of S. Marco.

But the earliest inscription of a *lector* is the following, the beautiful lettering of which is not later than the beginning of the third century:

235

FAVOR · FAVOR (anchor) LECTOR

Cemetery of S. Agnese.

The lowest offices are those of *notarius* and *exceptor*.

236

..... M · CALOPODIVS · NOTAR
..... ANN · XLVIII · DEPOS

Cloister of the basilica of S. Paolo.

This inscription gives the name of an ecclesiastical *notarius*, Calopodius, which may be noted for its rarity.

237

> . . . . . *vixi*T · ANNIS · XVIII
> . . . . . NOTARIO
> . . . . . *cu*N · MARTVRIBVS

Cemetery of Priscilla.

The *exceptores* were the shorthand writers of the chancery of the Roman Church. This office was held, it may be remarked, by the father of Damasus, as appears from the well-known inscription placed by that Pontiff in the workrooms of the Ecclesiastical Record Office situated near the theatre of Pompey : *Hinc pater exceptor, lector, levita, sacerdos*, etc. (See the chapter on Damasian inscriptions.)

§ 5

Inscriptions bearing on the various Classes of Christian Society

(*a*) VIRGINS

The whole community of the Faithful was included in the description *plebs Dei* ; within that, the members were divided into classes according to the positions of the individuals in relation to the Church.

One of the most highly esteemed classes within the bosom of the primitive Church was that of the virgins who had consecrated their lives to God, and who were therefore called *virgines Dei*, and (in later days) *sanctimoniales*; they received special mention in the public prayers, and had special seats reserved for them at divine service. We find records of them in many inscriptions.

238

QVIESCIT · IN *pace* PRAETEXTATA
VIRGO · SACRA . DEP*osi*TA · D · VII
ID · AVG · CONS · RV*sti*CI · ET · OLYBRI

From the Agro Verano.   Museum of the Capitol (A.D. 464).

Remark the name *Praetextata*, which connects this virgin with the Christian branch of the illustrious family of the Praetextati.

239

☧

NICELLA VIRGO DEI QVE VI
XIT ANNOS PM XXXV DE
POSITA XV KAL MAIAS BENE
MERENTI IN PACE

Lateran Museum.

240

HIC THEODVLE IACET ☧
VIRGO ANNORVM XVII
PVELLA DEP VI IDVS IANVARIAS

Cemetery of Cyriaca.   Lateran Museum.

241

BICTORIA FIDELIS BIRGO
QVE VIXIT ANNIS XVII
MENSIS VIII DIES V IN PACE
DEFVCTA VIDVS SEPTEMB

Lateran Museum.   (Plate XIII. 3.)

242

IENVARIE BIRGINI
BENEMERENTI IN
PACE BOTIS DEPOSITA

Galleria Lapidaria of the Vatican.

The words *votis deposita* refer to the prayers offered at the burial of this holy virgin.

243

AESTONIA VIRGO PEREGRI ☧
NA QVE VIXIT ANIS XL · I · ET · DS
VIII · IIII KAL · MAR DECESSIT
DE CORPORE

Lateran Museum.   (Plate XIII. 7.)

The expression *Virgo peregrina* shows that the holy virgin was a foreigner who had been received into the community of the Roman Church.

244

ADEODATE	ET QVIESCIT
DIGNAE ET	HIC IN PACE
MERITAE	IVBENTE
VIRGINI	$\overline{\text{XPO}}$ EIVS

Cemetery of Cyriaca.   Lateran Museum.   (Plate XIII. 5.)

Note the phrase *jubente Christo ejus*.

(*b*) WIDOWS

Widows were highly honoured in the primitive Church and were called sometimes *viduae Dei*, sometimes by their Greek name χῆραι. They devoted themselves to works of charity.

245

OC · TA · VI · AE · MA · TRONAE
VI · DV · AE · DE · I

Lateran Museum.   (Plate XIII. 6.)

246

DAFNE VIDVA Q · CVN VIX*it* . . . . .
ACLESIA NIHIL GRAVAVIT A . . . . .

Lateran Museum.   (Plate XIII. 4.)

Observe the praise bestowed on her for not having been a burden on the Church: *Ecclesiam nihil gravavit*.

(*c*) The Faithful

The Faithful (*fideles*, πιστοί) were all those who had been baptized and fully instructed in all the Christian mysteries.

247

> ΑΛΥΠΙΟϹ · ΠΙϹΤΟϹ · ΕΝ · ΕΙΡΗΝΗ

Cemetery of Cyriaca.   Lateran Museum.   (Plate XIV. 2.)

248

> B M
>
> PARTHENIO FIDELI IN PACE QVI BIXIT ANNIS XXVIII
> DEP · XVIIII · KAL · FEB

Lateran Museum.   (Plate XIV. 1.)

249

> DEPOSITVS ZOSIMVS
> FIDELIS ANNORVM
> OCTOGINTA
> X̄ KALENDAS DECEMBRES
>   IN PACE

Lateran Museum.

(*d*) Neophytes

The neophytes, from the Greek νεόφυτος (recently planted), formed the class of the Faithful who had but lately received baptism.

250

☧ PAVLINO NEOFITO
IN PACE QVI VIXIT ANOS VIII

Cemetery of Cyriaca.　　Lateran Museum.　　(Plate XIV. 4.)

251

MIRAE · IN*nocentiae* . . . . .
PVLCRITV(*dinis*) . . . . .
HAERMOG . . . . *vix ann* . . . . .
V · NEOFIT · BENE*merens*

Dittc.

252

ZOSIMO · Q · VIXIT · ANN
V · M · VIII · D · XIII · NEOF · IN · ☧
DONATVS · P · F · B · M
ET · IVSTA · M

Lateran Museum.

253

```
IVNIVS · BASSVS · V · C
IN · IPSA · PRAEFECTVRA · VRBIS
NEOFITVS · IIT · AD · DEVM
EVSEBIO · ET · IPATIO · CONSS
```

Grottos of the Vatican (A.D. 359).

This is the celebrated inscription of Junius Bassus, prefect of Rome in 359, who died a neophyte while holding his political office. It is cut on the magnificent sarcophagus, ornamented with striking sculpture, in which that official was buried.

254

```
BENEMERENTI
IN · PACE · LIBERA
QVAE · BIXIT · AN · VIII
NEOFITA · DEP · DIE
III · NONAS · MAIAS
CONS · GRATIANO · III
ET · EQVITIO
```

Kircherian Museum (A.D. 375).

(e) CATECHUMENS

The name catechumen (from the Greek κατηχέω, I instruct) was given to those who were making their initiate into the Faith and preparing to receive baptism. They were kept distinct from the Faithful, properly so called, and were only allowed to be present at certain portions of divine service. They were dismissed at the moment of oblation, whence S. Augustine says: *Fit missa catechumenis, manebunt fideles.* At Easter they received the rite of baptism in solemn form; those who were fit to be baptized were called *catechumeni competentes.*

255

.... LVCILIANVS BACIO VALERIO
.... QVI BISIT AN VIIII
.... VIIII DIES XXII CATECVM

Lateran Museum.

256

KITE · ΒΙΚΤΟΡ · ΚΑΤΗΧΟΥΜΕΝΟϹ
ΑΙΤΩΝ · ΕΙΚΟϹΙ · ΠΑΡΘΕΝΟϹ
ΔΟΥΛΟϹ · ΤΟΥ · ΚΥΡΙΟΥ · ΙΗϹΟΥ ☧

" Here lies Victor, a catechumen of twenty years of age, a bachelor, and a servant of the Lord Jesus Christ."

From a cemetery on the Via Tiburtina; now in the museum of the German cemetery in the Vatican.

This inscription was discovered by me in a vineyard near the Via Tiburtina; I published a special review of it, entitled " A Valuable and Unpublished Christian Inscription," in *Studi in Italia*, sixth year, vol. ii. No. 11, 1883.

§ 6

Slaves and Freedmen

One of the largest classes in old pagan society was that formed of slaves and freedmen (emancipated slaves) ; and both of these are very frequently mentioned in old pagan inscriptions. In old Christian inscriptions, on the other hand, records of slaves and freedmen are very rare, owing to the fact that the Faithful, in obedience to the great Christian principle of the equality of all men before God, eschewed social caste-distinctions, while the pagans were always for insisting on them. To show that Christianity abolished slavery in theory, even though unable to do so immediately in practice, we need only cite the evidence of Lactantius, who solemnly affirms the principle of Christian equality in these noble words: *Apud nos inter servos et dominos interest nihil ; nec alia causa est cur nobis invicem fratrum nomen impertiamus, nisi quia pares nos esse credimus.* (*Div. Ist.* v. 14-15.)

Accepting these views the Christians were not in the habit of mentioning in their inscriptions the status of slave or freedman ; they remembered, moreover, the words of S. Paul, "There is neither bondman nor free" (Gal. iii. 28). It is at any rate undeniable that these descriptions scarcely ever appear on Christian monuments.

There are, however, a few here and there which record the fact. In the cemetery of Priscilla an inscription was discovered in the eighteenth century commemorating the death of a girl, in which the parents state that they manumitted seven slaves at her funeral, *septem (servos) manomisimus*. The text runs thus:

257

```
SECVNDVS · ET · RVFINA
FILIAE · DVLCISIMAE
HVNC · F | VNVS · SCRITVRA
INTRA · NOS · VII · MANOMISIMVS
TV | AM · CARITATEM · FILIA
DVLCISSIMA · SIN · NA · III · K · S
```

(Boldetti, *Osservazioni*, p. 386.)

258

```
ALEXANDER
AVGG · SER · FECI
SE · BIVO · MARCO · FILIO
DVLCISSIMO · CAPVT · A
FRICE · SI · QVI · DEPVTA
BATVR · INTER · BESTITO
RES · QVI · VIXIT · ANNIS
XVIII · MENSIBVS · VIIII
DIEBV · V · PETO · A · BOBIS
FRATRES · BONI · PER
VNVM · DEVM · NE · QVIS
HVNC · TITE · LO · MOLES(*tet*)
POS · MOR (*sic*)
```

Cemetery of S. Hermes on the old Via Salaria.
Kircherian Museum.

The following speaks of an imperial freedman :

259

```
        M · AVRELIO · AVGG · LIB · PROSENETI
        A · CVBICVLO · AVG ·
        PROC · THESAVRORVM
        PROC · PATRIMONI · PROC
(a genius  MVNERVM · PROC · VINORVM          (a genius
support-   ORDINATO · A · DIVO · COMMODO      support-
ing the    IN · KASTRENSE · PATRONO · PIISSIMO ing the
tablet)                                        tablet)
        LIBERTI · BENEMERENTI
        SARCOPHAGVM · DE · SVO ·
        ADORNAVERVNT ·
```

On the front of a sarcophagus in the Villa Borghese in Rome ; found at the seventh milestone of the Via Labicana near Torre Nuova (A.D. 217).

259 (*a*)

```
PROSENES · RECEPTVS · AD · DEVM
  V · NON · aprILIS · SAuro in Camp
ANIA · PRAESENTE · ET · EXTRICATO · II
  REGREDIENS · IN · VRBE
    AB · EXPEDITIONIBVS · SCRIPSIT · AMPELIVS
    LIBertus
```

De Rossi decided that this inscription was Christian on account of the words *receptus ad Deum.* (*Inscr.* i. 5.)[1]

[1] Possibly Proxenes was secretly a Christian.

260

PETRONIAE · AVXENTIAE
C · F · QVAE · VIXIT | ANN
XXX · LIBERTI · FECERVNT
BENEMERENTI · IN · PACE

Cemetery of Callisto.

These were perhaps slaves who had been emancipated by the Lady Petronia Auxentia on the day of her baptism.

Alumni, a class often mentioned in Christian inscriptions, were children who had been deserted by pagan parents, and adopted and brought up as sons on charity in the families of the Faithful.

261

ΠΕΤΡΟC ·

ΘΡΕΠΤΟC ·

(dove) ΓΛ · Υ · Κ · Υ · ΤΑ · (dove)

ΤΟC · ΕΝ · ΘΕΩ · (*sic*)

"Peter, my foster-son, live in God!"

The Greek word θρεπτός answers to the Latin *alumnus*

262

```
EROTIS · ALVMNO
DVLCISSIMO · ET · PAMMVSO
CVMNICO · VALENTINES
FILIES · MEES · VIXIT · ANNOS
XVI
DEFVNCTVS · EST · IDIBVS
IVNIS · DIE · SATVRNI
ORA · NONA
(wreath)                    (palm)
```

Kircherian Museum.

§ 7

Inscriptions bearing on Offices and Professions carried on by the Faithful

The Faithful of the first centuries, while distinguished from the pagan world by their moral and religious principles and by their mode of burial, none the less took their part in public life, and were found in all offices and carrying on all professions, from the highest to the humblest. Hence Tertullian is able to say that the idolaters could find Christians in all places, in the army, the workshops, the civil service, everywhere except in their temples (*Apolog.* 42).

The various classes of society to which Christians belonged are recorded in the inscriptions.

One of the best known of these is that of an unknown consul and martyr named Liberalis who was buried on the old Via Salaria, and whose birth was so lofty that his very name added new dignity to the fasces of the consul. We shall quote this important text in dealing with the historical inscriptions.

The greater number of the inscriptions which record offices held by Christians belong, as is natural, to the times of peace. There are one or two, however, of earlier date, such as the following :

263

XVIII · KAL	AVRELIVS · PRIMVS
SEPT	AVG · LIB · TABVL ·
	ET · COCCEIA · ATHENAIS
	FILIAE · FECERVNT
	AVRELIAE · PROCOPENI
	QVAE · BIXIT ; ANN · XIII · MESIBVS · III
	DIEBVS · XIII · PAX · TECV

Cemetery of S. Hermes.   Kircherian Museum.

This records an imperial freedman, who was a *tabularius*, or keeper of the emperor's books and private papers.

In the cemetery of Priscilla there is also an inscription to an imperial freedman, *praepositus tabernaculariorum*, who, like Aquila and Prisca, and even S. Paul himself, carried on the trade of a tent-maker :

264

... AVG · LIB · PRAEPOSITVS · TABERNACVL(*ariorum*)
... IDI · SORORI · BENEMERENTI · QVAE · VIXIT · AN ...
.. SORORI · QVAE · VIXIT · ANN · XVII · SERAP ... etc.

The following are of a later date; they mention various employments:

265

Hic situs est VictoR FIDENS REMEARE SEPVLTOS
LAETIOR I*n coelum superam* QVI SVRGAT AD AVRAM
IMMACVLATA *piae conservans f*OEDERA MENTIS
CONCILIO SPLENDENS PR*udens et in urbe* SENATOR
INLVSTRES MERITO CEPIT VE*nerandus honor*ES
SVBLIMISQ COMES NOTVS *virtutibus aulae*
VIVIDVS ANNONAM REXIT C*anonemque probavit* (?)

Basilica of S. Sebastian.

This is on one Victor, a senator.

The following refer to employés in the administration, and in the offices of the emperor's establishment, after the reforms effected in the middle of the fourth century:

266

CALLIDROMVS · EX ·ıDISP · HIC · D*ormit* . . . . .
SIGNO · LEVCADI · ANIMA · BONA . . . . .
TIANVS · AVG · LIB · ADIVTOR · PROC · SVM*marum rationum* |
ET · SEIA · HELPIS · FILI · DVLCISSIMI · ET · *Valeria*
CRESCENTINA · COIVX · EIVS

From Ostia.   Lateran Museum.

From the tomb of a *dispensator*. The words *signo Leucadi* mean " with the sobriquet of Leucadius."

267

HIC · QVIESCIT · IN · PACE · LAVRENTIVS
SCRIBA · SENATVS · DEP · DIE · IIII · IDVVM · MART
ADELFIO · VC · CONS

(dove)

Porch of S. Maria in Trastevere.

On the tomb of a clerk to the senate.

268

HIC · QVIESCIT · IN · PACE · FL · CELERINVS
$\overline{VD}$ · SCRINIARIVS · $\overline{INL}$ · PATRICIAE · SEDIS
DEP · D · IIII · ID · NOVEMB · QVI · VIXIT · $\overline{ANN}$ · XXXIII · PLM
$\overline{DN}$ · $\overline{PL}$ · VALENTINIANO · VII · ET · AVIENO · $\overline{VCS}$

Basilica of S. Paolo (A.D. 450).
(De Rossi, *Inscr. christ.* i. No. 751.)

Scriniarius was a clerk of the archives.

269

(wreath) IN HOC LOCV DEPOSITVS EST
FARETER PROTECTOR DOMESTICVS
QVI VIXIT ANNVS XXV REQVIESCIT
IN PACEM   (tree)

Monastery of S. Paolo.

Protector domesticus was a member of the emperor's police.

270

```
.... ANASTASO BEN eme RENTI
.... N PACE DEPOSITVS IIII IDVS OCTOBR
.... ) MILITANS BESTEARV DOMINICV
```

Monastery of S. Paolo.

Vestiarius dominicus, like *vestitor* in the next inscription, means keeper of the imperial wardrobe.

271

```
HIC · POSITVS · EST · BENEMERITVS · EL · AS ....
VESTITOR · IMPERATORIS · QVI · VIX ....
DEPOSITVS · D · VIIII · KAL · SEPTEMBR consulatu
DOMINI · N · HONORI · AVG · VI · CCSS ....
```

Basilica of S. Paolo (A.D. 404).

(De Rossi, *Inscr. christ.* i. No. 531.)

272

```
+ HIC · REQVIESCIT · IN · PACE · IOHANNIS · V̅H̅
OLOGRAFVS · PROPINE · ISIDORI · QVI · VIX
A̅N̅N̅ · PLVS · M̅ · XLV · D̅E̅P̅ · X · K̅A̅L̅E̅N̅ · IVNIA
CONSVLATV · VILISARI · V̅S̅
```

In the Vatican grottos (A.D. 535).

The *olographus propinae* was the book-keeper at a tavern.

273

> CVCVMIO ET VICTORIA
> SE VIVOS FECERVNT
> CAPSARARIVS DE ANTONINIANAS

Cemetery of Domitilla.

The *capsararii* were the attendants who took charge of clothing at the public baths. The baths here mentioned are the Thermae Antoninianae, now known as the Baths of Caracalla, on the Via Appia.

The next inscription gives the name of a superintendent of roads on the Via Flaminia:

274

> HIC · POSITVS · EST · MAXIMVS · QVI
> VIXIT · ANNVS · P · M · LXX · PRAEPOSITVS
> DE · VIA · FLABINIA (*sic*)

Cemetery of S. Valentinus on the Via Flaminia.

Next are some epitaphs on soldiers:

275

> . . . . VDI XII ET AVRELIAE BARB . . . .
> . . . . CV QVE VIXIT AN XXVI MES VIIII DIES . . . .
> A*u*RELIVS BARBAS VET AVGG · NN · X · COHT · PR . . .
> . . . . KARISSI · M · SB · M · FECIT

Cemetery of S. Hippolytus on the Via Tiburtina.

This and the next mention two soldiers, veterans under two emperors.

276

> P · MARCELLO · BETERANO
> AAGG · NN · EQ · R

Cemetery of Priscilla.

Inscription No. 276 is still to be seen on its own tomb in the baptistery quarter of the cemetery of Priscilla. Besides having the title of *veteranus*, the deceased is also described as *eques Romanus* (cavalry soldier), a description seldom found in Christian inscriptions.

Here are two epitaphs of praetorian soldiers:

277

> LICINEIVS · MILX · PRETORIANVS
> AVR · PRICE · COIVGI · K · BENE
> MERENTI · IN · PACE · COH · VI ·

Larger cemetery of S. Agnese.

278

> . . . . IIS IVS MILEX COHS . . . .
> . . . . VSTVS FRTER F PATRV
> . . . . EMERENTI POSVIT QVI . . . .
> ANNIS XXX IN PACE

Cemetery of S. Nicomedes on the Via Nomentana.

The next is on the tomb of a soldier who had been recalled to service after discharge, *evocatus*, and attached to the tenth city cohort:

279

```
COMINIO · MAXI
MO · EVOCATO · COHO
RTIS · X · VRBANAI · QVI · DE
POSITVS · EST · DIE · XV · KAL · MART
```

Lateran Museum.

The two next inscriptions belong to *pneumatici*; a word which has had several different interpretations.

The first gives the name of the deceased, who was a physician ($\iota\alpha\tau\rho\acute{o}s$):

280

```
☧ ENΘA · KATAKITE · AΛEξAN
  ΔΡΟC · IATPOC · XPICTIANOs
  KAI · ΠNEϒMATIKOC ☧
```

(De Rossi, *Cod. vat. lat.* 10,517, fol. 190.)

Some think the word may be taken as meaning a "physician of the soul"; but more probably it refers to some special school of medicine, or what we call a "specialist" [? Christian scientist.—Tr.].

The second inscription, in which the same word occurs, is on one *Ablavios*, a native of Galatia:

281

ΕΝΘΑΔΕ · ΚΑΤΑΚΕΙΤΑΙ · ΑΒΛΑΒΗC

ΓΑΛΑΤΗC · ΧΩΡΙΟΥ · ΜΟΥΑΙΚΟΓΓΙΟC

ΦΩΤΙΝΟΥ · ΖΗΣΑΣ · ΕΤΗ · ΤΡΙΑΚΟΝΤΑ

ΠΝΕΥΜΑΤΙΚΟΣ · ΚΑΛΥΠΤΕΙ · ΓΗ

ΕΙΡΗΝΗ · ΣΟΙ

Some have suspected that the description may refer to the sect of *pneumatici*.

The last words, meaning "the earth hides thee: peace to thee!" are rare, but occasionally found even in Christian inscriptions.

282

*dep*OSITA PVLLA DIE III IDVS OCTOBRIS
*cons*VLATV CALYPI
*deposi*TVS SCOLASTICVS DIE VIIII KAL AVG
consulatu POSTVMIANI IN PACE

Cemetery of Pontianus (A.D. 447-448).

Scholasticus is possibly the name of a person; but it is also the name of a profession, meaning teacher, and it is used in this sense on other inscriptions.

283

MAECILIO HILATI DV	
LCISSIMO NVTRITORI CAE	AMATORI
IONIORVM PVSCIANAE C F	BONO QVI OM
ET CAMENICV QVI VIXIT AN	NES SVOS AM
LXXV M X FECIT MAE	ABIT CARISSIMO
CILIA ROCATA DOMINO PA	
TRI DVLCISSIMO MELLITO	

Cemetery of Priscilla.

No. 283 gives the name of one Maecilius Hilas who was *nutritor* (*angl.* tutor) in the family of the Ceionii. Observe that *mellitus* in the last line is synonymous with the preceding *dulcissimus*.

No. 284 speaks of one *Antimius*, who is called *papas*, or "father"; it is a mistake to take it as meaning Pontiff:

284

PERPETVAM · SEDEM · NVTRITOR · POSSIDES · IPSE
HIC · MERITVS · FINEM · MAGNIS · DEFVNCTE · PERICLIS
HIC · REQVIEM · FELIX · SVMIS · COGENTIBVS · ANNIS
HIC · POSITVS · PAPAS · ANTIMIO · QVI · VIXIT ·
ANNIS · LXX | DEPOSITVS · DOMINO · NOSTRO · AR-
CADIO · II · ET · FL · RVFINO
VVCC · SS · NONAS · NOBEMB

Cemetery of Cyriaca.

Galleria Lapidaria of the Vatican (A.D. 392).

285

PELICA

IN · PACE

(vessel in the   IN · FIDE · DEI

shape of a cask)   QVI · VIXIX ANIS

XXXIIII

PREPO

SITVS

MEDIAS

TINORVM · DE · MONETA · OFFICINA

PRIMA

Lateran Museum.

He was an employé in the imperial mint.

286

M

*bonae me*MORIE CATADROMARIVS

. . . . . MANIS QVI CATADROM

. . . . . CCXXI IN GLAVCE (palm branch)

S. Sebastian.

The epitaph of a racing charioteer of the "glauca," or blue faction.

In this inscription, as in those of pagan charioteers, there is a statement of the number of races won by the deceased for his faction, which was 221 at least, and possibly more.

287

DE BIA NOBA

(grave)

POLLECLA QVE ORDEVM BENDET IN BIA NOBA

Cemetery of Domitilla.

Scratched on the mortar of a grave. It gives the name of a barley-seller of the *via nova*. The only part of the inscription now existing is the expression *de bia noba*.

288

ARTIS · ISPECLARARIE ·	
SABINIVS · SANTIAS · ANIMA	(mirror)
DVLCIS · QVI · VIXIT · ANNIS · XLVI	

Cemetery of Pontianus on the Via Portuensis.

The epitaph of a mirror-maker.

289

. . . CRESCENTIO FERRARIVS DE SVB(*ura*)
. . . NQVE SIBI ET SVIS · QVI OMNIBVS . . .

S. Paolo.

The epitaph of a blacksmith who lived in the Subura.

The next is on a worker in marble:

290

IC POSITVS EST SILBANVS MARMORARIVS
Q VI AN XXX ET FECIT CVM VXXORE AN III
ET MENSIS III DEPOSITVS IIII KAL IVLIAS

Lateran Museum.

291

DEP III IDVS MAI IOSIMVS QVI
VIXIT ANNVS XXVIII QVI FECIT
CVM CONPARE SVA ANNVS SEPTE
MENSIS VIIII BENEMERENTI IN PACE CON
SVLATV NICOMACI FLABIANI LOCV MAR
MARARI QVADRISOMVM

Basilica of S. Paolo (A.D. 394).
Lateran Museum.

This worker in marble had made himself a tomb
to hold four bodies (*locus quadrisomus*).

292

LOCVS DONATI QVI
MANET IN SVBVRA
*m*AIORE AD NIMFA
LINTEARIVS BISOMV

Cemetery of Cyriaca.

This epitaph on a cloth-weaver is to be noted,
giving the name (*ad nymphas*) of a district in the
ancient Subura.

In the cemetery of Commodilla there is an epitaph on a fruiterer (*pomarius*).

Again we have an epitaph on a worker in ivory (*elephantarius*) :

293

> LOCVS · OLYMPI
> ELEFANTARI

Cemetery of Commodilla.

With these we close this series of inscriptions bearing on the occupations of the primitive Christian community.

§ 8

Instances of Christian Inscriptions mentioning Persons of High Rank or connected with Families of High Rank.

There can be no doubt that among the members of the first Christian congregations were to be found many of the nobility, and of those connected in some way with families of high rank, and even with the family of the emperor. Even in the time of S. Paul there were Christians in the imperial household : *salutant vos omnes sancti, maxime autem qui de Caesaris domo sunt* (Phil. iv. 22) : these were probably freedmen of Nero.

By the end of the first century Christianity had made its way into the illustrious home of the Acilii Glabriones, and into that of the Flavii, of which Vespasian Titus and Domitian were members ; and not long afterwards it had also reached the equal noble house of the Caecilii.

At the beginning of the third century there were many Christians in the Senate, as we are told by Tertullian, who mentions *clarissimi viri* and *clarissimae foeminae*; and Pontius the deacon in his life of S. Cyprian tells us that among the confessors to the faith in Africa there were many *egregii et clarissimi ordinis et sanguinis sed et saeculi nobilitate generosi.*

Many other Christians in the first centuries held high office in the state, or important municipal dignities. Flavius Clemens, a cousin of Domitian, was consul, as also was Acilius Glabrio; and in the reign of Commodus there was a senator, Apollonius by name, who read an Apology for Christianity to the Senate. Later there was another consul, Liberalis, who was also a martyr (see p. 409).

These facts are all corroborated by inscriptions in which these high and illustrious personages are mentioned. We will give some of them as specimens.

294

M · ACILIO · GLABRIONI
FILIO
· · · · · · · · · · · ·

Cemetery of Priscilla.

This belonged to a sarcophagus which was recovered in the subterranean vaults of the Acilii which run into the cemetery of Priscilla. It records one *Manius Acilius Glabrio*, who was probably the son or grandson of Manius Acilius Glabrio, consul in A.D. 91, and martyred under Domitian.[1]

[1] See on this point De Rossi, *Bull. di arch. crist.*, 1887-1889, p. 67.

295

```
M · ACILIVS · Verus
      V · C
PRISCILLA · C · F
```

Cemetery of Priscilla.

This speaks of one *Manius Acilius Verus vir clarissimus*, *i.e.* of senatorial rank; and of one *Priscilla clarissima foemina*, his wife.

This inscription shows that a connexion existed between the family of Pudens and Priscilla and that of the Acilii.

296

```
(Α)ΚΙΛΙΟC · ΡΟΤΦΙΝΟC
(Ζ)ΗCΗC · ΕΝ · ΘΕΩ
```

" Acilius Rufinus, mayest thou live in God ! "

Cemetery of Priscilla.

297

```
ΚΛ
ΑΚΕΙΛΙΟΤ ·
ΤΑΛΕΡΙΟΤ
veaΝΙCΚΟΤ
```

" The tomb of the youth Claudius Acilius Valerius."

Cemetery of Priscilla.

298

ΦΛ · CABEINOC · KAI ·
ΤΙΤΙΑΝΗ · ΑΔΕΛΦΟΙ

"Flavius Sabinus and Titiana, brother and sister."

Cemetery of Domitilla.

The personage here mentioned belonged to the Christian branch of the Flavii, and bore the same name as Flavius Sabinus, the elder brother of the Emperor Vespasian.

De Rossi has shown that the branch of the Flavii which was converted to Christianity as early as the first century was the very same that sprang from Flavius Sabinus, who was the father of Fabius Clemens, consul and martyr, and husband to Flavia Domitilla.[1]

299

TITVS · FLAVIVS
FELICISSIMVS
*hic depo*SITVS · EST

Cemetery of Priscilla.

Possibly belonging to a freedman of the Emperor Titus.

[1] *Bull. di arch. crist.*, 1875, pp. 37 *et seq.*

300

ΠοΜΠΩΝΙΟϹ · ΓΡΗκειvoϹ

" Pomponius Grecinus."

Cemetery of Callisto.

De Rossi thinks this person may have belonged to the same family as Pomponia Grecina, wife of the senator Aulus Plautius under Nero.

Other inscriptions, as well in Greek as in Latin, have been brought to light in the cemetery of Callisto, as to the gens Pomponia which was connected with the Caecilii.[1]

301

Q · CAE*cilio*

MAXIMO

C · P

(clarissimo puero)

" To Quintus Caecilius Maximus, a youth of senatorial family."

Cemetery of Callisto.

This was a relative of the celebrated martyr S. Caecilia, who was buried in the same cemetery on the Via Appia; that cemetery was constructed in a property belonging to the illustrious family of the Caecilii.

---

[1] *Roma sotterranea*, vol. ii. plates 41 and 69.

To the same family belong the following inscriptions of personages entitled to the prefix *clarissimi*:

302

. . . . . ATTICA
CAECILIANA · C · F · VIX
. . . . . A · XVII · M · III
. . . . . D · XX

Cemetery of Callisto.

303

POMPEIA · OC
(*t*)ABIA · ATTICA
*Ca*ECILIANA · C · P
VIXIT · MEN . . . .

Cemetery of Callisto.

304

*Octa*VIVS · CAECILIANVS · V · C
*in pa*CE · DEPOSITVS
*idu*S · MAIAS · VIX
annos XXXXIIII
menses VIII

Cemetery of Callisto.

In the cemetery of Callisto there is also the epitaph of Septimius Praetextatus Caecilianus,[1] of senatorial rank :

305

CΕΠΤΙΜΙΟC · ΠΡΑΙΤΕΞΤΑΤΟC

ΚΑΙΚΙΛΙΑΝΟC

. . . .

The two next belong to persons of the noble gens Annia :

306

ΑΝΝΙΑ · ΦΑΥCΤΕΙΝΑ

. . . .

Cemetery of Callisto.

307

ΑΝΝΙΟΣ · ΚΑΤΟΣ

Cemetery of Callisto.

Here is one of Licinia, a lady of rank :

308

ΛΙΚΙΝΙΑ · ΦΑΥCΤΕΙΝΑ

Cemetery of Callisto.

---

[1] The recovery of a further fragment makes it probable that we should read " Licilianus " instead of " Caecilianus."

The next is on a lady of the noble gens Emilia:

309

> EMILIA · PVDENTILLA

Cemetery of Callisto.

310

> ΟΥΡΑΝΙΑ · ΘΥΓΑΤΗΡ · ΗΡΟΔΗϹ

" Urania, daughter of Herodes."

Cemetery of Praetextatus.

De Rossi thinks this was the daughter of the celebrated Herodes Atticus, a man of rank, contemporary of Marcus Aurelius.[1]

We will add three epitaphs of ladies of senatorial family, *clarissimae foeminae*:

311

> AELIVS · SATVRNINVS
> CASSIAE · FARETRIAE · CLARISSIME
> FEMINE · CONIVGI · BENEME
> RENTI · DEPOSTIO · TERTIV · NO
> NAS · FEBRARIAS (*sic*)
>
> (dove)

Cemetery of Callisto.

---

[1] *Bull. di arch. crist.*, 1872, p. 625.

312

> PETRONIAE · AVXENTIAE · C · F · QVAE · VIXIT
> ANN · XXX · LIBERTI · FECERVNT · BENEMERENTI
> IN · PACE

Cemetery of Callisto.

One of the very rare Christian inscriptions which mention freedmen.

313

> LVRIA · IANVARIA · C · F
> CAELIO · FELICISSIMO · V · E
> COIVG · KARISS ·

"The Lady Luria Januaria, of senatorial rank, placed this to the memory of her beloved husband Caelius Felicissimus, of equestrian rank" (*egregius*).

Cemetery of S. Agnese.

Inscriptions of members of noble families become naturally more numerous in the peaceful times of the fourth and fifth centuries, when many other patrician families embraced Christianity, such as the Anicii, and many other nobles of the highest rank. And of these inscriptions a large number are still to be seen in various cemeteries. Those of the Anicii Bassi in the Vatican are specially to be noted. With these and others of the same sort we shall deal in the chapter treating of metrical inscriptions other than those of Damasus.

CHAPTER VI

IT is well known that the ancient Romans, while
they used the year of the foundation of the city
(*anni ab urbe condita*) as their chronological starting-
point for inscriptions, deeds, and letters generally,
used the "consular" reckoning.   It is further well
known that, as consuls were still nominated under
the empire, this method of marking the date
was continued into imperial times, and used by
Christians also.   Hence it is that in old Christian
inscriptions we find the names both of consuls of
subject rank, and of emperors who assumed that
dignity.

The Christians used the same indications of date
as the pagans ; and they placed on their inscriptions
the names alike of their great protectors and of their
cruellest enemies.   So we read therein not only the
names of Constantine, Jovianus, Gratianus, and
Theodosius, but also that of Julian the Apostate ;
and we find the years of the consulship even of
usurpers carefully noted.   Moreover, the Christians
did not even change the conventional titles ; nay,

[1] These preliminary notes are taken from the masterly
Preface to vol. i. of *Inscriptiones christianae*, by G. B. De Rossi.

they also used the word *Divi* to describe deceased sovereigns; and this not only in the case of Christian emperors, but also in that of Julian. But it must be noted that in the days before the peace of the Constantinian age the title of *Divus* given to the deceased ruler implied a superstitious and idolatrous worship, and therefore in that period it is never given to them in any Christian inscription. But after the empire had become officially Christian, the custom of describing the dead emperor as *Divus* was continued, but only as an honorific epithet; as we say in the present day, *sanctae memoriae, felicis recordationis, sanctissimae recordationis.*

In Rome the consuls had been in the habit of giving their names to their year of office; and thus it came about that generally in the Roman empire the years were thus designated. But there was this difference between Rome and the provinces of the empire, that whereas in Rome only the names of the consuls were used to distinguish the year, in the provinces we find the monuments naming emperors, and provincial presidents also. We may note that the years of the emperor's reign are not generally recorded before the middle of the sixth century; and if an inscription mentions them, there is always something in the history to account for the irregularity. Thus a Christian inscription contains the words *sub Maxentio*: now we know from history that the intrusion of this tyrant into the empire disturbed the regular order of the consuls, and this is the precise reason why the writer gave a mere general date, *sub Maxentio.*

In Rome then, as a general rule, the date of a monument was indicated by the names of the consuls only; and hence Christian inscriptions with consular date are very common in Rome. They are rarely found indeed in the first and second centuries; but in the third they begin to appear rather oftener; in the fourth and the beginning of the fifth they are very numerous; then they go on diminishing in number to the middle of the sixth century, after which time they return to their original rarity. Outside Rome it should be noticed that certain provinces had their own methods of marking dates. In Spain, Africa, Egypt, and in all the East, where there was a great variety of systems of chronology, consuls are very rarely mentioned: inscriptions from those regions bearing a consular date are very few in number, and nearly all of the sixth century.

Consuls were termed *ordinarii* when they began their duties on January 1st and gave their names to the year; they were called *suffecti* when they took the place of *ordinarii* leaving office for any reason whatever before the end of the year. In inscriptions the names of the consuls are sometimes abbreviated, sometimes set out in full; sometimes the year is designated by the names of both consuls, sometimes of only one; in some cases the proper order of the names is not maintained. Often, again, a period is reckoned from the year of the preceding consuls. The abbreviations to indicate consular dignity are many: COS, COSS, CONS, CONSS. It is worth notice that in some cases other titles of office are mentioned. Lastly, the conventional form may be used in the ablative or in the genitive case, *e.g. Titio et Caio consulibus*, or *consulatu Titii et Caii*. The conjunction *et* is always inserted between the names of the two consuls by constant and well-recognised usage;

there are very few cases of its omission. As for the number of the consulships served by one person, we should notice that when no number is stated, it is understood that the consul has not served before; if the number is placed after both names, *e.g.* PRAESENTE ET EXTRICATO II, it signifies that both consuls were holding the fasces for the second time. In these cases the word CONSVLIBVS is often omitted, as in the instance quoted above. Furthermore, where the abbreviation COS stands for two consuls, it may be inferred that the inscription is comparatively ancient, while the word CONSVLIBVS written in full only appears about the middle of the fourth century.

A large use was also made of the words DOMINI NOSTRI, DOMINORVM NOSTRORVM, applied to the Augusti and the Caesars. The doubled letters DD. NN. (*Dominis nostris*) begin to occur in the date-marks at the beginning of the third century, and the practice lasted to the end of the fifth. The abbreviations DOM. N. and especially DOMNO belong to a later period. The epithet *nobilissimi* was officially applied to the Caesars from the age of Commodus and Septimius Severus, but it does not appear in Christian inscriptions before the fourth century. At that time the sons of the Augusti (and also of the relatives of the Augusti) were styled *nobilissimi* before becoming Caesars. Under Constantine too the abbreviation N. P. makes its appearance, signifying *nobilissimus puer*. Deceased Augusti could receive the title of *Divi* by decree of the Senate. This before the age of Constantine signified actual bestowal of divinity and therefore is never found in Christian inscriptions anterior to the Peace ; but after Constantine, as we have already pointed out, it only means that the emperor referred to is dead.

In A.D. 305 the division of the Roman empire took place. Hereupon arose quarrels between the Augusti, who began by establishing separate administrations in the provinces that fell to their respective shares, and everything, including the creation and proclamation of consuls, fell into confusion. The old historians make no mention of these details and the consular fasti present many difficulties; but in the obscurity of the history the inscriptions, when read alongside of the fasti, give a certain amount of light. And some Christian inscriptions of the time of Maxentius enable us to detect a complete and sudden change in the ancient system of consular fasti.

For in the year A.D. 307 appears for the first time the formula *post consulatum*, the consuls mentioned being those of the previous year. This was the year in which the fierce dissensions arose between Maximianus Herculeus and his son Maxentius; the adherents of the latter, who was masters of Rome, were afraid to place the name of the consul Maximianus on public monuments; and hence was devised the formula *post consulatum*, which was officially sanctioned. After the defeat of Maxentius, Constantine and his sons maintained, in name at least, the unity of the Roman empire, and even during the struggle between Licinius and Constantine consuls continued to be proclaimed according to ordinary rule. If in A.D. 346 Christian inscriptions are dated *post consulatum Amantii et Albini* rather than by the consulship of the two Augusti, this was not by the whim of an individual, but by reason of the fact that in that year the consulship of the two Augusti was not proclaimed, in Rome and throughout the West, till the last months of the year: this is shown by the inscriptions, the tables of the fasti, and the Council of Cologne (Colonia Agrippina), which all show the same date-mark as above given. But the reason of the fact is still unknown to us.

In 350, after Constans had been slain, Nepotianus and Magnentius invaded the empire, and for this reason an epitaph written in the month of July gives the date *post consulatum Limenii et Catullini*.

In the year 360 Julian the Caesar was saluted as emperor by the troops in Gaul; and traces of the strife which arose between Julian and the Emperor Constantius on this account are to be found in some Christian inscriptions. Under Jovian and the other emperors up to Valentinian II. there were no disturbances that affected the consular fasti. In the year 375 Valentinian II. was saluted as emperor in Pannonia, but his sovereignty was not immediately recognised throughout the Roman world; in Rome and in Alexandria his name was inserted between those of the emperors after the beginning of the year 376, as we learn from a fragmentary Christian inscription.[1] The tyrant Maximus, after defeating Valentinian II., marched into Italy, and even to Rome; later on, after the slaughter of Valentinian, Eugenius usurped the Western empire. Of all these vicissitudes we find clear traces in the consular inscriptions of the time.

It has been often thought that immediately after the death of Constantine, and the division of the empire among several Augusti, the practice was adopted of nominating two consuls, one in the East,

---

[1] Cp. De Rossi, *Inscr. christ.* p. 254.

the other in the West; because towards the end of that century we find a habit of entering at one time the name of one consul, at another of two, at another again the form *post consulatum*. But this variety of usage, so far from being accidental, represents historical facts. From the year 366 to 386 the formula *post consulatum*, contrary to ancient practice, appears in Roman inscriptions, but only in the first months of each year, indicating that in those months the names of the consuls were not known. In the years in question, therefore, some change must have been made in the manner of proclaiming consuls, or else that ceremony was postponed for three or four months. And this last was exactly what had happened; and history explains why. Those were the days when the emperors were always at a great distance apart, and were incessantly engaged either in civil struggles or in wars with the barbarians; and thus, as is easily understood, the proclamation of consuls was hindered or belated. In fact matters came to such a pass that in the year 375 no consuls at all were nominated, a thing which had never before happened. S. Jerome, too, records this, writing in his *Chronicon* (for 375): *Quia superiore anno Sarmatae Pannonias vastaverant, iidem consules permansere.* Thus in that year, as the inscriptions show us, the date was given by *post consulatum*.

The college of consuls was maintained undivided till the year 399. Then began the division of the consulate, as the eunuch Eutropius, who had been nominated by the Emperor Arcadius as consul in the East, was not recognised in the West, where Theodorus only was recognised, on the nomination of the Emperor Honorius. And then, as it was contrary to usage to mark the date by one consular name only, we find inscriptions in which, while Theodorus alone is mentioned, he is given several names, *i.e.* Flavius Mallius Theodorus.

From that time onwards many variations were introduced in the fasti and on monuments. The proclamation of the Eastern consul in the West, as of the Western consul in the East, was largely neglected, so that in the first months of a year every one recorded the name of his own consul only; in fact the name of the other was often entirely left out. But, as the law required that the names of both consuls should be given, if the other was not known they had to use the words, *et qui de Oriente vel de Occidente fuerit nuntiatus.* This expression is well known in laws and in other historical records, but is very uncommon in inscriptions.

After the destruction of the Roman empire and the subjection of Italy to the barbarians, the creation of consuls continued as before; and this privilege was left by the barbarian kings exclusively to the Roman senate, which exercised it in conjunction with the Roman emperor of the East. Theodoric, however, used to nominate the Western consul himself; hence during his time the latter alone is mentioned and the Byzantine consul is entirely ignored. It follows that the names of consuls found on inscriptions dating from the rule of the Goths must be looked for on the fasti of the West.

In the year 535 Belisarius was elected consul of the East; he finished his year of office at Syracuse after wresting that city from the Goths and restoring it to the dominion of the Emperor Justinian. During the twenty years of the Gothic War great confusion reigned in the method of denoting the date by the names of the consuls. From the beginning of the war and the consulship of Belisarius in 535, the Gothic kings ceased to nominate a consul; and the Emperor Justinian, having taken possession of Italy and of Rome itself, on several occasions nominated two consuls for the Roman world. After the year 534, when the Emperor Justinian was consul in the East and Paulinus in the West, one consul was created every year by Justinian in the East, and another by the Roman Senate in the West; but in 536 and 537 there were no consuls appointed; in 538, 539, and 540 Johannes Appius Justinus was named, and in 541 Basilius; and with him the list of the ancient fasti closes. During the reign of Justinian the date was noted either by the single consul nominated by him, or by the years after a consulship. In the countries subject to the Goths, the names of Justinian's consuls could not be entered, as they were not recognised; and for this reason the years were numbered from the consulship of Paulinus, the last who was proclaimed and officially accepted in the West. The Burgundians and the Franks, out of respect for the Eastern empire, recognised the consuls of Justinian. After them began a period during which time was counted from the consulship of Basilius, who had been recognised throughout the Roman empire, and this lasted twenty-four years. On the death of Justinian, his successor Justinus took the office of consul into his own hands. But in the Gallic provinces and in Burgundy, time continued to be counted *post consulatum Basilii* for forty-six years; the custom, however, gradually died out, and the habit began of denoting time by the years

s

of the king's reign. In 568 the rule of the Lombards in Italy began, but it seems that the computation from the consulship of Justinus was continued even where the Lombards were in occupation; indeed an inscription of 575, belonging to the Lombard period, marks the year by the formula *post consulatum Justini imperatoris*.

As for the date at which each variety of this formula came into use, we must observe that in early times the word *consulibus* or *consule*, as the case might be, never preceded the names of the consuls, but always followed them; *e.g. Pisone et Bolano consulibus*, not vice versa. Then came in the practice of saying, *e.g., consulatu Juliani et Sallustii*, and even *consulatu Modesto et Ariuntheo*. The word *consulatu*, either in full or abbreviated, standing before the names of the consuls, and the names of the consuls in the genitive case, are marks of an age later than the middle of the fourth century. In Greek inscriptions it would seem that about from the middle of the fourth century the word ὑπάτοις is altogether dropped, and ὑπατεία regularly used.

To indicate the years after a consulship, from the middle of the fourth to the middle of the fifth century, the forms POST-CONS or POST CONSS (sometimes only POS), or again POST CON-SVLATVM or POST CONSVLATV in full, were used; sometimes POST or POS only was written with the names of the consuls in the genitive or ablative case. In the middle of the fifth century the abbreviation PC comes into use; and this lasted to the end of the sixth century. In the second half of that century the names of kings, and later also sometimes of Popes, are substituted for those of consuls to mark the date; the rare exceptions to this practice were due to the assumption of the consular title by the Byzantine emperors even at that late period.

We must now say a little on the chronological reckoning known as the *Vulgar era*, and on its origin.

*
* *

Of the Dionysian or Vulgar Era

In the first half of the sixth century the monk Dionysius, a native of Scythia, with a view to harmonising the practice of the Eastern and Western Churches as to the date of the celebration of Easter, introduced in the Latin Church the cycle of ninety-five years known as the Cyrillian; but while the cycle of Cyril took as its starting-point the first year of the reign of Diocletian, Dionysius selected for the starting-point of his cycle the birth of Christ, which he determined to be the year 754 from the foundation of Rome.[1] But the pious monk's calculation was found to be erroneous by the learned Sanclemente and other chroniclers; and it is now generally admitted that Christ was born A.U.C. 747. It is indeed quite clear that he was born in the reign of Herod, and that Herod died in A.U.C. 750; and, besides that,

[1] Cf. Sanclemente, *De emendatione temporum*, book iv. chap. viii. p. 458.—But the date of Christ's birth had naturally been already made the subject of calculation. Thus S. Augustine writes: "A nativitate autem Domini hodie computantur anni ferme quadringenti viginti, a resurrectione autem vel adscensione ejus anni plus minus CCCXC." (Aug., Epist. 199, 20).

the date-mark given in the Gospel of S. Luke, which says that Quirinus was president of Syria, and that of Tertullian, who mentions Sensius Saturninus as governor of that province, bring us back to the same date, 747. The conclusion we must therefore draw is that the Dionysian or Vulgar era is seven years in arrear, and hence that the year commonly known as 1910 is the year 1917 of the true and correct Christian era.

The Vulgar era was introduced by Dionysius in the year A.U.C. 1279, which he called A.D. 525; but it was not immediately brought into common use, and for a long time years were still marked by a consular or other similar date-mark. The Vulgar era is first recorded on Christian monuments of the seventh and eighth centuries; hence it is never to be met with in the inscriptions of the older subterranean cemeteries of Roman Christians, which were not used after the fifth century, nor in the open-air cemeteries of the Roman suburbs, in which ordinary burials ceased after the middle of the sixth century.

Olivieri, in his work on the inscriptions of Pesaro, records an inscription with the date-mark ERA · CCCC · LI ; but this inscription was afterwards admitted to be a forgery.

The oldest inscriptions hitherto known which contain a date of the Vulgar era are that in the baptistery of Brescia of 617 (SACRAE · SALVT · SAECVLO · CCCCCCXVII), and that in the basilica of S. Valentine at Terni of 727 (A · S · DCCXXVII).[1] But it should be noted that just at the time when the new era came into common

[1] Cf. Mai, *Scriptorum veterum nova collectio,* vol. v. part i. p. 157, 3 ; p. 170, 3.

use, there was a great variety and much confusion in the manner of denoting the year. Thus some gave a *post consulatum* of some sort along with the Indiction ; others joined to the Indiction the years of the reign of Roman pontiffs or of Byzantine emperors ; others, again, confined themselves to the cycle of Indictions, a method which is absolutely useless for chronological purposes.[1]

These few remarks on the Vulgar era will suffice, as we have already pointed out that it is never used in the inscriptions with which this Manual of Ancient Christian Epigraphy is concerned.

§ I

Of the Tables of Consular Fasti

The consular fasti are the list of the names of the consuls ; by the aid whereof any "consular" date may be at once expressed by the corresponding year of the era of the foundation of Rome, and therefore of the Vulgar era also. As we have to deal with consular inscriptions of the Christian era, it is obvious that we need not consider either the ancient marble fasti of the Capitol nor others of a very early date, but only the fasti of the imperial age which record the names of the consuls. Among these the best and earliest are those of Philocalus, edited for the first time by Bucher, and called the Bucherian on that account. They include the period A.D. 254-354.

[1] Cf. C. L. Visconti, *Dell' uso e della utilità dei monumenti cristiani cronologici anteriori all' uso dell' era volgare*, Roma, 1856, pp. 11-17.

The annals of the history of S. Athanasius give us his actual letters translated into Syriac, and also the year-names from 324 to 373; the letters were edited for the first time in 1848 by William Cureton, and afterwards translated into Latin by Cardinal Mai. The earlier part of this chronological list gives the gentile names of the consuls; for later years we find the cognomens only, as in the ordinary fasti.

Fasti of the Fifth and Sixth Centuries

Many compilations of the consular fasti were made in the fifth and sixth centuries, as they were needed by jurists for their editions of the statutes; and when the chronicles of Eusebius and Jerome came to be popularly known, that description of literature was much cultivated among Christians. The fifth century was above all remarkable for the violent discussions as to the date of the Easter festival in which Alexandria and Rome took so leading a part; these induced many learned men of the day to collect the particulars of the dates of previous Easters, in order to forecast those to come.

In these fasti, however, the older part must be carefully distinguished from the portion compiled in the fifth century; the former appears to be an original document, and a common basis to nearly all.

Thus the fasti called the Idatian and those in the paschal chronicle of Alexandria are undoubtedly taken from a common original; thus, again, the chronicles of Pompeius of Aquitania were made use of afterwards by Victorius (also of Aquitania); and again, too, those of Victorius were utilised by

Cassiodorus and others. But we had better confine ourselves to a consideration of the fasti of the fifth and sixth centuries, as it was especially in that period that great differences existed between the East and the West in the nomination of consuls.

Fasti of the West

I. The *Paschal Index*, covering the eighty-four years ending with A.D. 437 : Codex Vat. Reg. 2077, p. 79. Published by Manzi in *Apparatus ad Baronii Annales*, pp. 237-342.

This Codex was probably written in the seventh century. From A.D. 354 to 398 it records the names of both consuls ; from 399 to 437 the Western consul only is named.

II. *Paschal Table from the death of Christ to the year* 448.—This list was drawn up in 447 and 448, and gives the series of consuls for 420 years ; it goes back therefore to A.D. 29. The very little that is left of this valuable record is published by Haenel in *Kritische Jahrbücher für deutsche Rechtswissenschaft*, vol. i. (Leipsic, 1837), pp. 756-760.

III. *Fasti Prosperiani.*—These form part of the Chronicle of Prosperus of Aquitania. This chronicle is in two parts ; the first, from A.D. 28 to 378 ; the second appears to have been frequently re-edited with continuations ; the last revision by the original author is probably the one ending A.D. 455.

IV. *Fasti Idatiani.*—The work of Bishop Idatius is of great value for the consulships of the time of Maxentius, particularly if compared with the Index of Philocalus.

V. *Fasti Veronenses.*—Found in the parchment palimpsest LV. 53, of the famous library of the Cathedral of Verona; on p. 89 is a list of consuls from 439 to 486.

VI. *Chronicon Cuspinianaeum.*—Two consular lists which Cuspiniani was the first to use; the first runs to 493, the second to 539, but in Mommsen's opinion both are copies of the same work.

VII. *Cassiodori Senatoris Chronicon.* — Cassiodorus copied Victorius of Aquitania so far as the consuls are concerned; his list goes down to the time of Theodoric.

VIII. *Tabula paschalis Neapolitana.*—Found in Cod. Vat. Reg. 2077. It goes from 464 to 614. The method of designating the years shows that it comes from Southern Italy, which was nearly always under the sway of Byzantium. Furthermore, the precise indication of the months and days of the month on which eruptions of Vesuvius occurred point clearly to the city of Naples as the birthplace of this document.

Fasti of the East

I. *Marcellini comitis Chronicon ab ignoto auctore continuatum ad annum 566.*—From A.D. 421 onwards the two consuls are entered, the consul of the East taking precedence of the consul of the West.

II. *Victoris Tunnunensis Chronicon.*—This runs from 444 to 566. The fasti are Western up to 459; from that year to 500 (with the exception of 460) they are Eastern. Then, from 501 to 532, Victor makes use generally, though not always, of the Western fasti; and from 533 to 566 goes back to the Eastern. The dates, however, are very inaccurate, often more through the ignorance of the copyist than from the fault of the writer.

III. *Fasti Graeci Florentini majores ab anno 222 ad 630.*—Dodwell gave these the name of Heraclian. They are very useful, as they give all the Eastern consuls.

IV. *Chronicon paschale.*—In this the consul- ships are recorded historically.

N.B. — The list of consuls in the above- mentioned fasti is to be found in many chrono- logical works; but two works may be recommended as extremely practical:

Klein, *Fasti consulares inde a Caesaris nece usque ad imperium Diocletiani* (Leipsic, 1881).

Vaglieri, *I consoli di Roma antica.* (From the dictionary of inscriptions of De Ruggiero, Spoleto, 1905.)[1]

CATALOGUE OF THE NAMES OF CONSULS WHOSE NAMES MIGHT OCCUR IN CHRISTIAN INSCRIPTIONS

This synoptical catalogue contains the names of the consuls from the foundation of the Christian Church to the middle of the sixth century.

Birth of Christ, A.U.C. 747; death, A.U.C. 782, A.D. 29.

A.D.

29. L. Rubellius Geminus — C. Fufius Geminus.
30. M. Vinicius I. — L. Cassius Longinus.

---

[1] Vaglieri also gives an alphabetical index of the consuls, by means of which the year of our Lord corresponding to any consular date may easily be found.

[For reasons of convenience the subjoined list has been taken from the *Fasti consulares imperii Romani* (W. Liebenam, Bonn, 1909), and differs in some points from that given by S. Marucchi. —TR.]

A.D.

31. Tiberius Aug. V. — L. Aelius Seianus.
32. Cn. Domitius Aenobarbus — M. Furius Camillus Scribonianus.
33. Ser. Sulpicius Galba — L. Corn. Sulla Felix.
34. Paulus Fabius Persicus — L. Vitellius I.
35. C. Cestius Gallus — M. Servilius Nonianus.
36. Sex. Papinius Allenius — Q. Plautius.
37. Cn. Acerronius Proculus — Caius Petronius Pontius Nigrinus.
38. M. Aquila Iulianus — P. Nonius Asprenas.
39. Caius Caesar German. Caligula II. — L. Apronius Caesianus.
40. Caius Caesar German. Caligula III.
41. Caius Caesar German. Caligula IV. — Cn. Sentius Saturninus.
42. Tib. Claudius Aug. II. — Caius Cecina Largus.
43. Tib. Claudius Aug. III. — L. Vitellius II.
44. C. Passienus Crispus II. — T. Statilius Taurus.
45. M. Vinicius II. — T. Statilius Taurus Corvinus.
46. Valerius Asiaticus I. — M. Iunius Silanus.
47. Tib. Claudius Aug. IV. — L. Vitellius III.
48. Aulus Vitellius — L. Vipstanus Publicola.
49. C. Pompeius Longus Gallus — Q. Veranius.
50. C. Antistius Veto — M. Suillius Nerullinus.
51. Tib. Claudius Aug. V. — Serv. Corn. Orfitus.
52. Faustus Corn. Sulla Felix — Lucius Salvius Otho Titianus.
53. Decimus Iunius Silanus Torquatus — Quintus Haterius Antoninus.
54. M. Asinius Marcellus — Manius Acilius Aviola.
55. Nero Aug. I. — L. Antistius Vetus.
56. Q. Volusius Saturninus — P. Cornelius Scipio.
57. Nero Aug. II. — L. Calpurnius Piso.
58. Nero Aug. III. — M. Valerius Messala Corvinus.
59. C. Vipstanus Apronianus — C. Fonteius Capito.
60. Nero Aug. IV. — Cossus Cornelius Lentulus.
61. L. Caesennius Paetus — P. Petronius Turpilianus.
62. P. Marius Celsus — L. Afinius Gallus.
63. C. Memmius Regulus — L. Verginius Rufus I.

A.D.

64. C. Lecanius Bassus — M. Licinius Crassus.
65. A. Licinius Nerva Silianus — M. Vestinus Atticus.
66. C. Luccius Telesinus — C. Suetonius Paulinus II.
67. Fonteius Capito — C. Iulius Rufus.
68. Galerius Trachalus Turpilianus — C. Silius Italicus.
69. Galba Aug. II. — T. Vinius Rufinus.
70. Titus Fl. Vespasianus Aug. II. — Titus Caesar Vespasianus I.
71. Vespasianus Aug. III. — M. Cocceius Nerva.
72. Vespasianus Aug. IV. — Tit. Caesar Vespasianus II.
73. Domitianus Caesar II. — L. Valerius Catullus Messalinus.
74. Vespasianus Aug. V. — Titus Caesar Vespasianus III.
75. Vespasianus Aug. VI. — Titus Caesar Vespasianus IV.
76. Vespasianus Aug. VII. — Tit. Caesar Vespasianus V.
77. Vespasianus Aug. VIII. — Tit. Caesar Vespasianus VI.
78. L. Ceionius Commodus. — D. Novius Priscus.
79. Vespasianus Aug. IX. — Tit. Caesar Vespasianus VII.
80. Titus Aug. VIII. — Domitianus Caesar VII.
81. L. Flavius Silva Nonius Bassus — Asinius Pollio Verrucosus.
82. Domitianus Aug. VIII. — T. Flavius Sabinus.
83. Domitianus Aug. IX. — Q. Petillius Rufus II.
84. Domitianus Aug. X. — C. Oppius Sabinus.
85. Domitianus Aug. XI. — T. Aurelius Fulvus.
86. Domitianus Aug. XII. — Ser. Cornelius Dolabella Petronianus.
87. Domitianus Aug. XIII. — L. Volusius Saturninus.
88. Domitianus Aug. XIV. — Q. Minucius Rufus.
89. T. Aurelius Fulvus — Attrattinus.
90. Domitianus Aug. XV. — M. Cocceius Nerva II.
91. M. Acilius Glabrio — M. Ulpius Traianus.
92. Domitianus Aug. XVI. — Q. Volusius Saturninus.

A.D.

93. Pompeius Collega — Priscinus.
94. Lucius Nonius Torquatus Asprenas — T. Sextius Magius Lateranus.
95. Domitianus Aug. XVII. — T. Flavius Clemens.
96. C. Antistius Vetus — T. Manlius Valens.
97. Nerva Aug. III. — L. Verginius Rufus III.
98. Nerva Aug. IV. — M. Ulpius Traianus Caesar II.
99. A. Cornelius Palma I. — Q. Sosius Senecio I.
100. Traianus Aug. III. — Sex. Iulius Frontinus III.
101. Traianus Aug. IV. — Q. Articuleius Paetus.
102. L. Iulius Ursus Servianus II. — L. Licinius Sura II.
103. Traianus Aug. V. — M. Laberius Maximus II.
104. Sex. Attius Suburanus II. — M. Asinius Marcellus.
105. Tib. Iulius Candidus II. — C. Antius Iulius Quadratus II.
106. L. Ceionius Commodus Verus — Cerealis.
107. L. Licinius Sura III. — Q. Sosius Senecio II.
108. App. Annius Trebonius Gallus — M. Atilius Metellus Bradua.
109. A. Cornelius Palma II. — Q. Baebius Tullus.
110. Servius Scipio Salvidienus Orfitus — M. Peducaeus Priscinus.
111. C. Calpurnius Piso — M. Vettius Bolanus.
112. Traianus Aug. VI. — T. Sextius Africanus.
113. L. Publicius Celsus II. — C. Clodius Crispinus.
114. Q. Ninnius Hasta — P. Manilius Vopiscus.
115. L. Vipstanus Messala — M. Vergilianus Paedo.
116. L. Aelianus Lamia — Vetus.
117. Q. Aquilius Niger — M. Rebilius Apronianus.
118. Hadrianus Aug. II. — Cn. Pedanius Fuscus Salinator.
119. Hadrianus Aug. III. — Q. Iunius Rusticus.
120. L. Catilius Severus II. — T. Aurelius Boionius Arrius Antoninus.
121. M. Annius Verus II. — Arrius Augurinus.
122. Manius Acilius Aviola — Corellius Pansa.

A.D.
123. Q. Articuleius Paetinus — L. Venuleius Apronianus.
124. Manius Acilius Glabrio — C. Bellicius Torquatus Tebanianus.
125. Valerius Asiaticus II. — L. Epidius Titius Aquilinus.
126. M. Annius Verus III. — C. Eggius Ambibulus.
127. M. Gavius Squilla Gallicanus — T. Atilius Rufus Titianus.
128. Torquatus Asprenas II. — M. Annius Libo.
129. P. Iuventius Celsus II. — L. Neratius Marcellus II.
130. Q. Fabius Catullinus — M. Flavius Aper.
131. Ser. Octavius Laenas Pontianus — M. Antonius Rufinus.
132. C. Serius Augurinus — C. Trebius Sergianus.
133. M. Antonius Hiberus — P. Mummius Sisenna.
134. L. Iulius Servianus III. — T. Vibius Varus.
135. L. Tutilius Lupercus Pontianus — P. Calpurnius Atticus Atilianus.
136. L. Ceionius Commodus Verus — S. Vetulenus Civica Pompeianus.
137. L. Aelius Caesar II. — L. Caecilius Balbinus Vibullius Pius.
138. C. Pomponius Camerinus — K. Iunius Niger.
139. Antoninus Aug. II. — C. Bruttius Praesens II.
140. Antoninus Aug. III. — M. Aelius Aurelius Verus Caesar.
141. T. Hoenius Severus — M. Peducaeus Stloga Priscinus.
142. L. Cuspius Rufinus — L. Statius Quadratus.
143. C. Bellicius Torquatus — T. Claudius Atticus Herodes.
144. L. Lollianus Avitus — T. Statilius Maximus.
145. Antonius Aug. IV. — M. Aelius Aurelius Verus Caesar Aug. II.
146. Sex. Erucius Clarus II. — Cn. Claudius Severus Arabianus.

147. L. Annius Largus — C. Prastina Pacatus Messalinus.
148. C. Bellicius Torquatus — P. Salvius Iulianus.
149. Ser. Cornelius Salvidienus Scipio Orfitus — Q. Nonius Sosius Priscus.
150. M. Gavius Squilla Gallicanus — Sex. Carminius Vetus.
151. Sex. Quintilius Condianus — Sex. Quintilius Maximus.
152. M. Acilius Glabrio senior — M. Valerius Homullus.
153. C. Bruttius Praesens — A. Iunius Rufinus.
154. L. Aelius Aurelius Commodus — Titus Sextius Lateranus.
155. C. Iulius Severus — M. Iunius Rufinus Sabinianus.
156. M. Ceionius Silvanus — C. Serius Augurinus.
157. M. Ceionius Civica Barbarus — M. Metilius Aquil. Regulus.
158. Ser. Sulpicius Tertullus — Q. Tineius Sacerdos Clemens.
159. Plautius Quintillus — M. Statius Priscus.
160. Appius Annius Atilius Bradua — T. Clodius Vibius Varus.
161. M. Aelius Aurelius Verus III. — L. Aurelius Commodus II.
162. Q. Iunius Rusticus II — L. Plautius Aquilinus.
163. M. Pontius Laelianus — A. Iunius Pastor.
164. M. Pompeius Macrinus — P. Iuventius Celsus.
165. M. Gavius Orfitus — L. Arrius Pudens.
166. Q. Servilius Pudens — L. Fufidius Pollio.
167. L. Aurelius Verus Aug. III. — M. Ummidius Quadratus.
168. L. Venuleius Apronianus II. — L. Sergius Paulus II.
169. Q. Sosius Priscus Senecio — P. Caelius Apollinaris.
170. M. Cornelius Cethegus — C. Erucius Clarus.
171. T. Statilius Severus — L. Alfidius Herennianus.

A.D.

172. Ser. Calpurnius Scipio Orfitus — Quintilius Maximus.
173. Cn. Claudius Severus II. — Tit. Claudius Pompeianus II.
174. Gallus — Flaccus Cornelianus.
175. L. Calpurnius Piso — Salvius Iulianus.
176. T. Pomponius Proculus Pollio II. — M. Flavius Aper II.
177. L. Aurelius Commodus Aug. — M. Plaut. Quintillus.
178. Orfitus — Rufus Iulianus.
179. L. Aurelius Commodus Aug. II. — P. Martius Verus II.
180. L. Fulvius Praesens II. — Sex. Quintilius Condianus.
181. L. Aurelius Commodus Aug. III. — L. Antistius Burrus Adventus.
182. Petronius Mamertinus — Rufus.
183. Aurelius Commodus Aug. IV. — C. Aufidius Victorinus II.
184. L. Cossonius Eggius Marullus — Cn. Papirius Aelianus.
185. M. Com. Nigrinus Curiatius Maternus — T. Cl. Bradua Atticus.
186. Aurel. Commodus Aug. V. — M. Acilius Glabrio II.
187. L. Bruttius Quintus Crispinus — L. Roscius Aelianus.
188. Seius Fuscianus II. — M. Servilius Silanus II.
189. Duilius Silanus — Q. Servilius Silanus.
190. Aurel. Commodus Aug. VI. — M. Petronius Sura Septimianus.
191. Pedo Apronianus — M. Valerius Bradua Mauricus.
192. Aurel. Commodus Aug. VII. — P. Helvius Pertinax II.
193. Q. Sosius Falco — C. Iulius Erucius Clarus.
194. Septimius Severus Aug. II. — Clodius Septimius Albinus Caes. II.
195. Scapula Tertullus Priscus — Tineius Clemens.

A.D.

196. Domitius Dexter II. — L. Valerius Messalla Thrasea Paetus.
197. T. Sextius Lateranus — L. Cuspius Rufinus.
198. Saturninus — Gallus.
199. Cornelius Anullinus II. — M. Aufidius Fronto.
200. T. Claudius Severus — C. Aufidius Victorinus.
201. L. Annius Fabianus — M. Nonius Arrius Mucianus.
202. Septimius Severus Aug. III. — M. Aurelius Severus Antoninus Pius Aug.
203. Fulvius Plautianus II. — P. Septimius Geta II.
204. M. Fabius Cilo Fulcinianus II. — M. Annius Flavius Libo.
205. M. Aurel. Severus Antoninus Pius Aug. II. — P. Septimius Geta Caesar.
206. M. Nummius Primus Senecio Albinus — Fulvius Aemilianus.
207. Aper — Maximus.
208. M. Aurel. Sev. Antoninus Pius Aug. III. — P. Septimius Geta Caesar II.
209. Pompeianus — Avitus.
210. M. Acilius Faustinus — A. Triarius Rufinus.
211. Gentianus — Bassus.
212. C. Iulius Asper II. — C. Iulius Galerius Asper.
213. M. Aurel. Sev. Antoninus Pius Aug. IV. — D. Caelius Calvinus Balbinus II.
214. L. Valerius Messalla — C. Octavius Appius Suetrius Sabinus.
215. M. Maecius Laetus II. — Sulla Cerialis.
216. P. Catius Sabinus II. — P. Cornelius Anullinus.
217. C. Bruttius Praesens — T. Messius Extricatus II.
218. Macrinus Aug. — Oclatinius Adventus.
219. Imp. Caes. Aurelius Antoninus Pius II. — Q. Tineius Sacerdos II.
220. Imp. Caes. Aurelius Antoninus Pius III. — Valerius Eutychianus Comazon.
221. Vettius Gratus Atticus Sabinianus — M. Flavius Vitellius Seleucus.

A.D.

222. Imp. Caes. Aurelius Antoninus Pius IV. — M. Aurelius Severus Alexander Caesar.
223. Marius Maximus Perpetuus Aurelianus II. — L. Roscius Paculus Papirius Aelianus.
224. App. Claudius Iulianus II.—L. Bruttius Crispinus.
225. Ti. Manilius Fuscus II. — Sex. Calpurnius Domitius Dexter.
226. Imp. Caes. Aurelius Severus Alexander II.— L. Aufidius Marcellus II.
227. M. Nummius Senecio Albinus — M. Laelius Maximus Aemilianus.
228. Modestus II. — Probus.
229. Imp. Caes. Aurelius Severus Alexander III. — Cassius Dio Cocceianus II.
230. L. Virius Agricola — Sex. Catius Clementinus Priscillianus.
231. Claudius Pompeianus — T. Flavius Sallustius Paelignianus.
232. Lupus — Maximus.
233. Maximus II. — Paternus.
234. Maximus II. (*sic*) — Urbanus.
235. Cn. Claudius Severus — L. Ti. Claudius Aurelius Quintianus.
236. Imp. Caesar C. Iulius Verus Maximus — M. Pupienius Africanus.
237. Marius Perpetuus — L. Mummius Felix Cornelianus.
238. Fulvius Pius — Pontius Proculus Pontianus.
239. Imp. Caes. M. Antonius Gordianus — M. Acilius Aviola.
240. Sabinus II. — Venustus.
241. Imp. Caes. M. Antonius Gordianus II. — Pompeianus.
242. C. Vettius Gratus Atticus Sabinianus — C. Asinius Lepidus Praetextatus.
243. L. Annius Arrianus — C. Cervonius Papus.
244. Ti. Pollenius Armenius Peregrinus — Fulvius Aemilianus.
245. Imp. Caes. M. Iulius Philippus — Titianus.

T

A.D.

246. C. Brutius Praesens — Albinus.
247. Imp. Caes. M. Iulius Philippus II. — Imp. Caes. M. Iulius Severus Philippus fil.
248. Imp. Caes. M. Iulius Philippus III. — Imp. Caes. M. Iulius Philippus fil. II.
249. Fulvius Aemilianus II. — L. Naevius Aquilinus.
250. Imp. Caes. C. Messius Quintus Traianus Decius II. — Vettius Gratus.
251. Imp. Caes. C. Messius Quintus Traianus Decius III. — Q. Herennius Etruscus Messius Decius Caesar.
252. Imp. Caes. C. Vibius Trebonianus Gallus II. — Imp. Caes. C. Vibius Afinius Gallus Veldumnianus L. Volusianus.
253. Imp. Caes. C. Vibius Afinius Gallus Veldumnianus L. Volusianus II. — Maximus.
254. Imp. Caes. Licinius Valerianus II. — Imp. Caes. Licinius Egnatius Gallienus.
255. Imp. Caes. Licinius Valerianus III. — Imp. Caes. Licinius Egnatius Gallienus II.
256. L. Valerius Maximus II. — M. Acilius Glabrio.
257. Imp. Caes. Licinius Valerianus IV. — Imp. Caes. Licinius Gallienus III.
258. M. Nummius Tuscus — Pomponius Bassus.
259. Aemilianus — Bassus.
260. P. Cornelius Saecularis II. — C. Iunius Donatus II.
261. Imp. Caes. Licinius Egnatius Gallienus IV. — T. Petronius Taurus Volusianus.
262. Imp. Caes. Licinius Egnatius Gallienus V. — Faustinianus.
263. Albinus II. — Dexter.
264. Imp. Caes. Licinius Egnatius Gallienus VI. — Saturninus.
265. P. Licinius Cornelius Valerianus II. — Lucillus.
266. Imp. Caes. Licinius Egnatius Gallienus VII. — Sabinillus.
267. Paternus — Arcesilaus.
268. Paternus II. — Marinianus.
269. Imp. Caes. M. Aurelius Claudius — Paternus.

A.D.
270. Flavius Antiochianus II. — Virius Orfitus.
271. Imp. Caes. L. Domitius Aurelianus — Pomponius Bassus II.
272. Quietus — Veldumnianus.
273. M. Claudius Tacitus — Placidianus.
274. Imp. Caes. L. Domitius Aurelianus II. — Capitolinus.
275. Imp. Caes. L. Domitius Aurelianus III. — Marcellinus.
276. Imp. Caes. M. Claudius Tacitus II. — Aemilianus.
277. Imp. Caes. M. Aurelius Probus — Paulinus.
278. Imp. Caes. M. Aurelius Probus II. — Virius Lupus.
279. Imp. Caes. M. Aurelius Probus III. — Nonius Paternus II.
280. Messala — Gratus.
281. Imp. Caesar M. Aurelius Probus IV. — C. Iunius Tiberianus I.
282. Imp. Caes. M. Aurelius Probus V. — Victorinus.
283. Imp. Caesar M. Aurelius Carus Pius — Imp. Caes. M. Aurelius Carinus.
284. Imp. Caesar M. Aurelius Carinus II. — Imp. Caes. M. Aurelius Numerianus.
285. Imp. Diocletianus II. — Aurelius Aristobolus.
286. M. Iunius Maximus II. — Vettius Aquilinus.
287. Imp. Caes. Valerius Aurelius Diocletianus III. — Imp. Caes. M. Aurelius Valerius Maximianus Aug.
288. Imp. Caes. M. Aurelius Valerius Maximianus Aug. II. — Pomponius Ianuarinus.
289. M. Magrius Bassus — L. Ragonius Quintianus.
290. Imp. Caes. C. Aurelius Valerius Diocletianus Aug. IV. — Imp. Caes. M. Aurelius Valerius Maximianus Aug. III.
291. C. Iunius Tiberianus II. — Cassius Dio.
292. Afranius Hannibalianus — Asclepiodotus.
293. Imp. Caes. C. Aurelius Valerius Diocletianus Aug. V. — Imp. Caes. M. Aurelius Valerius Maximianus Aug. IV.

A.D.

294. C. Flavius Valerius Constantius Caesar —
Galerius Valerius Maximianus Caesar.

295. Nummius Tuscus — Annius Anullinus.

296. Imp. Caes. C. Aurelius Valerius Diocletianus
Aug. VI. — C. Flavius Valerius Constantius
Caesar II.

297. Imp. Caes. M. Aurelius Valerius Maximianus
Aug. V. — Galerius Valerius Maximianus
Caesar II.

298. Anicius Faustus II. — Virius Gallus.

299. Imp. Caes. C. Aurelius Valerius Diocletianus
Aug. VII. — Imp. Caes. M. Aurelius Valerius
Maximianus Aug. VI.

300. C. Flavius Valerius Constantius Caes. III. —
Galerius Valerius Maximianus Caesar III.

301. T. Flavius Postumius Titianus II. — Popilius
Nepotianus.

302. C. Flavius Valerius Constantius Caesar IV. —
Galerius Valerius Maximianus Caesar IV.

303. Imp. Caes. C. Aurelius Valerius Diocletianus
Aug. VIII. — Imp. Caes. M. Aurelius Valerius
Maximianus Aug. VIII.

304. Imp. Caes. C. Aurelius Valerius Diocletianus
Aug. IX. — Imp. Caes. M. Aurelius Valerius
Maximianus Aug. VIII.

305. C. Flavius Valerius Constantius Caesar V. —
Galerius Valerius Maximianus Caesar V.

306. Imp. Caes. C. Flavius Valerius Constantius Aug.
VI. — Imp. Caes. Galerius Valerius Maximianus
Aug. VI.

307. Imp. Caes. M. Aurelius Valerius Maximianus
Aug. IX. — Flavius Valerius Constantinus nob.
Caesar.

308. Imp. Caes. M. Aurelius Valerius Maxentius Aug.
— M. Valerius Romulus nob. puer.

309. Imp. Caes. M. Aurelius Valerius Maxentius Aug.
II. — M. Valerius Romulus nob. puer II.

310. Imp. Caes. M. Aurelius Valerius Maxentius Aug.
III. — Sicorius Probus.

A.D.
311. Eusebius — C. Ceionius Rufus Volusianus.
312. Imp. Caes. M. Aurelius Valerius Maxentius
Aug. IV.
313. Imp. Caes. Flavius Valerius Constantinus Aug.
III. — Imp. Caes. Galerius Valerius Maximinus
Aug. III.
314. C. Ceionius Rufus Volusianus II. — Petronius
Annianus
315. Imp. Caes. C. Flavius Valerius Constantinus
Aug. IV. — Imp. Caesar P. Valerius Licinianus
Licinius IV.
316. Sabinus — Rufinus.
317. Ovinius Gallicanus — Iunius Bassus.
318. Imp. Caes. Valerius Licinianus Licinius V. —
Flavius Iulius Crispus nob. Caesar.
319. Imp. Caes. C. Flavius Valerius Constantinus
Aug. V. — Valerius Licinianus Licinius nob.
Caesar.
320. Imp. Caes. C. Flavius Valerius Constantinus
Aug. VI. — Flavius Claudius Constantinus
junior nob. Caesar.
321. Flavius Iulius Crispus nob. Caesar II. — Flavius
Claudius Constantinus junior nob. Caesar II.
322. Petronius Probianus — Annius Anicius Iulianus.
323. Acilius Severus — C. Vettius Cossinius Rufinus.
324. Flavius Iulius Crispus nob. Caesar III. — Flavius
Claudius Constantinus junior nob. Caesar III.
325. Sex. Cocceius Anicius Faustus Paulinus II. — P.
Ceionius Iulianus.
326. Imp. Caesar Flavius Valerius Constantinus Aug.
VII. — Flavius Iulius Constantius nob. Caesar.
327. Flavius Caesarius Constantinus — Maximus.
328. Ianuarinus — Iustus.
329. Imp. Caesar Flavius Valerius Constantinus Aug.
VIII. — Flavius Claudius Constantinus junior
nob. Caesar IV.
330. Fl. Gallicanus — Aurelius Tullianus Symmachus.
331. Annius Bassus — Ablabius.
332. Papinius Pacatianus — Maecilius Hilarianus.

A.D.

333 Dalmatius — Zenophilus.
334. Optatus — Anicius Paulinus junior.
335. I. Costantius — Rufius Albinus.
336. Nepotianus — Facundus.
337. Felicianus — T. Fab. Titianus.
338. Ursus — Polemius.
339. Constantius Aug. II. — Constans Aug.
340. Acindinus — Proculus.
341. Marcellinus — Petronius Probinus.
342. Constantius III. — Constans Aug. II.
343. Placidus — Romulus.
344. Fl. Leontius — Fl. Sallustius Bonosus.
345. Amantius — Albinus.
346. Constantius Aug. IV. — Constans Aug. III.
347. Rufinus — Eusebius.
348. Philippus — Sallia.
349. Limenius — Catullinus.
350. Fl. Anicius Sergius — Nigrinianus.
351. Imp. Magnentius — Gaiso.
352. Decentius — Paulus.
353. Constantius Aug. VI. — Constantius II.
354. Constantius Aug. VII. — Constantius III.
355. Fl. Arbitio — Q. Fl. Lollianus Mavortius.
356. Constantius Aug. VIII. — Iulianus Caes.
357. Constantius Aug. IX. — Iulianus II.
358. Datianus — Cerealis.
359. Eusebius — Ypatius.
360. Constantius Aug. X. — Iulianus Caes. III.
361. Fl. Taurus — Fl. Florentius.
362. Cl. Mamertinus — Fl. Nevitta.
363. Iulianus Aug. IV. — Sallustius.
364. Iovianus Aug. — Varronianus.
365. Valentinianus — Valens Aug.
366. Gratianus — Dagalaifus.
367. Fl. Lupicinus — Iovinus.
368. Valentinianus II. — Valens II.
369. Valentinianus (nobilis puer) — Victor.
370. Valentinianus III. — Valens III.
371. Gratianus II. — Probus.

A.D.
372. Fl. Domitius Modestus — Fl. Arynthaeus.
373. Valentinianus IV. — Valens Aug. IV.
374. Gratianus III. — Equitius.
375. P. c. Gratiani III. — Equitii.
376. Valens Aug. V. — Valentinianus junior.
377. Gratianus IV. — Merobaudes.
378. Valens Aug. VI. — Valentinianus junior II.
379. Ausonius — Olybrius.
380. Gratianus V. — Theodosius Aug.
381. Fl. Syagrius — Eucherius.
382. Cl. Antonius — Fl. Syagrius.
383. Merobaudes II. — Saturninus.
384. Ricomeres — Clearchus.
385. Arcadius — Bauto.
386. Fl. Honorius — Euodius.
387. Valentinianus junior III. — Eutropius.
388. Imp. Theodosius II. — Maternus Cynegius *in Roma* Imp. Maximus II.
389. Timasius — Promotus.
390. Valentinianus Aug. IV. — Neoterius.
391. Fl. Tatianus — Q. Aur. Symmachus.
392. Arcadius Aug. — Fl. Rufinus.
393. Theodosius Aug. III. — Eugenius Aug.
394. Nicomachus Flavianus.
    — Arcadius III. — Honorius II.
395. Anicius Olybrius — Probinus.
396. Arcadius Aug. IV. — Honorius Aug. III.
397. Fl. Caesarius — Nonius Atticus Maximus.
398. Honorius IV. — Fl. Eutychianus.
399. Fl. Mallius Theodorus.
400. Fl. Stilicho.
401. Fl. Vincentius — Fravita.
402. Arcadius V. — Honorius Aug. V.
403. Theodosius Aug. — Fl. Rumoridus.
404. Honorius Aug. VI. — Aristaenetus.
405. Fl. Stilicho II. — Anthemius.
406. Arcadius Aug. VI. — Anicius Petronius Probus.
407. Honorius Aug. VII. — Theodosius Aug. II.
408. Anicius Bassus — Fl. Philippus.

A.D.

409. Honorius Aug. VIII. — Theodosius Aug. III.
410. Tertullus — Varanes.
411. Fl. Theodosius Aug. IV.
412. Honorius Aug. IX. — Theodosius V.
413. Heraclianus — Lucius.
414. Fl. Constantius — Constano.
415. Honorius X. — Theodosius VI.
416. Theodosius VII. — Iunius Quartus Palladius.
417. Honorius XI. — Constantius II.
418. Honorius XII. — Theodosius VIII.
419. Monaxius — Plinta.
420. Theodosius IX. — Constantius III.
421. Eustathius — Agricola.
422. Honorius XIII. — Theodosius X.
423. Fl. Avitus Marinianus — Asclepiodotus.
424. Fl. Castinus — Victor.
425. Theodosius XI. — Valentinianus Aug.
426. Theodosius XII. — Valentinianus Aug. II.
427. Hierius — Artabures.
428. Flav. Felix — Tauro.
429. Florentius—Dionysius.
430. Theodosius XIII. — Placidus Valentinianus Aug. III.
431. Anicius Bassus — Antiochus.
432. Aetius — Valerius.
433. Theodosius Aug. XIV. — Petronius Maximus.
434. Fl. Aspares — Ariavindus.
435. Theodosius XV. — Valentinianus Aug. IV.
436. Fl. Senator — Isidorus.
437. Fl. Aetius — Sigisvultus.
438. Theodosius XVI. — Anicius Acilius Glabrio Faustus.
439. Theodosius XVII. — Festus.
440. Valentinianus V. — Anatolius.
441. P. c. Valentiniani V. — Anatolii — Constantius Cyrus (in Oriente).
442. Dioscorus — Eudoxius.
443. Petronius Maximus II. — Paterius.
444. Theodosius Aug. XVIII. — Albinus.

A.D.
445. Valentinianus VI. — Nomus.
446. Aetius III.— Symmachus.
447. Calepius — Ardabur.
448. Rufus Praetextatus Postumianus — Fl. Zeno.
449. Asturius — Protogenes.
450. Valentinianus VII. — Avienus.
451. Adelfius — Marcianus Aug.
452. Fl. Bassus Herculanus — Sporacius.
453. Opilio — Vincomalus.
454. Aetius — Studius.
455. Valentinianus VIII. — Anthemius.
456. Ioannes —Varanes.
— Eparchius Avitus.
457. Fl. Constantinus — Rufus.
458. Maiorianus Aug. — Imp. Leo.
459. Ricimeres — Patricius.
460. Magnus — Apollonius.
461. Severinus — Dagalaiphus.
462. Leo Aug. II. — Severus Aug.
463. Fl. Basilius — Vivianus.
464. Rusticus — Olybrius.
465. Herminericus — Basiliscus.
466. Leo Aug. III. — Tatianus.
467. Puseus — Ioannes.
468. Anthemius Aug. II.
469. Marcianus — Zeno.
470. Severus — Iordanes.
471. Leo Aug. IV. — Probianus.
472. Festus — Marcianus.
473. Leo Aug. V.
474. Leo junior Aug.
475. Fl. Zeno Aug. II.
476. Basiliscus Aug. II. — Armatus.
477. P. c. Basilisci II. et Armati.
478. Illus.
479. Zeno Aug. III.
480. Fl. Basilius junior.
481. Rufius Placidus.
482. Severinus — Trocondus.

A.D.

483. Anicius Acilius Aginatius Faustus.
484. Venantius — Theodoricus.
485. Q. Aur. Memmius Symmachus.
486. Caecina Mavortius — Longinus.
487. Boethius.
488. Dynamius — Syfidius.
489. Petronius Probinus — Eusebius.
490. Fl. Probus Faustus junior — Longinus II.
491. Fl. Olybrius junior.
492. Anastasius Aug. — Rufus.
493. Albinus — Eusebius II.
494. Fl. Asterius — Praesidius.
495. Viator.
496. Paulus.
497. Anastasius Aug. II.
498. Paulinus — Iohannes (Scytha).
499. Iohannes (Gibbus).
500. Patricius — Hypatius.
501. Avienus — Pompeius.
502. Fl. Avienus junior — Probus.
503. Volusianus — Dexicrates.
504. Nicomachus Cethegus.
505. Fl. Theodorus — Sabinianus.
506. Fl. Messala — Dagalaifus.
507. Venantius — Anastasius III.
508. D. Marius Venantius Basilius — Celer.
509. Importunus.
510. Manlius Anicius Severinus Boethius.
511. Fl. Felix — Secundinus.
512. Paulus — Muschianus — post consul. Felicis.
513. Probus — Taurus Armonius.
514. Senator.
515. Fl. Florentius — Anthemius.
516. Fl. Petro.
517. Agapitus — Anastasius Paulus Probus.
518. Anastasius Paulus Probus — Moschianus Probus Magnus.
519. Fl. Eutharicus Cillica — Iustinus Aug.
520. Rusticius — Vitalianus.

A.D.
521. Valerius — Iustinianus.
522. Symmachus — Boethius.
523. Fl. Maximus.
524. Opilio — Iustinus Aug. II.
525. Probus junior — Philoxenus.
526. Fl. Anicius Olybrius.
527. Fl. Vettius Agorius Basilius Mavortius.
528. Fl. Iustinianus Aug. II.
529. Fl. Decius junior.
530. Lampadius — Orestes.
531. Post consul. Lampadii et Orestis.
532. Iterum p. c. Lampadii et Orestis.
533. Fl. Iustinianus Aug. III.
534. Fl. Dec. Paulinus jun. — Iustinianus Aug. IV.
535. P. c. Paulini junioris — Fl. Belisarius.
536. P. c. Belisarii.
537. P. c. Belisarii.
538. Iohannes.
539. Fl. Appion.
540. Fl. Iustinus.
541. Fl. Anicius Faustus Albinus Basilius.

This Basilius was the last regular consul in a private position. After A.D. 541 the consular date was expressed by *post consulatum Basilii* for 44 years, *i.e.* to A.D. 585, alternately with *post consulatum Justini Aug.*, and the latter was then continued in some records up to the 72nd year, A.D. 612. After that date all mention of consuls ceases.

In some ancient Christian inscriptions reference is made to the Easter festival, and also to lunations, both of which are matters connected with the Calendar. It will be as well, therefore, to give here some information on the subject of the Calendar.

§ 2

The Calendar

The astronomical or sidereal day is the interval of time between two successive transits of any star over the same meridian in the same hemisphere, and its length is 24 hours; the solar day is the interval of time between two transits of the sun over the meridian, amounting to 24 hours 3′ 56″. The sidereal year is the period of time at the end of which the earth returns to the same point in its orbit; the tropical or equinoctial year, again, is that between one spring equinox and the next, and is 365 days 5 hours 48′ 51″ in length; the sidereal year is a trifle longer, viz. 365 days 6 hours 8½′. The tropical year is the one accepted as the legal year, because it involves the periodical recurrence at identical intervals of time of the same phenomena, constituting the succession of the seasons. The ancients had only an approximate idea of the length of the tropical year; thus in the days of Romulus they made it only 304 days, which they divided into 10 months, beginning with March. According to tradition, Numa Pompilius, knowing that the measurement of the year was incorrect, added the two months of January and February; thus the year came to have 12 months, or 12 lunations, covering 355 days; some of the months contained 31 days, others 29, and others, again, 28. But there was still a deficiency of some 11 days between this and the true year, and that difference grew to 22 days in 2 years. It was therefore determined to insert an additional month of 22 days between the 23rd and 24th of February in every other year : this was called the *Mercedonian* month, and the duty of carrying out the intercalation was entrusted to the pontifices, who often lengthened or shortened the year without due reason. Matters remained thus up to the days of Julius Caesar, by which time the correct length of the year had been very nearly ascertained, and determined at 365 days 6 hours. Then the dictator, principally by the advice of Sosigenes, a celebrated astronomer of the school of Alexandria, undertook the task of regulating the Calendar, which had up to that time been in an uncertain condition : he ordained that the ordinary year should consist of 365 days, and in order to allow for the yearly defect of 6 hours, amounting in 4 years to the error of a whole day, he directed that every fourth or intercalary year should have 366 days ; and he inserted the supplementary day in the same place in the Calendar as the old *Mercedonian* month, *i.e.* between the 23rd and 24th of February. Now February 23rd was called " VII. Kalendas Martias," and the additional day would therefore be " VI. Kalendas," and the 24th would then be " bis VI. Kalendas," whence the year took its name of bissextile. Thus while Julius Caesar added some days to Numa's year, he retained his twelve months, only lengthening all of them, except February, in which for religious reasons he made no change. But even this intercalation does not bring the year into exact correspondence with the motion of the sun. Julius Caesar assumed the length of the year to be 365 days 6 hours, whereas its true length is 365 days 5 hours 48' 51.6" ; so that on his system it was still 11′ 8.4″ too long. This error meant that at the end of the civil year the actual year had been completed 11′ 8.4″ earlier; and hence after the lapse of 100 civil years, there had been an actual lapse of 100 years and a little more than 18 hours; and this deficiency when accumulated through many years made a serious alteration in the date of the annual recurrence of certain phenomena.

The Council of Nice, which met in A.D. 325, assumed, for the determination of the date of the Easter festival, that as the spring equinox had occurred in that year on March 21st, so it would always return on that day; whereas the above-named error of 11′ 8.4″ caused each equinox to fall 11′ 8.4″ earlier than in the previous year; and after the lapse of 1356 years, *i.e.* about the end of the sixteenth century, it made the equinox fall 10 days earlier; so that while the Calendar continued to describe it as occurring on March 21st, it had actually taken place on the 11th. It was obvious that a reform was required to regulate the Calendar and reorganise it on exacter data; and this reform was duly carried out by the most famous astronomers of the day, with Lilius and Clavius at their head, and under the patronage of Gregory XIII., from whom it derived the name of Gregorian. It was effected by adding the ten days' arrears which had accrued through the mistake as to the true length of the year, and thus making March 21st again coincide with the spring equinox; and it was carried out by a papal brief ordaining that the morrow of October 4th, 1582, should be called the 15th instead of the 5th. But the correction, though it remedied the past mischief caused by the Julian Calendar, did nothing to prevent its future recurrence, as the few minutes' difference between the Julian and the true year would still exist; a difference which in 400 years amounts to three days, *i.e.* three days more than actually occur in that period. It was therefore determined that in every 100 of the bissextile years which, according to the Julian system, would occur in 400 years, three should be cancelled, and this was done as follows: the "century" years, such as 1400, 1500, 1600, being all bissextile in the Julian Calendar because exactly divisible by 4, it was ordered that, for the future, of every four consecutive "century" years, one only should be of 366 days, and that it should be that one of the four the number of whose hundreds was exactly divisible by 4. By this method, known as the Gregorian reform, such a degree of exactness can be reached, that the spring equinox will be only one day too early 4000 years hence; an error which those then living may be left to deal with.

We may now pass to other matters closely connected with the Calendar. The solar cycle is a period of 28 years, after which time relations are restored to identically the same order as at its beginning; and the days of the month fall on the same days of the week. The starting-point of the solar cycle is assigned to B.C. 9, or, in other words, A.D. 1 was the tenth in the current solar cycle. So to find the place occupied in a solar cycle by any given year, all that is needed is to add 9 to the year and divide by 28; the quotient gives the number of completed cycles, and the remainder the place in the then current cycle. The solar cycle is used to find the day of the week, which is done by what is known as the Dominical or

Sunday letter. For this purpose every day in the year is distinguished by one of the first seven letters of the alphabet, from A to G, the first day being marked A, the second B, and so on up to the seventh; the eighth is again marked A, the 9th B, etc.; so that, as the year contains 52 weeks and 1 day, if the first day be marked A the last day will bear the same letter. Furthermore, during the whole year the same letter corresponds to the same day of the week; and the letter which corresponds to the Sundays is called the Sunday letter. Given the Sunday letter of a year, one may calculate on what day of the week the year began; *e.g.* if the Sunday letter be known to be A, the year will have begun with a Sunday; if B, with a Saturday, etc.; and this being known it is easy to calculate on what day of the week any given day of a month falls. But if the Sunday letter is not known, it can be discovered by a very simple calculation.

There is another very important astronomical period, viz. the lunar cycle of Meto, also called the cycle of the Golden Number. That astronomer, who lived about 430 B.C., observed that every 19 years the same phases of the moon recurred on the same day, and nearly at the same hour of the day, a fact depending on the retrograde motion of the lunar nodes, which take 19 years to return to the same position. This lunar or Metonic cycle was then introduced, and its superiority to all others in accuracy eventually brought it into universal use; it was called the cycle of the Golden Number, because, after having been lost and found again, it was carved in letters of gold in the Agora of Athens. This Golden Number denotes the place occupied by the year in the lunar cycle of Meto; *i.e.* if it was the 1st, 2nd, or 3rd in the cycle, it would have for Golden Number 1, 2, or 3, up to 19, after which there is a return to 1. It has been calculated that this cycle started in the year preceding A.D. 1, so that A.D. 1 had the Golden Number 2; and thus, if you wish to find the Golden Number of any given year, add 1 to the number of the year and divide by 19; the quotient gives the number of completed cycles, and the remainder is the Golden Number of the year.

By "lunar" year is meant a period of 12 re-currences of the new moon, or 12 lunations, *i.e.* the number of completed lunations in a solar year. As an average or mean lunation contains $29\frac{1}{2}$ days, the lunar year consists of 354 days, or 11 days less than an ordinary solar year, and 12 less than a bissextile. In fact, however, the *mean* lunation of $29\frac{1}{2}$ days is 44′ and a fraction shorter than the true lunation; and this error, multiplied by 12, amounts to a loss of $8\frac{3}{4}$ hours in the full lunar year, or of about 7 days in the 19 lunar years of the complete cycle of Meto. To make up for this loss, the number of the days is altered in 7 lunations in the course of the cycle of 19 years, six being in-creased by about a half-day from $29\frac{1}{2}$ days to 30, and one diminished by about a half-day to 29. (The lunations so altered are technically called embolismic.) To understand how this alteration corrects the above-mentioned loss of 7 days, it must be noted that an embolismic lunation of 30 days is longer than a true lunation by 11 hours and a fraction, giving for the six 30-day lunations an excess of $67\frac{1}{2}$ hours—call it 2 days 20 hours—and for the one lunation of 29 days a defect of $12\frac{3}{4}$ hours,

U

making a net gain on this account of $54\frac{3}{4}$ hours, or 2 days $6\frac{3}{4}$ hours. We have now to take into account the bissextile or leap years, of which there are about 5 in a cycle of 19 years; add 5 days on their account to the 2 days $6\frac{3}{4}$ hours previously arrived at, and we get a total net gain of, say, $7\frac{1}{4}$ days, which about compensates for the loss of 7 days which we found to exist owing to the difference between the true and the mean lunations.

The difference of 11 days between the solar and lunar years is kept constant by the addition of an intercalary day into the February lunation in a bissextile year. Now let us take for the first year of a cycle one in which a new moon falls on January 1st: the lunar year of 354 days being shorter than the solar by 11 days, the new moons will fall 11 days earlier in the following year; or to put it in another way, the last new moon of that year will fall on its 354th day, *i.e.* December 20th, and the moon will be 11 days old on the next January 1st; this age of the moon on January 1st is what is called the *epact*; and the 2nd year of the cycle will have the Epact XI., while the first year will have the Epact O. Then in the 3rd year of the cycle the new moons will again be 11 days earlier than in the 2nd, or 22 days earlier than in the first; therefore the Epact will be XXII. In the 4th the new moons will be 33 days earlier; but, as 30 days go to a lunation, the moon will be 3 days old on January 1st, and the Epact of the 4th year will be III. If the Golden Number of a year be known, its Epact can be found by multiplying the Golden Number minus 1 by 11, and dividing by 30; the remainder will be the Epact. Indeed, given any particular year, if it be required to express in terms of lunar years the fraction of a lunar cycle which has elapsed before it, it can be done thus: take 11 for each of the previous solar years of the cycle, or—more simply—multiply 11 by the Golden Number of the preceding year, divide the product by 30; the quotient will give us the number of the lunar years, and the remainder that of the day of the lunation coinciding with January 1st of the year in question, which is, in fact, the Epact. But care must be taken when dealing with a year antecedent to the Gregorian reform, to allow for the days deducted by virtue of that reform.

By the use of the Epact it is easy to find the new moons of a year : for this purpose the Epact of the year must be subtracted from the number of days in the lunation of the month whose new moon it is sought to ascertain, remembering that if the year begins with an incomplete lunation, that lunation always contains 30 days, and that the first lunation that falls entirely within the year is always of 29 days (unless the Epact is O or higher than XXIV., in which case such first lunation is of 30 days) ; after this the lunations are alternately of 29 and 30 days. There are some further small errors, which are corrected by adding 1 to the Epact at the beginning of a century when necessary.

The Council of Nice, which met a few years after the famous Edict of Milan, by which the Emperor Constantine officially recognised the Church, besides providing for other very material matters, thought it desirable to regulate also the date of the celebration of Easter, on which matter there had been some want of agreement among the Churches; and it was decreed that Easter should for the future always be celebrated on the Sunday immediately following the full moon occurring on or after March 21st. In order, then, to find Easter in any year the date of the March full moon must be found; if that occurs on or after the 21st, it will be the Easter full moon, and the following Sunday will be Easter; if it falls before the 21st, the next full moon must be found, and on the Sunday after that Easter will be celebrated.

Easter may therefore be ascertained for any year, past or future, by means of the materials we have described under the present heading; *i.e.* by finding the Sunday letter, the Golden Number, and the Epact in the way we have explained. And this method may easily be applied to verify the correctness of the inscriptions in which the festival of Easter is mentioned.

§ 3

Some Specimens of " Consular " Inscriptions

The completest series of Roman consular inscriptions is that given by De Rossi in vol. i. of *Inscriptiones christianae*, which includes those known up to 1861. Others were published by him in the *Bullettino di archeologia cristiana*, and by his successors in the *Nuovo Bullettino*. The sequel of the series with the above-mentioned and other additions will shortly appear, published by Comm. Giuseppe Gatti in vol. ii. of the *Inscriptiones*.

Here we propose to give only a small number as specimens; others may easily be found in the above-mentioned volume of De Rossi.

314

```
.... VESPASIANO · III · COS
```

Lateran Museum (A.D. 71). (Table XIX. 1.)

According to De Rossi this is the only Christian inscription as yet known which bears a consular date of the first century.[1]

315

.... *an*N · XXX · SVRA · ET · SENEC · COSS

(A.D. 107.)

Sura et Senecione consulibus.

316

SERVILIA · ANNORVM · XIII

PIS · ET · BOL · COSS

(A.D. 111.)

Pisone et Bolano consulibus.

The two preceding were transcribed by Boldetti, who states that they were "graffiti" on mortar in the cemetery of Lucina near the Via Ostiensis; but they have never been seen since. De Rossi considered them to be genuine and printed them as such.[2] There is now, however, some suspicion that they were incorrectly transcribed by Boldetti; but the point has not been yet cleared up. In any case, no other Christian consular inscription of the second century is known.

In the third century occasional Christian consular inscriptions begin to appear, but they do not

[1] De Rossi, *Inscr. christ.* i. No. 1.
[2] *Ibid.* i. Nos. 2, 3.

become frequent till later. One of the oldest appears to be one accepted as Christian by De Rossi, and quoted above, p. 225, with the date A.D. 217. We will go on to mention next a few others of the third century, and then some of a later date.

317

KΩϹΟΥΛΕ · ΚΛΥΔΙΩ
ΕΔ · ΠΑΤΕΡΝΩ · ΝΟΝΕΙϹ
ΝΟΒΕΝΒΡΕΙΒΟΥϹ · ΔΕΙ · Ε · ΒΕΝΕΡΕϹ ·
[ΛΟΥΝΑ · ΧΧΙΙΙΙ
ΛΕΥΚΕ · ΦΙΛΙΕ · ϹΗΒΗΡΕ · ΚΑΡΕϹϹΕΜΕ ·
[ΠΟϹΟΥΕΤΕ
ΕΔ · ΕΙϹΠΕΙΡΙΤΩ · ϹΑΝΚΤΩ · ΤΟΥΩ
· · · · · · · · · · · · · · · · · · · ·

Consule Claudio et Paterno nonis nobenbribus die Veneris Luna XXIIII. Leuca filiae Severae carissimae posuit et ispirito sancto tuo[1] . . .

A cemetery on the Via Salaria (A.D. 269).
Lateran Museum.

This Latin inscription, incorrectly transcribed in Greek characters, is remarkable for its date of 269, and for the further mention of the days of the month and of the week, and of the age of the moon.

[1] A postscript in smaller character states that she died at the age of about six years.

318

CVMCVMVIXIT · SEVERA · SELEVCI
ANE · CVM · AVRELIO · SABVTIO · ANNIS
DECE · ET · SEPTE · IMP · PROBO · AVG · III · ET · NONIO
PATERNO · BIS · CONS · QVOT · VIXIT · IN · SECVLO
ANNIS · TRIGINTA · ET · DVO · ET · MENSES · DVO · IMP
CLAVDIO · AVG · ET · PATERNO · CONSS

Museum of the Capitol (A.D. 269-276). (Plate XIX. 2.)

The next belongs to the time of Diocletian :

319

VIBIVS · FIMVS · R · KAL · SEP
DIC · IIII · ET · MAX · COS

Vibius Fimus recessit kalendis Septembris Diocle-tiano IIII. et Maximiano consulibus.

Cemetery of Callisto (A.D. 290).

320

CATILIAE · IN · PACE · FILIAE
DVLCISSIME · INGENV
A · MATER · FECIT · D ·
P · VIIII · K · IVL · DIO
CLETIANO · III · ET · MAXI
MIANO · II ·

Cemetery of S. Hippolytus (A.D. 290).   Lateran Museum.
(Plate XIX. 3.)[1]

---

[1] Here we have an instance of a consular date incorrectly stated (see De Rossi, *Inscr. christ.* i. pp. 22-23). [Cp. *Fasti consulares*, p. 275 *sup.*—TR.]

321

```
: ⊠ < TIBERIANO ET DI
: — ⋜ ONE CONSS qVIN
: ∽ ⋗ TV KAL DEC . . . . NTONI
: ○ ·
: ⌷ ·              . . . . ESIT
```

Cemetery of S. Agnese.   Lateran Museum.   (Plate XIX. 4.)

322

IVLIA EVSTOCHIA . . .
ET CAESIO LEONTIO . . .
BENEMERENTI DEP . . .
FAVSTO ET GALLO . . .

Lateran Museum (A.D. 298).

323

. . . . STAB · DVLCIS
*anima pi*E · SESES (*zeses*)
dep . . . . DECEM · POST · VI

Cemetery of SS. Peter and Marcellinus (A.D. 307 [? 306.—Tr.]).
Lateran Museum.   (Plate XIX. 5.)

Notable for the indicative *post sextum consulatum*,
which suggests the age of Maxentius (see above;
cp. De Rossi, *Inscr. christ.* i. p. 30).

324

> . . . . . *accer*
> *situs ab* ANGELIS QVI VI
> *xit* ANN XXII MESIS VIIII
> DIEB VIII IN PACE DEP IDI
> BVS DEC MAXENT III COS

Lateran Museum (A.D. 310).

After the peace of Constantine in 313 Christian inscriptions bearing consular dates become very common and may be counted by the hundred.

Here are some specimens of the fourth and fifth centuries, selected from those which give any special or remarkable indications as to date :

325

> ASELLVS · ET · LEA · PRISCO · PATRI · BENE
> MERENTI · IN · PACE |
> QVI · BIXIT · ANNIS · LXIIII · MENSIBVS · III
> ☧ IN · SIGNO ☧ DIES · N · XII
> V · K · OCT · D · BASSO · ET · ABLAVIO
> CONSS

Cemetery of S. Agnese (A.D. 331). Lateran Museum.

Observe in the last line but one the expression *in signo Christi*, evidently alluding to the name of Christ placed on the standard of Constantine, the memory of which was still fresh in men's minds.

326

CVBICVLVM · AVRELIAE · MARTINAE · CASTISSIMAE
ATQVE · PVDI | CISSIMAE · FEMINAE · QVE · FECIT
IN · CONIVGIO · ANN · XXIII · D · XIIII | BENEMERENTI
QVE · VIXIT · ANN · XL · M · XI · D · XIII · DEPOSITIO
EIVS | DIE · III · NONAS · OCT · NEPOTIANO · ET
FACVNDO · CONSS · IN · PACE

Lateran Museum (A.D. 336).   (Plate XX. 1.)

327

FL · BALBILLA · VIXIT · ANN · XXVIII
MENS · VII · D · XII · REQVIEVIT · IN · PACE
MAMERTINO · ET · NEBIDDA · COSS · PREF · VRB
MAXIMO · V · KAL · FEBR

Cemetery of Callisto (A.D. 362).

Remarkable as being a hitherto unique instance
of the use of the name of the prefect of Rome to
give the date : *praefecto urbis Maximo.* This tablet
is also important in connexion with the topography
of that portion of the cemetery to which it belongs.
It was discovered in a burial-chamber of the cemetery of Callisto, which has lately been very arbitrarily identified as the tomb of Pope Damasus,
an idea which I have shown to be utterly without
foundation.

328

```
HIC · IACET · NOMINE · MATRONA · C · F · IN · PACE
VXOR · CORNELI · PRIMICERI · CENARIORVM
FILIA · PORFORI · PRIMICERI · MONETARIO
RVM  QVE · VIXIT · ANN · P · M · XXIII · QVE · RECESSIT
DIE · MERCVRIS · ORA · VIII · ET · DEPOSITA · DIE
IOVIS · IDVVM · MAIARVM · INCONTRA
COLOMNA · VII · CONS · FL · HERCVLANI · VC
```

Monastery of S. Paolo (A.D. 452).   (Plate XX. 2.)

Noticeable for the offices recorded; also for the statement that this lady's tomb lay close to the seventh column of the basilica of S. Paul.

329

```
HIC · QVIISCIT · ROMANVS · PBB
QVI · SEDIT · PBB · ANN · XXVII · M · X
DEP · X · KAL · AVGVS
CONS · SEVERINI · V · CL

+
```

Cemetery of SS. Peter and Marcellinus (A.D. 461).
Lateran Museum.   (Plate XX. 3.)

The expression *qui sedit presbyter* is noticeable.

330

```
. . . . . ARIA · IN · PACE
que vixit anNVS · III · MENS · IIII
. . . . . (k)AL · SEP · CON · DMN
Basilisci et ARMATI · VV · CC
```

Cemetery of S. Valentinus in Rome (A.D. 476).

The consulship of Basiliscus and Armatus denote the year 476, in which Odoacer extinguished the Western empire.

Consuls continued to be named after the fall of the empire, under the rule of the barbarians, and later under Byzantine dominion, as we have already said, up to Basilius, who was the last private person to be invested with the consular dignity before its abolition by the Emperor Justinian. The habit continued for some years of dating inscriptions *post consulatum Basilii.* Here is one of the latest instances, which gives the year as the sixteenth after that consulship :

331

+ HIC REQVIESCIT IN PACE IVLIANVS $\overline{ARGT}$
QVI VISIT | ANNVS PLVS MINVS XLV DE-
POSITVS EST SVB D XVII $\overline{KAL}$ | NOBEMBRIS
$\overline{P}$ $\overline{C}$ BASILI $\overline{V}$ $\overline{C}$ ANNO XVI

Basilica of S. Agnese (A.D. 557).

Lateran Museum.   (Plate XX. 4.)

After the abolition of the consular dignity, we find dates indicated by the years of the emperor's reign ; as, for instance, in the last lines of the epitaph on Boethius, the son of the notary Eugenius :

332

```
+   DEP · EST · BOETIVS · CL · P · OCT · KAL · NOBR
    INDICT · XI · I͞M͞P | DOM · N · IVSTINO · PP · AVG
    ANN · XII · ET · TIBERIO · CONST · CAER | ANN · III
    DEP · EST · IN · PACE · ARGENTEA · MAT · S͞S · XIII
    KAL · DE͞C͞E͞MB | QVI · SS · BOETIVS · VIXIT · ANN · XI
    M · VIIII · D · XXIII · S · ET · MAT · EIVS · VIXIT · ANN
    XXXII · M · II · D · XIII
```

Rome.   Church of S. Angelo in Borgo (A.D. 578).
(Plate XXI. 1, 2.)

At the end of the present group of inscriptions we shall give some (though of an earlier date) which record the date by the name of the Pope. But it must be noted that such a practice is extremely rare.

333

```
SVB · IVLIO · Antistite . . . . . . . .
DRO · FOSSORE . . . . . . . .¹
        PERCVSS . . . . .
```

Cemetery of Callisto.

It mentions the pontificate of Julius I. (A.D. 337-352).

334

```
deFVNCTA EST EVPLIA QVAR
to idVS MAIAS QVE FVIT ANNORV
quinQVE DEPOSITA IN PACE SVB LIBE
RIO PAPA
```

Cemetery of Callisto.   Lateran Museum.   (Plate XXII. 1.)

The pontificate of Liberius was A.D. 352-366.

¹ . . . *comparavit ab Alexandro fossore* . . .

335

.... A CVMPARAVIT

.... ONVS SE BIBO

*sedent*E PAPA LIBERIO

Cemetery of Cyriaca.

336

ERENI QVE VIXIT ANN

PM XLV CVM CVPARE

SVO FECIT ANNVS VIII

QVE RECESSIT III NON IN

PACE SVB DAMASO EPISCO*po*

Lateran Museum (A.D. 366-384). (Plate XXII. 2.)

This records the pontificate of Damasus (A.D. 366-384), a period of great importance, as immediately preceding the final triumph of Christianity under Theodosius. Note that the deceased was called Irene, like the sister of Damasus.

337

SALBO · PAPA · N · IOHANNE · COGNOMEN
TO · MERCVRIO · EX · SCE · ECCL · ROM · PRESBYTE
RIS · ORDINATO · EX · TIT · SCI · CLEMENTIS · AD · GLO
RIAM · PONTIFICALEM · PROMOTO · BEATO · PETRO
AP · PATRONO · SVO · A · VINCVLIS · EIVS · SEVERS · PB
OPFERT | ET · IT · PC · LAMPADI · ET · ORESTIS · VV · CC
VRBI+CLVS · CEDRINVS · EST

Church of S. Pietro in Vincoli (A.D. 533). (Plate XXII. 3.)

A votive inscription which combines the indication of the date by the pontificate of John II. (*salvo papa Johanne*) with that by *post consulatum Lampadi et Orestis* (A.D. 533).

In the sixth century they began in some places to indicate the year by means of the names of the barbarian kings:

338

```
IN HOC TVM
OLO REQVIESCIT
IN PACE BONE
MEMORIAE IVLIA
NETA TRASIIT IN
ANNOS XXXXV
ANNO NONO X REG DOMNI
NOSTRI ALARICI
```

(A.D. 503.)

(Le Blant, *Inscriptions chrét. de la Gaule*, No. 569.)

So in Rome in the first half of the sixth century the name of King Theodoric is often given to indicate a date; and is often used as a stamp on bricks, thus:

REGNANTE · D · N · THEODORICO

FELIX · ROMA

After the sixth century the emperors alone are named; and finally in Rome the custom is started of recording only the names of the Popes.

The Christian era was never used in old Christian inscriptions; it does not begin to appear in inscriptions before the seventh century, as has been already stated.

We may add here a few inscriptions which bear some peculiar indications of date, as, for instance, the age of the moon, the sign of the zodiac, or sometimes the Easter festival:

339

```
PVER · NATVS
DIVO · IOVIANO · AVG · ET
VARRONIANO · COS (A.D. 364)
ORA · NOCTIS · IIII
IN(l)VXIT¹ VIII · IDVS · MAIAS
DIE · SATVRNIS · LVNA · VICESIMA
SIGNO · CAPIORNONOM² SIMP(li)CIVS
```

Cemetery of Giordano on the Via Latina.
(Boldetti, *Osservazioni*, p. 84.)

This inscription records the birth of the boy in 364, on Saturday, May 8th, when the moon was in the sign of Capricorn.

The next marks only the season (winter) and perhaps the days of the winter solstice:

340

```
PATER · FILIO · SILBINIANO
BENEMERENTI · IN · PACE
QVI · ABET · DEPOSSIONE · BRVMIS
```

Cemetery of Cyriaca.

¹ *Inluxit (dies natalis ejus)*, etc.

² *Signo capricorni.* Another inscription referring to Capricorn was published by me, together with others, from the cemetery of Commodilla in *Nuovo Bull.* Nos. 1-4 of 1904.

341

```
AVRELIVS · MELITIVS
INFANS · CRISTAEANVS
FIDELIS · PEREGRINVS · HIC
POSITVS · EST · QVI · VIXIT
ANNIS · IIII · DIES · DVO · QVI
DEFVNCTVS · EST · DIAE
SATVRNI · PASCAE · NOCTIS
IPSIVS · PERVIGILATIO · ORA
TIONE · QVINTA · VITA · PRIVATVS
EST · ET · SEPVLTVS · DIAE · SOLIS
      VI · KAL · APRIL · PP . . . . .
```

Cemetery of S. Mustiola in Chiusi.

The boy Aurelius Melitius died in the night of Easter Eve, in the fifth hour of that vigil, and was buried on Easter Sunday, March 27th. The year is omitted, but may be recovered by calculation from the date of Easter.

342

```
(hic) IACET · DECORA
MERCVRINA · QVAE
VIXIT · ANNOS · XX
OVIIT · XIII · KAL · MA
IAS · VIGELIA · PASCE
CALIPIO · V̅C̅ · CONS
```

Lyons in France (A.D. 447).

(Le Blant, *Inscr. chrét. de la Gaule*, No. 35.)

In the year 447, given in this inscription, Easter fell on April 20th, and *XIII. Kal. Maias* or April 19th was actually Easter Eve.

X

343

*in hoc se*PVLCRO · REQVIESCET · PVELLA · VIRGO
SACRA · B · M · ALEXA*ndra* | QVAE · RECEPTA
COELO · MERVIT · OCCVRRERE · $\overline{\text{XPO}}$ · AD · RESVR-
RECT*ionem* | *praemium aet*ERNVM · SVSCIPERE
DIGNA · HAEC · DEP · VII · KAL · AP(*rilis*) | *die*
*Sabba*TI · VIGILIAS · SACRAS · CONS · FL · ASTVRIO
V · C · CON(*sule*)

In the choir of the church of S. Prassede in Rome (A.D. 449).

The holy virgin Alexandra was buried on March 26th, 449, which was Easter Eve in that year; hence she is said to have been buried on the specially holy Vigil, *i.e.* the Vigil of Easter. Note also the beautiful statement that she was received in Heaven, and held worthy of appearing in the presence of Christ.

It would be easy to add further specimens, but those I have given are sufficient as samples of the more unusual expressions.

CHAPTER VII

INSCRIPTIONS SELECTED FOR CERTAIN SPECIAL EXPRESSIONS [1]

Ejaculations—Language bearing on the Conception of a Future Life

344

```
ΑΥΡΕΛΙΟϹ · ΘΕΟΔΟΥΛΟϹ
ΚΑΙ · ΚΕΚΙΛΙΑ · ΜΑΡΙΑ · ϹΥΜΒΙΟϹ
ΑΥΤΟΥ · ΖΩΝΤΕϹ · ΕΠΟΙΗϹΑΝ · Ε
ΑΥΤΟΙϹ · ΚΑΙ · ΤΟΙϹ · ΤΕΚΝΟΙϹ · ΑΥ
ΤΟΥ · ΟΥΡΒΙΚΟ · ΚΕ · ΒΟΝΙΦΑΤΙΕ
ΕΖΗϹΗΝ · ΔΕ · ΘΕΟΔΟΥΛΟϹ · ΕΤΗ
Ο · Β · ΚΑΤΑΚΕΙΤΕ ☧ Ζ · ΚΑΛ ·
ΝΟΕΝΒΡΙΩΝ · ΕΙϹ · ΑΓΑΠΗΝ
```

Cemetery of Callisto.

The inscription states that Aurelius Theodulus and Cecilia Maria his wife made a tomb for themselves and their children.

Observe the ejaculation in the last line EIϹ · ΑΓΑΠΗΝ, the hope that the deceased may be admitted to the mystical love feast of the Saints.

[1] In this chapter will be also recorded several inscriptions which have been left out of the groups already given.

In a Latin inscription the same ejaculation is found:

345

IVSTE · NOMEN
TVM · IN AGAPE (dove)

From the Via Salaria Nova.   Lateran Museum.
(Plate XXIII. 2.)

346

SPI
LIARA
EIΛΑΡ
A
ISPIRI
TVM · TVV
M · SANTVM

Cemetery of Praetextatus.

After the name Spiliara Ilara must be understood the words (*Deus suscipiat*) *spiritum tuum sanctum.*

347

DALMATIVS · IN · PA
CE · TE · PARADIS · SV (*sic*)
FIDELIS · IN · DEO
VIXIT · ANNIS

· · · · · · ·

In pace te paradisus (*suscipiat*).
Africa (Carthage).

348

DOMINE · NEQVANDO
ADVMBRETVR · SPIRITVS
VENERES · DE · FILIVS · IP
SEIVS · QVI · SVPERSTI
TIS · SVNT · BENIROSVS
PROIECTVS

Cemetery of Callisto.   Lateran Museum.   (Plate XXIII. 1.)

The prayer herein contained is noticeable as imploring that the soul of Veneria should not be left in the shadow of death, thus corresponding to the words of the Psalmist: "Give light to those who sit in darkness and in the shadow of death." The concluding sentence means that the inscription was put up by her surviving sons, Venerosus and Projectus.

349

SOLVS · DEVS · ANIMAM · TVAM
DEFENDAD · ALEXANDRE (*sic*)

Cemetery of Domitilla.

350

IN · HOC · SIGNO · SIRICI . . . .
☧

Cemetery of S. Agnese.
Museum of sacred objects, Vatican Library.

An ejaculation, reminding us of the words on the labarum of Constantine : *in hoc signo vinces.*

Here again is the same form of words:

351

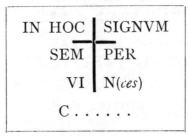

IN HOC | SIGNVM

SEM | PER

VI | N(*ces*)

C . . . . . .

Carthage.[1]

352

A ☧ Ω

NEGLICIA

PAX TECVM

CASTA

CHRISTIANA

Arles.[2]

353

A ☧ Ω

VICTRIS QVE VIXIT ANNIS

VIIII DEPOSITA ES PRIE NON

AS AVGVSTAS MANET IN PACE ET IN CRISTO

Cemetery of S. Felicitas.

Mark the beautiful expression "dwells in peace and in Christ."

[1] Cp. De Rossi, "De titulis Carthaginiensibus," in the *Spicilegium* of Pitra, iv. p. 516.

[2] Cp. Blant, *L'Épigr. chrétienne en Gaule et dans l'Afrique romaine*, Paris, 1890, p. 9.

Sometimes the prayer for peace is intended to apply to the survivors, as in the greeting of the liturgy *pax vobis*. Thus an inscription set up by one Salvius Ceppenius Vitalis to his wife Julia Veneranda closes with the beautiful words PAX OMIBUS (*pax omnibus*) (Lateran Museum, wall xvii. 1).

The following variant on the form *in pace* is noticeable :

354

IVLIA NICE QVE VICXIT ANNIS
XL IN PACE MECVM

Cemetery of Cyriaca.   Lateran Museum.   (Plate XXIII. 3.)

The next contains, again, another important variant :

355

DEPOSITVS · HERILA
COMES · IN · PACE · FIDEI
CATHOLICE · VII · KAL
AVG · QVI · VIXIT · ANN
PL · M · L · DN · SEVERI · AVG
PRIMO · CONS

Cemetery of S. Valentinus in Rome (A.D. 462).

(De Rossi, *Inscr. christ.* i. p. 807.)

The following figurative expression for death is very fine :

356

```
. . . rAPTA · AB · ANGELis . . .
    . . . AM · MARITO . . .
    . . . CAL · AVG . . .
```

" She was borne away by angels."

Cemetery of Cyriaca.

357

```
ΤΕΡΤΙ · ΑΔΕΛΦΕ
ΕΤΨΤΧΙ · ΟΤΔΙϹ
ΑΘΑΝΑΤΟϹ
```

" Tertius, my brother, be of good cheer, no man is immortal ! " This expression is found both in Christian and in pagan inscriptions.

Cemetery of Priscilla (in red paint on brick).

We may next notice some expressions of affectionate tenderness applied to the deceased, and referring to their innocence, their sweetness of disposition, etc. :

358

```
FLORENTIVS · FELIX
AGNEGLVS · DEI
```

" Florentius Felix, lamb of God ! "

Cemetery of S. Agnese.   Lateran Museum.   (Plate XXIII. 4.)

359

LAVRENTIA · MELIS · DVL
CIOR · QVIESCE · IN *pace*

Cemetery of Cyriaca.

A pretty phrase—" sweeter than honey."

Similarly, in an inscription of the cemetery of Praetextatus, very lately discovered, we find the epithet *mellitissima*, equivalent to *dulcissima* :

360

CALLIOPE
Q · V · A · XXVII
CASTISSIMA · ET
MELLITISSIMA

361

MACEDONIANO · FILIO
CARISSIMO · SVPER
OMNEM · DVLCITV
DINE · FILIORVM
DVLCIOR · QVI · VIXIT
IN · SECVLO · ANNIS
N · VIIII · DIES · N · XX
CARO · SVO · FECI
IN · PACE

Inscription on a sarcophagus in the cemetery of Callisto, standing in the chamber known as the cubiculum of the Apostles and erroneously supposed by some to belong to the family of Pope Damasus.

This tells that the deceased boy Macedonianus was the most charming of the family.

362

DASVMIA QVIRIACE BONE FEMINE PALVMBA
SENE FEL | QVAE VIXIT ANNOS LXVI DEPO-
SITA IIII KAL MARTIAS | IN PACE

Cemetery of Callisto.

Notice the pretty expression *palumba sine felle,* "dove without gall," to indicate the sweetness of character of the deceased.

363

ISPIRITO SANTO BONO
FLORENTIO QVI VIXIT ANNIS XIII
CORITVS MAGITER QVI PLVS AMAVIT
QVAM SI FILIVM SVVM ET COIDEVS
MATER FILIO BENEMERENTI FECERVNT

Via Salaria Nova.   Lateran Museum.   (Plate XXIV. 2.)

The soul of the youthful Florentius is here called *spiritus sanctus bonus.*

364

. . . .
MAI · DN · GRATIANO *Au*
G · IIII · ET · MEROBAVD*e*
CONSS · LAETVS · ANIM*o*
AMICVS · OMNIVM
SINE · VILE (*sine bile*)

Cemetery of S. Sebastian (A.D. 377).

This describes the deceased as the friend of all, cheerful of character, and devoid of "bile": *sine bile, sine ulla bile,* mean that his disposition was devoid of spitefulness; the expression is found in other inscriptions.

365

CECILIVS · MARITVS · CECILIAE
PLACIDINE · COIVGI · OPTIME
MEMORIAE · CVM · QVA · VIXIT · ANNIS · X
BENE · SENE · VLLA · QVERELA · ΙΧΘΥϹ

Cemetery of Basilia.   Lateran Museum.

Sine ulla querela, "without any bickerings."
The word ΙΧΘΥϹ at the end is tantamount to a profession of belief in the Divinity of Christ, as has been already pointed out under the head of doctrinal inscriptions.

366

HIC REQVIESCIT SVPERBVS
TANTVM IN NOMINE DICTVS
QVEM INNOCENTEM MITEMQVE SANCTI NO
VERE BEATI IN QVO MISERABILIS PA
TER OPTAVERAT ANTE IACERE DEPOS
V KAL AVG STILICHONE VC BIS C (1)

Cemetery of Praetextatus (A.D. 405).

The deceased, it says, was *Superbus* by name, but only by name, being in fact innocent and gentle.

Sometimes other word-plays on the name are found. Thus, for instance, in an inscription painted in the cemetery of Commodilla a matron by name *Turtura* is described as having been a very turtle-dove for amiability: *Turtura nomen habes sed turtur vera fuisti.* (See *Nuovo Bull. di arch. crist.,* 1904, Nos. 1-4.)

---

1 *Stilichone viro clarissimo bis consule.*

The two following inscriptions contain unusual expressions:

367

> CITONATA · IN · PACE
> QVE · VEX · ANN
> ET · QVATOR · MESES
> POSTERV · CALEDAS
> NOBEBES (*sic*)

Discovered in the cemetery of S. Felicitas, but since lost.

This baby of sixteen months old had been prematurely born (*cito nata*).

368

> APRICLA
> VISSIT · AN
> NOS · DECEOT
> TO · IN · DECENOBEM

Cemetery of Cyriaca.   Lateran Museum.   (Plate XXIV. 3.)

Notice the words *vissit* and *deceotto*, belonging to the rural dialect of Latin, from which the modern language has sprung.

It is just this trace of rural Latin which gives their value to some ancient Christian inscriptions. Thus we find *toti tres* (Ital. *tutti e tre*), *bocata so* for *vocata sum*, *cinque* for *quinque*, etc.

Sometimes the words *fatum facere* are used to express dying :

369

AGATE · FILIA · DVLCISSIMA · QVE
VIXIT · ANN · P · M · VIIII · ET · D · LXIII
FATVM · FECIT · PRID · IDVS · MART

Cemetery of Commodilla.   Lateran Museum.

In others we find mention of the "Brethren," meaning the Christian community, as in the fine inscription already given (No. 188) with the words *ecclesia fratrum.*

370

LEONTI
PAX · A · FRA
TRIBVS
VALE

Cemetery of Priscilla.

This expresses the last farewell of the Brethren to Leontius at his burial.

371

BENE QVIE
SQVENTI
FRATRI BAC
CHYLO IN PACE
FRATRES (palm branch)

Bene quiescenti fratri Bacchylo in pace, fratres (*posuerunt*).

Kircherian Museum.

Within the general community which we call the Church, to which all the Brethren belonged, there were then, as now, particular associations ; and we find records of some of these in the inscriptions ; that of the Eutychii, for instance, in an inscription in the cemetery of Callisto ; and the following as to the Pelagii :

372

AVREL · PETRO · FIL . . . .
DVLCISSIMO · QVI *vixit annos* . . . .
MENS · VII · VIRGO · AVR · M . . . .
AEL · DONATA · PARENT*es*
PELAGIORVM

Cemetery of Priscilla.

In some inscriptions allusion is made to the light that shall shine upon the departed in a future life ; and the day of their death is accordingly described as that which rose upon them in brightness. That is the sense of the following, which is apparently of considerable age :

373

. . . . (*Clau*)DIA · AGRIPPINA · REDD
. . . . CVIVS · DIES · INLVXIT
. . . . DEPOSITA · IDIBVS
. . . .

Cemetery of Callisto.

374

```
C · CLODIO · FABATO
MARITO · OPTIMO
ATILIA · MARCELLA
TERRENVM · CORPVS
CAELESTIS · SPIRITVS · IN · ME
QVO · REPETENTE · SVAM
SEDEM · NVNC · VIVIMVS · ILLIC
ET · FRVITVR · SVPERIS
AETERNA · IN · LVCE · FABATVS
```

(De Rossi, *Cod. Vat. Lat.* 10,530, fol. 38.)

According to De Rossi one part is at Niebla in Spain, and the rest at Rignano in the church of S. Abbondio.

There was a Greek inscription once to be seen in the cemetery of Priscilla, but now unfortunately lost, which expresses very beautifully the idea of the Eternal Light that shines on the Saints in a future life. It is very ancient, and it may be added to the list of doctrinal inscriptions :

375

```
ΜΑΡΙΤΙΜΑ · ΣΕΜΝΗ · ΓΛΥΚΕΡΟΝ · ΦΑΟΣ ·
ΟΥ · ΚΑΤΕΛΕΨΑΣ |
ΕΣΚΕΣ · ΓΑΡ · ΜΕΤΑ · ΣΟΥ   (fish and anchor)
ΠΑΝΑΘΑΝΑΤΟΝ · ΚΑΤΑ · ΠΑΝΤΑ |
ΕΥΣΕΒΕΙΑ · ΓΑΡ · ΣΗ · ΠΑΝΤΟΤΕ · ΣΕ ·
ΠΡΟΑΓΕΙ
```

"Sainted Maritima, thou didst not leave the pleasant light behind thee, for with thee thou didst bear (ἰχθύς) Him who is immortal in all things ; for thy piety has gone before thee everywhere."

(Boldetti ; see De Rossi, *Inscr. chr.* ii. pp. xxvii-xxviii.)

376

CL · CALLISTO · V · I (*viro illustri*)
SIVE · HILARIO · VXOR
ET · FILII · BENEMERENTI · FECER ·
VIR · BONVS · ET · PRVDENS · STVDIIS
IN · PACE · DECESSIT · NOMEM · DIGNI
TATIS · EXIMIVM · LAVDEMQ · SVPER
BAM · DEVM · VIDERE · CVPIENS · VIDIT
NEC · FRVNITVS · OBIIT · SIC · SIBI · VOLV
IT · AC · MERITIS · SVIS · FVNVS · ORNARI
OMNES · FILII · BONVM · PATREM · CLA
MITANT · QVERENTES · PARITER · ET
VXOR · LVGET · QVAERET · NON · IN
VENTVRA · QVEM · PERDIDIT
QVI · VIXIT · ANNIS · LXV
D · P · PRID · N · FEB ·

Cemetery of Domitilla.

Notice the statement that Claudius Calixtus, yearning to see God, attained to the sight of Him.

The following records the native country of the deceased and speaks of eternal life:

377

ΚΑΛΛΙϹΤΟϹ · ΑΠΟ · ΤΗϹ
ϹΙΚΕΛΙΑϹ · ΕΝΘΑΔΑΙ
ΚΙΜΕ · ΠΑΡΟΙΚΗϹΑϹ
ΕΤΕ · ΤΕϹϹΕΡΑΚΟΝ
ΤΑ · ΚΑΤΟΙΚΩ · ΤΟΝ
ΕΩΝΑ

" Here I lie, Calixtus of Sicily, forty years of age; I now dwell in eternity."

Greater cemetery of S. Agnese.

Another fine Greek inscription in the cemetery
of Priscilla concludes with the words:
. . . . EIC · ANACTACIN · AIΩNION
"till the resurrection into immortality."
(See *Bull. di arch. crist.*, 1892, p. 79.)

We will now add some other inscriptions
remarkable for even more unusual expressions;
we will give three as specimens. The first relates
to the veneration for the blood of the martyrs; the
second is that of a bishop, and mentions the
persecutions; the third belongs to an acolyte, and
speaks of the journeys he had made.

378

TERTIV · IDVS ☧ IVNIAS · DEPOSI
TIO · CRVORIS · SANCTORVM · MARTYRVM
QVI · SVNT · PASSI · SVB · PRAESIDE · FLORO · IN · CIVI
TATE · MILEVITANA · IN · DIEBVS · TVRIFI
CATIONIS · INTER · QVIBVS · HIC · INNOC
ens · EST . . . . IN · PACE

Mastar in Numidia.

"On June 11th was deposited here the blood of
the holy martyrs who suffered under Florus the
president in the city of Milevis in the days of the
incense-burning . . ."
This inscription shows that the Faithful of early
days were in the habit of preserving the blood of
the martyrs with special care, a fact confirmed by
Prudentius, who says that they kept it in their
houses, *domi ut reservent posteris.* There is also a
record of the days of "thurification" under Diocletian, when attempts were made to force the
Christians to burn incense before idols.
(Cp. Ottato di Milevi, *De schismate Donat.* iii. 8.)

379

We will now give a translation of the second specimen, which is in Greek ; it was discovered a short time ago by Calder in Lycaonia : [1]

"*I, Marcus Julius Eugenius, served in the army of Pisidia as a member of the forces of Cyrillus Celer the senator; I was the husband of Julia Flaviana, daughter of the senator Caius Nestorianus, and I completed my military career with honour. Then, Maximinus issued an order compelling Christians to do sacrifice but without abandoning their service in the army; and having suffered many annoyances from the General Diogenes, I resigned my military commission, holding fast to the Christian faith. After dwelling for a short time in Laodicea, I was by the will of God made bishop, and for twenty years I laboured in the episcopate with honour: I built the church from its foundations upwards, to wit, the porches, the fore-courts, the paintings, the sculptures, the font, the vestibule, etc.; and having completed all this, I renounced the life of man, and wrought myself a marble sepulchre; and I ordered that the aforesaid matter would be inscribed on the tomb built for myself and my issue.*"

This is important, because contemporary with the last persecutions, and because it gives us some information as to the persecution of Maximinus Daza, which took place about 311, shortly before the Peace of Constantine. The celebrated inscription of Aricanda also speaks of this period.[2]

[1] See the *Expositor* of London, Nov. 1908, pp. 385-408. The Greek text is given, with Ramsay's restorations, by P. Sisto Scaglia in his *Notiones archaeol. Christ.* vol. ii. part i. p. 271.

[2] O. Marucchi, " Un nuovo monumento della persecuzione di Diocleziano" in *Nuova Antologia*, June 1893.

The third inscription, which has been only lately brought to light, is very remarkable as referring to an acolyte, Annius Innocentius, who travelled on Church business in Greece and elsewhere, and finally died in Sardinia:

380

AN · INNOCENTIVS · ACOL · QVI · VIXIT · ANN · XXVI
HIC · OB · ECCLE | SIASTICAM · DISPOSITIONEM ·
ITINERIB · SAEPE · LABORABIT · NAM | ITER · VSQ ·
IN · GRAECIS · MISSVS · SAEPE · ETIAM · CANPANIA
CA | LABRIAM · ET · APVLIAM · POSTREMO · MIS-
SVS · IN · SARDINIAM | IBI · EXIT · DE · SAECVLO ·
CORPVS · EIVS · HVC · VSQ · EST · ADLATVM · DOR-
MIT | IN · PACE · VIII · KAL · SEPTB · AN · VINCEN-
TIVS · FRATER · EIVS · PRESB · CV | QVO · BENE ·
LABORABIT · FECIT (fourth to fifth century)

Cemetery of Callisto, under the Trappist Monastery.

We will now pass to inscriptions speaking of the tomb itself and its position:

381

M · ANTONI
VS · RESTVTV
S . FECIT · YPO
GEV · SIBI · ET
SVIS · FIDENTI
BVS · IN · DOMINO

Cemetery of Domitilla.

This speaks of a subterranean burial-chamber constructed by M. Antonius Restutus for himself and those of his family who, like him, trusted in the Lord.

382

```
MONVMENTVM · VALERI · M
ERCVRI · ET · IVLITTES · IVLIAN
I · ET · QVINTILIES · VERECVNDIES · LI
BERTIS · LIBERTABVSQVE · POSTE
RISQVE · EORVM · AT · RELIGIONE
M · PERTINENTES · MEAM · HOC · A
MPLIVS · IN · CIRCVITVM · CIRCA
MONVMENTVM · LATI · LONGE
PER · PED · BINOS · QVOD · PERTIN
ET · AT · IPSVM · MONVMENT
```

Cemetery of S. Nicomedes on the Via Nomentana.

383

```
          DIGNO ET MERITO
          PATRI ARTEMIDORO
D P VIII  CVIVS HAEC DOMVS    KAL AG
          AETERNA VIDETVR
          BENEMERENTI IN PACE
```

Lateran Museum.

In this, as in some other Christian inscriptions, the grave is called *domus aeterna*, but not, of course, in the pagan sense, which excluded the possibility of resurrection; in fact, in the present case the writer may have meant to say that the grave may seem to be *domus aeterna*, but is not so.

Indeed, another inscription describes the *domus aeterna* as made for the "refreshment" (*refrigerium*) of the deceased, because there prayers might be offered up for him:

384

M · AELIVS · TIGRINVS
OB · REFRIGERIVM
DOMVM · AETERNAM
VIVVS · FVNDAVIT

In the Cathedral of Terni.

Some inscriptions indicate the exact location of the tomb, and are therefore very valuable for topographical purposes.

For instance, on the two next an old Christian cemetery of Rome is mentioned by name, and the purchase of the site is spoken of:

385

SABINI · BISO
MVM · SE · BIBVM
FECIT · SIBI · IN · CYME
TERIVM · BALBINAE
IN · CRYPTA · NOBA

"Sabinus in his lifetime made a tomb for two bodies in the cemetery of Balbina in the new crypt" (*i.e.* in the new gallery).

Lateran Museum.

386

```
FELIX · FAVSTINIAN
VS · EMIT · SIBI · ET · VX
ORI · SVAE · FELICITA
TI · A · FELICE · FOSSORE
IN · BALBI(nae)
```

"Felix Faustinianus purchased for himself and his wife Felicitas of Felix the fossor this tomb in the cemetery of Balbina" (close to S. Callisto).

Museum of the Capitol (Hall of Christian Inscriptions).

Sometimes the location of the tomb in the cemetery is more precisely indicated, *e.g.*:

387

```
VNDECIMA · CRYPTA
PILA · SECVNDA
GREGORI
```

"The tomb of Gregorius in the eleventh gallery and on the second wall."

A "graffito" inscription on the mortar of a grave in the cemetery of Priscilla.

This inscription is specially valuable as telling us that the old excavators called *crypta* what we now term a gallery, and gave the name of *pila* to the wall in which the graves were cut.

The positions of the tombs had to be entered on the registers kept in the managers' offices for each cemetery, as may be gathered from the next inscription :

388

LOCVM · VINCENTI
  QVEM · CVMPARA
  VIT · CVM · SVIS · SI
  QVI · VOLVERIT · REQVI
  RERE · VENIAT · IN · CLE(*meterium*)

" Property of Vincentius. . . . Any one wishing to examine (the purchase-deed) should attend at the cemetery " (*i.e.* at the manager's office).

(See De Rossi, *Roma sotterranea*, iii. p. 545.)

In some the position of the tomb in the cemetery is indicated by some particular feature, thus :

389

EGO · EVSEBIVS · ANTIOCENO
AN · PL · M · LXX · COMPARAVI · E
GO · SS · VIVVS · IN · CATACVMBAS · AD
LVMINAREM · A · FOSSORE · OC
APATOSTANEES · AMICV · (*sic*)
    S · D · III · IDVS · SEPT
     (*sic*)

Cemetery of S. Sebastian ; now in the courtyard of the Ambrosian Library at Milan.

This Eusebius of Antioch had purchased a tomb in the catacombs "near a skylight."

390

```
LOCVS TRI
SOMVS VIC
TORIS IN CRV
TA DAMASI (sic)
```

From a vault in the Via Ardeatina.
(Seen and copied by Marini, but now lost.)

This refers to a tomb for three bodies (*locus trisomus*) bought by one Victor, valuable as telling us that the tomb was in the vault under the mausoleum of Pope Damasus (*in crypta Damasi*).

This mausoleum has not yet been discovered; it consisted probably of a monument built above-ground, like so many others. At any rate it is now certain that the burial-chamber recently discovered under the Trappist monastery cannot be called the tomb of Damasus, as some have rather too hastily imagined.

391

```
+ LOCA ADPERTENENTE (sic) . . .
    AD CVBICVLV GERMVLAN . . . .
```

Cloister of S. Paolo fuori le Mura.

The tombs here mentioned stood in a burial-chamber owned by a certain Germulanus.

392

FL · TATIANO · ET · QVINTO

AVR · SVMMACO · VIRIS

CLARISSIMIS · EGO · ZITA

LOCVM · QVADRIC

SOMVM · IN · BSLIC(*a*)

ALVA EMI

Cemetery of Domitilla (A.D. 391).

This inscription says that a lady named Zita purchased a site for four bodies (*quadrisomum*) *in basilica*, *i.e.* in the great basilica of the cemetery of Domitilla, near the tombs of the martyrs Nereus and Achilleus.

The last line ALVA · EMI is interpreted by De Rossi as = *salva emi*, "I bought it in my lifetime." But it is better explained as meaning that the tomb purchased stood *in basilica alba*, *i.e.* "in the white basilica." This was the above-named basilica, which had been erected just at that date, and was called white, because it had been lately white-washed, which is tantamount to saying that it was newly built. Now we know from other sources that the basilica in question was not built before 390 ; and this inscription is of 391.

In the same way, another inscription of the same date, belonging to the same basilica, speaks of a tomb constructed *in basilica nova*.

I may add here the text of an African inscription, in which a portion of a basilica is mentioned, and a martyr of the name of Casta is recorded. It must, however, be observed that it is a votive and not a sepulchral inscription :

393

AD HANC DO
MVM DEI TR
IBVNAL BASI
LICAE DOMI
NAE CASTAE
SANCTAE AC
VENERANDE
MARTIRI (palm branch)
SABINIANVS
VNA CVM CON
IVGE ET FILIS
VOTVM PER
FECIT (palm branch)

From Henchir-Chorah (Africa). On a pilaster of the basilica.
(See *Nuovo Bull. di arch. crist.*, 1906, p. 15.)

Very important on account of the notice of the martyr Casta, which occurs also in the martyrology of Jerome ;[1] and also for the mention (of which there is no previous instance) of the *tribunal basilicae*, or choir of the church, which was usually raised above the general level of the building, exactly like the *tribunal* in the civil basilica.

[1] This martyr is commemorated on the 21st and 24th of February, 1st and 2nd of June, and 31st of October.

Let us return to sepulchral inscriptions. The following speaks of a tomb in the shape of an arcosolium :

394

DOMVS · ETERNALIS
AVR · CELSI · ET · AVR · ILAR
ITATIS · CONPARI · M
EES · FECIMVS · NOBIS
ET · NOSTRIS · ET · AMIC
IS · ARCOSOLIO · CVM · P
ARETICVLO · SVO · IN · PACEM

Kircherian Museum.

The *parieticulum* was the wall next to the arcosolium, in which graves were also cut, as we often see in underground cemeteries.

395

ANNIBONIVS · FECIT · SIBI · ET · SVIS
LOCVM · HOMIBVS · N · VIII · INTRO · FORMAS (*sic*)
EC · TON · EMON · PANTON · TVTO · EMON

Cemetery of Domitilla ; now in the basilica
of S. Maria in Trastevere.

"Annibonius made for himself and his family a tomb to contain eight in the *formae*," or graves cut in the pavement.

The last line is a Greek sentence in Latin characters, meaning, "Of all that I had this alone is mine," *i.e.* the tomb.

In some inscriptions we are told of the mode of burial practised. Thus in one from Civita Vecchia we read :

396

+ HIC · REQVIESCIT · IN · PACE · APOL
LONIVS · QVI · VIXIT · PL · M · ANNOS · LXX
ET · CVM · VXVRE · SVA · DVLCAIA · AN
NOS · XL · ET · DEFVNCTVS · EST · IPSAS
KAL · MAIAS · ITEM · POST · MORTE
IPSIVS · MORTVA · EST · NEPVS
EIVS · NOMINE · PASCASIA · ET
REPOSITA · EST · SVPER · PEC
TVM · ABVNCVLO · SVO · IN · PACE
ET · CVM · MARITO · SVO · VIXIT · MENSIS
NOVE · QVI · DEMISIT · LVCTVM · SEM
PITERNVM · PATRI · VEL · MATRI · ET · A̅B̅

Civita Vecchia—palace of the sub-prefect.

This tells us that Pascasia was buried on the bosom of her uncle Apollonius.

397

*benemer*ENTI · SABINAE · ALVMNA*e* · *quae*
vix · *an*N · P · M · XXX · D · XXIII · SVPER · PATRO*num*
DEC · III · IDVS . . . . .

"To the worthy foster-child Sabina, who lived . . . and was buried above the tomb of her foster-father."

Cemetery of S. Agnese.

398

CAELIDONIVS · HIC · D*or*
MIT · QVI · BIXIT · ANNIS · XXV
MES · VIII · DIAES · XVIIII · LOCA
QVAE · IPSE · CLVSIT

Ostia.

This tells us that Celidonius was the last to be buried in the family tomb, and so "closed" the list of excavated graves.

Next come some inscriptions which speak of tombs purchased from the grave-diggers, and of the price paid for them, which is often expressed in gold solidi.

These inscriptions show that in the fourth and fifth centuries the fossores or grave-diggers had the right to dispose of tombs in the catacombs, and that they carried on a regular business in them; a practice of which there is no trace in earlier times.

399

EGO TIBERIVS . . . .
NVS CONPARABI . . . . *ab Exu*
PERANTIVM FO*ssore* . . . .
MVM DEPOSITA E . . . .

"I, Tiberius, purchased this tomb from the fossor Exuperantius . . ."

Cemetery of Commodilla.

400

... *em*PTVM EST AB IPOLYTVM FOSSORE

.... VIXIT AN III

.... PANCRATIVS QVI

.... *n*ONAS MAIAS

*Valen*TINIANO III

et Valente III M GERONTI

Cemetery of Pontianus (A. D. 370) ; now in the museum
of the Teutonic cemetery.

The tomb was purchased of a fossor named
Hippolytus.

401

EMPTVM LOCVM AB AR

TAEMISIVM VISOMVM

HOC EST ES PRAETIVM

DATVM FOSSORI HILA

RO IDEST $\overline{\text{FOL}}$ $\overline{\text{N}}$ MD PRAE

SENTIA SEVERI FOSS ET LAVRENT

Museum of the Capitol.

This speaks of a "double" tomb, bought by a
certain Artemisius of a fossor Hilarius for 1500
folles[1] in the presence of two other fossors, Severus
and Laurentius, who acted as witnesses to the
contract and to the payment of the purchase
money.

[1] *Follis* was the smallest coin in use.

402

CONSTANTIVS ET SOSANNA
SE VIVI LOCVM SIBI EMERVNT
PRAESENTIS A ☧ Ω OMNIS FOS
SORES · (*sic*)

"Constantius and Susanna in their lifetime purchased this tomb in the presence of all the fossors," *i.e.* of all the fossors of this cemetery.

The insertion of the monogram of Christ between the letters A and Ω in the middle of this inscription is curious.

Cemetery of Commodilla.   Lateran Museum.

403

AVR · EXSV
PERANTIVS
COSTAT · ME
EMISSE · A · FO
SSORIS · DISC
INDENTIB(*us*)

Cloister of the basilica of S. Lorenzo.

This declares that, according to certain written documents, that tomb had been purchased from the family of the fossor.

This confirms the supposition that in every cemetery there was an office in which the register of the purchase of tombs was kept, as at present.

Some tombs were bought with the expressed assent of the chaplains of the cemetery:

404

L · FAVSTINI QVEM COM
PARAVIT A IVLIO
MANSONARIO SVB
CONSCIENTIA PRES
BYTERI MARCIANI

Kircherian Museum.

405

☧

CAIANVS · EMIT · CVM · VIVIT
SIBI · ET · VXORI · SVAE · AB · ADEO
DATO · FOSSORE · SVB · PRAESEN
TI · SANCTI · MAXIMI · PRESBYTERI (*sic*)
· ·

Cemetery of Commodilla.

406

✝ FL · MAXIMO · V · C · CON*sule* . . .
CONCESSVM · LOCVM · P . . . .
ROME · EXTRB · VOLVP . . . .
ET · CONIVGI · EIVS · IOHAN . . . .
PAPA · HORMISDA · ET · TRA . . . .
PRAEPST · BASC · BEATI · PETRI . . . .

In the grottos of the Vatican (A.D. 523).

This records a person described as *tribunus voluptatum* to the Court, to whom a tomb had been granted by the *praepositus* of the Vatican basilica in the time of Pope Ormisdas (A.D. 514-523).

In some inscriptions there are threats of penalties for the profanation of the tomb. The oldest instance is the one already quoted in the inscription of Abercius, p. 129 *et seq.*, which declares the amount of the fine to be paid to the treasury if another body be placed above that of the owner. But these minatory expressions are found more frequently in Christian inscriptions of a late date. Thus the following, of the year 430, ordains the payment of a fine to the Church chest if another body is placed in that tomb:

407

```
HIC REQVIESCIT IN PACE DVION ANCILLA BA
LENTE SE SPONSA DEXTRI DEPOSITA EST III
IDVS SEPTB CONSVLATV DN THEODOSIO
AVG XIII ET VALENTINIANO AG BES CC SS ADIV
RO PER DEVM ET PER LEGES CRESTEANOR
VT QVICVMQVE EXTRANEVS VOLVERIT AL
TERVM CORPVS PONERE VOLVERIT DET
ECLESIE CATOLICE SAL AVR III
```

" *Adjuro per Deum et per leges christianorum* . . . that he who dares to place there another body pay *Ecclesiae Catholicae Salonitanae aureos III.*" (three gold pieces).

Cemetery of Salona in Dalmatia (A.D. 430).

The mention of a *lex Christiana* and of a "Church chest" are both very noticeable.

Z

In other inscriptions, also of a late date, actual imprecations against possible violators of the tombs are to be met with.   Thus:

408

ADIVRO VOS OMNES XR̄IANI | ET TE CVSTODE
BEATI | IVLIANI PER DM ET PER TREMENDA DIE |
IVDICII VT HVNC SEPVLCRVM VIOLARI | NVNQVAM
PERMITTATIS SED CONSERVETVR | VSQVE AD FI-
NEM MVNDI VT POSIM | SINE IMPEDIMENTO IN VITA
REDIRE | CVM VENERIT QVI IVDICATVRVS EST VI-
VOS | ET MORTVOS

One fragment of this is in the Palazzo Ghirardi, Como.
The remainder has been preserved by Peiresc.
(Bibliothèque Nationale de Paris, MS. 8957, f. 16.)

Christians are here adjured not to profane the tomb.

409

. . . . MALE PEREAT INSEPVLTVS IACEAT NON RE-
SVRGAT · CVM IVDA PARTEM HABEAT SI QVIS
SEPVLCRVM HVNC VIOLAVERIT

From the Roman catacombs.
(Published by Bosio in *Roma sotterranea*.)

This imprecation of the fate of Judas upon the culprit is to be met with in other texts, also of a late date.

I will close this series of inscriptions remarkable for out-of-the-way expressions with one recently discovered, in which an abbess of the convent of S. Maria in Trastevere in Rome is mentioned, apparently of the sixth century. It is one of those referred to above as containing curses upon the profaners of the tomb :

410

```
+  HIC · REQVIESCIT · IN · PA
   CE · ARGENTIA · QVI (sic) BIX
   IT · PLVS · MINVS · ANNOS · XL · LO
   CVM · BERO · QVEM · SIBI · BENERABI
   LIS · ABBATISSA · GRATIOSA · PREPA
   RABERAT · SE · VIBAM · MIHI · EVM · CES
   SIT · CONIVRO · PER · PATREM · ET · FI
   LIVM · ET · SPIRITVM · SCM · ET · DI
   EM · TREMENDAM · IVDICII · VT · NVL
   LVS · PRESVMAT · LOCVM · ISTVM
   VBI · REQVIESCO · VIOLARE · QVOD
   SI · QVI · POT (post) ANC (sic) CONIVRA
   TIONEM · PRESVMSERIT · ANA
   TEMA · ABEAT · DE · IVDA · ET · RE
   PRANAMANSYRIABEAT [1] (sic)
```

In the Casa Colafranceschi near S. Cecilia in Trastevere.

The meaning is clear, except for the last line, which evidently contains a further curse on the profaner of the tomb, in addition to that of sharing the end of Judas. Possibly it may refer to the end of Haman, which was the same as that of Judas ; but perhaps the conjecture of Bacci is preferable, who reads these words as containing an imprecation of the leprosy of Naaman : *et lepra Naman Syri habeat* (*repra* for *lepra*).

[1] The words in this inscription run one into the other without intervening points, as in the last line.

CHAPTER VIII

THE DAMASIAN INSCRIPTIONS

DAMASUS, one of the most famous Pontiffs, was Pope from 366 to 384. The *Liber pontificalis* calls him a Spaniard, *natione Hispanus*; but this must be understood as meaning of Spanish blood, for he was most probably born in Rome.[1] His father was one of the ecclesiastics working in the archives of the Roman Church, the offices of which were situated near the theatre of Pompey; he filled the offices of clerk, lector, deacon, and bishop successively, as Damasus himself tells us in the inscription placed on the spot:

Hinc Pater exceptor, lector, levita, sacerdos
Creverat hinc meritis quoniam melioribus actis, etc.[2]

Damasus spent his youth in these same offices, and he seems to have belonged to the party opposed to Liberius; hence it was that, on his election as Pope at the death of Liberius, an anti-pope, named Ursinus, was put forward against him. Damasus, however, succeeded in putting an end to

---

[1] Any one wishing to find a collection of all the more important historical notices relating to Damasus may consult a recent work of mine, *The Pontificate of Pope Damasus and the History of his Family, etc.*, Rome, Pustet, 1905.

[2] *Carm.* xxxv. (*P.L.* vol. xiii. col. 409).

all the quarrels that had vexed the Church ; and attributing his success to the protection of the martyrs, he at once set himself to protect, beautify, and restore their tombs; he uncovered those which had been hidden under ruins, he widened galleries, opened fresh lights, built staircases near the historical crypts, and thus fulfilled the vow that he had made to the martyrs on the healing of the schism :

Pro reditu cleri Christo praestante triumphans
Martyribus sanctis reddit sua vota sacerdos.[1]

But, above all, Damasus was the poet of the martyrs, an elegant versifier, says S. Jerome : *elegans in versibus scribendis.*[2] At the same time he was a conscientious historian, and a diligent student of the traditions of the Roman Church ; his metrical panegyrics have preserved to us many precious pages of the history of the persecutions, which but for him would have been forgotten.[3]

The information given us by Damasus concerning the martyrs is of great value, seeing how well he must have been acquainted with the historical evidence of the persecutions kept in these Church muniment-rooms in which he had spent all his youth.

The ancient collections of inscriptions have handed down to us the texts of his inscriptions, which have been published by Fabricius (1562), Sarazani (1638), Rivino (1652), Meranda,[4] Migne

[1] *Carm.* xvi. (*P.L.* vol. xiii. col. 390).
[2] *De scriptor. eccles.* ciii. (*P.L.* vol. xxiii. col. 701).
[3] On the metrical inscriptions of Pope Damasus, see De Rossi, *Roma sotterranea*, vol. i. pp. 118-122 ; *Patrol. Lat.* vol. xiii.
[4] *Damasi papae opuscula et gesta*, Romae, 1754.

(*Patr. Lat.* xiii.), and Ihm (*Damasi epigrammata,* 1895).

These inscriptions are nearly all written in hexameters, but the rules of prosody are not always strictly followed. They have a style of their own, and certain expressions recur very frequently, *e.g. rector* for Pope, *fateor, supplex, mira fides,* etc. S. Jerome says that Damasus was an admirer of the poet Vergil, *Vergilii non incuriosus*; and no doubt there are in his poems several reminiscences of the *Aeneid.*[1]

Aeneid vi. 325: . . . *aeternumque tenet per saecula nomen.*

Damasus: . . . *teneant proprium per saecula nomen.*[2]

Aeneid ii. 39: *Scinditur incertum studia in contraria vulgus.*

Damasus: *Scinditur in partes populus gliscente furore.*[3]

Aeneid xii. 427: *Non haec humanis opibus, non arte magistra.*

Damasus: *Non haec humanis opibus, non arte magistra.*[4]

The Damasian inscriptions were cut in marble, in very beautiful lettering of a special type. The name of the artist to whom the execution of them was entrusted was discovered by De Rossi (Plate

[1] Hertz, *Analecta ad Horatium,* iv. p. 19.
[2] Ihm, No. 57.
[3] *Idem,* No. 18.
[4] *Idem,* No. 5. Damasus himself had imitators. Cp. Weymann, "De carminibus Damasianis et pseudo-Damasianis observationes" in *Revue d'hist. et de littérat. religieuse,* 1896, pp. 58 et seq. Stornaiolo, *Literary and Philological Notes on the Damasian Inscriptions,* Rome, 1886. Ihm, *Damasi epigrammata,* 1895.

XXVI. 1). He recognised him as the celebrated Furius Dionysius Philocalus, whose name is recorded in a fragment placed by Marini in the midst of the pagan inscriptions of the Vatican, which he restored thus : *scripsit Furius Dion(isius Philocalus)* (Plate XXVI. 2). Moreover, the inscription of Pope Eusebius, discovered in the cemetery of Callisto in 1856, proves that this was actually the name of the artist employed by Damasus. Some archaeologists used to call all letters Damasian which were ornamented with tendrils, but erroneously. It is well recognised now that the true Damasian lettering has a very peculiar character, as may be seen in Plate XXVI. 1, already referred to. For instance, vertical lines are always terminated by a wavy line forming three curves ; the letters are deeply cut, and invariably keep the same proportion between height and width ; the letter M has its side lines quite or almost vertical, while of the oblique lines one is thick and the other thin ; lastly, in the letter R there is a minute space between the oblique foot-line and the curve above. This old-fashioned hieratic lettering was generally reserved for the inscriptions of martyrs, and was only exceptionally used by Damasus in some other cases, *e.g.* in that of *Projecta*, preserved in the Lateran Museum. On the other hand, the inscriptions that were cut for him before he began to embellish the tombs of martyrs exhibit the ordinary lettering of the fourth century, as may be seen in the two inscriptions of his mother and sister, which will occupy our special attention later on. It is clear too that Furius Dionysius Philocalus did not work for Pope Damasus exclusively, but that he carved other inscriptions in this lettering, and

accepted the commissions of others besides
Damasus, *e.g.* the inscription of the priest
Timotheus in the cemetery of S. Hippolytus. An
attempt was made in later days to imitate this
lettering of Philocalus, but the results always
turned out inferior to the original.

Damasian inscriptions have been found in well-
nigh all the Roman catacombs, and also within the
walls of Rome, as, for instance, at S. Clemente.
But it does not appear that any existed on the
tombs of the Apostles Peter and Paul; possibly
because those monuments did not need any
special indication. If Damasus placed an inscription to the Apostles in the Platonia, this was
perhaps done from fear that the record of the
simultaneous burial of the two Apostles there
might be lost.

Next in order we propose to give a selection of
some of the principal Damasian inscriptions found
in the Roman cemeteries, beginning at the Vatican
and then passing round by the Via Pinciana to the
Via Ostiensis.[1]

The first is that in the baptistery of the Vatican,
where Damasus tells us how he drained that spot,
which was previously water-logged; he gives the
description *mons* to the place. Now this is an
important detail, as it informs us that the part of
the Vatican on which the basilica stands was also
called "monte," and establishes that the evidence
for the Apostle Peter having been crucified "in
monte" may well refer to the Vatican.

---

[1] After each text I shall state whether, and where, the inscription now exists, or if it is known from the Codexes only.

411

CINGEBANT LATICES MONTEM TENEROQVE MEATV |
CORPORA MVLTORVM CINERES ATQVE OSSA RIGA-
BANT | NON TVLIT HOC DAMASVS COMMVNI LEGE
SEPVLTOS | POST REQVIEM TRISTES ITERVM PER-
SOLVERE POENAS | PROTINVS AGGRESSVS MAGNVM
SVPERARE LABOREM | AGGERIS IMMENSI DEIECIT
CVLMINA MONTIS | INTIMA SOLLICITE SCRVTATVS
VISCERA TERRAE | SICCAVIT TOTVM QVIDQVID MA-
DEFECERAT HVMOR | INVENIT FONTEM PRAEBET
QVI DONA SALVTIS | HAEC CVRAVIT MERCVRIVS
LEVITA FIDELIS

Preserved entire in the caves of the Vatican. (Ihm, No. 4.)

On the Via Pinciana, otherwise the old Via
Salaria, there were two inscriptions in honour of
SS. Protus and Hyacinthus:

412

EXTREMO TVMVLVS LATVIT SVB AGGERE MONTIS |

HVNC DAMASVS MONSTRAT SERVAT QVOD MEMBRA

PIORVM | TE PROTVM RETINET MELIOR SIBI REGIA

COELI | SANGVINE PVRPVREO SEQVERIS HYACINTHE

PROBATVS | GERMANI FRATRES ANIMIS INGENTIBVS

AMBO | HIC VICTOR MERVIT PALMAM PRIOR ILLE

CORONAM

One half is kept in the church of the Quattro Coronati ; the
other is known from the Collections. (Ihm, No. 49.)

The martyrdom of the brothers Protus and Hyacinthus is assigned to the persecution of Valerian (A.D. 257-258).

The next records the work done in the cemetery of S. Hermes, near the tomb of the above-mentioned saints ; it seems, however, to be somewhat later in date, and is possibly not a genuine Damasian :

413

ASPICE DESCENSVM CERNES MIRABILE FACTVM | SANCTORVM MONVMENTA VIDES PATEFACTA SE-PVLCRIS | MARTYRIS HIC PROTI TVMVLVS IACET ATQVE HYACHINTHI | QVEM CVM IAMDVDVM TE-GERET MONS TERRA CALIGO | HOC THEODORVS OPVS CONSTRVXIT PRESBYTER INSTANS | VT DO-MINI PLEBEM OPERA MAIORA TENERENT

Kept in the cemetery of S. Hermes.   (Ihm, No. 96.)

In the cemetery of Priscilla used to exist the epitaph on SS. Felix and Philippus, the sons of S. Felicitas (A.D. 162). The first five verses are a summary of the Apostles' Creed ; the rest speak of the Saints.

414

QVI NATVM PASSVMQVE DEVM REPETISSE PA-
TERNAS | SEDES ATQVE ITERVM VENTVRVM EX
AETHERE CREDIT | IVDICET VT VIVOS REDIENS
PARITERQVE SEPVLTOS | MARTYRIBVS SANCTIS
PATEAT QVOD REGIA COELI | RESPICIT INTERIOR
SEQVITVR SI PRAEMIA CHRISTI | CVLTORES DOMINI
FELIX PARITERQVE PHILLIPVS | HINC VIRTVTE PA-
RES CONTEMPTO PRINCIPE MVNDI | AETERNAM PE-
TIERE DOMVM REGNAQVE PIORVM | SANGVINE
QVOD PROPRIO CHRISTI MERVERE CORONAS | HIS
DAMASVS SVPPLEX VOLVIT SVA REDDERE VOTA

From the Collections.

Once erroneously believed to form two inscriptions.
(Ihm, Nos. 91 and 47.)

In the same cemetery was to be found the inscription of Pope Marcellus (A.D. 309), which touches on the question of the *lapsi* and on the exile of the Pope:

415

VERIDICVS RECTOR LAPSOS QVIA CRIMINA FLERE |
PRAEDIXIT MISERIS FVIT OMNIBVS HOSTIS AMARVS |
HINC FVROR HINC ODIVM SEQVITVR DISCORDIA
LITES | SAEDITIO CAEDES SOLVVNTVR FOEDERA
PACIS | CRIMEN OB ALTERIVS CHRISTVM QVI IN
PACE NEGAVIT | FINIBVS EXPVLSVS PATRIAE EST
FERITATE TYRANNI | HAEC BREVITER DAMASVS
VOLVIT COMPERTA REFERRE | MARCELLI VT PO-
PVLVS MERITVM COGNOSCERE POSSET

From the Collections. (Ihm, No. 48.)

The next stood on the tomb of S. Agnes in the Via Nomentana:

416

FAMA REFERT SANCTOS DVDVM RETVLISSE
PARENTES | AGNEN CVM LVGVBRES CANTVS
TVBA CONCREPVISSET | NVTRICIS GREMIVM
SVBITO LIQVISSE PVELLAM | SPONTE TRVCIS
CALCASSE MINAS RABIEMQVE TYRANNI |
VRERE CVM FLAMMIS VOLVISSET NOBILE
CORPVS | VIRIBVS IMMENSVM PARVIS SV-
PERASSE TIMOREM | NVDAQVE PROFVSVM
CRINEM PER MEMBRA DEDISSE | NE DOMINI
TEMPLVM FACIES PERITVRA VIDERET | O
VENERANDA MIHI SANCTVM DECVS ALMA
PVDORIS | VT DAMASI PRECIBVS FAVEAS
PRECOR INCLYTA MARTYR

Preserved entire in the basilica of S. Agnese.
(Plate XXVII. 1.)   (Ihm, No. 40.)

This inscription speaks of the length of time which has elapsed since the martyrdom of Agnes, of her youth, and of her death by fire; it alludes also to the attempted outrages on her modesty; and thus it may be read so to harmonise both with the traditional story given by Ambrose and with that which Prudentius followed. The closing prayer to the martyr to intercede for Damasus is noticeable. The martyrdom of Agnes is said to have taken place in the third century, but the precise date is unknown.

In the tomb of S. Lawrence, on the Via Tiburtina, stood an inscription which confirms the truth of the story of the condemnation of that martyr to death by fire during the persecution of Valerian (A.D. 258):

417

VERBERA CARNIFICIS FLAMMAS TORMENTA CATE-
VINCERE LAVRENTI SOLA FIDES POTVIT   [NAS
HAEC DAMASVS CVMVLAT SVPPLEX ALTARIA DO-
MARTYRIS EGREGIVM SVSPICIENS MERITVM [NIS

From the Collections. (Ihm, No. 32.)

A rare instance in Damasian inscriptions of pentameters alternating with hexameters.

In a neighbouring cemetery there was an inscription of S. Hippolytus:

418

HIPPOLYTVS FERTVR PREMERENT CVM IVSSA TY-
RANNI | PRESBYTER IN SCISMA SEMPER MANSISSE
NOVATI | TEMPORE QVO GLADIVS SECVIT PIA VI-
SCERA MATRIS | DEVOTVS CHRISTO PETERET CVM
REGNA PIORVM | QVAESISSET POPVLVS VBINAM
PROCEDERE POSSET | CATHOLICAM DIXISSE FIDEM
SEQVERENTVR VT OMNES | SIC NOSTER MERVIT
CONFESSVS MARTYR VT ESSET | HAEC AVDITA
REFERT DAMASVS PROBAT OMNIA CHRISTVS

From the Collections. (Ihm, No. 37.)

Some fragments of this are in the cloister of the Lateran.

Damasus here tells us that what little he knew of the history of Hippolytus was uncertain and obscure, and closes by saying that Christ alone knew the truth of the matter.

From the Via Tiburtina we pass to the Via Labicana; where, on the tombs of SS. Peter and Marcellinus, stood the following:

419

MARCELLINE TVOS PARITER PETRE NOSSE TRIVM-
PHOS | PERCVSSOR RETVLIT DAMASO MIHI CVM
PVER ESSEM | HAEC SIBI CARNIFICEM RABIDVM
MANDATA DEDISSE | SENTIBVS IN MEDIIS VESTRA
VT TVNC COLLA SECARET | NE TVMVLVM VE-
STRVM QVISQVAM COGNOSCERE POSSET | VOS
ALACRES VESTRIS MANIBVS MVNDASSE SEPVLCRA |
CANDIDVLO OCCVLTE POSTQVAM IACVISTIS IN
ANTRO· | POSTEA COMMONITAM VESTRA PIETATE
LVCILLAM | HIC PLACVISSE MAGIS SANCTISSIMA
CONDERE MEMBRA

From the Collections.   (Ihm, No. 29.)

Of importance as containing the affirmation of Damasus that he had heard the story of these martyrs from the actual executioner who put them to death in the persecution of Diocletian.

In the same cemetery on the Via Labicana was to be seen the inscription of the martyr Gorgonius, of whose history, however, Damasus tells us nothing:

420

MARTYRIS HIC TVMVLVS MAGNO SVB VERTICE
MONTIS | GORGONIVM RETINET SERVAT QVI AL-
TARIA CHRISTI | HIC QVICVMQVE VENIT SANCTO-
RVM LIMINA QVAERAT | INVENIET VICINA IN SEDE
HABITARE BEATOS | AD COELVM PARITER PIETAS
QVOS VEXIT EVNTES

From the Collections.   (Ihm, No. 31.)

From the Via Labicana we pass to the Via Appia, where Damasus set up many inscriptions, most of them in the cemetery of Callisto. The following is that of Pope Eusebius (A.D. 310):

421

DAMASVS EPISCOPVS FECIT

HERACLIVS VETVIT LAPSOS PECCATA DOLERE

EVSEBIVS MISEROS DOCVIT SVA CRIMINA FLERE

SCINDITVR IN PARTES POPVLVS GLISCENTE FVRORE

SEDITIO CAEDES BELLVM DISCORDIA LITES

EXTEMPLO PARITER PVLSI FERITATE TYRANNI

INTEGRA CVM RECTOR SERVARET FOEDERA PACIS

PERTVLIT EXILIVM DOMINO SVB IVDICE LAETVS

LITORE TRINACRIO MVNDVM VITAMQVE RELIQVIT

EVSEBIO EPISCOPO ET MARTYRI

Some fragments of the original Damasian inscription and a copy made in the sixth century are kept in the cemetery of Callisto.

(Plate XXVII. 2, 4.) (Ihm, No. 18.)

On the right and left of the main inscription, in two vertical lines, the sculptor has placed his name and a testimony to his affection for Pope Damasus:

FVRIVS DIONYSIVS FILOCALVS SCRIBSIT
DAMASI PAPAE CVLTOR ATQVE AMATOR

In this inscription Damasus relates an unknown episode in the life of the heresiarch Heraclius, and also alludes to the question of the *lapsi*, as in the inscription of Marcellus, No. 415. He adds that Eusebius died in exile in Sicily.

In the next Damasus speaks of the various categories of martyrs buried in the cemetery of Callisto :

422

HIC CONGESTA IACET QVAERIS SI TVRBA PIORVM | CORPORA SANCTORVM RETINENT VENERANDA SEPVLCRA | SVBLIMES ANIMAS RAPVIT SIBI REGIA CAELI | HIC COMITES XYSTI PORTANT QVI EX HOSTE TROPAEA | HIC NVMERVS PROCERVM SERVAT QVI ALTARIA CHRISTI | HIC POSITVS LONGA VIXIT QVI IN PACE SACERDOS | HIC CONFESSORES SANCTI QVOS GRAECIA MISIT | HIC IVVENES PVERIQ SENES CASTIQVE NEPOTES | QVIS MAGE VIRGINEVM PLACVIT RETINERE PVDOREM | HIC FATEOR DAMASVS VOLVI MEA CONDERE MEMBRA | SED CINERES TIMVI SANCTOS VEXARE PIORVM

In the crypt of the Popes in the cemetery of Callisto.
(Ihm, No. 12.)

There was another inscription there which described the scene of the surprise of Pope Sixtus II. in the cemetery (A.D. 258):

423

TEMPORE QVO GLADIVS SECVIT PIA VISCERA MATRIS | HIC POSITVS RECTOR COELESTIA IVSSA DOCEBAM | ADVENIVNT SVBITO RAPIVNT QVI FORTE SEDENTEM | MILITIBVS MISSIS POPVLI TVNC COLLA DEDERE | MOX VBI COGNOVIT SENIOR QVIS TOLLERE VELLET | PALMAM SEQVE SVVMQVE CAPVT PRIOR OBTVLIT IPSE | IMPATIENS FERITAS POSSET NE LAEDERE QVEMQVAM | OSTENDIT CHRISTVS REDDIT QVI PRAEMIA VITAE | PASTORIS MERITVM NVMERVM GREGIS IPSE TVETVR

From the Collections.   (Ihm, No. 13.)

In the same cemetery Damasus placed the following inscription on the tomb of Tarsicius, a youth
who was martyred in defence of the Eucharist, whom
he likens to the proto-martyr Stephen.   It is of great
value in its bearing on the doctrine of the Eucharist,
as he calls the Eucharistic elements *coelestia membra.*

424

PAR   MERITVM   QVICVMQVE   LEGIS   COGNOSCE
DVORVM | QVIS DAMASVS RECTOR TITVLOS POST
PRAEMIA REDDIT | IVDAICVS POPVLVS STEPHA-
NVM MELIORA MONENTEM | PERCVLERAT SAXIS
TVLERAT   QVI   EX   HOSTE   TROPAEVM | MARTY-
RIVM PRIMVS RAPVIT LEVITA FIDELIS | TARSI-
CIVM SANCTVM CHRISTI SACRAMENTA GEREN-
TEM | CVM   MALE   SANA   MANVS   PETERET   VVL-
GARE PROFANIS | IPSE ANIMAM POTIVS VOLVIT
DIMITTERE CAESVS | PRODERE QVAM CANIBVS
RABIDIS COELESTIA MEMBRA

From the Collections.   (Ihm, No. 14.)

The next, of Pope Cornelius, records the work
done upon his tomb :

425

ASPICE   DESCENSV   EXTRVCTO   TENEBRISQVE
FVGATIS | CORNELI MONVMENTA VIDES TVMV-
LVMQVE SACRATVM | HOC OPVS AEGROTI DA-
MASI PRAESTANTIA FECIT | ESSET VT ACCESSVS
MELIOR POPVLISQVE PARATVM | AVXILIVM SAN-
CTI ET VALEAS SI FVNDERE PVRO | CORDE
PRECES DAMASVS MELIOR CONSVRGERE POS-
SET | QVEM NON LVCIS AMOR TENVIT MAGE
CVRA LABORIS

The fragments containing the last portion are in the cemetery of Callisto.   (The restoration is by De Rossi, *Roma
sotterranea*, i. 291.)

On the same road, in the cemetery of Praetextatus, has been discovered the inscription of
S. Januarius, the elder of the sons of S. Felicitas
(A.D. 162). It consists of a simple dedication
placed close to the tomb:

426

BEATISSIMO · MARTYRI
IANVARIO
DAMASVS · EPISCOP ·
FECIT

Still in situ.   (Ihm, No. 22.)

Here also were some verses in honour of the
martyrs Felicissimus and Agapitus, deacons to
Sixtus II. (A.D. 258), which ran as follows:

427

ASPICE ET HIC TVMVLVS RETINET CAELESTIA
MEMBRA | SANCTORVM SVBITO RAPVIT QVOS
REGIA COELI | HI CRVCIS INVICTAE COMITES
PARITERQVE MINISTRI | RECTORIS SANCTI ME-
RITVMQVE FIDEMQVE SECVTI | AETHERIAS PE-
TIERE DOMOS REGNAQVE PIORVM | VNICA IN
HIS GAVDET ROMANAE GLORIA PLEBIS | QVOD
DVCE TVNC XYSTO CHRISTI MERVERE TRIVM-
PHOS | FELICISSIMO ET AGAPITO DAMASVS

From the Collections.   (Ihm, No. 23.)

Hard by, in the cemetery of S. Sebastian, Damasus placed the next inscription, to preserve the memory of the spot where the bodies of the Apostles Peter and Paul had been deposited for some time in the year 258 :

428

HIC HABITASSE PRIVS SANCTOS COGNOSCERE DEBES | NOMINA QVISQVE PETRI PARITER PAVLI QVE REQVIRIS | DISCIPVLOS ORIENS MISIT QVOD SPONTE FATEMVR | SANGVINIS OB MERITVM CHRISTVMQVE PER ASTRA SECVTI | AETERIOS PE-TIERES SINVS REGNAQVE PIORVM | ROMA SVOS POTIVS MERVIT DEFENDERE CIVES | HAEC DA-MASVS VESTRAS REFERAT NOVA SIDERA LAVDES

From the Collections.   (Ihm, No. 26.)

Another, placed close to it, describes the cruel death of the martyr Eutychius :

429

EVTYCHIVS MARTYR CRVDELIA IVSSA TYRANNI | CARNIFICVMQVE VIAS PARITER TVNC MILLE NOCENDI | VINCERE QVOD POTVIT MONSTRAVIT GLORIA CHRISTI | CARCERIS INLVVIEM SEQVITVR NOVA POENA PER ARTVS | TESTARVM FRAG-MENTA PARANT NE SOMNVS ADIRET | BIS SENI TRANSIERE DIES ALIMENTA NEGANTVR | MITTI-TVR IN BARATHRVM SANCTVS LAVAT OMNIA SANGVIS | VVLNERA QVAE INTVLERAT ¡MORTIS METVENDA POTESTAS | NOCTE SOPORIFERA TVRBANT INSOMNIA MENTEM | OSTENDIT LA-TEBRA INSONTIS QVAE MEMBRA TENERET | QVAERITVR INVENTVS COLITVR FOVET OMNIA PRAESTAT | EXPRESSIT DAMASVS MERITVM VENERARE SEPVLCRVM

Kept in the basilica of S. Sebastian.   (Ihm, No. 27.)

There is again another inscription by Damasus in honour of a set of unknown martyrs, two copies of which he set up, one on the Via Appia, the other on the Via Salaria, to celebrate the healing of the schism :

430

SANCTORVM QVICVMQVE LEGIS VENERARE SE-
PVLCRVM | NOMINA NEC NVMERVM POTVIT RE-
TINERE VETVSTAS | ORNAVIT DAMASVS TVMV-
LVM COGNOSCITE RECTOR | PRO REDITV CLERI
CHRISTO PRAESTANTE TRIVMPHANS | MARTY-
RIBVS SANCTIS REDDIT SVA VOTA SACERDOS

From the Collections. (Ihm, No. 42.)

On the neighbouring Via Ardeatina, in the cemetery of Domitilla, the inscription of SS. Nereus and Achilleus was once to be seen ; two important fragments of it have been recovered in excavating near the tombs of those martyrs :

431

MILITIAE NOMEN DEDERANT SAEVVMQVE GE-
REBANT | OFFICIVM PARITER SPECTANTES IVSSA
TYRANNI | PRAECEPTIS PVLSANTE METV SER-
VIRE PARATI | MIRA FIDES RERVM SVBITO
POSVERE FVROREM | CONVERSI FVGIVNT DVCIS
IMPIA CASTRA RELINQVVNT | PROIICIVNT CLY-
PEOS PHALERAS TELAQVE CRVENTA | CONFESSI
GAVDENT CHRISTI PORTARE TRIVMPHOS | CRE-
DITE PER DAMASVM POSSIT QVID GLORIA CHRISTI

The restorations have been made from the Collections.
(Ihm, No. 8.)

The inscription gives us some particulars con-cerning these martyrs which are not to be found in their legendary history. It tells us that they had been in the army and had taken part in the persecution of the Christians.

Between the Via Appia and the Ardeatina, Damasus had erected a tomb for himself by the side of those of his mother and his sister Irene, and there he placed some very noteworthy inscriptions. But with these we shall deal in the following chapter and its special appendix on the family history of Damasus.

And now completing our round, we reach the cemetery of Commodilla, near the Via Ostiensis, where Damasus placed an inscription in honour of SS. Felix and Adauctus, martyred under Diocletian, whose tomb has been recently discovered in that spot. The text of it, with which we shall conclude this series, is as follows:

432

O SEMEL ATQVE ITERVM VERO DE NOMINE FELIX | QVI INTEMERATA FIDE CONTEMPTO PRINCIPE MVNDI | CONFESSVS CHRISTVM COELESTIA REGNA PETISTI | O VERE PRE· TIOSA FIDES COGNOSCITE FRATRES | QVA AD COELVM VICTOR PARITER PROPERAVIT ADAVCTVS | PRESBYTER HIS VERVS DA- MASO RECTORE IVBENTE | COMPOSVIT TV- MVLVM SANCTORVM LIMINA ADORNANS

One fragment is in the Lateran Museum ; the rest is taken from the Collections. (Ihm, No. 7.)

It may be added that Damasus undoubtedly wrote other inscriptions in honour of martyrs, the contents of which are unknown to us. Thus, a

Damasian fragment was recently discovered near the Via Flaminia on the tomb of the martyr S. Valentinus (Plate XXVI. 1).[1]

For conciseness' sake I omit many more that could be added to the inscriptions already quoted; they can be found in the various Collections, and especially in that compiled by Ihm, so often referred to already.

The reader does not need my help to run rapidly over the texts that I have printed above, and at once to appreciate their immense value. It is not too much to say that they have preserved for us whole pages of the stories of martyrs; they contain expressions illustrative both of doctrine and of liturgy, which demonstrate the antiquity of the dogma of the Communion of Saints, and the existence of a cult of the martyrs; furthermore, they help us to locate the most venerated tombs in the respective cemeteries. They have thus a threefold value—for doctrine, for history, and for topography: for doctrine, in respect of the confession of faith which they contain; for history, on account of the particulars of the martyrs which they give us; and lastly for topography, in respect of the position of their tombs in the catacombs.

In proof of this, let me arrange the Damasian inscriptions above quoted in a synoptic form, showing the relation of each to one or other of the triple order of conceptions I have mentioned—the doctrinal, the historical, and the topographical.

[1] Cp. Marucchi, "On an unknown Damasian inscription in honour of the martyr S. Valentine," *Nuovo Bull. di arch. crist.*, 1905, p. 103.

§ 1. *Doctrinal Inscriptions*

No. 414. The baptismal creed; a profession of faith in the incarnation of Christ, in redemption through Him, in His resurrection and ascension into Heaven (ll. 1-5). The cult of the saints (last line).

416. Invocation of a martyr and prayer for intercession addressed to her (last line).

417. Cult of saints and oblations on their altars.

418. The unity of the Catholic Church.

419. Cult of the relics of martyrs (last lines).

420. Cult of saints (ll. 3-5).

422. Reverence for the tombs of saints (last two lines).

424. Real Presence of Christ in the Eucharist (ll. 5-8).

429. Cult of the tombs and relics of martyrs, intercession of the saints (last two lines).

430. Invocation of martyrs (last line).

432. Veneration of the tombs of martyrs (last line).

§ 2. *Expressions of Historical Value*

412. Simultaneous martyrdom of the brothers Protus and Hyacinthus.

415. Story of Pope Marcellus; banished by Maxentius for his views on the *lapsi*.

416. Allusion to the cruel persecution in which S. Agnes was put to death, and description of her martyrdom.

417. Allusion to the martyrdom of S. Lawrence by fire.

418. Obscure and doubtful account of S. Hippolytus the martyr; allusion to the Novatian schism by which he had been led away before his martyrdom, and his bold profession of faith before death.

419. Martyrdom of Peter and Marcellinus; their

place of sepulture originally concealed, afterwards transferred elsewhere.

420. Schism of Heraclius in the Roman Church. Exile of Pope Eusebius, and his death in Sicily.

423. Surprise of Sixtus II. in the cemetery on the Via Appia while teaching his flock ; his forcible removal, and subsequent martyrdom under Valerian.

424. Martyrdom of Tarsicius, "martyr of the Eucharist," who was stoned like Stephen the proto-martyr.

425. Allusion to the martyrs Felicissimus and Aga-pitus as companions to Sixtus II. in his martyrdom.

426. Temporary deposit of the bodies of the Apostles Peter and Paul on the Via Appia, and solemn testi-mony to the foundation of the Roman Church by the two Apostles from the East, who were both martyred in Rome, and hence were called " Roman citizens."

429. Detailed description of the martyrdom of S. Eusebius.

430. Allusion to the close of the schism created by the anti-pope Ursinus and to the return of the clergy to the unity of the Church.

431. Important statement that Nereus and Achilleus were originally soldiers, and took part in a persecution (possibly that of Nero) ; that they were afterwards converted, and left the army ; that then they confessed Christ, and were martyred.

432. Allusion to the episode of Adauctus bringing about his own martyrdom along with that of the priest Felix.

§ 3. *Information of Special Topographical Value*

411. Construction of a baptistery on the Vatican.

412-413. Discovery of the tombs of the martyrs Protus and Hyacinthus by Damasus.

420. Location of the tomb of Gorgonius under a high hill.

422. Classification of martyrs in the well-known tombs of the cemetery of Callisto.

425. Ornamentation of the tomb of Pope Cornelius.

429. Tomb of the martyr Eutychius successfully searched for and restored to veneration by Damasus.

432. Ornamentation of the tombs of the martyrs Felix and Adauctus in the cemetery of Commodilla.

This seems to me to be a good opportunity for the introduction of a special investigation of certain Damasian inscriptions, from which we may derive some important conclusions on the personal history of Pope Damasus and his family ; the more so as this investigation includes sundry new inferences of my own, made in consequence of recent discoveries.

This digression will have its own use in the present manual, inasmuch as it gives a practical example of the value of the study of ancient inscriptions for historical purposes.

CHAPTER IX

APPENDIX TO THE DAMASIAN INSCRIPTIONS

§ I

The Sepulchral Inscriptions of Damasus and his Family

THE *Liber pontificalis* tells us that Damasus was buried on December 11th, 384, in a basilica which he had himself erected in the Via Ardeatina, and that he was buried close to his mother and his sister: *qui etiam sepultus est via Ardeatina in basilica sua III. Idus decembris juxta matrem suam et germanam suam.*[1]

The body of Pope Damasus was still lying in the same tomb on the Via Ardeatina in the seventh century, and the fact is noted in the Itineraries.[2] But we also know, on the authority of the *Liber pontificalis*, that in the days of Pope Adrian I.

---

[1] Note that this basilica was built by Damasus after he became Pope, as is evident from the text of the *Liber pontificalis*.

[2] *Et dimittis viam Appiam et perveniens ad S. Marcum papam et martyrem et postea ad S. Damasum papam (et martyrem) via Ardeatina. Et propre eandem viam (Ardeatinam) S. Damasus papa depositus est,* etc. *Inter viam Appiam et Ostiensem est via Ardeatina, ubi sunt Marcus et Marcellianus, et ibi jacet Damasus papa in sua ecclesia* (v. De Rossi, *Roma sotterranea*, i. pp. 180-181).

(772-795) it had already been placed in the church of S. Lorenzo in Damaso, where it is still venerated.[1] It is probable, therefore, that the body was transferred from the Via Ardeatina to the interior of Rome in the Pontificate of Paul I. (757-767).

The original tomb of Damasus as well as that of his sister once bore the metrical inscriptions with which we were already acquainted, as they have been preserved to us by the old Collections. The epitaph of Irene, the sister of Damasus, is singularly beautiful and affectionate; but with that epitaph I shall deal later on.

I come now to the inscription written by Damasus for himself, which for a long time adorned his original tomb. It contains a solemn profession of belief in the doctrine of the Resurrection, declaring that the writer would assuredly rise again from the dead by the merits of the Redeemer, who walked on the waters with unwetted feet, who causes the seeds of earth to revive, who bade Lazarus rise from his tomb.

433

QVI · GRADIENS · PELAGI · FLVCTVS · COMPRESSIT ·
AMAROS | VIVERE · QVI · PRAESTAT · MORIENTIA ·
SEMINA · TERRAE | SOLVERE · QVI · POTVIT LA-
ZARO · SVA · VINCVLA · MORTIS | POST · TENE-
BRAS · FRATREM · POST · TERTIA · LVMINA · SOLIS |
AD · SVPEROS · ITERVM · MARTHAE · DONARE ·
SORORI | POST · CINERES · DAMASVM · FACIET ·
QVIA · SVRGERE · CREDO

---

[1] "(Hadrianus) renovavit etiam et tectum basilicae S. Laurentii quae appellatur Damasi . . . simulque et aliam vestem de post altare fecit, ubi requiescit corpus S. Damasi" (*Lib. pont.*, ed. Duchesne, i. p. 500).

The cemetery in which Damasus was buried is marked by De Rossi as being in one of the divisions of the cemetery of Domitilla on the right of the Via Ardeatina, but Wilpert has since placed it on the left of that road, owing to the discovery on that spot of the sepulchral inscription of the mother of Damasus, whom we know to have been buried in the cemetery in which the monument of that Pontiff afterwards stood.[1]

This inscription has come down to us in a very curious way: the original marble was lost, but an impression of it was preserved on the mortar by which a piece of marble had been at some later time joined to the slab bearing the inscription; the piece with the mortar on it was afterwards thrown into the ditch in which it was eventually discovered.

This short epitaph consists of four hexameters, cut in the ordinary lettering of the fourth century, and not in the elegant alphabet of Philocalus.

434

HIC · DAMASI · MATER · POSVIT · LAVRE*ntia memb*RA
QVAE · FVIT · IN · TERRIS · CENTVM · MINV*s octo*
                        [*per an*NOS (?)
SEXAGINTA · DEO · VIXIT · POST · FOE*dera sancta* (?)
PROGENIE · QVARTA · VIDIT · QVAE *laeta nepotes* (?)[2]

[1] I must observe, however, that the tomb of Damasus was not at the place where this inscription was found, as has been arbitrarily supposed; the inscription was not on its own site, and must have come from some neighbouring spot.

[2] The capitals represent the imprint on the mortar, with the exception of the letters on the right hand . . . RA . . . NOS, which come from a fragment of the original stone, identified as such by Wilpert.

We may infer with certainty from the newly discovered text that the name of the mother of Damasus was *Laurentia*, that she lived to a great age, probably of 89, possibly of 92 years, and that she lived to see a fourth generation, *progenie quarta*.

It is certain in any case that Laurentia lived for 60 years under vows to God, for this must be the meaning of the words *Sexaginta* (annos) *Deo vixit*, *i.e.* that she had taken the vow of chastity 60 years before her death. We shall see later where and why she took this vow.

These biographical notices are scarcely sufficient to satisfy our curiosity as to the minor details respecting the family of the great Pontiff; but at any rate when carefully examined, and taken in connexion with some others which we already possess, they will lead us to some useful conclusions.

First of all, I think I can establish one point very material to the present inquiry, viz. that Laurentia, the mother of Damasus, died during her son's Pontificate. We know that he was Pope for 18 years, from October 366 to December 11th, 384; and we have it on the authority of S. Jerome that he died at the age of 80.[1] He was born, then, in 305, and ascended the Pontifical throne at the age of 61. Now as his mother had taken the vows 60 years before her death, her youngest son cannot have been under 60 years of age at her death, probably indeed not under 61, for it is unlikely that she consecrated herself to a religious life immediately after the birth of her youngest child.

[1] *Propre octuagenarius sub Theodosio principe mortuus est.* (*De viris illustribus*, 103.)

Furthermore, Damasus was not the youngest of the family, for it is probable that his sister Irene, of whom we shall shortly speak, was younger.[1] So at the death of his mother Damasus could not have been under, and was probably over, 61 years of age, and therefore he was already Pope; it follows, therefore, that his mother died after October 366. And hence one can understand why on her sepulchral inscription he described her as *Damasi mater*; the reason being that Damasus had already become a personage of note; for it would have been the height of presumption to use the expression while he was no more than a private individual.[2] And on the same reasoning I conclude that the inscription of his sister Irene, in which she is called *soror Damasi*, was also placed there after his election as Pope, as I will explain at greater length hereafter. And no difficulty need arise from the fact that both inscriptions, of mother and sister, are cut in the ordinary lettering, and not in that of Philocalus. Indeed, De Rossi insists that Damasus used the ordinary lettering for all the inscriptions of his first period; and he further expresses the opinion that he only adopted the lettering of Philocalus after having become Pontiff.[3]

[1] I shall speak of the details of the life of Irene when I come to quote her inscription.

[2] That as early as the time of Damasus the Pope was held to be a personage of eminence, even from a civil point of view, appears from the celebrated reply of Praetextatus, prefect of Rome, when Damasus himself invited him to embrace Christianity: "*Facite me Romanae urbis episcopum et ero protinus Christianus.*" (Hieron. contra Johann. Jerosolim. 8.)

[3] *Roma sott.* iii. p. 241. *Bull. di arch. crist.*, 1888-1889, pp. 146-151.

And to this indeed we may now add that he continued to use the ordinary lettering for his inscriptions even after the beginning of his Pontificate. And this, so far from being improbable, is, on the contrary, consistent with all we know of him. Damasus had, as is well known, to meet the opposition of his rival Ursinus and his followers: this schism lasted for some time after his election; and it was because he attributed the settlement of it to the intercession of the martyrs that he proceeded to adorn their tombs with his poems. In all probability, then, it was at that period when he had at last gained the victory over his opponents that he began to use for these votive monuments the beautiful lettering designed by Furius Dionysius Philocalus, as a sort of triumphal alphabet.

It was natural that Damasus, when he had become Pope, should begin to think of constructing his own tomb. As we know, he would have liked to place it in the Papal vault. But, as he says himself in his well-known verses, he refrained from so doing out of reverence for so holy a place: *Hic fateor Damasus volui mea condere membra, sed cineres timui sanctos vexare piorum.* And now we learn from the discovery recently made that he selected a spot at no great distance off, near the Via Ardeatina.

The *Liber pontificalis* tells us that the tombs of the mother and sister of Damasus were on the Via Ardeatina; but nothing is said of his father, who was certainly not buried there, otherwise there would be some memorial of him. From this we may infer that his father had died long before, and was buried elsewhere. Damasus has left us a passing remark on the subject of his father in the inscription on the Archives, in the place where he built the basilica dedicated to the martyred S. Lawrence, *juxta theatrum* (S. Lorenzo in Damaso). And I must now proceed to discuss that inscription, because upon it the whole of my argument hinges.

The original of the inscription is no longer in existence; we know its contents from the Palatine Collection, and from that of Verdun, but the two copies differ on a point of great importance.[1]

The entire text as given in the first-named Collection is as follows:

435

HINC · PATER · EXCEPTOR · LECTOR · LEVITA · SA-
CERDOS | CREVERAT · HINC · MERITIS · QVONIAM
MELIORIBVS · ACTIS | HINC · MIHI · PROVECTO · CHRI-
STVS · CVI · SVMMA · POTESTAS | SEDIS · APOSTO-
LICAE · VOLVIT · CONCEDERE · HONOREM | ARCHI-
BIS · FATEOR · VOLVI · NOVA · CONDERE · TECTA |
ADDERE · PRAETEREA · DEXTRA · LAEVAQVE · CO-
LVMNAS | QVAE · DAMASI · TENEANT · PROPRIVM
PER · SAECVLA · NOMEN

In the codex of Verdun, on the other hand, the first verse, which, owing to laceration of the sheet, is the only one preserved, runs thus:

Hinc puer exceptor, lector, levita, sacerdos.

[1] De Rossi, *Inscr. christ.* ii. p. 135, 7; p. 151, 23.

Scholars are divided into two camps, the one preferring *pater*, the other *puer*. It is obvious that according to the first reading Damasus would be speaking, first of his father, and afterwards of himself; while on the second view he would be speaking throughout of himself. De Rossi, who had at first preferred the reading *puer*, gave it up afterwards for that of *pater*;[1] and this last reading was followed also by Duchesne, Ihm, and Rade.[2] And the reading *pater* may be demonstrated to be the only true one for the following reasons:

1. The context of the poem shows that Damasus is speaking of two persons: one who *creverat* (had grown up) from that place into some higher dignity, whom he compares with himself, who had only left it to ascend the Apostolic throne.

2. If in the first two verses Damasus were speaking of himself when a boy (*puer*) or *puer exceptor*, we must necessarily hold that after having been lector and deacon he had become a bishop or at least a priest (for *sacerdos*, as we shall see, may mean priest, though better used to signify bishop), and that from that rank of priest (or bishop) he had risen to the Apostolic throne. Now it is quite inconceivable that he had been a bishop before becoming Pope, for it is notorious that in those times this would have been contrary to ecclesiastical etiquette, and that the first bishop who was made Pope was Formosus in the ninth century. Nor can we allow that Damasus was ever a priest, as this also was contrary to the practice of the time,

[1] *Bull. di arch. crist.*, 1881, pp. 48 *et seq.* ; 1883, p. 62 ; 1884-1885, p. 24.

[2] Duchesne, *Lib. pont.* in *Damaso.* (note) ; Ihm, *Damasi epigrammata*, p. 58 ; Rade, *Damasus Bischof von Rom* (1882), p. 6.

which was to select the Pope from among the deacons. Thus Liberius was made Pope when a deacon, and the same occurred in the case of Syricius, as their sepulchral inscriptions testify. We know also that Damasus before becoming Pope had been deacon to Liberius; he is called *diaconus ejus* at least twice in a contemporaneous work, *Libellus precum Faustini et Marcellini.*[1]

From this work we may also draw the conclusion that Damasus was archdeacon at the death of Liberius, because it declares that it was he who summoned to his assistance *arenarios et fossores.* Now the archdeacon was just the officer who had jurisdiction over the Papal cemetery; and it was likewise a recognised practice of the early centuries that the archdeacon should be chosen as Pope.[2] My conclusion therefore is that the *lector, levita, sacerdos* of the inscription on the Archives could not have been Damasus, and must have been some one else; which means that we must read *pater* and not *puer.*

It has been argued in favour of the reading *puer* that this reading agrees excellently with the expression *pueri exceptores,* which was sometimes used; and we are asked to compare the expression in the Damasian inscription of S. Peter and S. Marcellinus: *Percussor retulit Damaso mihi cum puer essem.*

But it must be remembered that *pueri exceptores* have nothing to do with *pueri* properly so called,

[1] Migne, *P.L.* xiii. pp. 81 *et seq.* The only record of the name of Damasus among the priests is in a document of much later date and of little historical authority, the *Acta Liberii* of the sixth century.

[2] See De Rossi, *Bull. di arch. crist.*, 1866, pp. 8 *et seq.*; *ib.*, 1890, pp. 119 *et seq.*

for in that phrase *puer* means, not child, but servant. It is common knowledge that the ancients used *puer* for servant; so much so that in earlier times slaves were called, *e.g.*, *Gaipor* (Gai puer) or *Marcipor* (Marci puer). The word is used in the same sense in the version of the psalm *Laudate pueri Dominum*, where the Hebrew text gives *gavdim* (servants).[1]

It follows from this that there is no reason why *puer* in the Damasian inscription of S. Peter and S. Marcellinus should have anything to do with *puer exceptor*; in that inscription he may very well be speaking of his own childhood, when he heard the story of the martyrdom of the two saints told by their executioner. And even if it were argued that Damasus was *puer exceptor*, in the sense explained above, at the time when he heard the executioner's tale, the most that can be made of that is that he became *exceptor* at some later date, as his father had done before him.

Moreover, we know that the *exceptores* in the ecclesiastical organisation corresponded to notaries, who were bound to be of a certain age, and could not be children.

In confirmation of this we may cite two inscriptions of notaries of about the time of Pope Damasus, which prove that they might be of a tolerably mature age.

The first is at Spoleto:

---

[1] Cp. *puer meus jacet in domo paralyticus*, Matt. viii. 6.

436

```
HIC · REQVIESCIT · BRITTIVS
DALMATIVS · NOTARI
VS · AECLESIAE · ANNIS · V
L · M . . . . . . XXXII
PRAECESSIT · IN · SOMNO
PACIS · XII · KAL · IVNIAS
CONSVLATV · HONORI (A.D. 386) 1
```

The second is in Rome in the cloister of S. Paolo fuori le Mura, and records a notary of 48 years of age:

437

```
. . . . . CALOPODIVS · NOTAR
ANN · XLVIII · DEPOS . . . . .
```

But if *exceptores* were notaries, it is manifest that the duty of an *exceptor* does not involve any extreme youth in the holder, and indeed is incompatible with early manhood. Indeed, it is not likely that youths would be entrusted with the business of taking minutes of church conferences, which was the duty of *exceptores*. And therefore from the phrase *cum puer essem* of the inscription of S. Peter and S. Marcellinus no decisive argument can be drawn in favour of *puer exceptor* as against *pater exceptor* in the inscription of the Archives; and the correctness of the latter reading is demonstrable quite independently by the arguments stated above.

¹ De Rossi, *Bull.* p. 113. Even admitting that the figures giving the age in this inscription stand for 32 and no more, the deceased seems to have been made a notary at the age of 28.

To all these reasons for denying that Damasus was speaking of himself in the first two verses of the inscription of the Archives may be added another. The word *creverat* shows that he is speaking of another person, and the word *meritis* confirms the view. Damasus never used the word *meritum* except as applying it to Saints, or to deceased persons who had led a saintly life ; and he would never have applied it to himself.[1]

There is, again, another argument for *pater* in the place of *puer*. The transcriptions of the Palatine codex are more accurate than those of Verdun, however superior the latter codex may be in the correctness of its topographical classification of the inscriptions. The codex of Verdun, with all its topographical correctness, is very inaccurate ; it gives many variants in the language, and seems itself to be copied from another codex.

To give instances from the poems transcribed in S. Lorenzo in Damaso, the Verdun codex writes *saepius auxilio* by mistake for *saeptus auxilio*, the mistake occurring in exactly the same letter, T, as in the blunder of writing *puer* for *pater*.[2] Here we may see that either the first transcriber who copied the inscriptions on the spot, or the amanuensis who wrote the codex which has come down to us, was guilty of some carelessness in mistaking one letter for another.

[1] He used it in his eulogies on the following persons : S. Sixtus II., S. Stephen and S. Tarsicius, S. Felicitas, Felicissimus and Agapitus, S. Peter and S. Paul, S. Eutychius, S. Lawrence, S. Marcellus, S. Mark, and lastly in that on Irene, to whose intercession he commends himself.

[2] Among other mistakes of transcription in the Verdun codex I may mention *geminatus* for *geminatum, lumina* for *limina, lumine* for *flumine*, etc.

And everybody will agree that in copying a partly effaced inscription, or one which is placed far above the eye, it would be easier to read PATER as PUER than vice versa, supposing the second and third letters to have been somewhat worn.

My conclusion is therefore that, as at present advised, we should adopt the reading *pater*, which is accepted by most critics, and take it that Damasus is here speaking of his father, describing him as having been *lector, levita, sacerdos*.

I have already pointed out that in the language of the age immediately following the Peace of Constantine the proper significance of the word *sacerdos* is "bishop," the priest being simply called presbyter. I may give the following (among many) illustrations.

Damasus himself, in his well-known verses in the crypt of the Popes, says of Pope Miltiades, *Hic positus longa vixit qui in pace sacerdos*;[1] and in the inscription of certain martyrs on the Via Salaria, he speaks of himself after his consecration as Pontiff: *Martyribus sanctis reddit sua vota sacerdos.*[2]

In the inscription of Syricius, the successor to Damasus, we read: *Fonte sacro magnus meruit sedere sacerdos.*[3] The epitaph of *Spes*, bishop of Spoleto in the fourth century, speaking of the duration of his episcopate, says that *vixit in sacerdotio.*[4]

Lastly, in the inscription of Marea the priest,

[1] Ihm, No. 12.   [2] Ihm, No. 49.   [3] *Ib.* No. 93.
[4] This is the text of the inscription :

DEPOSITIO · SANC | TAE · MEMORIAE · VE | NERABILIS · SPEI | AEPISCOPI · DIE · VIIII | KAL · DECB · VI | XIT · IN · SACERDOT | IO · ANNIS · XXXII ·

(De Rossi, *Bull. di arch. crist.*, 1871, p. 113, Table VII.)

vicar to Pope Vigilius, which records how he forbade, in the name of the Pope, a second administration of the rite of confirmation, the bishops are called *sacerdotes*:

Tuque sacerdotes docuisti chrismate sancto, Tangere bis nullum judice posse Deo.[1]

Rufinus, when relating the election of Damasus, says that *post Liberium, sacerdotium in urbe Roma susceperat*;[2] so also Marcellinus, when naming Pope Liberius, calls him *sacerdos urbis Romae.* Moreover, it is common knowledge that the episcopate is the true completion of the priesthood, and that the bishop is always the true priest : the proper title of priests is invariably *presbyter*, whence in the official language of the Church *presbyteratus* is to this day the title of the order which we generally now call the sacerdotal. Thus the Pope is *sacerdos magnus*, as he is called in an inscription of Syricius, and the *plenus summusque sacerdos* spoken of in the inscription of Liberius.[3]

Nor does the fact that the father of Damasus must have passed straight from the diaconate to the episcopate constitute any difficulty ; for besides the instance of several Popes given above, there are many others showing that the practice was common enough in those days.

Therefore if this interpretation of *sacerdos* be accepted—and it is the most natural one—we have it on the authority of Damasus himself in his inscription on the Archives that his father was a bishop ; a circumstance of the utmost import for my subsequent argument.

[1] De Rossi, *Bull. di arch. crist.*, 1869. [2] *H.E.* ii. 10.
[3] See De Rossi, *Inscr. crist.* ii. pp. 83, 85 ; cp. *Bull. di arch. crist.*, 1883, pp. 5 *et seq.*

And, again, if this be admitted, we have an excellent explanation of a metaphorical expression used in an inscription discovered a few years ago in the cemetery of S. Hippolytus, the meaning of which has not been hitherto clearly made out. It describes the work done in the cemetery and invites the Christian world to give thanks to God for these works, which it states were executed by the order of Pope Damasus.

438

LAETA · DEO · PLEBS · SANCTA · CANAT · QVOD · MOENIA · CRESCVNT | ET · RENOVATA · DOMVS · MARTYRIS · IPPOLITI | ORNAMENTA · OPERIS · SVR-GVNT · AVCTORE · DAMĀSO | NATVS · QVI · AN-TISTES · SEDIS · APOSTOLICAE · etc.[1]

De Rossi explained the words *natus antistes sedis apostolicae* as meaning that Damasus, as the son of one who was already attached to the Church, had been in a sense predestined to the episcopal throne. And this bold metaphor finds a good parallel in the sepulchral inscription of Pope Anastasius II. (498), who was the son of a priest; it says of him:

Presbytero genitus delegi dogmata vitae
Militiaeque Dei natus in officiis.[2]

From a comparison of these two passages it is clear that the expression *natus* to an ecclesiastical office was the precise term used of any one whose father was an ecclesiastic. And if it could be said of Anastasius, the son of a *presbyter*, that he was

---

[1] De Rossi, *Bull. di arch. crist.*, 1883, pp. 60 *et seq.*
[2] De Rossi, *Inscr. christ.* ii. p. 126.

natus in officiis militiae Dei, much more could it be said of Damasus, the son of a bishop, that he was *natus antistes*; and the expression must be taken to allude to the episcopal status of his father.

This at any rate is another argument in favour of the view that Damasus was the son of one who at least held some office in the Church, and thus it strengthens the belief that the *sacerdos* of the inscription on the Archives was his father.

To proceed, if on the strength of the ordinary meaning of *sacerdos*, and of what has been said above, we are to allow that the father of Damasus was a bishop, it may well be inferred that he was bishop of one of the many small sees near Rome.

Now it is well known that when a married man took holy orders he was bound by the rules of the Church to separate from his wife ; the celebrated canon of the Council of Elvira held in 306 is clear on this point at any rate.[1] Wherefore De Rossi, when discussing the question of a married man taking holy orders, says in so many words, "He who is acquainted with the ancient ecclesiastical discipline knows well that in such cases not only bishops, but also priests and deacons, were obliged to renounce marital intercourse."[2] On the basis of this reasoning, then, I think I may safely assert

[1] "Placuit in totum prohibere episcopis presbyteris et diaconibus vel omnibus clericis positis in ministerio abstinere se a coniugibus suis et non generare filios. Quicumque vero fecerit, ab honore clericatus exterminetur" (Labbe, *Coll. Concil.* i. col. 1231, canon 33). Cp. le lettere di papa Siricio ad Himerium Terraconensem ; Coustan, "Ep. Rom. Pont. di Innocenzo I. ad Victric Rothomag," *ibidem* ; Leo Magnus, *Epist.* 14, cap. 4 ; V. Tommasini, *Veteris et novae Ecclesiae disciplina,* pars i. lib. ii. cap. 61.

[2] *Bull. di arch. crist.,* 1864, p. 55.

that the father of Damasus (whoever he was), after receiving holy orders, was obliged to separate from his wife, whose name we now know was Laurentia ; it naturally follows that she must then have entered on a life of chastity ; so that it might well have been said of her that from that moment *vixit Deo*. Hence it appears that the expression *sexaginta Deo vixit post foe(dera)* does not mean that she was an actual widow for sixty years, as some would explain it ; for this would imply that she did not consecrate herself to God till after the death of her husband, in other words, that she had lived maritally with her husband to the date of his death. But this was impossible, because the father of Damasus took orders and must have lived for several years separated from his wife ; these years, therefore, must be included in the sixty which she consecrated to God. The period of sixty years must begin from the separation of the spouses, and must take in the years between that separation and the death of the husband as well as the years during which she survived him. It may be suggested that the words *post foedera* mean after the natural end of her married life, *i.e.* after the death of the husband. But this interpretation is impossible if we admit the validity of the proof that the father of Damasus had taken holy orders. And even apart from that, it is unsound. *Post foedera* (even allowing that *foedera* could mean matrimony here) does not mean *post soluta foedera* (upon the close of the contract), but simply *post inita foedera* (at some time after the contract was made) ; it does no more than give the date of the marriage of Laurentia as the point of time after which something happened ; and if the missing word after *foedera* be *prima* (which is by no means certain) it would show that this was her first and only marriage, and that subsequently to this she devoted herself to God. And the word "subsequently" may also mean subsequently to her marital life, and to the birth of her children. In other words, I believe this laconic phrase to be the equivalent of the following: "Laurentia married and bore children; at some subsequent time she consecrated herself to God, *and in this new state*, i.e. *of consecration to God, she lived for sixty years.*"

Wilpert has pointed out that Damasus has used the expression *post foedera prima* in another inscription, that of Projecta (Ihm, 53), to mean *after the dissolution of the marriage by death*; and he argues that we must interpret the same phrase in the inscription of his mother in the same sense. But, in the first place, the word *prima* after *foedera* in the inscription of Laurentia is conjecturally supplied; and, in any case, in the inscription of Projecta, which I shall examine later, the expression has not the meaning suggested.

So far it is clear that in the inscription of Laurentia the words *sexaginta Deo vixit post foedera* cannot be explained to mean a widowhood of sixty years in length; for if the father of Damasus was a *levita* and *sacerdos*, he must have separated from his wife on taking holy orders, and Laurentia could not have continued to live with him up to his death.

Her consecration to God (*Deo vixit*) therefore began before the death of her husband. And from this it follows that we cannot argue that Laurentia only began her self-dedication to God at the death of her husband, without giving up the reading *hinc pater* in the inscription of the Archives; now that reading has been demonstated to be the correct one by good arguments quite independently of this question, and we are bound to take it as such till the contrary is proved.

Again, if we are to infer from the lately discovered text that her actual widowhood lasted for sixty years, we must conjecture that the lost words in the inscription were *post foedera soluta*, or to that effect; for the simple expression *post foedera*, or even *post foedera prima*, if that reading could be accepted, would not of itself mean that the marriage had then come to an end.

But, as has been already pointed out, the restoration *post foe(dera prima)* in the inscription of Laurentia, although taken from the verses on Projecta and therefore Damasian in style, is really conjectural. We may observe here that *foedus* by itself means any compact or contract, and not essentially marriage. So true is this that when Damasus wished to use *foedus* in the sense of marriage, as in the inscription of Projecta, he wrote *thalami post foedera*. And he might easily have used the same expression in the inscription on his mother in a hexameter which would have come spontaneously to his pen, *sexaginta Deo thalami post foedera vixit*.

Probably then, as he did not add *thalami* to *post foedera* in the inscription to his mother, he meant to speak of some other *foedus*.

Damasus in fact actually used the word *foedus* in his verses in other significations, all very different from that of marriage. Thus in the inscription of Eusebius he says "integra cum rector servaret *foedera pacis*"; and in that of Marcellus, "solvuntur *foedera pacis."* In the verses on S. Paul he uses the same word, "cum lacerat sanctae matris *pia foedera* coecus"; and so in the inscription of S. Saturninus, "qui sciret sanctae servare *foedera matris.*" [1]

But what is more important for the purpose of the present case is that in the time of Damasus the word *foedus* was used specially to signify the vow of chastity; and S. Jerome uses it in this sense when, writing to Demetrias the virgin, he says, "nunc autem quia saeculum reliquisti . . . serva FOEDUS quod pepigisti." [2] It is again used in the same sense in the Vulgate: "pepigi *foedus* cum oculis meis ut ne cogitarem quidem de virgine" (Job xxxi. 1). I can also add an instance from an inscription of about the age of Damasus, now in the basilica of S. Sebastian, in which the expression *immaculata* [piae conservans] *foedera mentis* [3] is used to express the vow of chastity.

If, then, *foedus* can include a vow of continence, we may reasonably fill the gap in the third line of the inscription of Laurentia thus: *sexaginta Deo vixit post foe(dera sancta)*; understanding by *foedus sanctum* the vow to live a life of chastity, a vow which, when a married couple is in question, must be the subject of a common agreement and a mutual compact; for this reason it would be a *foedus* in the true sense, and one which might properly be described as *sanctum*, seeing that not

---

[1] In a metrical inscription of the age of Damasus or thereabouts, found near the basilica of S. Paul, the words *publica post docuit Romani foe(dera juris)* are used with reference to the Roman civil law.

[2] Hieron. *Epist.* 130; *P.L.* xxxiii. col. 113 *et seq.*

[3] *C.I.L.* vi. 32,052. Cp. O. Marucchi, *Le Catacombe romane*, 1905, p. 213. See above, No. 265, p. 229.

even matrimony deals with a condition of life more perfect and more holy. If, then, we accept the arguments stated above, and if we admit the reading *hinc pater* in the inscription of the Archives, we establish the fact that the parents of Damasus must have taken the vows described, and entered into a new compact (*foedus*) together. When it is thus interpreted all difficulty disappears, and the notion that the inscription of Laurentia refers to a widowhood of sixty years is shown to be false.

It is evident that nothing but the discovery of the missing fragment will enable us to complete with certainty that third line, *sexaginta Deo vixit post foe(dera)*; but even if the word thus found could be used to show that *post foedera* meant "after the marriage," this would in no way alter my view of the meaning—and that for the reasons already given—unless it should turn out to be *post foedera soluta* or some similar expression; in that case it would be necessary to explain it otherwise. But until this happens we must understand that Laurentia after her marriage (not immediately, but after more or less of an interval from its celebration) entered upon a life dedicated to God, apart from her husband, and that she lived that life for sixty years.

The words *progenie quarta vidit quae* . . . seem to me to suggest that Laurentia died immediately after seeing a fourth generation, and they might be completed thus: *progenie quarta vidit quae laeta nepotes*; meaning that Laurentia died after having been cheered by the appearance of a fourth generation.

I will add nothing on this point for the present, but I shall return to it later, when I come to deal with the restoration of this line in connexion with another Damasian inscription.

There are other important facts connected with the family history of Damasus which we may learn from the remarkably fine inscription which he set on the tomb of his sister Irene in the same cemetery of the Via Ardeatina in which his mother was buried.

The text of this inscription was already known from the Collections of Inscriptions; but a small fragment of the original slab was recovered in 1880 in the church of SS. Cosma and Damiano on the Forum Romanum, the lettering of which is not in the style of Philocalus, but the ordinary lettering of the fourth century. For clearness' sake I will quote here the entire text, marking the portion which has come down to us: [1]

439

Hoc tumulo sacrata D*EO* NV*nc membra quiescunt,*
*Hic soror est Damasi no*MEN SI QVA*eris Irene.*
*Voverat haec sese Christ*O CVM VITA MA*neret*
*Virginis ut meritum san*CTVS PVDOR IPS*e probaret.*
*Bis denas hiemes necdum complev*ERAT *aetas,*
Egregios mores vitae praecesserat aetas,

---

[1] The entire text, written in cursive hand, is known to us through the Palatine Collection of the Vatican Library (cp. Ihm, No. 10). The fragment of inscription, which had gone astray after 1880, was rediscovered by me in 1900 among the marbles of the Forum ; and at my request it was presented by the Baccelli Ministry to the Commission of Sacred Archaeology. It was at first placed in the basilica of S. Petronilla, and afterwards near the fragment of the inscription of Laurentia.

Propositum mentis pietas veneranda puellae,
Magnificos fructus dederat melioribus annis.
Te germana soror nostri tunc testis amoris,
Cum fugeret mundum, dederat mihi pignus honestum.
Quam sibi cum raperet melior sibi regia caeli,
Non timui mortem, caelos quod libera adiret,
Sed dolui, fateor, consortia perdere vitae.
Nunc veniente Deo nostri reminiscere virgo
Ut tua per Dominum praestet mihi facula lumen.

On one point I am sure, namely, that the words of the fifth verse, *Bis denas hiemes necdum compleverat aetas*, are not to be taken, as some think, in the sense that Irene died before she was twenty ; in my opinion it must be understood as saying that she was barely twenty when she made her profession as a holy virgin.   The fact is that in the opening lines Damasus is speaking only of the dedication of Irene to virginity ; in the line that follows *Bis denas hiemes*, etc., he says that her manner of life was beyond her years, and then he goes on to say that *in following years* she displayed the blessed fruits of her self-dedication.[1]   All this seems to me to explain sufficiently that Damasus, when thus speaking of his sister's tender age, meant the age at which she made her profession.   After saying this, he goes on to state that Irene had been commended to his care by some one on his or her deathbed.   And surely had he wanted to tell us the age of Irene at her death, he would have put it at the end of the poem.

But if line 13 is to be read as an expression of the grief of Damasus over the death of Irene, as

---

[1] Both PEREZ and BIRAGHI think that the twenty years mentioned refer to her consecration to God.   See De Rossi, *Bull. di arch. crist.*, 1888-1889, p. 159.

his life-companion, *dolui fateor consortia perdere vitae*, it involves the conclusion that he had spent a great part of his life in her company; and this Damasus could not possibly have said if Irene had died in her twentieth year, since he could then have been only some two years older.

There is withal the further consideration on which I have already dwelt, that the words *Hic soror est Damasi* show that Damasus was already Pope when he composed this inscription. It is open, however, to the reply that he might have written the epitaph long after the death of his sister. In all probability, however, it was not written later, but placed immediately after her death on the tomb which Damasus had already made. For these reasons I am of opinion that both the mother and the sister of Damasus died towards the beginning of his Pontificate.

And this view is strengthened by lines 9-10, which say that some one who had witnessed the mutual affection of Damasus and Irene had, on his or her death-bed, commended the sister to the care of the brother : *Te germana soror nostri tunc testis amoris Cum fugeret mundum dederat mihi pignus honestum.*

The most obvious explanation of this is that the person in question was their mother, who, as their father was dead, commended Irene to the care of her brother.[1] Bücheler, however, proposes to explain *Germana soror* as the name of another sister who had given this injunction.[2]

But it is difficult to accept this, seeing that, as

---

[1] See De Rossi, *Bull. di arch. crist.*, 1888-1889, pp. 140 *et seq.*; Duchesne, *L.P.* i. p. 215.

[2] Ihm, *Damasi epigrammata*, p. 17.

we now know from the mother's inscription, she did not die young, as once might have been supposed, but at an advanced age; that being so, it is difficult to suppose that Irene should have been commended by this supposed sister to the brother while the mother was still living. Besides this, the word *pignus* in the language of the inscriptions of that date always means offspring.[1] Finally, Damasus uses *germanus* in the sense of "brother in blood" elsewhere, as, for instance, in the inscription of S. Protus and S. Hyacinthus, where he says, *Germani fratres animis ingentibus ambo.*[2]

De Rossi has given a very ingenious, and to my mind satisfactory, explanation of lines 11-13, referring them to the death of the mother; he completes them thus: *Quam (matrem) sibi cum raperet melior sibi regia coeli, non timui mortem coelos quod libera adiret, sed dolui fateor consortia perdere vitae*; observing that the verbs in the third person, *raperet, adiret*, cannot be construed as referring to the vocative *germana soror.*[3] And his allusion to his grief on the death of his mother comes in very naturally after the reference to the death of her who gave him her dying injunctions.

To sum up: the verses on Irene speak of the injunction given to Damasus by his dying mother; then they allude to her death; and they conclude with a prayer to the deceased sister. And the words *consortia vitae*, it may be added, are most appropriate as applied to a mother who had lived with her son up to extreme old age.

[1] "*Pignus*, in the sepulchral language of that time, means offspring" (De Rossi, *Bull. di arch. crist.*, 1885-1889, p. 151).

[2] Ihm, No. 49. See above, No. 412, p. 345.

[3] De Rossi, *Bull. di arch. crist.* l.c.

It may be objected that as Laurentia was at least 89 years of age at her death, and had taken the vow of chastity 60 years before, Irene could not have been less than 60 at her mother's death; and some may perhaps consider that a commendation of a woman of such advanced years to the care of another is rather improbable. But this is not a serious difficulty: an aged sister may well be commended to a brother, not as needing guardianship and advice like a girl, but as possibly wanting material aid and sustenance.

And if *testis amoris* does not mean the mother, it must, by virtue of the meaning assigned above to *pignus*, refer to the father; and indeed the injunction would come perfectly well from a father, as head of the family, even in the lifetime of the mother. This, if admitted, would be another argument in support of the contention that the father of Damasus could not have died 60 years before his wife Laurentia; for in that case Irene and Damasus would both have been children at the date of his death, and he would scarcely have commended one child to the care of the other.

And this seems to be the opinion of Wilpert, who thinks that the inscription of Irene was the first to be placed in the sepulchral vault, and he infers from this that she died before her mother. If so, the *testis amoris* who commended to Damasus the *pignus honestum* must have been the father; the latter must therefore have died when Damasus was of an age to accept such a commission, and not at the time of Laurentia's consecration to God, about 307, when Damasus was only about two years old. And I cannot see how Wilpert reconciles his opinion on this point

with his contention that Laurentia became a widow
60 years before her death ; for 60 years before her
death Damasus was still a child.[1]

However, the *testis amoris* who gave the injunction was a woman, and not a man, as the expression *libera adiret* undoubtedly refers to that person ;
and as this *testis* must have been one of the parents,
it could only have been the mother.   It was therefore the mother who commended Irene to Damasus
on her death-bed ; it was therefore the mother who
died first.   And here is another proof of the un-
soundness of Wilpert's conjecture that Laurentia
was buried in the cubiculum known as the
Apostles', near which was found the slab bearing
her inscription ; for that cubiculum had certainly
been previously used for burials, and could not
therefore have been the sepulchral monument
erected by Damasus for his mother, his sister, and
himself.

All these inferences are logically deducible from
the inscriptions in which Damasus himself is
certainly speaking of his own family ; and if my
inquiry were to stop here, I might still present it as
an adequate comment on the newly discovered
Damasian text.   To summarise it, then, so far as
we have gone, I think I have reached the following
conclusions :

1. The mother of Damasus was named Laurentia,
and lived to 89, or rather 92 years of age ; she gave
up marital life at the age of 29 at least, or more
probably of 32, and then dedicated herself to God,
because her husband had taken holy orders.

[1] Wilpert, I should say, has now given up his interpretation
of the inscription of Laurentia.   See *Römische Quartalschrift*,
1908, pp. 73 *et seq.*

2. Her husband, the father of Damasus, was a notary of the Church, lector, deacon, and finally *sacerdos*, *i.e.* bishop.

3. He died before his wife.

4. Laurentia died towards the beginning of the Pontificate of Damasus.

5. Irene, younger sister to Damasus, dedicated herself to God at about the age of 20, and died in advanced years after her mother, and therefore while Damasus was Pope.

6. The parents of Damasus had other children besides Damasus and Irene, inasmuch as Laurentia "saw the fourth generation," *i.e.* descendants through some other son or daughter.

7. Damasus was buried near his mother and his sister in a tomb of great pretensions, which he had erected after becoming Pope, and which, whether it was above ground or subterranean, was thought worthy of the title of basilica. This building must have stood on the Via Ardeatina on the left hand as one leaves Rome, near the cemetery of Callisto, and almost opposite that of Domitilla. The exact spot cannot be as yet identified with certainty, but in any case it could not have been in the cubiculum in which Wilpert rather prematurely boasted that he had rediscovered it.[1]

---

[1] Wilpert's mistake arose from his assuming that the inscription of Laurentia belonged to that cubiculum, whereas it was in. fact brought from elsewhere, and laid on a block of travertine, in the ordinary course of building.

§ 2

Inscriptions possibly referring to the Father of Damasus

I can now take a farther step, and having thrown some light on the inscription of the mother of Damasus, I may go on to inquire into the personality of the father of the great Pontiff, a subject of much historical and epigraphical importance.

And I must start with the prefatory observation that as the father of Damasus was a man of some mark, as a bishop, it is most probable that his son wrote an inscription in his honour, as he did for his mother and his sister; and further, that a copy of such inscription is probably preserved in the ancient Collections. Another preliminary remark must be made, that as the father of Damasus was not buried in the cemetery of the Via Ardeatina, with the mother and sister, it is extremely likely that he had predeceased them and been buried in some other place, from which his son had been unwilling to move his body owing to the invariable custom of not changing a burial-place without the gravest of reasons. And here I will remark on one or two coincidences which struck me, on my first reading the inscription of *mater Damasi*, as existing between that same inscription and another well-known one, which has not, however, as yet been examined with sufficient care.

The name of *Laurentia*, which is now ascertained

to be that of the mother of Damasus, set me
thinking at once of an inscription in which mention
is made of an individual who must have had
personal relations with Damasus, an unknown
bishop of the name of Leo, whose tomb is on the
Via Tiburtina in the *agro Verano* near the basilica
of S. Lawrence, and who happened to have a wife
named Laurentia.

This inscription had been already known through
the existing Collections, and a great part of it was
actually recovered in the later excavations on the
agro Verano near the above-mentioned basilica.
De Rossi published it in the *Bulletino* of 1864,
and pronounced it to be Damasian; his words are
as follows: "I think it cannot be doubted that
Pope Damasus wrote these verses. His style has
a distinctive mark which can be recognised among
a thousand. If I cared to enter into a philological
discussion, I could prove in every line that the
metre and the language belong to Damasus."[1]
To this I may add that the inscription of this Leo
cannot possibly be a later imitation of Damasus.
In fact, its lettering shows that it is not later than
the Pontificate of Damasus, and is more likely
earlier; De Rossi attributes it to the age of Liberius.
But as it contains expressions which are unmistak-
ably Damasian, it may be set down with certainty
as the production of Damasus himself, and not an
imitation of his style.

I will now give the text of this striking inscription, putting in italics the portion which, though
perished, is known through the Collections, and in
capital letters the portion which still exists.

[1] *Bull. di arch. crist.*, 1864, pp. 54-56.

440

OMNIA QVAEQ*ue vides proprio quaesita labore*
CVM MIHI GENTIL*is jamdudum vita maneret*
INSTITVI CVPIENS *censum* COgnoscere *mundi*
IVDICIO POST MV*lta Dei meliora se*CVTVS
CONTEMPTIS OPI*bus malui cogno*SCERE CHRIS*tum*
HAEC MIHI CVR*a fuit nudos vest*IRE PETENTES
FVNDERE PAVP*eribus quid quid con*CESSERAT ANNVS

No. 1, discovered in 1881.[1]

440 (*a*)

PSALLERE ET IN POPVLIS VOLVI M*odulante*
[PROFETA
SIC MERVI PLEBEM CHRISTI RETI*ne*RE SACERDOS
HVNC MIHI COMPOSVIT TVMVLVM LAVRENTIA
[CONIVNX
...V̄ MORIBVS APTA MEIS SEMPER VENERANDA FI-
[DELIS
INVIDIA INFELIX TANDEM COMPRESSA QVIESCET
OCTOGINTA LEO TRANSCENDIT EPISCOPVS AN-
DEP · DIE PRID · IDVS MARTIAS   [NOS

No. 2, discovered in 1857.[2]

[1] The fragment No. 1 was discovered in 1881 in the *agro Verano* in two pieces. I made for De Rossi the first transcription, which is preserved among his papers now in the possession of Prof. Gatti, his successor in the editorship of the *Inscriptiones christianae*. The supplementary portion is taken from the Collections (*v.* Ihm, No. 33). I have placed it in the Lateran Museum.

[2] The fragment No. 2 was found in the *agro Verano* in 1857, and is preserved in the Lateran Museum, where I have lately attached it to fragment No. 1, with the additions which belong to it (bottom of Wall X. of the Loggia).

The person here commemorated had been originally an idolater and given up to worldly pursuits; he was then converted to Christianity, took holy orders, and became successively reader, deacon, and bishop. Though the two first-mentioned offices are not recorded in their proper order (no doubt to suit the metre) they are nevertheless clearly indicated. *Haec mihi cura fuit* suggests an office held by the deceased; and the office which involved the duty of distributing food and clothing to the poor was exactly that of the deacon. *Psallere in populis modulante propheta* points obviously to the office of lector.[1] Lastly, it is recorded that he became a bishop; and here the use of *sacerdos* in the sense of "bishop," for which I have argued above, besides being suggested by *retinere Christo plebem* is made a matter of certainty by the last line: *octoginta Leo transcendit episcopus annos.*[2]

Thus the unknown Leo, who was buried on the Via Tiburtina, was the honoured subject of a Damasian eulogy; was *lector, levita, sacerdos*, like the father of Damasus; was buried at the charge of his wife, by name Laurentia, like the mother of the great Pontiff, who, as we have seen, survived her husband. Moreover, Laurentia, the mother of

---

[1] There is no reason why the office of deacon should not be named before that of lector, to suit the verse; there are other instances of the same. Another Damasian inscription (to which I shall return later), speaking of a deacon called Florentius, describes him first as in *sacris famulus* (deacon) and afterwards as lector. Cp. Ihm, *Epigr.* No. 34, pp. 39-40.

[2] Damasus uses the verb *retinere* for "to preserve," "quis mage virgineum placuit *retinere* pudorem"—"nomina nec numerum potuit *retinere* vetustas." So *retinere plebem Christi* means "to keep, guard, govern" the people of Christ.

Damasus, lived for 60 years a life consecrated to God, *sexaginta Deo vixit*; and the same is clearly suggested of Laurentia, the wife of Bishop Leo, of whom the inscription says that her tenor of life corresponded to that of her husband, as they were both dedicated to the service of God; that she was *fidelis* and of venerable age : *moribus apta meis semper veneranda fidelis.*[1]

Another point of similarity between the two cases may be noticed. In the inscription of the Archives Damasus says of his father, " Creverat hinc meritis quoniam *melioribus actis* "; and in the epitaph on Bishop Leo, Damasus uses the same expression of his idea, " Judicio post multa Dei *meliora secutus.*" Now it is remarkable that Damasus uses the word *meliora* in the sense of "a higher life" (*acta meliora*) three times only, once in the verses on S. Tarsicius, again in those on the Archives which speak of his father, and finally in these on Bishop Leo. The poem on Tarsicius says of the protomartyr Stephen, *Judaicus populus Stephanum meliora monentem perculerat saxis*, etc., evidently meaning Stephen's discourse in which he exhorted the Jews to turn to Jesus Christ.[2] In the verses on Bishop Leo *meliora secutus* must be understood as *acta meliora secutus*, referring no doubt to his conversion, as the inscription tells us that he was so converted: *Contemptis opibus malui cognoscere Christum.*

Arguing by analogy, then, I come to the conclu-

[1] The epithet *fidelis* is used of persons dedicated to God. Cp. *Virgo fidelis* in inscriptions, *e.g.* VIXIT PURA FIDE VIRGO FIDELIS (*Roma sotterranea*, iii. p. 230).

[2] Acts vii. The inscription has been already quoted above— No. 424, p. 353.

sion that in the poem of the Archives too, when he says of his father, *Creverat hinc meritis quoniam melioribus actis*, the words *melioribus actis* refer to his conversion. Thus Damasus appears to allude here to the conversion of his father; while we learn from the inscription that Bishop Leo was converted from paganism to Christianity; the coincidence is perfect. We may also remark that Damasus only uses the word *meritum* of Saints, or people of saintly life. Here, too, the words of the Archives inscription, *creverat hinc meritis*, would be admirably suited to describe Bishop Leo, who was afterwards venerated as a Saint.[1]

It must be allowed that the details of these two lives present an astounding resemblance which it is difficult to account for as the result of mere accident. From this harmony of coincidences the thought naturally arises that the unknown bishop of the *agro Verano* may have been the father of the great Pontiff. And another inference again may be drawn from the words, *invidia infelix tandem compressa quiescet*, used in the inscription of Bishop Leo, which clearly allude to persecutions and slanders. We know from the disputes which arose in the time of Pope Liberius that Damasus was always a mark for his enemies' hatred, even before ascending the Pontifical throne; thus the *Liber pontificalis* says of him, "Accusatus *invidiose* incriminatur de adulterio." Damasus alludes to this hostile feeling again in the inscription of the martyr S. Felix of Nola: *hostibus extinctis fuerant qui falsa locuti*.[2] The odium against the son may have embittered the life of the aged father also,

---

[1] See De Rossi, *Bull. di arch. crist.* p. 56.

[2] Ihm, No. 61.

and it may be to this circumstance that the verse in the inscription of Leo refers.

But I must not ignore the objections that have been made in some quarters; indeed I cannot state them more clearly than by showing that there is a very good answer to them.

No 1. Damasus inserted his own name in the inscriptions of his mother and his sister; why should he have omitted it in that of his father?

My reply is, first, in the epitaph of Leo the deceased is represented as speaking, not the writer of the inscription; and it would have been rather strange for him to state that he was the father of Damasus. Next, the tomb was made by Laurentia, his wife, and not by his son. Thirdly, the inscription of Bishop Leo has not come down to us entire; and the fragment preserved in the Lateran Museum shows that besides the verses there must have been some words in prose, and more especially a dedication, of which nothing remains but the letters VV (*viro venerabili*). Now these dedications were not always transcribed in the Collections; *e.g.* in the Damasian inscription of S. Eusebius there is an entire omission of two lines containing the dedication by Pope Damasus and the signature by Furius Dionysius Philocalus. We are therefore at liberty to believe that the original monument, which must have been of some magnificence, and decorated with pierced marble screens, bore the name of Damasus. And if his father died, as is probable, some years before his mother, when the son was still only in minor orders, a prose dedication, *e.g.*, *Damasus patri suo*, etc., would seem more natural than a statement in verse that the deceased was *pater Damasi*—an expression which would savour of arrogance before Damasus attained to the Pontificate ; and it would in no way increase the dignity of a bishop to be known as father of a deacon. But if the verses were written by Damasus while he was a mere deacon, they read as naturally as possible.

No. 2. Bishop Leo was over 80 when he died, leaving Laurentia, the mother of Damasus, a widow of 29 or 32 years of age : Leo then could not have been the husband of a lady so much younger than himself. I have already anticipated the answer to this objection, which might seem one of some gravity, by proving it to be a perfectly gratuitous assumption that Laurentia was still young when she became a widow, inasmuch as *sexaginta Deo vixit* cannot mean that she was an actual widow for 60 years before her death ; and that, on the contrary, these 90 years are to be reckoned from the date of her separation from her husband, on his taking orders. When this is understood, it matters not whether you supply the lacuna in the line as *post foedera sancta* or as *post foedera prima*, in neither case would any difficulty arise owing to the age of Leo. Suppose him separated from his wife when she was 29 or 32 years of age, and he perhaps a trifle older ; he may well have lived many years longer, and after passing through all the grades of the hierarchy he may have died at the age of 80.

No. 3. Bishop Leo of the Via Tiburtina had been an idolater, then had made a fortune, and, lastly, on conversion had taken holy orders. On the other hand the father of Damasus had been *exceptor* and after that *lector* ; but *exceptores* took that office in early youth, and it would therefore have been difficult for him to find the time to do all he did before becoming *exceptor*; it follows that the life-

career of the father of Damasus does not correspond
with that of Leo.

This also I answered when I showed that
exceptores were really notaries, and that the latter
might be 40 years of age, as shown by inscriptions.
If then we suppose that the father of Damasus was
converted in his 30th year, he clearly had plenty
of time to give to business and to make money
before his conversion. And we must not omit to
notice that the words of the inscription of Leo,
censum cupiens cognoscere mundi, rather suggest a
youth starting in business than a man with the
experience of many years. If this be so, Leo at
his conversion was not of advanced age, but still
young. Now the father of Damasus was not a
child when he entered the clerical profession.
And in this connexion I may cite the very
opportune remark of Perez [1] on the words " Hinc
pater *exceptor, lector, levita, sacerdos*," which, he
maintains, enumerate the offices which he held in
their correct order; in short, that he was first *exceptor*, then *lector*. And he observes that, as a rule,
youths who entered for the clerical profession first
became *lectores*, and from the *lectores* were afterwards selected the *exceptores*. To support this he
quotes a passage of Ennodius which relates how
Epiphanius of Pavia, after having filled the office
of *lector*, was nominated *exceptor*.[2] And hence
Perez infers that if the father of Damasus was
exceptor before being *lector*, he could not have
entered the clerical profession as a boy, but must

[1] *Damasus et Laurentius Hispanis asserti et vindicati*
(1756), p. 46.
[2] Ennodius, *In vita Epiphanii Ticinensis*. Ed. Paris,
1611, p. 360.

have been of mature years, and competent to transact the difficult duties of *exceptor*. And we have already noticed that an office which was practically that of a notary and a stenographer could not possibly be filled by boys, and therefore that the expression *puer exceptor* must be understood to refer to anything rather than youthfulness of the official. And it is impossible, at any rate, to assert that a *lector* must necessarily be of very tender years, for the inscriptions inform us that there were *lectores* of over 30 years of age, and that some of them were married.[1]

So, too, there is no force in the argument derived from the fact that the Archives inscription describes the father of Damasus as *exceptor, lector, levita, sacerdos*, while that of Leo in the Via Tiburtina records *lector, levita, sacerdos* only. For assuming the two people to be identical, there was a reason for mentioning in the Archives inscription the office of *exceptor*, which the father of Damasus had filled on that spot, a reason which did not apply to his sepulchral inscription, where it was enough to mention his full holy orders.

No. 4. *Liber pontificalis* says that Damasus was born *ex patre Antonio*; therefore Bishop Leo could not have been his father.

My answer is that *Antonius* is a gentile name, while Leo is a cognomen; the father of Damasus may very well have been named Antonius Leo; and as the use of more names than one was rather common, he might have been called *Antonius qui*

---

[1] HIC · REQVIESCIT · RVFINVS · LECTOR | QVI ·VIXIT ANNIS · P · M · XXXI | *dep*OSITVS · IN · PACE · IIII · IDVS | SEPT | *arc*ADIO · ET · HONORIO · AVGG · V · CONSS · (A.D. 402). (From the Cemetery of S. Hermes.)

et Leo, as may be seen on many inscriptions.[1] Finally, Leo may have been his personal name.

Furthermore, he may also, as was often done, have changed his name at baptism, having been previously an idolater ; this is the more possible as Leo had a Biblical meaning and was therefore more used by Christians than by pagans.

If this hypothesis is correct, the *Liber pontificalis* would be following its own practice in recording the gentile name only of the father of Damasus, as it does in the case of other Popes. I may add that, in the opinion of Duchesne, the registers of the families of the Popes in the *Liber pontificalis* are not of much value before the Pontificate of Felix III. (483-492), a century later than Damasus.[2]

I have already observed on the fact that the inscription of Leo was carved on two separate screens, and had a dedication in prose (now lost) ; hence it is possible that the gentile name Antonius actually appeared in the dedication, while the personal name of Leo was used in the actual epitaph for the convenience of the verse.[3]

[1] In an inscription of the year 352, and therefore contemporary with Damasus, we read of a MASCLINIVS LEO (Wilmans, *Exempla inscriptionum*, No. 2283).

[2] See Duchesne, *Lib. pont.* i. (Les Sources, p. lxxvi).

[3] With regard to *Antonius*, the father of Damasus, it is worth noticing that, according to the *Liber pontificalis*, Damasus endowed the church which he built *juxta theatrum*, where his father's house stood (S. Lorenzo in Damaso), with a *possessio Antoniana in territorio Cassino*. Could this have been a family property? If so, it would harmonise with the fact that Bishop Leo had been a business man in his youth, *censum cupiens cognoscere mundi*, was a man of wealth, *contemptis opibus*, and property, *omnia quaeque vides proprio quaesita labore*, etc. One of the charges made against Damasus by his detractors was of *porrectae in longum possessiones* (cp. *Libellus precum* already quoted).

It might also be objected that had Damasus been the son of an ecclesiastic the *Liber pontificalis* would not have failed to record the fact, as in the cases where it was true of other Popes. I can answer to this, that the Papal biographies are often silent on this point, possibly because the writer failed to notice it. Thus it is clear that it was omitted in the biography of Anastasius II. (496-498), where the *Liber pontificalis* only says "ex patre Petro"; whereas it is perfectly well known from his inscription quoted above that his father was a priest.[1] If, then, a point of this sort is left unnoticed in the portion of the work which is accepted as fairly authoritative on the genealogies of Popes, we need not be surprised if it is left equally unnoticed in the portion which has less historical authority.

This is, I hope, an exhaustive answer to all the difficulties raised.

And here it is important, I think, to notice, that if we accept the suggested identification of Bishop Leo with the father of Damasus, it may be gathered from what has been said above that the separation from his wife took place in A.D. 307, when she was about 32 years of age. Now he was probably but little older than his wife; and if he died at over 80 (*octoginta Leo transcendit episcopus annos*), we may conjecture, always on the assumption aforesaid, that he did not die before 350, when Damasus was a deacon. Clearly then, if he was converted at the age of 30, he had had plenty of time before that to devote himself to worldly affairs, and if he took orders in 307 and died about 350, he may very well have passed through all the steps

[1] *Presbytero genitus*, etc.; see Duchesne, *Lib. pont.* i. p. 258.

of the Hierarchy, and have been successively *exceptor, lector, levita, sacerdos.*

It is worth attention that the verses on Bishop Leo, although Damasian in style, are cut in the ordinary lettering of the fourth century, exactly like the epitaphs of the mother and sister of Damasus; and thus this fact, which might have raised some difficulties against my hypothesis, had we not known all about the originals of the two last-mentioned, now, on the contrary, turns out to agree with the practice of Damasus up to a certain time in his life; for we have shown that he did not adopt the lettering of Philocalus till later.

But notice should also be taken of the fact that on the precise spot in the *agro Verano* where the fragments of the inscription on Bishop Leo came to light, there were also found many fragments of inscriptions in the genuine and unmistakable lettering of Philocalus, which have no reference to the local martyr S. Lawrence.[1] One of these fragments, still in situ, was found in absolutely the same place as the fragments of the epitaph of Leo; it runs as follows:

441

MARMORIBVS VESTITA *novis?*
QVAE INTEMERATA FIDES . . . . .
HIC ETIAM PARIES IVSTO . . . . .
OMNIA PLENA VIDES . . . . .

I seem to recognise some connexion between

[1] Ihm, No. 35. I have been able to recognise a few more fragments as Damasian, or of that school, in my searches in the cemetery of Cyriaca.

this fragment and the epitaph on Leo. Indeed the last line of the fragment, *omnia plena vides*, recalls the first line of the epitaph, *omnia quaeque vides* ; and the words *intemerata fides* in the second line of the fragment remind one of the eulogy on Laurentia, the wife of Leo, *semper veneranda fidelis.*

Furthermore, the poem to which the words *omnia plena vides* belonged goes on to speak of a splendid monument, decorated with marble, *marmoribus vestita . . .,* and it would appear that this monument had been erected by the person described as having *intemerata fides.*

And no doubt the tomb of Bishop Leo was splendid, seeing it was erected on his own property purchased by his own money ; and it was prepared for him by a spouse *veneranda fidelis.* We may well suspect, then, that the Damasian metrical inscription containing the words *marmoribus vestita* was placed on the actual tomb of Leo. If so, it might be inferred that Damasus, who wrote his first poem in honour of that worthy while still using the ordinary fourth-century lettering, put up another inscription to the same person after adopting the alphabet of Philocalus ; and this would confirm the idea that he held him in special affection. All which would, according to my hypothesis, be very natural and intelligible.

Another detail which must not be neglected is that the tomb of Bishop Leo stands near that of the martyr S. Lawrence. It is true that he had, while still a pagan, bought himself a property there with no reference to the sanctuary of the Saint ; but it is also true that he did not construct his own tomb there, this having been done many years after, when he died *Christi sacerdos*, by his wife

Laurentia, who took charge of his funeral. The wife's very name might explain the choice of the spot, close to the martyr whose name she bore ; but we must also remember that the family of Damasus must have had a special devotion to the martyr S. Lawrence on account of their Spanish origin, which they shared with that heroic deacon of the Roman Church.[1] This explains the magnificence of the gifts made by Damasus to the altar of S. Lawrence (*cumulat altaria donis*) and the consecration of a basilica by Damasus to that martyr on the site of his father's house (S. Lorenzo in Damaso).

And if we suppose that the tomb of the father of Damasus stood near so venerable and holy a spot, where he must have expressly desired to be buried, we shall understand why Damasus, though then Pope, and though he had founded a family tomb on the Via Ardeatina, should nevertheless have been unwilling to remove his father's bones from the place where they had lain for so many years.

I will conclude this investigation with a few additional remarks.

De Rossi, who was the first to publish the epitaph of Bishop Leo, published shortly afterwards another Damasian inscription on a young deacon of 38 years of age, Florentius by name, whom he made out to be a son of the above-mentioned bishop who died before his father. A fragment of this inscription was preserved in the Lateran Museum, and another was recovered in the *agro Verano*. The complete text is supplied in the Corbeian Collec-

---

[1] See Perez, *Damasus et Laurentius Hispanis asserti et vindicati* (Romae, 1756).

tion at St. Petersburg (*Bull. di arch. crist.*, 1881, p. 34):

442

Quisque vides tumulum vitam si quaeris operti
Ter morior denos et post bis quattuor annos
Servatum Christo reddens de corpore munus
Cuius ego in sacris famulus vel in ordine lector
Officio levita fui Florentius ore
Qui pater in terris item mihi sancte SACERD*os*
Contigit et natum tenuit IAM SORTE SECVNDA
HOC SVPERA*nte meo discedi*T SPIRITVS ORAE
ISTE SENI *Casus gravis est mi*HI MORTE BEATVS
QVOD PATRIS *hospitio bene nunc mea membra quie-*
DEP · DIE · PR . . . . . .[1]   [*scunt.*

De Rossi explains *natus sorte secunda* as meaning that Florentius was both the actual and the spiritual son of Leo, being deacon to him. But it is better perhaps to take it as meaning that he was his second son.

If my hypothesis is true, then he would be brother to Damasus; and this would agree with what has been said above, that Damasus had other brothers and sisters besides Irene. And no difficulty arises from the fact that the inscription of Florentius is in the lettering of Philocalus, for as Damasus may have written a second and " Philocalian " epitaph on his father in later years after becoming

[1] One fragment of the inscription of Florentius is the property of the Lateran Museum ; the other has been lost, but I have lately recovered two pieces of it, one from the municipal stores, the other from the cemetery of Cyriaca. I have put the three fragments together, and placed them on the walls of the Lateran Museum by the side of the inscription of Leo.

Pope, so he may have written another for his brother also, after adopting this style.

De Rossi, moreover, insisted that Damasus must have written the inscription of Florentius many years later, after the death and beatification of his father Leo, as it describes the son as *beatus* for finding a resting-place in the paternal tomb; and this would explain satisfactorily the use of the " Philocalian " character.

But we may get some more light from the actual name of Florentius. It is well known that we often find similar names in the same family, *e.g. Florus, Florentius*; *Valens, Valentinianus*; *Constantinus, Constans, Constantius*, etc. Now it is worth noting that Damasus wrote another beautiful poem commemorative of the death of a young married lady of 16 years of age, of the name of *Projecta*, and she, be it observed, was the daughter of one *Florus*. This inscription, to which attention has been called already, bears the consular date of the year 383, and is cut in very elegant " Philocalian " character.

For greater clearness I will quote the text of this beautiful epitaph, which is in the Lateran Museum :

443

QVID LOQVAR AVT SILEAM PROHIBET DOLOR IPSE
FATERI | IIIC TVMVLVS LACRIMAS RETINET CO-
GNOSCE PARENTVM | PROIECTAE FVERAT PRIMO
QVAE IVNCTA MARITO | PVLCRA DECORE SVO
SOLO CONTENTA PVDORE | HEV DILECTA SATIS
MISERAE GENITRICIS AMORE | ACCIPE QVID MVL-
TIS THALAMI POST FOEDERA PRIMA | EREPTA EX
OCVLIS FLORI GENITORIS ABIIT | AETHERIAM CV-
PIENS COELI CONSCENDERE LVCEM | HAEC DA-
MASVS PRAESTAT CVNCTIS SOLACIA FLETVS |
VIXIT ANN · XVI · M · IX · DIES · XXV · DEP · III · KAL · IAN ·
FL · MEROBAVDE · ET · FL · SATVRNIN · CONSS (a.d. 383)

Damasus was very aged when he composed this poem, being in the last year but one of his Pontificate: he deplores bitterly the death of the young bride, saying that his very grief forbade him to decide whether he should speak or be silent. *Quid loquar aut sileam? prohibet dolor ipse fateri.* Now I confess that the excessive grief of the aged Pontiff (who had already lost all his own relations) for the death of this young lady seems rather unnatural, unless she was connected with him by some family tie. If this be admitted, we must suppose that *Florus*, the father of Projecta, was a relative of Damasus, probably his nephew, in which case Projecta would have been his great-niece.

And on that hypothesis the youthful Projecta would represent, as regards the mother of Damasus, the fourth generation, *i.e.* exactly the *progenies quarta* recorded in the inscription of the mother of Damasus, lately found in the cemetery near the Via Ardeatina [No. 434, p. 364]. In that case the restoration of that line which I suggested in the first part of this work, *Progenie quarta vidit quae laeta nepotes*, would be extremely suitable, as it would be equivalent to saying that Laurentia died shortly after the birth of Projecta.

The inscription of Projecta tells us that she died on December 30th, 383, at the age of 16 years 9 months and 25 days; she was therefore born on March 5th, 367; and therefore Laurentia, on the hypothesis stated, must have died shortly after that date. But Damasus was elected Pope in October 366; these conjectures, then, would be in perfect agreement with the view I have maintained from the beginning, that Laurentia died at the commencement of the Pontificate of Damasus, that she left her husband in 307, and that she subsequently lived a consecrated life for 60 years. It is remarkable, at any rate, that the birth of Projecta (367), who may reasonably be supposed to have been connected with Damasus, and, as far as the dates go, might very well represent the fourth generation of his family (the *progenies quarta* named at the end of the inscription), is *exactly* 60 *years* after the date (307) which we have already fixed on other grounds as the beginning of Laurentia's consecration to God, which lasted exactly 60 years. This coincidence of dates is undoubtedly of great value in solving the problem before us, and in establishing a connexion between the inscription of Projecta and the family of Damasus.

De Rossi had already conjectured that some connexion existed between Damasus and Florus: in the opinion of my honoured master, Florus, the father of Projecta, was the person who placed a fine inscription on the tomb of Liberalis, consul and martyr, in a cemetery on the old Via Salaria. (See for this inscription De Rossi, *Inscr.* i. 2, pp. 145-146.)

444

MARTYRIS HIC SANCTI LIBERALIS MEMBRA QVIE-
SCVNT | QVI QVONDAM IN TERRIS CONSVL HONORE
FVIT | SED CREVIT TITVLIS FACTVS DE CONSVLE
MARTYR | CVI VIVIT SEMPER MORTE CREATVS HO-
NOR | PLVS FVIT IRATO QVAM GRATO PRINCIPE
FELIX | QVEM PERIMENS RABIDVS MISIT AD ASTRA
FVROR | GRATIA CVI DEDERAT TRABEAS DEDIT
IRA CORONAM | DVM CHRISTO PROCERVM MENS
INIMICA FVIT | OBTVLIT HAEC DOMINO COMPONENS
ATRIA FLORVS | VT SANCTOS VENERANS PRAEMIA
IVSTA FERAT | QVAMVIS PATRICIO CLARVS DE GER-
MINE CONSVL | INLVSTRES TRABEAS NOBILITATE
TVAS | PLVS TAMEN AD MERITVM CRESCIT QVOD
MORTE BEATA | MARTYRIS EFFVSO SANGVINE
NOMEN HABES | ADIVNCTVSQVE DEO TOTA QVAM
MENTE PETISTI | ADSERTOR CHRISTI SIDERA IVRE
COLIS | SIT PRECOR ACCEPTVM QVOD POST·DISPEN-
DIA BELLI | IN MELIVS MANVS RESTITVERE FLORI

This is a most important document, as it tells us of a consul altogether unknown, who became a martyr for the faith of Christ, and who is complimented on his illustrious birth, which, it is said, shed glory even on the fasces of a consul.

This epitaph also states that Florus built a basilica on that spot COMPONENS · ATRIA · FLORVS; and it would be very natural that a relative of Damasus should follow his splendid example in showing devotion to the tombs of the martyrs.[1]

[1] De Rossi calls our attention to a piece of funerary glass, on which one Florus is represented by the side of Damasus, and he suggests that this person may have been the author of the poem and the father of Projecta (*Bull. di arch. crist.*, 1894, p. 37).

These noble lines, which might well have been written by a contemporary of Damasus, conclude with a prayer to the martyr to accept the labour bestowed on his tomb *post dispendia belli*:

Sit precor acceptum quod post dispendia belli
In melius manus restituere Flori.[1]

De Rossi thought *dispendia belli* may refer to the sack of Rome by Alaric in 410; and even accepting this view, Florus may have been a nephew of Damasus. But the inscription might actually date from the time of the Pontiff. And, for my part, I am inclined to think that the words *post dispendia belli* allude to the serious quarrels which arose at the beginning of the Pontificate of Damasus through the schism of Ursinus. Indeed, the struggle against the Ursinians was actually called *bellum* by the historian Rufinus, whose words are these:

"Quo ex facto tanta seditio immo vero tanta *bella* coorta sunt a alterutrum defendentibus populis ut implerentur humano sanguine orationum loca" (*H.E.* ii. 10).

And Damasus himself, in describing similar contests between the followers of Pope Eusebius and those of the heresiarch Heraclius, uses an identical expression: "Seditio caedes *bellum* discordia lites."

This being so, I see no difficulty in inferring that Florus meant by *post dispendia belli* to refer to the end of the schism of Ursinus, when, following the

---

[1] The codex gives *disperandia*, but *dispendia* is evidently the correct reading: De Rossi, *Inscr. christ.* ii. p. 104. The last line, *In melius manus restituere Flori*, has been added.

example of Damasus, he set himself to decorate the tombs of the martyrs just as Damasus had done when he wrote the line *Pro reditu cleri Christo praestante triumphans.* This, then, is one more link between Florus and Pope Damasus.

And if Florus was nephew or grand-nephew to Damasus, we find ourselves getting nearer to Florentius, whose name suggests that they belonged to the same family ; and he again brings us back to Bishop Leo as his possible father: this at least is the opinion of De Rossi.

Finally, I may remark that the name of his mother Laurentia may indicate that she also belonged to the family of the Florentii, as we find in that family a Florida and a Laurentius.[1]

To all this I may add one final observation. In the inscriptions relating to Pope Damasus himself years are not mentioned ; these are only taken into account, and that with great exactness, in the inscriptions of his mother Laurentia, of his sister Irene (which gives, as I pointed out, the date of her profession), of Bishop Leo, of Florentius the deacon, who was probably the son of Leo, and of Projecta the daughter of Florus.[2] And we know of no other inscriptions of private individuals that can be certainly assigned to Damasus besides those which

[1] See Riese, *Anthol. Lat.* ii. pp. 211-212. I have had occasion elsewhere to dwell on the importance of a burial-place of the family Flori Florentii near the cemetery of Callisto, a burial-place that had been previously discovered by De Rossi, *Roma sotterranea*, iii. p. 40.

[2] "Centum minus (octo per ?) annos " (Laurentia).
"Bis denas hiemes necdum compleverat aetas " (Irene).
"Octoginta Leo transcendit episcopus annos" (Leo).
"Ter morior denos et post bis quatuor annos " (Florentius).
"Vixit annos XVI., menses IX., dies XXV." (Projecta).

I have here recorded ; which so far justifies a certain inference that some family tie existed among the subjects of these various private inscriptions composed by Damasus, on account of which he wished to record the minutest details concerning them.[1]

The rigorously logical result of my argument is this : if we admit the most reasonable, most natural, and most generally accepted interpretation of the inscription on the Archives, *Hinc pater exceptor, lector, levita, sacerdos,* and if we accept the evidence of the inscription of *mater Damasi,* even in its present condition, we cannot but recognise an extraordinary combination of coincidences between the facts we know about the father of Damasus and the statements about Bishop Leo in his inscription in the *agro Verano,* coincidences which have struck all to whom I have submitted this inquiry.[2]

[1] From this inquiry, and especially from the comparison of these inscriptions, and on the hypothesis above stated, a possible chronological table might be drawn up of the proximate dates of the events in the lives of the individuals in question.

Proposed Table

275-278. Birth of Laurentia, mother of Damasus. — 305. Birth of Damasus. — 306. Birth of Irene. — 307. Separation between Laurentia and her husband on his taking orders ; Laurentia being then 29 or 32 years of age, and her husband a little older. — 350 (or later). Death of the father of Damasus, over 80 years of age. — 366 (October). Election of Damasus to Pontificate at the age of 61. 367 (March 5th). Birth of Projecta, daughter of Florus and (perhaps) grand-niece of Damasus. — 367. Death of Laurentia (after March 5th), aged 89 or 92. — 368-9. Death of Irene, aged 62 or 63. — 383 (December 30th). Death of Projecta, aged 16 years 9 months and 25 days. — 384 (December 11th). Death of Damasus, aged about 80.

[2] All archaeologists whom I have consulted agree in my proposed identification. I may add that even Wilpert, while

Indeed, if all that has been said be accepted, we have these two persons living at the same time, each celebrated by Damasus in an epitaph, each going through the same steps of an ecclesiastical career, each married to a wife named Laurentia who took Professional Vows, each having children, each predeceasing his wife; and while one is expressly declared to have been converted from idolatry, allusion to the same circumstance is made in the case of the other.

And it is undeniable that these coincidences are sufficient to give my hypothesis an air of great probability, and of great importance for the study of the life of Damasus.

I must hold that until it be demonstrated that the inscription on the Archives reads *puer*, and not *pater*, it must be admitted that the father of Damasus was *lector, levita, sacerdos*; that until another fragment of the inscription of the mother of Damasus be recovered to show that *post foedera* means *post soluta foedera mortis causa*, the most natural explanation of the words *sexaginta Deo vixit* is that which I propose; and thus, that pending new and conclusive discoveries, my hypothetical identification of Bishop Leo with the father of Damasus must be accepted as reasonable and probable.

In this fashion we may, by careful investigation of some of the Damasian texts, arrive at a reconstruction of some important pages in the history of

contesting its correctness, is obliged to allow that his interpretation of the verses on the Archives, and of the inscription of Laurentia, which provided the principal arguments against my theory, could no longer be supported (See *Römische Quartalschrift*, 1908, pp. 128-129).

certain great personalities of the Roman Church in the fourth century. And with this important inquiry into a subject hitherto untouched I close my treatise on Damasian epigraphy, and I pass to the consideration of other classes of ancient Christian inscriptions.

CHAPTER X

ILLUSTRATIONS OF HISTORICAL (NON-DAMASIAN) INSCRIPTIONS FROM THE FOURTH TO THE SIXTH CENTURY

I WILL begin this chapter with the long and very beautiful sepulchral inscription which De Rossi very properly attributes to Pope Liberius (352-366). The text of it is reported in the Corbeian Collection now in St. Petersburg ; and it stood in the cemetery of Priscilla, in which that Pope was buried.[1]

445

Quam Domino fuerant devota mente parentes [2]
qui confessorem talem genuere potentem
atque sacerdotem sanctum, sine felle columbam,
divinae legis sincero corde magistrum.
Haec te nascentem suscepit Ecclesia mater,
uberibus fidei nutriens de[vo]ta beatum,
qui pro se passurus eras mala cuncta libenter.
Parvulus utque loqui coepisti dulcia verba,
mox scripturarum lector pius indole factus,
ut tua lingua magis legem quam verba sonaret,
dilecta a Domino tua dicta infantia simplex,
nullis arte dolis sceda fucata malignis
officio tali iusto puroque legendi.

[1] De Rossi, *Inscr. christ.* i. 2, pp. 83-86.
[2] Owing to the length of this inscription, it is not printed in uncial type.

Atque item simplex adolescens mente fuisti,
maturusque animo ferventi aetate modestus,
remotus, prudens, mitis, gravis, integer, aequus ;
haec tibi lectori innocuo fuit aurea vita.
Diaconus hinc factus iuvenis meritoque fideli,
qui sic sincere, caste, integreque pudice
servieris sine fraude Deo, [qui] pectore puro
atque annis aliquot fueris levita severus,
ac tali iusta conversatione beata,
dignus qui merito inlibatus iure perennis
huic tantae sedi Christi splendore serenae
electus fidei plenus summusque sacerdos
qui nivea mente immaculatus papa sederes
qui bene apostolicam doctrinam sancte doceres
innocuam plebem caelesti lege magister.
Quis, [t]e tractante, sua non peccata reflebat?
In synodo cunctis superatis victor iniquis
sacrilegis, Nicaena fides electa triumphat.
Contra quamplures certamen sumpseris unus
catholica praecincte fide possederis omnes.
Vox tua certantis fuit haec sincera, salubris :
atque nec hoc metuo neve illud committereque opto ;
haec fuit haec semper mentis constantia firma.
Discerptus, tractus, profugatusque sacerdos,
insuper ut faciem quodam nigrore velaret
nobili falsa manu portantes aemula caeli,
ut speciem Domini foedare[t] luce corusc[am].
En tibi discrimen vehemens non sufficit annum,
insuper exilio decedis martyr ad astra,
atque inter patriarchas praesagosque prophetas,
inter apostolicam turbam martyrumque potentum.
Cum hac turba dignus mediusque locatus [honeste]
mitter[is in] Domini conspectu[m], iuste sacerdos.
Sic inde tibi merito tanta est concessa potestas,
ut manum imponas patientibus, incola Christi,

daemonia expellas, purges mundesque repletos,
ac salvos homines reddas animosque vigentes
per Patris ac Filii nomen, cui credimus omnes.
Cumque tu[um] hoc obitum praecellens tale videmus,
spem gerimus cuncti proprie nos esse beatos,
qui sumus hocque tuum meritum fidemque secuti.

The poet begins by calling Liberius a *Confessor* of the Faith :

Quam Domino fuerant devota mente parentes
qui confessorem talem genuere potentem.

Then, after alluding to his early ecclesiastical career, he speaks of his election to the Apostolic See :

Huic tantae sedi Christi splendore serenae
electus fidei plenus summusque sacerdos
qui nivea mente immaculatus papa sederes.

He goes on to refer to a synod called together in Rome by Liberius, in which he triumphantly asserted the Creed of Nicaea :

In synodo cunctis superatis victor iniquis
sacrilegis, Nicaena fides electa triumphat.

Moreover, he stood alone to fight for the purity of the Catholic Faith against its many foes ; and here allusion is made to the condemnation of the Council of Rimini :

Contra quamplures certamen sumpseris unus
catholica praecincte fide possederis omnes.

The poet then asserts that these had always been the opinions of the Pontiff, and that he ever remained steadfast in the true doctrine :

Haec fuit haec semper mentis constantia firma.

And he concludes by saying that he died a martyr to his faith, not positively in exile, but in consequence of it : *Insuper exilio decedis martyr ad astra.*

From these words we may gather that there had been some accusations levelled against him, which his encomiast wished to refute ; thus he goes on to say that the Pope was driven into exile, and that attempts were made to make him sully the spotlessness of his faith : *ut faciem quodam nigrore velaret.* But he testifies, and solemnly declares, that the Pontiff's belief remained pure ; he calls him a Confessor of the Faith ; glorifies him as having his seat in Heaven among the patriarchs, prophets, apostles, and martyrs ; and he finally declares that God had been working great miracles at his tomb through his intercession.

The emphasis on these last words may be attributed without doubt to the enthusiasm of the partisans of Liberius ; but at any rate such a contemporary memorial of the Pontiff thus publicly exhibited in Rome is a splendid testimony to the belief of the Roman Church in Liberius as a champion of the Nicene faith and a stout fighter for Catholic truth.

In my opinion, however, this inscription was placed on the tomb of Liberius some years after his death ; this may have been done in the days of Pope Syricius, who was his faithful companion, and doubtless also his admirer, inasmuch as his own epitaph makes express mention of Liberius, as we shall see later.

Liberius certainly received the honour of "Veneration," at any rate at a later period ; his name is to be found in the martyrology of Jerome at least twice, on September 24th, the day of his death, and May 17th, the anniversary of his ordination.

It could not, however, be said that he was admitted to the rank of saint in the fourth century immediately after his death; as the honour of immediate beatification was reserved to martyrs only. It is true that in his sepulchral eulogy he is called *martyr*; but this must be taken merely as an emphatic way of speaking on the part of the writer, who was evidently an admirer of the Pontiff and who expressed the opinion of his other admirers. But from the rather exaggerated language of the eulogy (in which, by the way, justice was at last done to this unconquerable and much-calumniated Pontiff) it must not be inferred that Liberius was really placed on the same level as the martyrs in the fourth century, for the purposes of public worship. And it is difficult to accept the suggestion recently made, that the portrait of that date found on a tomb in the cemetery of Prae-textatus is a likeness of Liberius.[1]

Inscription of Pope Syricius
(385-399)

Pope Syricius was buried in the cemetery of Priscilla, according to the *Liber pontificalis*; the precise spot was near the tomb of Silvester, *ad pedes Sylvestri*, as noted in one of the Itineraries.[2]

The text of his sepulchral inscription, which is

[1] See *Nuovo Bull. di arch. crist.*, 1908, p. 77, note 1.

[2] " Qui etiam sepultus est in cymiterio Priscillae via Salaria," *L.P.*, Duchesne's ed., i. p. 216. De Rossi, *Roma sotterranea*, i. p. 176.

modelled on the style of Damasus, is known
to us through the two Collections of Lorsch and
Verdun, which say that the verses were placed *ad
S. Silvestrum ubi ante pausavit super illo altare.*
This shows that the transcription was made after
the relics of Silvester had been taken up thence
and transported within the city, which took place
in the Pontificate of Paul I. (757-767).

The poem runs thus:

446

LIBERIVM LECTOR MOX ET LEVITA SECVTVS |
POST DAMASVM CLARVS TOTOS QVOS VIXIT IN
ANNOS | FONTE SACRO MAGNVS MERVIT SEDERE
SACERDOS | CVNCTVS VT POPVLVS PACEM TVNC
SOLI CLAMARET | HIC PIVS HIC IVSTVS FELICIA
TEMPORA FECIT | DEFENSOR MAGNVS MVLTOS VT
NOBILES AVSVS | REGI SVBTRAHERET ECCLESIAE
AVLA DEFENDENS | MISERICORS LARGVS MERVIT
PER SAECVLA NOMEN | TER QVINOS POPVLVM
QVEM REXIT IN ANNOS AMORE | NVNC REQVIEM
SENTIT COELESTIA REGNA POTITVS[1]

From the old Collections.

This inscription is very well known, but it has
not hitherto been thoroughly investigated.

It begins by saying that Syricius was first lector,
and then deacon to Pope Liberius; that afterwards
he served in the same office of deacon to his successor Damasus; and that he was distinguished in
the performance of these duties (*clarus*) throughout the Pontificate of the latter (366-384).

We may next note the expression *fonte sacro
magnus meruit sedere sacerdos, cunctus ut populus*

[1] For the text of the poem see De Rossi, *Inscr. christ.* i. 11,
p. 102, No. 30; p. 138, No. 21.

pacem tunc soli clamaret. These words must refer to some solemn recognition of Pope Syricius having taken place close to a memorial baptistery.[1]

Inscription of Pope Coelestinus
(423-432)

Celestine succeeded Boniface I. in 423 ; he ruled the Church up to 432, and was buried in the cemetery of Priscilla, *et sepultus est in cymiterio Priscillae via Salaria.*[2] His sepulchral inscription is known from the Collections of Tours and Lorsch, but it does not contain the slightest allusion to the history of his Pontificate.[3] The epitaph confines itself to saying that the Pontiff earned the veneration of the Christian world, that he ruled for ten years, and then passed into that eternal life which is the guerdon of saints ; that his body lies in the tomb, but will rise from it one day, and that meanwhile his spirit enjoys the vision of Christ. The text is as follows :

447

PRAESVL APOSTOLICAE SEDIS VENERABILIS OMNI | QVEM REXIT POPVLO DECIMVM DVM CONDERET ANNVM | CAELESTINVS AGENS VITAM MIGRAVIT IN ILLAM | DEBITA QVAE SANCTIS AETERNOS REDDIT HONORES | CORPORIS HIC TVMVLVS RE-QVIESCVNT OSSA CINISQVE | NEC PERIT HINC ALIQVID DOMINO CARO CVNCTA RESVRGET | TER-RENVM NVNC TERRA TEGIT MENS NESCIA MORTIS | VIVIT ET ASPECTV FRVITVR BENE CONSCIA CHRISTI

From the ancient Collections.

[1] See *Nuovo Bull. di arch. crist.*, 1908, pp. 79 *et seq.*
[2] *Lib. pont.*, Duchesne's ed., i. p. 231.
[3] De Rossi, *Inscr. christ.* i. 2, p. 62, 1 ; p. 101, 19.

There would be remarkably little to say about the tomb of Celestine, were it not for the memories which his name revives of the great Council of Ephesus held under him. To that Council he sent Philip the priest by special appointment as legate of the Apostolic See, who then as representative of the Pope solemnly and publicly asserted the supremacy of the Church of Rome over all other churches of the world; and the Council acknowledged that supremacy by its acceptance of Philip's unqualified and solemn declaration: "Nulli dubium imo omnibus saeculis notum est quod Petrus apostolorum princeps et caput, fidei columna, Ecclesiae catholicae fundamentum, a Domino nostro Jesu Christo claves regni accepit . . . et semper in suis successoribus vivit et judicium exercet." [1]

And we find an echo of this solemn statement in a monument of the age of Celestine, viz. the dedicatory inscription on the basilica of Santa Sabina on the Aventine, where that Pontiff is called "the first bishop of the world": *Culmen apostolicum cum Coelestinus haberet—primus et in toto fulgeret episcopus orbe.*

The following is the inscription placed by the above-named Philip, priest, in his titular church of S. Pietro in Vinculis; it contains an allusion to the Council of Ephesus:

---

[1] *Coll. dei Concili*, Coleti's ed. vol. iii. p. 1154.

448

CEDE PRIVS NOMEN NOVITATI CEDE VETVSTAS |
REGIA LAETANTER VOTA DICARE LIBET | HAEC
PETRI PAVLIQVE SIMVL NVNC NOMINE SIGNO |
XYSTVS APOSTOLICAE SEDIS HONORE FRVENS |
VNVM QVAESO PARES VNVM DVO SVMITE MV-
NVS | VNVS HONOR CELEBRET QVOS HABET VNA
FIDES | PRESBYTERI TAMEN HIC LABOR EST ET
CVRA PHILIPPI | POSTQVAM EPHESI CHRISTVS
VICIT VTRIQVE POLO | PRAEMIA DISCIPVLIS ME-
RVIT VINCENTE MAGISTRO | HANC PALMAM FIDEI
RETTVLIT INDE SENEX

From the Collections of Inscriptions (De Rossi, *Inscr.* i. 2,
p. 110).

In this inscription Sixtus III. is named as the successor to Celestine; and it is to Sixtus III. (Pope 432-440) that the following refers:

449

VIRGO MARIA TIBI XYSTVS NOVA TEMPLA DICAVI |
DIGNA SALVTIFERO MVNERA VENTRE TVO | TE GE-
NITRIX IGNARA VIRI TE DENIQVE FETA | VISCERI-
BVS SALVIS EDITA NOSTRA SALVS | ECCE TVI TE-
STES VTERI SIBI PRAEMIA PORTANT | SVB PEDIBVS
IACET PASSIO CVIQVE SVA | FERRVM FLAMMA FE-
RAE FLVVIVS SEVVMQVE VENENVM | TOT TAMEN
HAS MORTES VNA CORONA MANET

In the basilica of Santa Maria Maggiore.
From the Collections of Inscriptions.[1]

This inscription records the work carried out by Sixtus III. in the basilica of Liberius, which he had

[1] De Rossi, *Inscr. christ.* i. 2, pp. 71, 98.

dedicated to the Virgin as a memorial of the above-mentioned solemn decision of the Council of Ephesus.

The composition of it is very good, besides being of the greatest value as evidence of the cult of the Virgin. Moreover, it describes the mosaics which the Pontiff had ordered to be made for the basilica, representing martyrs, with the emblems of their martyrdom.

These mosaics have perished, but those of the great chancel arch are still preserved; they represent the Virgin in the scene of the Epiphany; and above the arch are still to be read the words in which the Pope dedicated the building to the people of Christ:

XYSTVS · EPISCOPVS · PLEBI · DEI

Next to this I will quote another inscription of the time of Pope Leo the Great (440-461):

450

```
CVM · MVNDVM · LInquENS · DEMetrias · ANNIA ·
virgo | CLAudERET · ExtREMVM · NON · MORItura ·
diem | HaeC · TIBI · PAPa · LEO · VOTORVM · EX-
TREMA · suorum | TradiDIT · uT · sacrAE · SVR-
GERET · AVla domus | MaNDaTI · COMPLEta · FIDES ·
SED · GLORia · major | InTERIVS · VOTVM · SOL-
VERE · QVAM · PROPAlam | INdidERAT · cVLMEN ·
STEPhanVS · QVI · PRIMVS · IN · ORbe | RAPTVS ·
MORTe · trVCI · REGNat · IN · ARCE · poli | PrAE-
SVLIS · HAnc · jussV · TIGRINVS · Presbyter · aulam |
EXcOLIT · INSigNIS · MENTE · LABOre · vigens
```

In the basilica of S. Stefano on the Via Latina.[1]

---

[1] The letters in italics represent restorations of the text.

We learn from this inscription that the noble maiden Demetrias, belonging to a Roman family of rank, at her death bequeathed to the Church one of her farms, for the erection thereon of a basilica, in honour of the protomartyr Stephen ; and that after the pious lady's death Pope Leo undertook the duty of carrying out her wish. The magnificent ruins of this sacred edifice still exist : it was basilical in shape, consisting of three aisles with an apse, a chapel of the relics, and an adjoining baptistery: the remains of these were brought to light in 1857. The erection of this suburban church, which is recorded in *Liber pontificalis*, like the restoration of other churches which was carried out by the same Pope Leo, must be attributed to the last period of the life of the Pontiff, when he devoted himself to the repair of the mischief, material as well as moral, which the Church of Rome had suffered from the invasions of the barbarians ; and for this reason the basilica of S. Stefano with the inscription of Demetrias may be looked upon as records of the occurrences which shed eternal glory on the Pontificate of the great Leo.

Not long after the Pontificate of Leo the Western Empire fell (476), and barbarian rule over Italy began. To Odoacer succeeded Theodoric ; and the following inscription is an important record of the relations between the Roman Pontiffs and the Ostrogoth government :

451

AVLA · DI · CLARIS · RADIAT · SPECIOSA · METALLIS
IN · QVA · PLVS · FIDEI · LVX · PRETIOSA · MICAT
MARTYRIBVS · MEDICIS · POPVLO · SPES · CERTA · SA-
[LVTIS
VENIT · ET · EX · SACRO · CREVIT · HONORE · LOCVS
OPTVLIT · HOC · DNO · FELIX · ANTISTITE · DIGNVM
MVNVS · VT · AETHERIA · VIVAT · IN · ARCE · POLI

In the apse of SS. Cosmo and Damiano in the Forum
Romanum (letters in mosaic).

This inscription is a record of Pope Felix IV.
(526-530), who decorated and consecrated this
church, and whose Pontificate is of much historical
importance. He succeeded John I., who was
martyred through the senile jealousy of Theodoric;
and he was elected to the Papacy by the express
direction of the king of the Goths. This is the
first instance of the interference of the civil
power in the election of Popes; a practice which
was carried on by the king's successors, which
passed from them to the Byzantine emperors, and
thence again to the mediaeval German emperors,
thus causing the secular dissensions between Church
and Empire. This inscription also bears witness
to one of the oldest instances of the transformation
of a pagan public edifice of the Forum into a
Christian church; for the existing church is formed
by combining parts of two ancient constructions
of different dates, one being the temple of Romulus,
the son of Maxentius, built on the side of the Via
Sacra, of which the circular *cella* still exists, and
the other being the *templum sacrae urbis*, the
entrance to which was on the Forum of Peace,

and in which were found the fragments of a plan of Rome on marble executed in the days of Septimius Severus.[1]

452

Cum peritura Getae POSVISSENT · CASTRA · SVB · VRBE
*Moverunt sanc*TIS · BELLA · NEFANDA · PRIVS
Istaque sacrilego VERTERVNT · CORDE · SEPVLCHRA
*Martyribus quo*NDAM · RITE · SACRATA · PIIS
*Quos mostrante Deo Da*MASVS · SIBI · PAPA · PROBATOS
Affixo monuit carmine jure coli
Sed periit titulus confracto marmore sanctus
Nec tamen his iterum posse perire fuit
Diruta Vigilius nam mox haec papa gemiscens
Hostibus expulsis omne novavit opus

In the Lateran Museum.[2]

This inscription tells us that the Goths, while encamped under the walls of Rome, laid waste some of the martyrs' tombs, and destroyed the marble slabs bearing the epitaphs placed thereon by Pope Damasus, and that these injuries were made good by Vigilius, after the enemy had been driven out.

This destruction took place in 537-538, at the time when Vitiges had placed his Goths in permanent camp under the walls of Rome; indeed *Liber*

[1] Cp. O. Marucchi, *Le Forum romain et le Palatin*, pp. 249 *et seq*.

[2] The only surviving fragment of this inscription was found in the cemetery of S. Peter and S. Marcellinus on the Via Labicana, and is kept in the Christian Museum of the Lateran (3rd compartment). The restorations are taken from the Codex Palatinus of the Vatican, No. 833, where this inscription is copied in its entirety among many others ; but it appears to have been transcribed from another original existing in the Via Salaria in the ninth century.

pontificalis, in describing the siege, says that *ecclesiae et corpora sanctorum martyrum exterminata sunt a Gothis* (see life of Silverius).

It was an easy matter for the barbarian soldiery to go down into the Roman catacombs, as their cantonments lay along the high roads, close to the entrances of these underground galleries ; thus not only the cemetery on the Via Salaria, where this inscription was seen by the compiler of the Palatine Collection, but also that of S. Peter and S. Marcellinus, where all that is left of the original marble was discovered, was contiguous to the two cantonments of the Gothic forces.

There can be no doubt as to the date of the restoration of the Damasian inscriptions through the efforts of Vigilius ; it must have been at a date subsequent to March 538, when Vitiges, after raising the siege, was defeated and taken to Rome as prisoner by Belisarius, there received the sworn promise that his life would be spared, and was thence taken to Constantinople. At the same time, it cannot be much later than that date, as that was the last occasion on which Pope Vigilius stayed in Rome for any time ; after leaving Rome, he visited the Imperial court to discuss the famous question of the *Three Chapters*, and never returned to his See. As we know of two identical copies of this inscription found in two different and widely separated cemeteries, we may infer that the Damasian inscriptions restored by Vigilius after the siege of Vitiges were fairly numerous; thus one of these restorations which was found in the cemetery of Callisto is a counterpart of the epitaph on the Pope and martyr S. Eusebius which has been already quoted.

The ruin wrought by the barbarians, and the work of repair carried out in the Roman catacombs and in the suburban basilicas after their departure, are also commemorated in other metrical inscriptions known to us through the Palatine Collection ; I will quote one specimen which used to stand in one of the cemeteries of Via Salaria, on the tomb of the martyrs Chrysanthus and Daria :

453

HIC VOTIS PARIBVS TVMVLVM DVO NOMINA SER-
[VANT
CHRISANTI DARIAE NVNC VENERANDVS HONOR
EFFERA QVEM RABIES NEGLECTO JVRE SEPVLCHRI
SANCTORVM TVMVLOS PRAEDA FVRENTIS ERANT
PAVPERIS EX CENSV MELIVS NVNC ISTA RESVRGVNT
DIVITE SED VOTO PLVS PLACITVRA DEO
PLANGE TVVM GENS SAEVA NEFAS PERIERE FV-
[RORES
CREVIT IN HIS TEMPLIS PER TVA DAMNA DECVS

From the Collections.

(De Rossi, *Inscr. christ.* i. 2, pp. 84, 87, etc.)

This tells us of some restoration effected at the expense of a private individual, and we have no means of determining whether it belongs to the same period as the one last quoted, or is later than the other sieges which Rome had to endure from the forces of Totila ; in the latter case it would belong to the period of tranquillity which followed the fall of the Gothic domination.

454

Devastata ITERVM SVMMOTA *plebe precantum*
  Priscum PERDIDERANT ANTRA *sacrata decus*
*Nec tua jam ma*RTYR POTERANT *venerande sepulcra*
  Huic mundo LVCEM MITTERE *qua frueris*
Lux tamen ista TVA EST QUAE NESCIT *fu*NE*ra sed quo*
  *Perpe*TVO CRESCAT NEC MINVA*tur ha*BE*t*
Nam nigra NOX TRINVM STVPVIT PER SPECVLA
                                  [LVMEN
  *Admittunt*QVE NOVVM CONC*ava* SAXA DIEM
*Frustra ba*RBARICIS *fremuerunt* AVSIBVS HOSTES
  Foedaruntque SACRVM *tela* CRVENTA LOCVM
Inclyta SED MELIVS *splendescit* MARTYRIS AVLA
  AVCTOREMQVE *gravant imp*IA FACTA SVVM
PRAESVLE VIGILIO SVMPS*erunt* ANTRA DECOREM
  PRESBYTERI ANDREAE CVRA PEREGIT OPVS

This inscription was found in the cemetery of S. Hippolytus on the Via Tiburtina, where it still stands. It speaks of the work done there in the Pontificate of Vigilius (*praesule Vigilio*) by a priest of the name of Andreas, who restored the crypt (*antra sacrata*).[1]

The particular work here recorded is the opening of skylights into the vaulting of the small underground basilica, so as to remedy its defective light. And when that historic crypt was once more uncovered, in 1881, the traces were once more seen of this splendid work carried out under Pope Vigilius at the charge of Andreas the priest, who proposed by these restorations to repair the injuries done to these monuments by Gothic barbarism.

[1] For the restorations of the text, see De Rossi, *Bull. di arch. crist.*, 1882, p. 60.

455

DIGNE TENES PREMIVM MARAE PRO NOMINE XPI
 VINDICE QVO VIVIT SEDES APOSTOLICA
PRAESVLIS IN VICIBVS CLAVSISTI PECTORA SAEVA
 NE MANDATA PATRVM PERDERET VLLA FIDES
TVQVE SACERDOTES DOCVISTI CHRISMATE SANCTO
 TANGERE BIS NVLLVM IVDICE POSSE DEO
TE QVAERVNT OMNES TE SAECVLA NOSTRA RE-
                                    [QVIRVNT
 TV FVERAS MERITVS PONTIFICALE DECVS
PAVPERIBVS LARGVS VIXISTI NVLLA RESERVANS
 DEDISTI MVLTIS QVAE MODO SOLVS HABES
HOC TIBI CARE PATER *debita* PIETATE NOTAVI
 VT RELEGANT CVNCTI QVAM BENE CLARVS ERAS
REQVIESCIT IN PACE MAREAS PB QVI
. . . . ST BASILI INDC III

In the church of Santa Maria in Trastevere.

This important inscription was found in 1869 in
the restoration of the pavement of the church of
Santa Maria in Trastevere, and is now to be seen
in the porch of that basilica; the text of it was
already known through the Palatine Collection.[1]
It is a laudatory epitaph on a priest of the name
of Marea, who died in a year distinguished by the
words *post consulatum* of Basilius, and of the 3rd
Indiction, circumstances which agree with the year
555, being the fourteenth year after that consulship;
thus the period of life of this worthy corresponded
pretty nearly with the stormy years of the Gothic
war. From the general tenor of the inscription
we learn that Marea the priest was a man of
great influence in Rome, that he was firm in

[1] De Rossi, *Bull. di arch. crist.*, 1869, No. 3, pp. 17 *et seq.*

asserting the authority of the Apostolic See (*vindice quo vivit Sedes Apostolica*), that he preserved the purity of the faith, gave liberally of his riches to the poor, and restrained the fury of the barbarians as vicar of the Pope (*praesulis in vicibus clausisti pectora saeva*). These details point to a time when Rome was without its shepherd, and torn by wars, sieges, and other great calamities, a date which corresponds with the second period of the Gothic war, when the barbarian Totila on no less than two occasions treacherously obtained possession of the city by bribing the Isaurian mercenaries who held its gates. It was just at this time that Pope Vigilius, who had left Rome for Constantinople to discuss the question of the *Three Chapters* and had stopped for a few days in Sicily on his way, had despatched Valentinus, bishop of Selva Candida, as his vicar with some shiploads of corn to meet the needs of the besieged city; but the ships were captured by the Goths in the port of Rome, and the unfortunate bishop was cruelly mutilated.[1] History does not give us the name of the successor of Bishop Valentinus in the administration of the Church in Rome as vicar of the absent Vigilius; but from this inscription we learn that it was Marea the priest, either on an express appointment by the Pope or by the election of the Roman clergy, we cannot say which. Marea, as the epitaph tells, worthily upheld his office: he bridled the fury of the Goths, and perhaps induced the furious Totila to spare the unfortunate city from the destruction with which he had threatened it; he maintained the standard of faith and discipline, and ever stood up for the authority of the absent Pontiff. This is

[1] Procopius, *De bello Gothico*, iii. c. 16.

a bright record for so gloomy a period, when this unfortunate city had fallen into the depths of misery of all sorts, so that Procopius (though with obvious exaggeration) could say that after the first entry of Totila into the city in 546 it remained for more than forty days an absolute desert and a mass of ruins inhabited only by wild beasts.[1] The following inscription throws some light into the obscurity of those days, and reveals to us the name of an individual who deserved well of his country in that dark time :

456

DEMOVIT DOMINVS TENEBRAS VT LVCE CREATA
    HIS QVONDAM LATEBRIS SIC MODO FVLGOR INEST
ANGVSTOS ADITVS VENERABILE CORPVS HABEBAT
    HVC VBI NVNC POPVLVM LARGIOR AVLA CAPIT
PRAESVLE PELAGIO MARTYR LAVRENTIVS OLIM
    TEMPLA SIBI STATVIT TAM PRETIOSA DARI
MIRA FIDES GLADIOS HOSTILES INTER ET IRAS
    PONTIFICEM MERITIS HAEC CELEBRASSE SVIS
TV MODO SANCTORVM CVI CRESCERE CONSTAT
                                                        [HONORES
    FAC SVB PACE COLI TECTA DICATA TIBI

In the apse of the basilica of S. Lorenzo on the Via Tiburtina (restored by the aid of the Collections).[2]

This inscription is to be read in the mosaic of the apse of the suburban basilica of S. Lorenzo in the *agro Verano* : the last distich is all that remains of the original ; the remainder was supplied on the authority of ancient and authoritative copies. The inscription states that Pope Pelagius II. (578-590)

[1] Procopius, *De bello Gothico*, iii. c. 22.
[2] De Rossi, *Inscr. christ.* i. 2, pp. 63, 106.

enlarged and adorned the basilica of S. Lorenzo. We know from *Liber pontificalis* that this restoration was on a very considerable scale, and consisted of the enlargement of the old basilica of Constantine, and the cutting away of the rising ground of the *agro Verano* above it, which made the church damp and dark. Yet these works were carried out amid the din of hostile arms that were threatening the very existence of Rome, *gladios hostiles inter et iras*; words which carry us in thought to the memorable time of the Lombard invasion of Italy, when those rude conquerors, after occupying the southern provinces of the peninsula, were threatening to overrun it from one end to the other. And we learn also from this record that the Lombards were considered general enemies, that their advance was looked for with terror, and that recourse was had to the intercession of the Saints to obtain peace, *fac sub pace coli tecta dicata tibi*.

This inscription of Pelagius, which stands above the mosaic, speaks of the work done for improving the light of the old Constantinian basilica of S. Lorenzo ; another inscription placed by the same Pontiff round the chancel arch of that building contains a distich comparing the light thus restored to the martyr's church to the glow of the flames in which he suffered martyrdom :

MARTYRIVM·FLAMMIS·OLIM·LEVITA·SVBISTI·
IVRE·TVIS·TEMPLIS·LVX·VENERANDA·REDIT.

I will now give another specimen of the inscriptions of the same period, which is placed on the tomb of a notary of the Roman Church, by name Eugenius. It bears the date of the twelfth year of the reign of Justinus (578):

457

+SEPVLCHRVM EVGENI $\overline{\text{NOT}}$ CVM SVIS
+IMPIA MORS RAPIENS TENERIS TE NATE SVB ANNIS
INVIDIT MERITIS CRISCERE MAGNA TVIS
TE EORALE DECVS PRIMO CVM CARMINE CEPTO
DOCTOREM DOCTOR   VIDIT ET OBSTIPVIT
VICISTI PRISCOS LONGEVA ETATE PARENTES
ANNIS PARVE QVIDEM   SED GRAVITATE SENEX
NON LVXVS TIBI CVRA FVIT NON GRATIA PONPAE
DOCTILOQVM CVPIDVS   CARMINIS ARDOR ERAS
TV MERITIS ORNATE TVIS MONVMENTA RELINQVIS
QVAE RECOLENS SEMPER   SIT SINE FINE DOLOR
MORTE TVA GENITRIX OPTAVIT SVMERE MORTE
SE QVOQVE FELICEM   SI POTERITVR AIT
TER DENOS PRIMVM QVAM LVNA RESVMERET IGNES
CONIVNCXIT MEMBRIS   MEMBRA SEPVLTA TVIS
NVNC COMMVNE NOBIS CVSTVS TV SERVA SEPVL-
[CRVM
QVE NOS HEC TECVM   MOX TEGET ORNA SIMVL
+$\overline{\text{DEP}}$ EST BOETIVS $\overline{\text{CL}}$ $\overline{\text{P}}$ OCT KAL NOBR $\overline{\text{INDICT}}$ XI
[$\overline{\text{IMP}}$
$\overline{\text{DOM}}$ $\overline{\text{N}}$ IVSTINO $\overline{\text{PP}}$ AVG ANN XII ET TIBERIO CONST
[CAER
$\overline{\text{ANN}}$ III DEP EST IN PAC ARGENTEA MAT $\overline{\text{SS}}$ XIII KAL
[$\overline{\text{DECEMB}}$
QVI $\overline{\text{SS}}$ BOETIVS VIXIT ANN XI $\overline{\text{M}}$ VIIII D XXIII ET
[$\overline{\text{MAT}}$ EIVS VIXIT ANN XXXVI $\overline{\text{M}}$ II D XII

In the church of Sant' Angelo in Borgo (*sic*).
(Plate XXI. Nos. 1 and 2.)
(De Rossi, *Inscr. christ.* i. No. 1122.)

This contains a turgid eulogium of Boethius, the son of the notary Eugenius, who had distinguished himself in early youth by his industry and poetical talent.

There are two circular slabs on the two sides of the inscription, on which are engraved two extracts from the will of Eugenius, containing some important instructions as to certain funds belonging to his estate, which were to be expended on oblations at his family tomb. The text of these is as follows :

On the left : *Deputavimus in ista sepultura nostra extremam paginam ad oblationem vel luminaria nostra Orti transtiberini uncias sex foris muros iuxta porta Portuense, quod fuit ex iure quondam Micini Cancellari inlustris urbanae sedis patris mei.*

On the right : *Sed quatuor uncias fundi Eucarpiani quod est constitutum iuxta sanctum Ciprianum in via Labicana inter affines fundi Capitiniani iuris Sanctae Ecclesiae Romanae, sed et fundi Flaviani iuris publici iuxta Sabinianum. Explicit.*

Finally, as the last inscription of the sixth century I will give the epitaph of Pope Gregory the Great :

458

```
SVSCIPE TERRA TVO CORPVS DE CORPORE SVMPTVM
  REDDERE QVOD VALEAS VIVIFICANTE DEO
SPIRITVS ASTRA PETIT LETI NIL IVRA NOCEBVNT
  CVI VITAE ALTERIVS MORS MAGIS IPSA VIA EST
PONTIFICIS SVMMI HOC CLAVDVNTVR MEMBRA SE-
                                      [PVLCHRO
QVI INNVMERIS SEMPER VIVIT VBIQVE BONIS
ESVRIEM DAPIBVS SVPERAVIT FRIGORA VESTE
ATQVE ANIMAS MONITIS TEXIT AB HOSTE SACRIS
IMPLEBATQVE ACTV QVIDQVID SERMONE DOCEBAT
  ESSET VT EXEMPLVM MYSTICA VERBA LOQVENS
AD CHRISTVM ANGLOS CONVERTIT PIETATE MA-
                                      [GISTRA
ADQVIRENS FIDEI AGMINA GENTE NOVA
HOC LIBER HOC STVDIVM HAEC TIBI CVM HOC
                                  [PASTOR AGEBAS
VT DOMINO OFFERRES PLVRIMA LVCRA GREGIS
HISQVE DEI CONSVL FACTVS LAETARE TRIVMPHIS
  NAM MERCEDEM OPERVM IAM SINE FINE TENES
HIC REQVIESCIT GREGORIVS I PP QVI SEDIT ANNOS
MENS VI DIES X DEPOSITVS III ID MART    [XIII
```

Some fragments of this exist in the grottos of the Vatican. The text is taken from the Collections (De Rossi, *Inscr.* i. 2, pp. 52-78, etc.).

The few remaining fragments of this metrical epitaph from the tomb of the great Pope Gregory I. were discovered by Sarti and Settele, the learned investigators of the grottos of the Vatican, in which they are now kept. The entire eulogy was already known, having been recorded in the biography of that Pope written by John the Deacon in the ninth century, and also in the Palatine Codex of the Vatican, No. 833.

The period of the Pontificate of Gregory, recorded in this inscription (590-604), is memorable for the continuous advance of the Lombards, who threatened to overrun the whole of Italy; in fact, the forces of Agilulphus all but reached the walls of Rome in 593, and laid waste the Campagna.[1] This siege is vividly described by the Pope in a letter to the archbishop of Ravenna, in which he tries to induce him to move the exarch to ask for aid from Constantinople; it tells us how in that mournful time Gregory had to look to everything, even to the posting of the guards on the city walls.[2]

But there is another of the notable deeds of Gregory to which this inscription bears witness, and one that was of great importance to the whole civilised world; viz. the conversion of England to the Christian faith: *Ad Christum Anglos convertit pietate magistra, adquirens fidei agmina gente nova.* In order to spread the light of the Gospel among the *divisos toto orbe Britannos*, Gregory despatched the monks from his private monastery on the Caelian Hill, under the command of Augustine, to make their way into regions which

[1] See *S. Gregorii homil. vi.* book ii. on Ezekiel; Epist. xxx. book iv. to Mauritius.

[2] Ep. xxxii. book ii. ind. x.

the unshaken legions of Claudius and Severus had
never penetrated.   It is to this high-hearted though
humble expedition that the noble British nation
must look for the source of its civilisation : this it
is that justifies the application to this great Pontiff
of the title, given in this inscription, of "the
triumphing Consul," "a Consul not of man, but of
God," whom the poet bids rejoice in his triumphs :
Hisque Dei consul factus laetare triumphis.

With the inscription of Gregory—"the last of
the Romans"—we have reached the limit laid
down by De Rossi to the ancient Christian
epigraphy of Rome.   We propose, however, to add
two more chapters to the present selection.   In the
first we shall give specimens of the "graffiti," or
inscriptions rudely scratched by pilgrims to the
catacombs, whose visits were still tolerably
numerous in the sixth and seventh centuries.   In
the second we shall add an appendix on some of
the last of the inscriptions running from the dawn
of the Middle Ages up to the ninth century.

CHAPTER XI

"GRAFFITI" OR INSCRIPTIONS SCRATCHED BY
EARLY VISITORS IN THE ROMAN CATACOMBS

THE subterranean sanctuaries of the martyrs situated in the Roman catacombs were always the
objects of the veneration of visitors; but it would
seem that the practice of scratching a record of
their visits on the plaster of the walls did not come
in till the period of tranquillity. Then from the
fourth century on at least to the eighth century we
find a constant habit of scratching the visitor's name
and a prayer of some sort on the walls of the crypts
or near the stairs that led to them. These inscriptions, known as the "visitors' graffiti," are of great
importance as testifying to the unceasing veneration
exhibited towards the tombs of the martyrs, and as
indicating to us the places of historical interest in
the underground cemeteries. Of these graffiti there
were certainly a vast number in every cemetery; but
at the present time only a few remains of them
are here and there to be seen. We shall here reproduce some of the most important, classifying
them according to their position in the cemeteries
of Rome.

Cemetery of Callisto.[1] The following graffiti are

[1] For these graffiti, see De Rossi, *Roma sotterranea*, vol. ii.
pp. 17, 18, etc.

still to be seen near the door opening into the well-known crypt of the Popes in this cemetery (see Plate XXVIII.).

The following is a transcription of the names in order beginning from the top; they may be compared with the facsimile on Plate XXVIII.:

459

*Maria*NVS BONIZO

... I VIV*as*

FEL*ic*I PBR PECCATOR

POYΦINA

SANCTE XVC*te*

*M*AXIMI   EN Θεω METαΠANTων αγιων

A   επισκοπων

*Pri*MITI V   ΠONTIANE ZHCHC SANC*te Suste*

PRO Λ ЬINIANI   *in men*

TE ABEAS IN ORATIONE

Tε εIC MIAN

*pe*TE*p*ROME EVSTA*chi*VM

PRIMITI NONNANЬC   SANTE SVSTE IN MENTE

*A*MANTI   HABEAS IN HORATIONES

NA   NA   AVRELIV REPENTINV

IERVSALE CIVITAS ET

A PETE PRO MARCIANVM ALVMNV IIM

ANASTATXA

ORNAMENTVM

CARA MATER

MARTYRV̄ D NABALTARIA

CVIVS...   BER TALLA

SANCTE SVSTE...

... REPENTI*num*

SVCCESSVM RVFINVM AGAPITVM E

SANCTE XYSTE

*in me*NTE HABEAS IN HO*rationes*

SVSTE SAN*cte*

VT AELIBERA

SVCC . . . SVM RVFINVM AGAPITVM   SA

RV   ☧   FINVM   CROCEO
                     ΓΕΛΑϹ ΙΖΗ ϹΕΝΕ
BYΛ . . .   ΚV   θεω
VT QVOD   CONTRI   ΔΙΟΝΥϹΙ ΖΗϹΕϹ
ITERAVI*mus*   FACER   CIA
                     BIBAC IN θεω
IN P*ace* ASTRA PETE   ΤΥΧΙϹ
       ELIA
NTE   BIBAC
E SATVR   IN ΔΕΟ   MARCIANVM
ARANTIAM AQ
ORTA   MAX   SVCCESSVM
        TVA   ANCTA
VT VERICVNDVS CVM SVIS SEVERVM SPIRITA ☧

ARMEN   BENE NAVIGET

(figura graffita) ☧   SEBATIA
                       ΡΑΤωΝΙ   (palm)   SANCTA IN MENTE
                         ΧΙϹ   HAVETE ET OM
           AICXIONAC   NES FRATRES NOS
      AΔΡΙΑΝΟϹ   TROS (palm) LEONTIVIB*as*
ΛΕΟ   AVIVS   IN VITA
                        ☧

The most important expressions used are as follows:

Sancte Suste (an invocation of the martyr Sixtus II).

ἐν θεῷ μετὰ πάντων ἁγίων
ἐπισκόπων Ποντίανε ζήσῃς

(an invocation of the Pope and martyr Pontianus).

Sancte Siste in mente habeas in orationes Aureliu Repentinu (a prayer addressed to Sixtus II.).

Ierusale civitas et ornamentum martyrum Dei.

An enthusiastic exclamation, showing the veneration felt towards that great sanctuary of martyrs.

Sancte Siste . . . Siste Sancte (another invocation
to Sixtus II.).

Spirita Sancta in mente havete et omnes fratres
(a direct prayer to the martyrs on behalf of all
the brethren).

There too a pilgrim of old, before entering the
principal sanctuary, wrote : " Sophronia vivas . . .
cum tuis" (Sophronia, live, thou and thine)! A
little farther on, on the door of another chapel, he
repeated the wish in more pious language :
"Sophronia (*vivas*) in Domino " (live in the Lord)!
Farther on still, close to the tomb in another
chapel, the last in fact which pilgrims of those
days visited, he wrote in capital letters and in a
larger and more regular hand these affectionate
words, "Sophronia dulcis semper vives in Deo "
(sweet Sophronia, thou shalt ever live in God); and
immediately below he repeats it, as if unable to
leave the thought, "Sophronia vives." Here we
have on these walls the tender and touching story
of the emotions that filled the soul of that pious
pilgrim, one succeeding the other, perhaps uncon-
sciously to himself, during his visit to the tombs
of the martyrs; first he tells us of his regret, his
love, his constant thought of her, his tender hope-
fulness; then, under the softening influences of the
holy places, the hope turns into an affectionate faith,
thence into certainty, and finally is transfigured into
a shout of triumph and love, enlightened by faith.[1]

---

[1] Northcote-Allard, *Rome souterraine*, p. 196 : " *Semper
vives Deo*: the last sublime greeting, expressing, not the hopeless
eternal farewell of the pagan, but the hope and faith of the
Christian." De Rossi, *Roma sotterranea*, vol. ii. p. 15.

Cemetery of Praetextatus.—Graffito on a stone forming part of the tomb of the martyrs Felicissimus and Agapitus:

460

FELI . . . . .

FELICISSIMVS ET AGAPITVS

$+$ A . . . . STI . . . . PRESB

$+$ EO LEO P̄R̄B̄ PETRI . . . .[1]

In the apse of the *spelunca magna* (great cave), on the plaster:

461

SVCVRIT*e* . . . . VT

VINCA . . . . IN DIE IVD (*icii?*)

Cemetery of S. Peter and S. Marcellinus.[2]—In the historic crypt of the martyrs:

462

MARCELLINE

PETRE PETITE

(*p*)RO GALL . . . .

(*c*)HRISTIANO . . . .

---

[1] Deciphered and published by Armellini, *A Historic Graffito in the Cemetery of Praetextatus*, Rome, 1874.

[2] For these graffiti, see O. Marucchi, *Nuovo Bullettino di archeologia cristiana*, 1898, pp. 162 *et seq.*

Then come these from the same cemetery:

463

✝ O ΘΕΩC ΤΗ ΠΡΕСΒΗΑ
ΤΩΝ ΑΓΩΝ ΜΑΡΤΥΡΩΝ ΚΑΙ ΤΗС
ΑΓΗΑС ΕΛΗΝΗС СΟСΩΝ
ΤΟΥС СΟΥ ΔΟΥΛΟΥС
ΙΟΑΝΝΗ . . . . . (*sic*)

. . . .

"Oh Lord, on the intercession of the martyred Saints and of S. Helena, save thy servants John," etc.

464

DOMINE LIBERA
VICTOREM
TIBVRTIVS IN ☧
CVN SVIS
AMEN
DOMINE CONSERBa
CALCIDIONE IN NOm
INE TVO SANCTO . . . . .

465

VICTORINE FOSOR
PERDVCAT TE VSOR TVA . . . . .

466

☧

CRISTE IN MENTE HABEAS MAR
CELLINV PECCATORE ET IOBI
NV SEMPER VIVATIS IN DEO

Cemetery of S. Hippolytus.—On the wall of the entrance gate of the historic crypt:

467

IPPOLYTE IN MENTE (*habeas*)
PET*rum* *p*EC*cato*Rem

In the apse of that crypt:

468

+ CRISAFIVS MENOR
TEARIVALITVS PR̄EP

469

BENE SERBVS D̄I

Cemetery of Priscilla.—On the arch of the baptistery:

470

QVI SITET VEN(*iat ad me et bibat*)

471

VRSE VIBAS
FELICISSIME
DONATA VI
VATIS IN ☧

On the lower side round the arch:

472

*s*CRIPSIT ASELLVS SERB*us* D*e*

Near the burial-chamber of the martyr Crescentio:

473

SALBA ME
DOMNE
CRESCENTIONE
MEAM LVCE . . . . .

474

CITO CVNCTI SVSCIPIA*ntur v*OT*is*
DOMNAE PRISCILLAE BE*a*TE . . . . .
(*de*)LICTI KAVSIS AGI VO . . . . .
. . . . . ATTINVS ET . . . . .

The next is noticeable as recording a libation made on the spot in February 375:

475

. . . . . IDVS FEBR
CONSS GRATIANI III ET EQVITI (A.D. 375)
. . . . . FLORENTINVS FORTVNATVS ET
FELIX AD CALICE BENIMVS

In the burial-chamber of the martyr Crescentio:

476

PAVLINA REQVIESCAS IN PACE
ET FILI TVI OMNES DEVM HABEANT
PROTECTOREM . . . . . .

. . . .

Cemetery of S. Hermes.—In the burial-chamber of the martyrs Protus and Hyacinthus:

477

AGATIO SVBD PECCATORI MISERERE $\overline{\text{DS}}$

"God be merciful to the subdeacon Agatius, a sinner!"

Cemetery of Pontianus on the Via Portuensis.—
Over a painting representing the martyrs Peter and
Marcellinus:

478

EVSTATIVS HVMILIS PECCATOR PRESBYTER SERVITOR
BEATI MARCELLINI MARTYRIS ET TV QVI LEGIS ORA
ME ET HABEAS DEVM PROTECTOREM   [PRO
. . . . . HVMILIS PECCATOR PRESB VESTER

On the other wall:

479

DIE IIII NAT · $\overline{\text{SCI}}$ · MILIX MART ALDVS SERVVS DEI . . . .
BEATA ANIMA IN PACE

*Cemetery of Commodilla.—*In the recently opened
crypt of the martyrs Felix and Adauctus:

480

+ LEO CESVFLVS CLERICVS BIBAT IN $\overline{\text{DO}}$
SEMP ET TV QVI LEGIS ORA PRO ME
MEMENTO $\overline{\text{DNE}}$
PETRI IND D (*indigni diaconi?*)

481

. . . . . CRISTOFORV
+ DEVS DEDI $\overline{\text{PRB}}$ + GAIDO
$\overline{\text{PBR}}$ + EGO IOAN . . . . . . VSTR (*presbyter vester*)
BIBA IN $\overline{\text{D}}$ . . . . . MAVRVS
$\overline{\text{PBR}}$ + EGO MINNA
. . . . . CEHORGIOS + EGO DICO
BOBI(*s*) LETAMINI
+ EGO . . . . . SERBVS $\overline{\text{DI}}$

482

+ EGO PETRVS BIBA IN D̄Ō

— EGO FVSCINNVS — COSTANTINVS

SERBV D̄Ī EGO DOMINICVS P̄RB

483

+ D̄S̄ DONA P̄R̄B PECCATOR [1]

These are only a few specimens of the inscriptions scrawled by visitors of old on the walls of the catacombs. Their dates fall between the fourth century and the eight and ninth centuries, when the transfer of the bodies of martyrs into the interior of the city was effected; hence the latest of them may be taken to be the last inscriptions made in the Roman catacombs. Thus they mark for us the passage of Christian Epigraphy from one period to another; and they suggest that we may give at least a few specimens of the inscriptions of the early Middle Ages which record either restorations of Christian churches or donations then made to them, or the translation of the bodies of martyrs from the suburban cemeteries; and this we shall do in the following Appendix.

[1] For these and other graffiti of the cemetery of Commodilla, see O. Marucchi, *Nuovo Bull. di arch. crist.*, 1904, p. 149.

APPENDIX

WE will begin with an inscription of the seventh century :

484

```
AVREA CONCISIS SVRGIT PICTVRA METALLIS
  ET COMPLEXA SIMVL CLAVDITVR IPSA DIES
FONTIBVS E NIBEIS CREDAS AVRORA SVBIRE
  CORREPTAS NVBES RVRIBVS ARVA RIGANS

VEL QVALEM INTER SIDERA LVCEM PROFERET IRIM
  PVRPVREVSQVE PAVO IPSE COLORE NITENS
QVI POTVIT NOCTIS VEL LVCIS REDDERE FINEM
  MARTYRVM E BVSTIS HINC REPPVLIT ILLE CHAOS

EVRSVM  VERSA  NVTV  QVOD  CVNCTIS  CERNITVR
                                          [VSQVE
  PRAESVL HONORIVS HAEC VOTA DICATA DEDIT
VESTIBVS ET FACTIS SIGNANTVR ILLIVS ORA
  EXCITAT ASPECTV LVCIDA CORDA GERENS
```

Basilica of S. Agnese on the Via Nomentana.

This inscription is in the mosaic of the apse of the suburban basilica of S. Agnese, and refers to the splendid work executed there under the care of Pope Honorius I. (625-638). Above the inscription is the figure, also in mosaic, of the youthful martyr to whom the church is dedicated, richly dressed, and near her the symbols of her martyrdom, fire and the sword. On the two sides of her are two Pontiffs clad in chasubles ; the one, Symmachus, who restored the basilica at the end of the fifth century, the other, Honorius, who rebuilt it almost entirely at a later date ; he is therefore depicted in the act of presenting the building to the saint. The style of the draughtsmanship, as well as that of the dedicatory inscription, may give us a fair idea of the depths of degradation into which arts and literature had fallen in the seventh century under Byzantine dominion ; we see evident traces of this influence in the handling of the mosaic, and in the identity of the robes of the saint with those of the Empresses of Constantinople.

To the same Pontiff Honorius belongs the following inscription, which he placed in the apse of the basilica of S. Pancratius. It is of material importance, as it records certain work done there in honour of the martyr ; his tomb, which originally stood obliquely to the axis of the building, was placed under a new altar at right angles thereto.

485

OB INSIGNE MERITVM ET SINGVLARE BEATI PAN-
CRATII MARTYRIS BENEFICIVM BASILICAM VETV-
STATE CONFECTAM EXTRA CORPVS MARTYRIS
NEGLECTI ANTIQVITATIS EXTRVCTAM · HONORIVS
EPISCOPVS DEI FAMVLVS ABRASA VETVSTATIS
MOLE RVINAQVE MINANTE A FVNDAMENTIS NOVI-
TER PLEBI DEI CONSTRVXIT ET CORPVS MARTYRIS
QVOD EX OBLIQVO AVLAE IACEBAT ALTARI INSI-
GNIBVS ORNATO METALLIS LOCO PROPRIO COL-
LOCAVIT

" In absida Sancti Pancratii." (Einsiedeln Collection.)

Here is a specimen of an inscription as to a donation to the funds of a church :

486

---

*Dilectissimo filio Iohanni presb. tit. s. vir*GINIS ET
[MARTYRIS XPI SVSAN-
nae et per eum eidem ven. eccl. SERGIVS EPISC. SER-
[VVS SERVORVM DI
*Dum. apost. Pont. Div. p*ROVIDENTIAE SVAE DIGNA-
[TIONE DNS
N. I. C. *eccl. suae regimen e*T ECCLESIASTICARVM
[RERVM DISPEN-
*sationem comm. pro data potest*ATE QVI VICEM APO-
[STOLORVM PRIN-
cipis gerit lib. perpendat opus EST VT PERAEQVARI
[DEBEANT EC-
*cles. sub quaestus et indi*GENTIAM SVSTINENTI SVC-
[CVRRI
quatenus non altera lauto reditu gaudeal, altera angustiis premalur inopiae. Quocirca considerantes ecclesiam sanctae virginis et martyris Susannae quae in regione quarta ad duas domnos . . . . *constituta est* . . . .

The surviving fragment of this inscription is in the Galleria Lapidaria of the Vatican Museum, and formed part of a long inscription recording the donations made by Pope Sergius I. (687-701) to the church of S. Susanna on the Quirinal; it was seen in that church in an almost perfect condition and copied by Panvinius, and also by the anonymous Spaniard. It has been printed by De Rossi, who comments thereon with his customary learning. The act of donation is addressed to John, titular priest of S. Susanna, and states that the Pope, being aware of the smallness of the endowment attached to that title (having held it himself before becoming Pope), assigned to it several plots of lands forming part of sundry estates held by the Roman Church. The interest of this inscription is topographical, inasmuch as it goes on to give a long list of the names of these plots, with their respective situations ; and thus the record is of great value to students who are trying to reconstitute the topography of the neighbourhood of Rome in the dark ages. The value of the donation of Sergius, from the historical standpoint, lies in the evidence it gives of the vast and rich possessions of the Roman Church in the neighbourhood of Rome, and of the amount of rural population and of churches which they contained. The following properties are named : *patrimonium Sabinense, patrimonium Tusciae, patrimonium Appiae.* Another fact, of which we have no other evidence but this inscription, is that the Holy See had also some *urban* property, in the shape of orchards and vineyards within the walls.[1] And the long list of cultivated lands in districts which were once crowded with population paints for us in lively colours the extreme degradation, the squalor, and ruin into which the wretched city of Rome was ever plunging deeper, now that it was reduced to the status of a provincial town depending on the distant Byzantium. As we read the long schedules of church property on which a large portion of the entire population were enjoying peace and security, we cease to wonder at the enormous influence which the Popes came gradually to acquire, or to be surprised that they, who had long been accepted as the mainstays of Rome and Italy, should in

---

[1] *Item ex patrimonio urbano intra hanc urbem Romam domum et hortum quae appellatur quondam Catelli, Siricari . . .*

the next century have developed into temporal sovereigns.

The next is an inscription recording the donation of sundry articles to the church of S. Clemente which took place under Pope Zacharias (741-752):

487

HISRAHELITICVS DEO OFFEREBAT POPVLVS RVRI	
ALIVS QVIDEM AVRVM	ALIVS NAMQVE AR-[GENTVM
QVIDEM QVOQVE AES	QVIDAM VERO PI-[LOS CAPRARVM
INFELIX AVTEM EGO	GREGORIVS PRIMVS [PRESBYTER ALMÆ
SEDIS APOSTOLICÆ	HVIVSQVE TITVLI [GERENS
CVRAM AC BEATI	SVPPREMVS CLIENS [CLEMENTIS
OFFERO DE TVIS	HAEC TIBI X̅P̅E̅ THE-[SAVRIS
TEMPORIBVS S̅C̅I̅S̅S̅	ZACCHARIÆ PRÆ-[SVLIS SVMMI
PER MARTVREM ET SANCTVM	PARVA MVNVSCVLA [TVVM
CLEMENTEM CVIVS MERITIS	MEREAR DELICTIS [CARERE
ATQVE AD BEATAM ÆTERNAM INGREDI VITAM	
AISTI QVANTVM HABES REGNVM VALET CŒ-[LORVM	
SVSCIPE HOS DOMINE VELVT MINVTA VIDVÆ QVESO	
VETERIS NOVIQVE TESTAMENTORVM DENIQVE [LIBROS	
OCTATEVCHVM REGVM PSALTERIVM AC PROFE-[TARVM	
SALOMONEM ESDRAM HISTORIARVM ILICO PLENOS	
REQVIRE SYLLABARVM LECTOR SEQVENTIAM HARVM	

In the church of S. Clemente.   (Plate XXX. 1.)

It was put up by a parish priest of S. Clemente,

by name Gregorius, who presented to his titular
church a volume of the books of the Old and New
Testament. Amongst them is mentioned by name
the "Octateuch," the Book of Kings, the Psalter,
and the Book of the Prophets, "Solomon and
Esdras"; and it is mentioned that these books
were illustrated, *historiarum ilico plenos.*[1]

Next is the epitaph on Pope Adrian I. (772-795)
composed by Charlemagne:

488

Hic Pater Ecclesiae Romae decus inclitus auctor
  Hadrianus requiem papa beatus habet.
Vir cui vita Deus pietas lex gloria Christus
  pastor apostolicus promptus ad omne bonum.
Nobilis ex magna genitus iam gente parentum
  Sed sacris longe nobilior meritis,
Exornare studens devoto pectore pastor,
  semper ubique suo templa sacrata Deo.
Ecclesias donis populos et dogmate sancto
  imbuit et cunctis pandit ad astra viam.
Pauperibus largus nulli pietate secundus,
  et pro plebe sacris pervigil in precibus
Doctrinis opibus muris erexerat arces,
  urbis et orbis honos inclita Roma, tuas,
Mors cui nil nocuit Christi quae morte perempta est
  ianua sed vitae mox melioris erat.
Post Patrem lacrimans Carolus haec carmina scripsi;
  tu mihi dulcis amor, te modo plango Pater.
Tu memor esto mei, sequitur te mens mea semper,
  cum Christo teneas regna beata poli.
Te clerus populus magno dilexit amore,
  omnibus unus amor optime praesul eras.

[1] Cp. Bartolini, *Di S. Zaccaria papa*, Ratisbon, 1879, p.
261, doc. lett. A.

Nomina iungo simul titulis clarissime nostra
   Hadrianus Carolus, rex ego tuque Pater.
Quisque legas versus devoto pectore supplex
   amborum mitis dic miserere Deus.
Haec tua nunc teneat requies carissime membra,
   cum sanctis anima gaudeat alma Dei.
Ultima quippe tuas donec tuba canet in aures,
   principe cum Petro surge videre Deum.
Auditurus eris vocem scio iudicis almam
   intra nunc Domini gaudia magna tui.
Tum memor sis tui nati, Pater optime, posco,
   cum Patre dic natus pergat et iste meus.
O pete regna Pater felix coelestia Christi,
   inde tuum precibus auxiliare gregem.
Dum sol ignivomo rutilus splendescit ab axe,
   laus tua sancte Pater semper in orbe manet.
Sedit beatae mem. Hadrianus papa, annos XXIII.,
   mens X., d. XVII., obiit VII. Kal. Ian.

In the portico of S. Peter's.

Adrian died at Christmas time A.D. 795, to the grief of Charlemagne, with whom his friendship had been long and close: in the present inscription we find an expression of the tender affection of the Frankish hero for the deceased Pontiff, combined with language of magnificent eulogy, and a pious commendation of himself to the prayers of the beloved one departed.

It is only right that such an inscription should stand in the portico of S. Peter's: looking upon it, one may imagine the hero kneeling in the old basilica of Constantine, while he makes a solemn gift of his conquests to the Pontiff over the tomb of the Apostles; the Pope meanwhile proclaiming him Defender of the Church, and already dreaming of restoring in his person the ancient majesty of the Empire — a magnificent idea, which was realised later in the coronation of Charles by Leo III. (800).

An inscription recording the restoration of a church and the translation of relics from the suburban cemeteries:

489

EMICAT AVLA PIA VARIIS DECORATA METALLIS
PRAXEDIS DOMINO SVPER AETHRA PLACENTIS
[HONORE
PONTIFICIS SVMMI STVDIO PASCHALIS ALVMNI
SEDIS APOSTOLICAE PASSIM QVI CORPORA CON-
[DENS
PLVRIMA SANCTORVM SVBTER HAEC MOENIA PONIT
FRETVS VT HIS LIMEN MEREATVR ADIRE PO-
[LORVM

In the church of S. Praxede.

This inscription in mosaic is still to be seen in the apse of the basilica of S. Praxede on the Esquiline. This graceful building, which we may consider with another not far from it, S. Maria in Domnica (la Navicella), and a third, S. Cecilia in Trastevere, reminds us of the Pontificate of Pascal I., the successor of Leo III. (817-824), who completely restored it, and adorned it with pictures in mosaic, among which is still preserved the authentic portrait of that Pope.

These churches also recall the many translations of the bodies of martyrs by Pascal I. from the suburban cemeteries (which meant the catacombs) to the interior of the city.

In the inscription before us it is stated of Pascal, *passim qui corpora condens plurima sanctorum subter haec moenia ponit*, *i.e.* he placed them in the church of S. Praxede.   In that church there is also preserved a marble slab inscribed with a long catalogue of these relics; it states that the Pontiff had taken more than two thousand bodies of martyrs from the cemetery crypts that had been deserted and gone into decay, and had placed them under various altars of that famous basilica, especially in the magnificent chapel of S. Zeno, which he had built as a burial-place for his mother, *Theodora episcopa*, whose portrait in mosaic is also placed therein.

The reader will find a reproduction on Plate XXX., No. 2, of the upper part of this celebrated inscription, containing the long list of names of the martyrs whose bodies had been brought from the catacombs.

The whole text is as follows:

490

✠ *In nomine Domini Dei Salvatoris nostri Iesu Christi.   Temporibus sanctissimi ac ter beatissimi et apostolici Domini Paschalis Papae infraducta sunt veneranda sanctorum corpora in hanc sanctam et venerabilem Basilicam beatae Christi virginis Praxedis quae praedictus Pontifex diruta ex cymiteriis seu cryptis iacentia auferens et sub hoc sacrosancto altare summa cum diligentia propriis manibus condidit in mense Iulio die XX. indictione decima. Nomina vero Pontificum haec sunt Urbani Stephani Antheri Meltiadis Faviani Iulii Pontiani Siricii Lucii Xysti Felicis Anastasii et Coelestini.   Item nomina episcoporum Stratonici Lucii et Optati. Quamquam presbyterorum et levitaru Nicomedis archipresbyteri Iustini et Cyrini Cyriaci diaconi Nemesii atque Iachei.   Etiam et martyrum nomina*

*ista sunt Zotici Herenei Iachinti Amanti Mari
Audifax Abbacu ac sanctorum octingentorum quorum nomina scit omnipotens Castuli Felicis militis
Gordiani Epimachi Serviliani Sulpicii Diogenis
Basti et alii LXII. Marcelliani Marci Festi et alii
duo Tertullini Fausti Bonosi Mauri Calumniosi
Iohannis Exsuperantii Casti Cyrilli et septem Ger-
manos Honorati Theodori Basilii Crescentii Largi
Smaragdi Crescentionis Iasonis Mauri Yppoliti
Pontiani Chrysanti et alii LXVI. simul que et alii
mille centum et vigintiquatuor quorum nomina sunt
in libro vitae Mauri Arthemii Polionis et alii sexaginta duo martyres. Nomina quoque virginum scilicet et viduarum Praxedis Pudentianae Iulianae
Synphorosae Feliculae Marinae Candidae Paulinae
Dariae Basillae Paulinae Memmiae Marthae Eme-
rentianae Zoe et Tiburtiadis. Quocirca et in ipso
ingressu Basilicae manu dextra ubi utique beni-
gnissimae suae genitricis scilicet Domnae Theodorae
Episcopae corpus quiescit condidit iam dictus praesul corpora venerabilium haec Zenonis presbyteri
et aliorum quorum. Pariterque et in oratorio beati
Iohannis Baptistae manu leva praenominatae Basilicae qui et secretarium esse dinoscitur condidit
corpora scilicet Mauri et aliorum quadraginta martyrum. Simili modo et in oratorio beatae Christi
virginis Agnetis quod sursum in monasterio situm
est ipse Pastor eximius posuit corpora piorum
martyrum videlicet Alexandri Papae atque Eventii
et Theoduli presbyteri. Hos omnes Dei electos
frequentius deprecans quatenus per eorum valeat
preces suae post funera carnis ad caeli conscendere
culmen amen. Fiunt etiam insimul omnes sancti
duo milia CCC.*

This long inscription may be looked upon as the most complete of those of the class recording the translation of relics taken from the catacombs.

The next records the well-known translation of the martyr S. Caecilia and her companions:

491

HAEC DOMVS AMPLA MICAT VARIIS DECORATA
[METALLIS
OLIM QVAE FVERAT CONFRACTA SVB TEMPORE
[PRISCO
CONDIDIT IN MELIVS PASCHALIS PRAESVL OPIMVS
HANC AVLAM DOMINI FIRMANS FVNDAMINE CLARO
AVREA GEMMATIS RESONANT HAEC DINDYMA
[TEMPLI
LAETVS AMORE DEI HIC CONIVNXIT CORPORA
[SANCTA
CAECILIAE ET SOCIIS RVTILAT HIC FLORE IVVENTVS
QVAE PRIVS IN CRYPTIS PAVSABANT MEMBRA
[BEATA
ROMA RESVLTAT OVANS SEMPER ORNATA PER
[AEVVM

In the basilica of S. Cecilia in Trastevere.

In this basilica, below the Byzantine mosaic, on which the portrait of Pope Pascal I. once again appears, the above inscription in verse may be read, referring to the restoration of the church: it states that the bodies that Pascal placed therein were those of martyrs taken from the catacombs, *quae prius in cryptis pausabant membra beata,* and that the whole city made joyful festival over these solemn translations, *Roma resultat ovans, semper ornata per aevum.*

In the vaults of the same basilica may be seen

another and later inscription, placed there in memory of the translation of the bodies of S. Caecilia and Valerianus, Tiburtius and Maximus, on whom the Romans bestowed much affection and veneration : *Hos colit egregios devote Roma patronos*.

This translation of the remains of Caecilia from the catacombs of the Appian Way to the Transtiberine basilica is one of the most moving episodes in the life of Pascal : the story of it was told to the Roman people by the Pope himself in a charming letter, in which he relates how he had searched for the sarcophagus of the martyr in vain among the ruins of the cemetery of Callisto, and had concluded that it had been carried off by the Lombards during their siege of Rome in 755 under Astolphus ; how the noble descendant of the Caecilii appeared to him in a vision and pointed out to him the exact place of her tomb ; and how he returned to the crypt and discovered her body near the sepulchral chamber of the Popes.

And with this we may conclude this Appendix on the Christian inscriptions of early mediaeval times. We have reached the date at which the ancient cemeteries of the suburbs were abandoned, and the great works on the urban churches had begun ; at that point ancient Christian Epigraphy, the subject of this manual, ends, and Mediaeval Epigraphy, properly so-called, begins. It is to be hoped that it may be dealt with in another work of the same description.

☧

Plate I.   *Ancient Christian Sepulchres*

Fig. 1.—Gallery in the cemetery of Priscilla.

FIG. 2.—Chamber (*cubiculum*) in the cemetery of Callisto.

FIG. 3.—Wall-grave (*loculus*) in the cemetery of Callisto.

PLATE II.   *Emblems cut   Inscriptions*

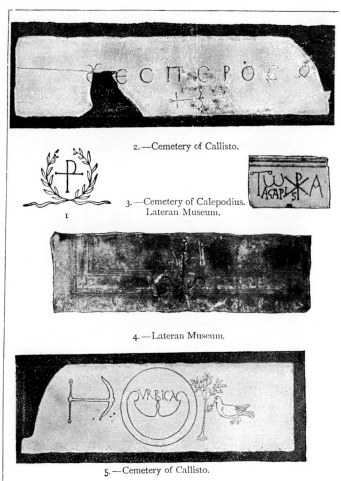

2.—Cemetery of Callisto.

3.—Cemetery of Calepodius.
Lateran Museum.

I

4.—Lateran Museum.

5.—Cemetery of Callisto.

N.B.—Where the name of the original site is omitted, unknown.

6.—Lateran Museum.

7.—Cemetery of Cyriaca.   Lateran Museum.

8.—Lateran Museum.

PLATE III. *Emblems cut in Inscriptions*

1.—Cemetery of Callisto.

3.—Cemetery of Cyriaca. Lateran Museum.

4.—Cemetery of S. Hermes. Lateran Museum.

2.—From the Via Appia.   Lateran Museum.

5.—Cemetery of Gordianus.   Lateran Museum.

PLATE IV. *Emblems cut in Inscriptions*

2.—Lateran Museum.

4.—Cemetery of S. Agnese.   Lateran Museum.

7.—Lateran Museum.

9.—Lateran Museum.

1.—From the Via Salaria
Nova.   Lateran Museum.

3.—Cemetery of Cyriaca.
Lateran Museum.

5.—Lateran Museum.

6.—Cemetery of Priscilla.
(Monogram of Rufilla.)

8.—Cemetery of Priscilla.
(Monogram of Rusticus.)

PLATE V. *Emblems cut in Inscriptions*

1.—Cemetery of Callisto.   Lateran Museum.

3.—From the Via Salaria Nova.   Lateran Museum.

5.—Cemetery of Priscilla.

2.—Lateran Museum.

4.—Cemetery of Callisto.

2

3

4

5

6

PLATE VII.   *Doctrinal Inscriptions*

1.—Cemetery of Callisto.   Lateran Museum.

From the Via Salaria Nova.   Lateran Museum.

2.—From the Via Salaria Nova.   Lateran Museum.

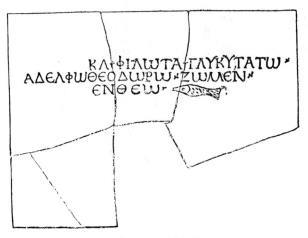

4.—Cemetery of Priscilla.

PLATE VIII. *Doctrinal Inscriptions*

1.—Fragment of the inscription of Abercius,
Lateran Museum.

2.—Museum of Aquileia.

PLATE IX. *Sepulchral Inscriptions*

1.—Pope Anteros (A.D. 236).
Cemetery of Callisto.

3.—Pope Cornelius (A.D. 253).
Cemetery of Callisto.

2.—Pope Fabianus (A.D. 250).
Cemetery of Callisto.

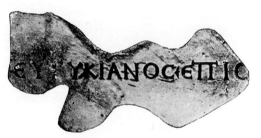

4.—Pope Eutychianus (A.D. 283).
Cemetery of Callisto.

PLATE X. *Sepulchral Inscriptions*

1.—Pope Pontianus (A.D. 236).
Cemetery of Callisto.

2.—Pope Lucius (A.D. 255).
Cemetery of Callisto.

PLATE XI.   *Inscriptions of Priests*

1.—From the church of S. Pudentiana.   Lateran Museum.

LOCVS PRESBYTERIBASIUTITVI SABINE

2.—Museum of Inscriptions at S. Paolo fuori le Mura.

LOCVSVALENTINIPRAESB

3.—Basilica of S. Agnese on the Via Nomentana.

PLATE XII. *Inscriptions of Priests*

1.—Basilica of S. Agnese on the Via Nomentana.

2.—Cemetery of Callisto.

3.—Basilica of S. Agnese on the Via Nomentana (A.D. 456).

PLATE XIII. *Inscription of a Deacon*

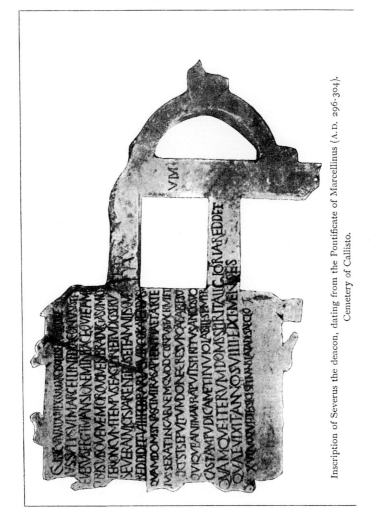

Inscription of Severus the deacon, dating from the Pontificate of Marcellinus (A.D. 296-304).
Cemetery of Callisto.

PLATE XIV. *Inscriptions of Lectors,*

1.—From the cemetery of Callisto.
Lateran Museum. (A.D. 461 or 482.)

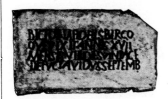

3.—Lateran Museum.

6.—Lateran Museum.

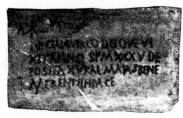

4.—Lateran Museum.

2.—Lateran Museum.

5.—From the cemetery of Cyriaca.
Lateran Museum.

7.—Lateran Museum.

PLATE XV. *Inscriptions of Brethren,*

1.—Lateran Museum.

2.—From the cemetery of Cyriaca.   Lateran Museum.

4.—From the cemetery of Cyriaca.   Lateran Museum.

3.—From the cemetery of S. Sebastian.
Lateran Museum.

5.—From the cemetery of Cyriaca.
Lateran Museum.

PLATE XVI. *Inscriptions with Titles and*

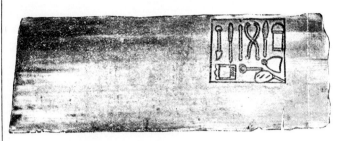

1.—Cemetery of Praetextatus.   Lateran Museum.

3.—Cemetery of Cyriaca.   Lateran Museum.

5.—Cemetery of Domitilla.   Lateran Museum.

2.—Lateran Museum.

4.—From the Via Salaria Nova.   Lateran Museum.

6.—Lateran Museum.

PLATE XVII. *Inscriptions with Titles and*

1.—Lateran Museum.

2.—Cemetery of Callisto. Lateran Museum.

4.—Lateran Museum.

3.—From the Via Salaria Nova.   Lateran Museum.

5.—Lateran Museum.

PLATE XVIII. *Inscriptions with Titles and*

1.—Cemetery of Cyriaca.
Lateran Museum.

4.—Lateran Museum.

5. —Lateran Museum.

2.—Cemetery of Cyriaca.
Lateran Museum.

3.—Lateran Museum.

6. —Lateran Museum.

PLATE XIX. *Specimens of Dated Inscriptions*

1. —Lateran Museum.   (A.D. 71.)

3.—Lateran Museum.   (A.D. 290.)

2.—Capitoline Museum. (A.D. 279.)

4.—From the cemetery of SS. Peter and Marcellinus
Lateran Museum. (A.D. 307.)

PLATE XX. *Specimens of Dated Inscriptions*

1.—Lateran Museum. (A.D. 336.)

2.—In the monastery of S. Paul. (A.D. 452.)

4.—From the basilica of S. Agnese. Lateran Museum. (A.D. 557.)

3.—From the cemetery of SS. Peter and Marcellinus.
Lateran Museum. (A.D. 461.)

PLATE XXI. *Specimens of Dated Inscriptions*

1.—Inscription of Eugenius the notary. (A.D. 578.) Church of S. Angelo in Borgo.

2.—Enlargement of the last four lines of the above inscription, exhibiting the consular date A.D. 578.

PLATE XXII. *Specimens of Dated Inscriptions*

1.—From the cemetery of Callisto. Lateran Museum.

The words SVB LIBERIO PAPA have been ascertained by the discovery of the fragment containing the left-hand portion of the inscription; and they fix the date as A.D. 362-366.

2.—Lateran Museum.

In the last line : SVB DAMASO EPISCO(*po*)
(A.D. 366-384.)

3.—Church of S. Pietro in Vincoli. (A.D. 533.)   It contains the name of Pope John II.

PLATE XXIII. *Inscriptions containing*

1.—From the cemetery of Callisto.
Lateran Museum.

2.—From the Via Salaria Nova.   Lateran Museum.

3.—From the cemetery of Cyriaca.   Lateran Museum.

4. —Lateran Museum.

PLATE XXIV. *Inscriptions containing*

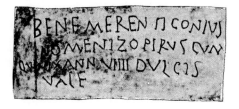

1.—From the cemetery of Cyriaca.
Lateran Museum.

3.—From the cemetery of Cyriaca.
Lateran Museum.

2.—From the Via Salaria Nova.
Lateran Museum.

4.—Lateran Museum.

PLATE XXV. *Inscriptions on Tombs*

1.—Lateran Museum.

3.—Lateran Museum.

4.—From the cemetery
of Cyriaca.
Lateran Museum.

5.—Monastery of S. Paolo fuori le
Mura.

2.—Cemetery of Priscilla (*v.* page 178, No. 164).

PLATE XXVI.

1.—Specimen of Damasian lettering.
Cemetery of S. Valentinus on the Via Flaminia.

2.—Fragment of a Damasian inscription.
Lateran Museum.

PLATE XXVII. *Damasian Inscriptions*

```
† A MARI-ERI SANCTOSDVDVMRETVLISSEPARENTES
A GNENCVMLVGVBRESCANTVSTVBACONCREPVISSET
N VTRICISGREMIVMSVBITOLIQVISSEPVELLAM
SPONTETRVCISCALCASSEMINASRABIEMQ·TYRANNI
VRERECVMFLAMMISVOLVISSETNOBILECORPVS
VIRIBINMENSVMPARVISSVPERASSETIMOREM
NVDAQVEPROFVSVMCRINEMPERMEMBRADEDISSE
NEDOMINITEMPLVMFACIESPERITVRAVIDERET
OVENERANDAMIHISANCTVMDECVSALMAPVDORIS
VTDAMASIPRECIBFAVEASPRECORINCLYTAMARTYR
```

1.—Inscription of S. Agnese.
Basilica of S. Agnese.

3.—Inscription by Pope Vigilius commemorating
his restoration of certain Damasian inscriptions
(6th century). Lateran Museum.

2.—Original fragments of the inscription
of S. Eusebius with modern additions.
Cemetery of Callisto.

4.—Copy of the above inscription of
S. Eusebius made in the 6th century.
Cemetery of Callisto.

PLATE XXVIII.

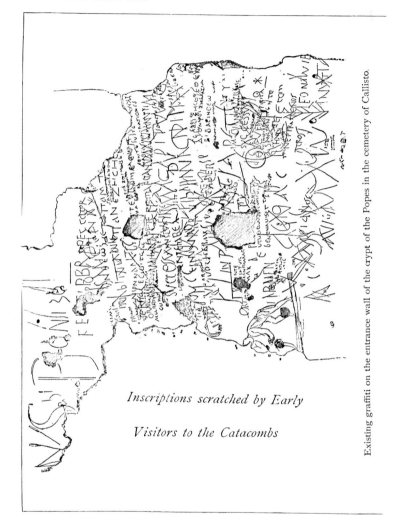

Inscriptions scratched by Early

Visitors to the Catacombs

Existing graffiti on the entrance wall of the crypt of the Popes in the cemetery of Callisto.

PLATE XXIX.

Existing graffiti on the wall of a chamber in the cemetery of
Priscilla under the basilica of S. Silvestro.

PLATE XXX.

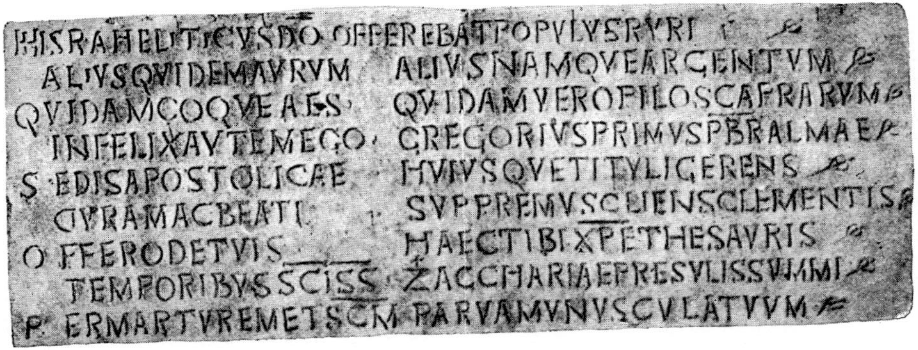

1.—Church of S. Clemente.   Donations of the time of Pope Zacharias (A.D. 741-752).

2.—Church of S. Prassede.   Transfer of relics in the time of Pope Pasqualis I. (A.D. 817-824).